GETTING IN IS NOT ENOUGH

A *Feminist Formations* Reader

Getting In Is Not Enough

Women and the Global Workplace

EDITED BY **Colette Morrow and Terri Ann Fredrick**

The Johns Hopkins University Press
Baltimore

© 2012 The Johns Hopkins University Press
All rights reserved. Published 2012
Printed in the United States of America on acid-free paper
9 8 7 6 5 4 3 2 1

The Johns Hopkins University Press
2715 North Charles Street
Baltimore, Maryland 21218-4363
www.press.jhu.edu

ISBN 13: 978-1-4214-0635-0 (paperback: alk. paper)
ISBN 10: 1-4214-0635-7 (paperback: alk. paper)

Library of Congress Control Number: 2012931110

A catalog record for this book is available from the British Library.

Special discounts are available for bulk purchases of this book. For more information, please contact Special Sales at 410-516-6936 or specialsales@press.jhu.edu.

The Johns Hopkins University Press uses environmentally friendly book materials, including recycled text paper that is composed of at least 30 percent post-consumer waste, whenever possible.

Contents

Introduction: Women and Public Work
COLETTE MORROW AND TERRI ANN FREDRICK   1

PART I **Getting In Is Not Enough: The Limits of Women's Access to Public Work**

1. The Cost of Being a Girl: Gender Earning Differentials in the Early Labor Markets   25
   YASEMIN BESEN-CASSINO

2. Retail on the "Dole": Parasitic Employers and Women Workers   40
   LYNN S. DUGGAN

3. Economic Development Policies and Women Workers: Filipina Workers in a Japanese Transplant   61
   NIZA LICUANAN-GALELA

4. The Rise of the Bangladesh Garment Industry: Globalization, Women Workers, and Voice   73
   FAUZIA ERFAN AHMED

5. Wading through Treacle: Female Commercial School Graduates in Egypt's Informal Economy   85
   MOUSHIRA ELGEZIRI

6. The Gender Gap in Patenting: Is Technology Transfer a Feminist Issue?   128
   SUE V. ROSSER

7. Is Sisterhood Conditional? White Women and the Rollback of Affirmative Action   148
   TIM WISE

PART II **Beyond Getting a Foot in the Door: Women Workers Accessing Power**

8. Progressive or Neo-Traditional? Policewomen in Gulf Cooperation Council Countries   177
   STACI STROBL

9. Motivational and Attitudinal Factors among Latinas in
   U.S. Electoral Politics   202
   SONIA R. GARCÍA AND MARISELA MÁRQUEZ

10. Feminists and the Welfare State: Aboriginal Health Care Workers
    and U.S. Community Workers of Color   213
    NANCY A. NAPLES AND MARNIE DOBSON

11. Lesbians in Academia   235
    ESTHER D. ROTHBLUM

12. Secretarial Work, Nurturing, and the Ethic of Service   242
    IVY KEN

13. Between L=A=N=G=U=A=G=E and Lyric: The Poetry of
    Pink-Collar Resistance   264
    KAREN KOVACIK

14. "Growing the Size of the Black Woman": Feminist Activism
    in Havana Hip Hop   282
    FARI NZINGA

List of Contributors   295
Index   299

GETTING IN IS NOT ENOUGH

Introduction: Women and Public Work

COLETTE MORROW AND TERRI ANN FREDRICK

Work has long been a touchstone issue for feminists because women's relationship to work is a question of power: how does women's labor enable or constrain their access to personal, economic, social, and political influence? In *Feminism without Borders: Decolonizing Theory, Practicing Solidarity*, Chandra Talpade Mohanty suggests that work offers feminists a site where they can forge transnational and cross-cultural solidarity, resist oppression, and make empowering social change without recourse to reductionist and essentializing notions of identity: the "intersection of gender and work, where the very definition of work draws upon and reconstructs notions of masculinity, femininity, and sexuality, offers a basis of cross-cultural comparison and analysis that is grounded in the concrete realities of women's lives" (2003, 144). Two hundred years before *Feminism without Borders* (2003) was published, Mary Wollstonecraft, in *Vindication of the Rights of Women* (1792), also linked women's labor to their well-being and civil and economic rights. In the years that separate these two paradigm-setting feminists, innumerable others have explored the possibilities and problems of gender and work. In the United States and other high-income countries with "advanced" free-market economies, middle-class, mainstream feminists relied on a strategy of framing their quest for gender equity in terms of rights to paid employment, contributing to popular misconceptions that entering the workforce is *the* Western feminist project, an end in itself rather than a means of attaining equality. In this book, we call this approach to empowering women via the right to public work "access-based feminism."[1]

Other feminists—concerned that employment constrains rather than empowers women, especially poor and working-class women, immigrants, and disenfranchised minorities in both developing countries and "advanced," capital-intense economies—argue that access-based feminism perpetuates injustice. Rather than campaigning for increasing women's resources and power by means of greater access to paid work, they advocate for systemic change that will "fundamentally transform" existing socioeconomic and political structures (Moghadam 2009, 111). This approach is characteristic of transnational and women of color feminisms, which, depending on practitioners' research and activist concerns, ideology, social locations, and sites of praxis (including the United States), may also be shared by social justice, liberatory, socialist, Marxist, borders/borderless, "Third World," multicultural, international, and global feminisms (Lock Swar and Nagar 2010, 4). To avoid confusion, we will use the nomenclature *transformative feminism(s)* to identify this approach.

Women's empowerment as conceptualized by access-based and transformative feminisms has been a focus of *Feminist Formations* (formerly the *NWSA Journal*) since its inception, and the journal consistently publishes research that investigates the complex nature of women's relationship to labor. Drawn from almost two decades of *Feminist Formations*, the articles included in this book critically examine women's paid work in terms of both access and a broader agenda of achieving feminist social change worldwide. In aggregate, the essays reveal, and in this volume we argue, that discussions of the ways in which women affect and are affected by work consider three major spheres:

- Economic: How does women's pay compare to others' earnings in their community? What roles do forms of power such as race and ethnicity, class, nation, migration, ability, sexuality, and religion play in the value assigned women's work? Are women able, through their work, to control the money they earn?
- Social: Do women experience positive, workplace-supported connection to others within their workplace? What connections and/or value do they experience within their homes and communities as a result of their work?
- Political: How much agency do women exercise in their jobs? Are they able to affect change within their workplaces? Does women's work increase their leverage to enact change in their communities and cultures?

Responses to these queries republished in this book offer a range of perspectives that (1) reject U.S. popular culture definitions of feminism, (2) frequently critique access-based feminism, (3) advocate for transformative social change, and (4) rectify widely held misinterpretations of feminist ideas about work, beginning with the myth that concepts such as "woman" and "work" are discrete, uncomplicated categories. This scholarship demonstrates the roles that race and ethnicity, class, sexuality, corporate practices, government policies, and economic systems play in women's experiences of work. Furthermore, the retrospective addresses diverse women's work experiences in the United States and other parts of the world. Our focus is on representing a wide range of viewpoints in the scholarship as well as on the multiplicity of women's work experiences. In this introduction, we briefly discuss the history, implications, and limits of access-based and transformative feminisms before introducing the articles, which, taken together, provide a critical and complex view of women and public work.

Access-Based Feminism: A Historical Overview

Access-based and transformative feminisms both respond to the rise and historical development of capitalism, a system that distributes power on the basis of wealth. While transformative feminism rejects capitalist economics as fundamentally oppressive, the goal of access-based feminism is for women to capture an equitable share of capitalism's benefits, which traditionally were reserved for men only. Hence, it tends to appeal to women living in and *profiting* from capitalist economies. For this reason and because access-based feminism developed in tandem with liberalism (a philosophy that posits collective concerns should not limit individual choice), it attracted relatively large followings in Western societies where modern capitalism first became a major force and that are now organized around neo-liberal capitalism (sometimes referred to as late capitalism).

During the seventeenth and eighteenth centuries, when modern capitalism was maturing, it was twinned with liberalism by European philosophers such as John Locke and Adam Smith, who claimed that men are citizens with "natural" rights—property ownership and the consent to be governed—because of their ability to reason and their participation in the marketplace and political sphere. In contrast, women were sequestered to the private sphere and denied the status of citizen because their ability to reason was deemed inferior and their primary activities—reproduction and child rearing—had no market value. Given these contexts, the conclusion that access to the market—paid work—would enhance women's power and status was a culturally familiar strategy that English and U.S. feminists from the eighteenth century through today have leveraged to demand political and economic rights. For instance, in 1792, Wollstonecraft, though she never campaigned for women to work outside the home, turned liberalism on itself (without challenging its basic tenets) by arguing that women's ability to fulfill traditional gender roles rested equally on personal virtue and having "a civil existence in the state" (1988, 149). This, along with her contention that women's capacity for reason equals men's, was the basis for Wollstonecraft's demands for women's education and emancipation. By being recognized as men's intellectual "fellows," women would be better able to execute their traditional domestic "duties" and the responsibilities of citizenship: "Would men but generously snap our chains, and be content with rational fellowship instead of slavish obedience, they would find us more observant daughters, more affectionate sisters, more faithful wives, more reasonable mothers—in a word, better citizens" (150).

Over the decades, scores of feminists adopted Wollstonecraft's access-oriented arguments and expanded them to include work outside the home. During the mid-twentieth-century, access became synonymous with U.S. feminism in part because the media, which gave greater coverage to the population wishing to enter the workforce—white, middle-class, heterosexual women—than groups with less privilege, made access-based feminism a conspicuous element of U.S. mass culture. Additionally, the feminist notion that the personal is political, suggesting that "all aspects of personal life have social dimensions, just as all political power relations have personal dimensions," thrust issues traditionally considered private into public discourse (Gordon and Hunter 2002, 249). What previously had been an individual concern became a social movement for employment. The rationale driving this movement was that, in a capitalist economy, paid work would increase women's earning capacity and give them power to enact change in the home, workplace, government, and community. To this end, access feminists from the 1960s through today have sought to reform rather than replace capitalist structures. Much of their platform entails initiatives that make working outside the home tenable. For instance, access proponents demand affordable childcare, family leave policies, and stop-the-clock policies that shield women from penalties incurred when they take family leave. Other reforms include ending the sexual division of labor, discriminatory hiring, sexual harassment, the gender wage gap, and sex segregation and gender hierarchies in the workplace.[2]

Today, access feminists' insistence that jobs—especially leadership positions at the highest levels of government, business, and other institutions—are the key to attaining gender equality continues to be the most recognizable form of U.S. feminism. It has succeeded in some respects but not others. In the United States, the Equal Pay Act of 1963 proscribed sex-based wage discrimination. It was soon followed by the Civil Rights Act of 1964, which expanded prohibitions against discrimination to multiple areas and which the Supreme Court has interpreted as disallowing sexual harassment at work. The U.S. Congress then passed the Education Amendments of 1972, which ban discrimination against females by federally funded schools: "No person in the United States shall, on the basis of sex, be excluded from participation in, be denied the benefits of, or be subjected to discrimination under any education program or activity receiving Federal financial assistance" (Family Educational and Privacy Rights Act of 2010). In 1981, the United Nations put in force the Convention on the Elimination of Discrimination against Women (CEDAW), which codifies international law pertaining to women's rights: "The Convention provides the basis for realizing equality between women and men through ensuring women's equal access to, and equal opportunities in, political and public life—including the right to vote and to stand for election—as well as education, health and employment"[3] (United Nations Commission on the Status of Women 1979).

Such laws and persistent feminist activism have enabled women who historically were blocked from public work—typically middle-class white women—to enter the workforce at high rates, particularly in the United States.[4] Furthermore, work and access to work have increased many women's economic, social, and political power, especially when that work arises in response to the economic and labor needs of their communities. In "Gender Distortions and Development Disasters: Woman and Milk in African Herding Systems," Bonnie Kettel demonstrates, for instance, that women whose work serves an important role within their communities may be able to parlay that work into greater social and economic standing (1992). Additionally, the increased presence of women in government and corporate leadership can be attributed to access-based feminism. For instance, Sonia R. García and Marisela Márquez (chapter 9) illustrate that increasing numbers of Chicana politicians—motivated by concerns regarding their families and communities—have been making inroads into traditional, mainstream politics, an area of work that in the U.S. has traditionally been dominated by white men.

Nevertheless, gender equity is far from complete. Women everywhere continue to be underrepresented in powerful, high-paying leadership positions, and wage parity is unlikely to materialize anytime in the foreseeable future. Yasemin Besen-Cassino (chapter 1) demonstrates that in the United States wage disparities between men and women begin during the teen years. In addition, women's lifetime earnings are far less than men's, and, as a group, men do not participate equally in women's traditional household duties, including child rearing and caring for aged or ill family members. In fact, most women now shoulder the double burden of full-time work in and outside the home, but few societies have accommodated working mothers' needs for safe, affordable childcare and adequate paid family leave or adopted policies and institutions that enable women to achieve a tenable work-life-family balance. Janine A. Parry, in "Family Leave Policies: Examining Choice and Contingency in Industrialized Nations," shows that U.S. family leave policies are woefully inadequate because hostility to limiting the free market far outweighs the influence of women leaders and unions and, we would add, any real allegiance to so-called family values (2001). Even First Lady Michelle Obama—a Princeton and Harvard graduate and working mother—has spoken openly about her struggle to juggle family and career.

These conditions have prompted some progressive feminists to argue that historically access-based feminism has served the needs of the U.S. economy to a much greater extent than it has facilitated women's empowerment. The United States, for example, could not have sustained its role in World War II without a 57 percent increase (from 1940 to 1944) in the number of women employed in all sectors of the economy. However, U.S. women who readily stepped up to this economic challenge faced discrimination and, as a group, did not realize lasting improvements in life quality, such as long-term financial independence, because returning veterans reclaimed their jobs after the war's end (Altbach 1974, 65). Another example is that midway through the twentieth century, as the U.S. economy shifted from manufacturing to the service sector, its ability to sustain productivity rates and avoid recession depended in part on securing a new pool of workers. From this perspective, white, middle-class women's en masse entrance into the workplace clearly benefited the national economy while creating new challenges with regard to women's traditional child rearing and other work in the home (Douglas 2007).

Another troubling failure is that women who have achieved success as the result of access-based feminism often do so on the backs of disenfranchised women. Colleen Canty-Mack points out that "poor women of color and/or immigrant women [are] laboring in the domestic sphere of other women's homes . . . [at a] much greater rate today . . . to facilitate the entrance into the public sphere of more privileged . . . women," which promotes class competition rather than mutually beneficial alliances (2004, 166). That workplace success can increase divisions among women is further borne out by Melissa Wright's findings that, once promoted from "blue collar" jobs to managerial positions, women internalize corporate cultures and distance themselves from former coworkers on the production line rather than opening doors for them (2000, 209, 221). Clearly, women's greater access to paid employment in the United States and other highly developed capitalist economies shows that paid work is no panacea for gender inequality.

Transformative Feminism and Views on Women's Labor

Transformative feminists argue that access-based feminism's failures are at least partially due to its close ideological affiliation with liberalism and capitalism. One area where liberalism and access-based feminism overlap is the primacy they give to the idea of the "individual" with rights and liberty. A central concept of liberalism, this principle contributes to access-based feminism's emphasis on the right of the female citizen (as an individual) to freedom, which both liberalism and capitalism define as economic opportunity. This prominence of the individual preempts the possibilities for collective action, which transformative feminists believe is more effective and a greater good in and of itself. Another key factor in access-based feminism's failures, suggest transformative feminists, is its reliance on reform—creating spaces for women in existing institutions—rather than making thoroughgoing, deeply rooted change. Significantly, transformative feminist economic agendas far exceed the goals of access-based feminism (though transformative feminists unequivocally support specific access-based initiatives, such as eliminating the gender wage gap). At its core, transformative feminism, a catchall term that encompasses the principles of transnational, women of color, and other liberatory-oriented feminisms, is committed to dismantling systems that inequitably distribute power because of racism, class bias, capitalism, imperialism, patriarchalism, sexism, heterosexism, and other forms of oppression as they are manifest in local and global contexts. Ultimately, transformative feminists seek to disassemble oppressive socioeconomic and political structures and replace them with just institutions.

Transformative feminisms' historical roots lie in multiple intellectual and political traditions, while transformative praxis is shaped by local and global contexts. For example, women of color feminisms are particularly prominent in the United States and other regions where power and wealth are apportioned according to intersections of race, class, and gender. Resistance to imperialism and colonization is a hallmark of transformative feminisms in regions with a history of being colonized. Transformative feminists everywhere generally oppose neo-liberalism, the governmental and corporate movement to impose radical free market capitalism throughout the globe, because it is a form of socioeconomic imperialism that intensifies the stratification of resources and power and (re)colonizes the world's most vulnerable populations.

From at least the mid-twentieth century, transformative feminists in the United States, especially practitioners of women of color feminism, have critiqued access-based feminism for privileging white, middle-class, able-bodied, heterosexual women's concerns and issues. Scholars such as Patricia Hill Collins (1990), bell hooks (1984), and Audre Lorde (1998) point out that the access-based movement primarily benefited the populations who advocated for it. For instance, affirmative action has advanced white women more than other groups that it covers (Wise, chapter 7), and the glass ceiling—an invisible but real barrier that keeps qualified people out of top leadership—is less penetrable by women of color than by white women. As a result, in the United States, there is a substantial, persistent wealth gap between white women and women of color. As Patricia Hill Collins explains in *Black Feminist Thought*, women of color encounter a racial as well as sexual division of labor, a point underscored by Heather Boushey and Robert Cherry, who establish that even during the U.S. economic expansion of the 1990s "the position of African-American women deteriorated relative to white women . . . [and] the economic advances of professional women have outpaced the advances of working-class women" (2003, 49).[5]

Boushey and Cherry's findings also highlight the important role that class plays in access-based feminism. Their research demonstrates that women who hold jobs defined as lower-class and/or "deskilled" often find work more limiting than empowering. In fact, as scholars such as Lynn Duggan (chapter 2) demonstrate, the women most often hired for these positions experience low wages, few benefits, unsafe work conditions, and lack of job security, all of which *reduce* their access to power.

Transformative feminists whose practice is oriented around world issues critique access-based feminism for its almost exclusive concern with conditions in the United States and a concomitant lack of attention to global macroeconomics, particularly the negative effects of neo-liberalism on poor and working-class women in developing countries. In fact, many transformative feminists argue that U.S. women's economic opportunities are made possible, in part, by the worldwide spread of neo-liberalism, which the United States has led as it has pursued international market dominance since World War II. They contend that globalization of the free market has significantly added to "America's breathtakingly disproportionate wealth and economic power" (Chua 2004, 232), while "reduc[ing] the ability of women around the world to find paid work that offers security and dignity" (Desai 2002, 32). An oft-cited example is U.S.-based corporations' efforts to boost profits by locating production in developing countries that have a large pool of "cheap" labor. For instance, Ahmed (chapter 4) demonstrates that sweatshops prefer to employ women because they can be paid less and are perceived to be more easily "controlled." Unions are usually banned and, in the absence of health and safety laws, employees work in dangerous conditions and commonly experience abuses ranging from harassment to sexual assault. If employees and local activists protest, corporations relocate. Transformative feminists argue that this system exacerbates the stratification of global wealth by moving capital from poorer to richer nations—particularly to high-income countries with "advanced" free-market economies where traditional socioeconomic patterns distribute it to already privileged groups, including women who have accumulated resources and power through access-based feminist reforms. At the same time, sweatshops in countries like Bangladesh (see Ahmed, chapter 4) and the Philippines (see Licuanan-Galela, chapter 3) perpetuate class oppression and gendered hierarchies rather than empowering women in their families and communities. The sweatshop example, transformative feminists argue, is proof that access-based reform is an insufficient remedy for women's disenfranchisement globally and, worse, that it diminishes the possibilities for global feminist solidarity by reinforcing class and national divisions rather than dismantling inequalities.

The divisive potential of access-based antidotes to inequality increases when the language of access and empowerment is coopted and deployed in service of governments and global financial institutions such as the International Monetary Fund (IMF), World Bank, World Trade Organization (WTO), and even U.N. agencies whose stated mission is to empower women. For instance, Alexandra Hrycak's research on women's organizing in post-Soviet Russia shows how the women's movement weakened when the United States and its subcontractors imposed the access-based model through aid and development initiatives (2002, 70–79). These projects concentrated resources on promoting leadership among elite women (the nouveau riche of Russia's free market capitalism) while disenfranchising grassroots activists who had successfully used maternalist collective action—a model that was defined in part by women's traditional role as mother and used collective decision making and advocacy strategies—to campaign for social justice during the final years of the Soviet era. The U.S. approach silenced seasoned, effective activists and put the women's movement in the hands of a relatively small population of emerging professionals who were profiting from neo-liberalization of Russian markets, an economic "therapy" whose aggregate effect was the feminization of poverty. Without practiced activists, the post-Soviet women's movement was significantly weaker than its predecessor. Moreover, in the new economy, the number of women's advocacy groups shrank to less than 1 percent of all Russian nongovernmental organizations (NGOs), and they exercised little power in local and national policymaking.

Another chilling example pertains to the Iraq War, specifically, President George W. Bush's claims that it was undertaken to liberate women, and the creation of "puppet" women's NGOs to advance the ruling coalition's agendas (Zangana 2007, 11). Bush's conflation of feminist ideas and language with U.S. economic imperialism produced a discourse that has since become commonplace. For example, atrocities against Afghan and Pakistani women and girls routinely have been invoked to justify "unpiloted drone bombings" that inflict heavy civilian casualties along the two countries' border. Likewise, violations of Iranian women's human and civil rights have been used to solidify anti-Muslim, anti-Iranian sentiment and to cultivate "war fever" when tensions escalate between the United States and Iran: in 2009, when opposition parties protested Iranian election results and, before that, in 2007–2008, when Vice President Richard Cheney urged military action against Iran. Furthermore, institutions and governments ranging from the United Nations to the Western media have picked up this refrain, citing women's political—but not economic—rights to legitimize the expansion of neo-liberal economics. (See, for example, *Time* magazine's cover story on August 9, 2010, "What Happens if We Leave Afghanistan?") As a result, feminists working outside the United States, particularly in the Middle East and South Asia, have developed the false perception that U.S. feminists support their government's militarization as well as neo-liberal "solutions" to poverty. Needless to say, this obstructs transnational feminist alliance building and subverts transformative feminists' program of pervasive social change. As Haifa Zangana explains, throughout the Middle East and South Asia, "Women's rights claims are seen by . . . women [in those regions] as the second supply line of U.S. colonial policy . . . with NGOs, especially those oriented to women's issues, damaging the possibilities for the much-needed work by genuine organizations" (2007, 11).

Such divisions, suggests Allison Jaggar, are fueled by access feminism's roots in liberal philosophies that conceptualize personhood as rational and autonomous and that value individual agency over collective action (1983, 28). According to this view, access-based feminism diverts attention away from dismantling structural inequities and overemphasizes individual women's aspirations. Such solipsism plays into the oppositions that neo-liberalism imposes on women: wealthier women are consumer "citizens," and poorer women are producer "citizens" (a deeply ironic twist in light of early access feminists' use of liberal philosophy to attain the status of citizen in capitalist economies). Not only does this dehumanize women by diminishing them to the status of economic units, but it also broadens real and perceived differences between women in developing and developed nations (Mohanty 2003, 141). This impedes the creation of feminist alliances, which, in turn, militates against the feminist goal of ending multiple forms of oppression. In contrast, transformative feminism, a method of praxis and a mode of analysis in which collaboration and collectivity are central, is less vulnerable to ruptures and cooptation by the very systems it aims to undo. For example, Mohanty, one of the first and most influential champions of transnational feminism in the United States, suggests that the interests and needs of women across the globe can converge in and through the institution of work to create opportunities for "constructing feminist solidarities across national, racial, sexual and class divides" (1997, 4, 19).

These tensions between access-based and transformative feminisms provide a useful context for examining core debates in women's and gender studies worldwide. First is whether idealizing and embracing a single social change strategy that reflects the interests of select populations is as effective as deploying manifold, multidimensional tactics that empower diverse groups with disparate social locations, needs, and desires. In light of the U.S. experience that the patriarchal organization of the public sphere and the family have been left intact by pursuing access to work outside the home, another question (one that for decades has characterized many other topics in feminism) is the degree to which change can be made within institutions and systems or whether feminists should focus on transforming socioeconomic structures and developing alternative paradigms. Additionally, of course, understanding the roots and evolution of access-based feminism and the reasons why it has been favored by some groups and not others reveals the diversity of U.S. feminisms and, to some degree, accounts for the different foci, goals, and methods that distinguish access feminisms from both transformative feminisms (wherever they are practiced) and variants of feminism that are shaped and differentiated by their particular responses to local and global concerns.

Rethinking Access-Based Feminism through *Feminist Formations*

The articles in this book take on the questions raised here as well as others; these articles include contemporary criticisms of access-based feminism that expand, detail, and add to the critiques we discussed in the previous section. In keeping with *Feminist Formations'* close relationship with the National Women's Studies Association, whose membership consists mostly of transformative feminists who teach and conduct research in women's and gender studies, many of the essays in this retrospective are informed by transformative feminist thinking. We have divided the book into two sections to demonstrate the complicated relationships between women's access to work and women's economic, social, and political power. Part I includes articles that outline how access-based feminism has failed to achieve its goals: the ways in which the work that women do re-inscribes patriarchal structures and/or limits women's power. Part II describes ways that women have exploited available work opportunities to benefit themselves and their communities. This section evaluates workplace alternatives that have been positively transformed through government initiatives, grassroots efforts, or women workers themselves. Even here, however, this transformation is not without cost, and the authors evaluate that cost in detail.

Part I. Getting In Is Not Enough: The Limits of Women's Access to Public Work

The articles in part I analyze how the promise of access has failed different groups of women based on their race, education and skill level, nationality, or age. These articles expose the ways in which access to work has been a false promise for many women, one that has not led to increased autonomy and power in the workplace, in families, or in their communities. Taken together, these articles offer a sobering critique of access-based feminism, yet the authors remain hopeful that work, under different circumstances, might empower more women. To that end, most of the articles in this section conclude with alternative possibilities or a call to action to change workplaces.

In chapter 1, Yasemin Besen-Cassino analyzes the gender wage gap and how her research on teens' work coincided with the institutionalization of Girls Studies in the United States. As Besen-Cassino points out, most research on the gender wage gap until that point had measured only adult employment, but most people have their first work experiences in high school. She finds that, beginning at age 14, boys earn more money hourly and per annum than do girls. Traditional explanations for this gap are flawed, since girls and boys at this age show no difference in education, skills, credentials, productivity, or hours worked and most teen girls do not have childbearing or child-rearing responsibilities. Besen-Cassino concludes that a small portion of these differences is explained by gender segregation, but much of this disparity is attributable to sex discrimination: "the cost of being a girl."

While Besen-Cassino focuses on analyzing gender, class, and race inequities that continue to exist (in terms of power and pay) among workers, the remaining articles in this section explore the specific causes of such injustice. Lynn Duggan, Niza Licuanan-Galela, and Fauzia Erfan Ahmed examine the role(s) played by corporate and government policies, educational systems, organized religion, and cultural attitudes toward both women and particular kinds of work. Sue Rosser considers the external and internal factors that might keep women in the sciences and engineering from pursuing patents. Finally, Tim Wise addresses attitudinal factors that can hinder women's empowerment.

Duggan draws on the work of turn-of-the-last-century economists in her analysis of the retail sales industry in the United States, which she characterizes as parasitic. It pays little and offers few benefits, which increases workers' reliance on food stamps, Medicaid, and other social benefits. Duggan claims that the 1996 Personal Responsibility and Work Opportunity Reconciliation Act (welfare "reform") limits poor women's access to education and, through tax breaks, provides advantages to companies that hire recipients of Temporary Assistance for Needy Families (TANF). Duggan ends by calling for major changes to industry and government, such as regulation of part-time labor, universal health care, expansion of unionization, and pay equity legislation.

In an article on Filipina workers in a Japanese factory, Niza Licuanan-Galela exposes the false promises of economic globalization. According to Licuanan-Galela, 80 percent of export industrialization workers in the Philippines are women, but their density in this workforce has not improved most women's economic or social opportunities. Similar to Duggan's claim that U.S. retail industries prefer inexpensive female laborers willing to work irregular hours for lower pay and no benefits, Licuanan-Galela demonstrates that the Japanese factory employs women for assembly line work because management believes women have greater dexterity and are more docile than men. According to Licuanan-Galela, a patriarchal Japanese organizational culture combines with the Filipino value of "get[ting] along with others" to create a female workforce with low job security, little mobility, and no leverage to make change. In addition, recruiting practices rely on male village leaders, which further marginalizes women by rendering them dependent on these men.

Fauzia Erfan Ahmed makes claims similar to Licuanan-Galela's in her study of women workers in the Bangladesh garment industry. The rise of this industry has provided employment for huge numbers of women, but jobs do not translate to greater power in the workplace or at home. According to Ahmed, garment industrialists create factories that offer low job security and segregate women according to gender and class, which discourages unionization. Outside of the factory, young, unmarried women may experience some economic freedoms as a result of their employment, but married women must give their income to their male partners. Ahmed stresses that the creation of a "sweatshop workforce" might benefit individual women and families, but it impedes efforts to secure women's rights in Bangladesh.

While Ahmed and Licuanan-Galela study women in manual labor factory jobs, Moushira Elgeziri writes about young women workers whose educational background would seem to afford them access to more skilled positions that meet middle-class ideas of work as "renumerative, fulfilling, and empowering" (chapter 5). Drawing from interviews with 60 women who work in Egypt's informal (nongovernmental) labor market, Elgeziri explores the experiences of female commercial school graduates, concluding that access to education and employment act as a false promise, in that they do not advance these women's professional, social, or political roles. Elgeziri identifies several factors that contribute to the disempowering nature of the work available to these women: outdated educational systems, a reduced public sector market that disproportionately affects women and lower-class Egyptians,[6] increasing divides between the educational opportunities available to middle- and lower-class Egyptians, and governmental and religious pressures on women to leave the public workforce for the home.

Even when women *are* granted equivalent access to the workplace, Sue Rosser demonstrates that access alone may not lead to equality. Rosser studies patenting rates among women in science, technology, engineering, and mathematics (STEM). She notes that, while rates of women earning degrees and working in STEM fields have risen over the past three decades, women's patenting rates lag significantly behind not only men's patenting rates but also women's rate of entrance into STEM fields. Drawing on published data and interviews with ten professionals in technology companies, Rosser demonstrates that this pattern of lower patenting rates—and, she notes, lower publication rates—holds true across all disciplines and across all countries. The problem with this low patenting rate, according to Rosser, is twofold: (1) prestige, advancement, and financial compensation in STEM fields are often tied to one's patenting, and (2) underrepresentation of women in the patenting process "hurts scientific innovation, technology, and competitiveness overall." Rosser ends her article with a detailed list of suggestions for women scientists, corporations and venture capitalists, male faculty, and educational institutions.

In the final chapter in part I, Tim Wise reminds us that "women" does not refer to a coherent, stable category in the workplace any more than it does in other contexts. Specifically, Wise looks at inequities between white women and women of color by focusing on attitudes toward affirmative action. Wise considers California's Proposition 209, which in 1996 ended affirmative action in state hiring, contracting, and college admissions, to explore why white women oppose affirmative action en masse despite being the population that has most benefited from it. He also investigates reasons for increased resistance to affirmative action among white women from the mid-1980s to the mid-1990s. He identifies five reasons, including sexist and heterosexist attitudes, and advocates for building cross-racial coalitions supporting affirmative action.

Part II. Beyond Getting a Foot in the Door: Women Workers Accessing Power

Despite the challenges of working in traditionally patriarchal environments, women's access to these milieus sometimes empowers them and almost always spurs change. The articles in part II examine women's experiences in traditional and nontraditional work and consider the direct and indirect effects of women's presence in these jobs. In addition, all of these articles focus on how institutions—law enforcement, politics, public sector community care, academia, business, food service, and entertainment—shape and are shaped by women who work in them.

Staci Strobl presents a historical overview of women's entrance into policing throughout the Gulf Cooperation Council (GCC) countries since the 1970s.[7] She demonstrates that the process of integrating women into these police forces has entailed negotiating and adapting to traditional mores about women's modesty and honor. She argues that this model of change is significantly different from the story of access-based feminism, which is typically framed in terms of heroic individuals overtly resisting sexism. Integrating women into nontraditional work in the GCC countries, writes Strobl, is more a matter of "backroom politicking based on notions of bottom-up voluntary deference and social exchange, as well as top-down state feminism" (chapter 8). In addition to changing policing itself, the means by which GCC women entered this field, Strobl suggests that her findings offer scholars a new way of conceptualizing how gender diversification of police forces in modern nation-states occurs, a process that until recently was understood solely through Western women's experiences and described as inevitable and linear. Strobl concludes by offering an alternate, culturally specific model of gender integration that accounts for multiple internal and external variables ranging from neo-traditional to progressive forces. Strobl's work is an important reminder of the negative consequences of intellectual and feminist imperialism.

In their article on "the increasing presence of Latinas and Chicanas in U.S. electoral politics," Sonia R. García and Marisela Márquez demonstrate how women's commitment to their communities can have statewide and national effects. Beginning in the 1980s, Latinas and Chicanas were winning races for public office at a rate higher than the overall percentage of women in elected positions. In a study of 51 Latina and Chicana activists, García and Márquez explore why and how these women created this access. The authors argue that Latinas and Chicanas take a unique approach to politics by blending traditional motivations for involvement (to elect particular candidates and to address specific issues) with community-based reasons (to serve and give back to Latino/a communities and their own families) and personality factors (high levels of confidence). As a result, García and Márquez claim, Latinas and Chicanas bring a grassroots focus to their political involvement.

Nancy Naples and Marnie Dobson find that community care workers of color in the United States and Aboriginal health care workers in Australia who occupy government-funded jobs are similarly motivated by concern for their communities. Through a comparative cross-cultural study that conceptualizes "community caretaking" as a form of activist mothering, Naples and Dobson reveal that, although female health care and community workers do not exercise as much influence over policymaking and resource distribution as women higher up the government bureaucracy, their collectivist approaches to social change offset the disadvantages of lower rank. Hence, the authors conclude that, in specific circumstances, the state can serve as a resource for poverty-eradication, anti-racist, and feminist movements. Naples and Dobson also suggest that scholars' traditional focus on definitions of citizenship that emphasize the individual discounts the extent and effectiveness of collectivism, which, offering lessons for creating alliances across differences, is the better model for resisting neo-liberalism on a global scale.

While the essays by García and Márquez and by Naples and Dobson examine access in the context of women's situation in and commitment to their communities, Esther Rothblum considers the advantages and disadvantages of decentering one's relationship to the dominant culture by identifying as a member of a sexual minority in the workplace. In a brief report on three major issues facing lesbians in academia, she illustrates how feminists have used work spaces to model self-acceptance, leadership, and success. Published in 1995, Rothblum's article discusses three decisions faced by the academic women she interviewed: whether to (1) come out to colleagues, (2) research gay and lesbian issues, and (3) discuss gay and lesbian issues and their own sexuality in different academic spaces. Rothblum reviews the choices lesbians make and their potential consequences, while acknowledging the role that institutions play in determining what is feasible.

The next two articles in this section contrast the experiences of U.S. female employees in pink-collar jobs. Based on interviews with 49 secretaries, Ivy Ken challenges two representations of women who employ a nurturing style in the workplace: the patriarchal view that women are naturally nurturing and the feminist perspective that women are socialized to perform nurturing behaviors. When this article was first published in 2006, Ken's focus on women's self-perceptions rather than others' attitudes added to the literature on gendered modes of leadership styles. The majority of the working-class interviewees, a racially and ethnically diverse group, reported that they do not engage in on-the-job nurturing, but some said they embrace this style at work. Ken argues that such nurturing constitutes an ethic of service rather than collusion with the patriarchy. She concludes by observing that class status affects whether women's service is respected or devalued and exploited.

Like Ken, Karen Kovacik examines women's workplace nurturing, but she interviews employees who have been forced to adopt caring roles. Kovacik reports that women in low-status, underpaid jobs often resent and resist mandates to "care" by caricaturing women's traditional gender roles. She subsequently analyzes poems by pink-collar workers whose texts critique demands to nurture customers and clients. Kovacik ends by citing scholarly assessments of these poems, which are largely negative, to indict the classed nature of literary criticism in the United States.

The final selection in part II examines how female performers in Cuba are feminizing hip hop while using their art to resist state and social patriarchalism. Las Krudas, an all-female hip-hop group, is the focus of Fari Nzinga's article on *raperas*, whose music is catalyzing public discussion of racism, sexism, and class bias in Cuba. The members of Las Krudas expose the government-generated myth of Cuban egalitarianism by rapping about hip hop's male-dominated culture, their experiences of homophobia, sexism, and racism, and the state's use of women's sexual, domestic, and emotional labor to navigate the postsocialist era. Las Krudas also appropriates the language of the Cuban Revolution and unapologetically infuses it with a feminist inflection, urging women to speak out against their oppression, distinguishing the *raperas* from their commercially successful counterparts in the United States.

All these assertions and counterclaims about feminism's use of work to achieve individual empowerment and social change create a "prevailing awareness that the world is increasingly complicated by the intricate workings of power, and we are all too implicated by its web to fit into the model of a perfect feminism, which is, of course, a fictitious construct" (Purvis 2004, 105). This mindfulness of the complex nature of power and our relationships with it, as Jennifer Purvis suggests, prompts us to interrogate "how to be a feminist." For more than 20 years, *Feminist Formations* has played a leading role in raising and discussing questions about "how to be a feminist" in relation to questions surrounding gender and work. We hope that the chapters in this book prompt continued conversations about the ways in which work benefits and complicates women's lives and shapes different feminist perspectives throughout the world.

As with any collection of research, however, questions and gaps remain. Several key issues are central to future analysis of women and work but are mentioned only briefly in this anthology. The first issue, and one that has been addressed by several scholars, is the important connection between women's public and family work, including (1) the nature of child rearing and housework as forms of (usually) uncompensated work, (2) the intractability of the traditional gendered division of labor, (3) the negative personal, social, and macroeconomic consequences of the (im)balance of work and motherhood, such as health risks and mothers' lower life quality, status, and income, and (4) in countries like India, Japan, and the United States, the persistent structural difficulties caused by the lack of affordable, safe institutional childcare. Because a book on motherhood was planned for the *Feminist Formations* retrospective series, we do not delve into these topics in this text. The articles included here, however, do reveal the influence that family and motherhood have on women workers. For example, García and Márquez note the influence of familial responsibilities on Chicana and Latina women's involvement in U.S. politics. Similarly, Naples and Dobson define work for social change as a form of activist mothering and point out that the public and private are not separate spheres despite the opposition posited between them by patriarchal views of family and work. Any continued research on women's work published in *Feminist Formations* must explore the challenges faced by working mothers not only in terms of their individual situations but also in the context of the economics of neoliberal market globalization.

Second, few articles published during the past two decades of *Feminist Formations* have addressed women's sexual minority status vis-à-vis formal employment and their unpaid work in the family (especially in their roles as mothers). Rothblum (chapter 11) and Diana Bilimoria and Abigail Stewart (2009) discuss lesbians and work, but both of these articles focus specifically on academic women in U.S. colleges and universities. Cultural beliefs about gender are complicated by diverse sexualities, and there is a need for research that addresses intersections of sexual minority status with class, nation, race, and ethnicity across diverse fields of work.

Finally, we turn to Mohanty's claims that suggest that work offers feminists a site for forging transnational and cross-cultural solidarity that facilitates empowering social change and resistance to oppression. Mohanty's ideas have been taken up by many transformative feminist scholars, but we were unable to find any articles in *Feminist Formations* that show or analyze the sort of transnational collaborations that Mohanty envisions. Sue Rosser's article (chapter 6) comes closest when she describes the case of Sal Calfit, who created a transnational community of women engineers who support one another through the patent process. Clearly, *Feminist Formations*' audiences will benefit from examining similar models of solidarity and adapting positive lessons to their own academic-activist endeavors.

Of course, books and journal articles that critique flawed, colonizing, and neo-imperialist projects and describe how transnational feminisms *should* operate are abundant, but material on successful, mutually beneficial partnerships is relatively unavailable for typical readers of *Feminist Formations*. Publications that look at effective, just transnational alliances among feminist practitioners who focus on gender and work are even rarer. Rather than characterizing this as a deficit, we consider it an opportunity. For instance, there is an urgent need to debunk the notion that U.S. feminists are complicit in the government and media's cooptation of women's oppression (discussed previously). Also, African studies is grossly underrepresented in women's and gender studies curricula in the United States, and remedying this gap is imperative. Certainly, articles on successful instances of transnational solidarity could serve as the starting point of both projects.

Feminist Formations, which made explicit its commitment to collaborative women's and gender studies initiatives around the world when it changed its name in 2010, is the ideal forum to host such future discussions, particularly conversations that center on gender and labor, and our readers are encouraged to submit their articles on this topic to the journal.

Notes

1. We are reluctant to use wording, such as "Western," that reinscribes perceived oppositions among feminists; however, access-based feminism is widely associated with feminisms in the United States and several European countries. Of course, its main proponents historically have been relatively privileged women in these regions, but, as this introduction argues, access

feminism is only one of many feminisms practiced in the United States, in particular.

2. Access feminists, of course, are not the only activists who back these reforms. Much feminist social change is accomplished through strategic alliances that cross ideological and other lines.

3. As of this writing, the United States, along with Sudan and Iran, is one of very few nations that has not ratified CEDAW because of conservative opponents who fear that it will undermine the nuclear family and promote abortion.

4. Obviously, women of color and poor women were waged workers for many years prior to the mid-twentieth century women's movement, and African American women labored as unpaid slaves for much of U.S. history.

5. A follow-up to Boushey and Cherry's research on the 1990s "boom" is that initial studies of the effects of the 2008 recession show that African Americans and other people of color—women and men—are the population most negatively affected by unemployment and narrowing opportunities for economic advancement.

6. Published in Fall 2010, Elgeziri's article predates by only a few months the mass protests in Egypt that led to the removal of President Hosni Mubarak. These protests saw labor strikes throughout the country, with strikers calling for better pay, working conditions, and access to employment. At the time of this writing, it is not yet known which, if any, of the criticisms leveled in Elgeziri's article will be addressed by the new Egyptian government.

7. The Gulf Cooperation Council includes Saudi Arabia, Kuwait, Bahrain, Qatar, the United Arab Emirates, and the Sultanate of Oman.

References

Altbach, Edith Hoskins. 1974. *Women in America*. Lexington: D. C. Heath.
Bilimoria, Diana, and Abigail Stewart. 2009. "Don't Ask, Don't Tell": The Academic Climate for Lesbian, Gay, Bisexual, and Transgender Faculty in Science and Engineering." *Feminist Formations* 21(2): 85–103.
Boushey, Heather, and Robert Cherry. 2003. "The Economic Boom (1991–1997) and Women: Issues of Race, Education, and Regionalism." *NWSA Journal* 15(1): 34–53.
Canty-Mack, Colleen. 2004. "Third-Wave Feminism and the Need to Reweave the Nature/Culture Duality." *NWSA Journal* 16(3): 154–179.
Chua, Amy. 2004. *World on Fire: How Exporting Free Market Democracy Breeds Ethnic Hatred and Global Instability*. New York: Random House.
Collins, Patricia Hill. 1990. *Black Feminist Thought: Knowledge, Consciousness, and the Politics of Empowerment*. Boston: Unwin Hyman.

Desai, Manisha. 2002. "Transnational Solidarity: Women's Agency, Structural Adjustment, and Globalization." In *Women's Activism and Globalization: Linking Local Struggles and Transnational Politics*, ed. Nancy Naples and Manisha Desai, 2–33. New York: Routledge.

Douglas, Susan. 2007. "The Mommy Myth: The Idealization of Motherhood and How It Has Undermined Women." Paper presented at a Women's History Month lecture on 5 March, at Northern Illinois University, DeKalb, Illinois.

Family Educational and Privacy Rights Act. U.S. Code 20 (2010), § 1232g. www.law.cornell.edu/uscode/20/1232g.html.

Gordon, Linda, and Allen Hunter. 2002. "Sex, Family, and the New Right: Anti-Feminism as a Political Force." In *Public Women, Public Words: A Documentary History of American Feminism*, ed. Dawn Keetley and John Pettegrew, 3:237–250. Lanham, MD: Rowman & Littlefield.

hooks, bell. 1984. *Feminist Theory: From Margin to Center*. Boston: South End.

Hrycak, Alexandra. 2002. "From Mothers' Rights to Equal Rights: Post Soviet Grassroots Women's Associations." In *Women's Activism and Globalization: Linking Local Struggles and Transnational Politics*, ed. Nancy Naples and Manisha Desai, 64–82. New York: Routledge.

Institute for Women's Policy Research. 2005. "African-American Women Work More, Earn Less: New Census Data Show Economic and Educational Status of African-American Women Still Lags Far behind White Women." News Release. Retrieved 5 March 2006, from www.iwpr.org/pdf/IWPRRelease3_29_05.pdf.

———. 2008 August. "The Gender Wage Gap: 2007." Fact Sheet C350. Retrieved 8 April 2009, from www.iwpr.org/pdf/C350.pdf.

Jaggar, Allison. 1983. *Feminist Politics and Human Nature*. Toronto: Rowman & Littlefield.

Kettel, Bonnie. 1992. "Gender Distortions and Development Disasters: Women and Milk in African Herding Systems." *NWSA Journal* 4(1): 23–41.

Lock Swar, Amanda, and Nagar, Richa. 2010. *Critical Transnational Feminist Praxis*. SUNY Series Praxis: Theory in Action. Albany: State University of New York Press.

Lorde, Audre. 1998. "Age, Race, Class, and Sex: Women Redefining Difference." In *Race, Class, and Gender*, 3rd ed., ed. Margaret L. Andersen and Patricia Hill Collins, 187–195. Belmont: Wadsworth.

Moghadam, Valentine. 2009. *Globalization and Social Movements: Islamism, Feminism, and the Social Justice Movement*. Lanham, MD: Rowman & Littlefield.

Mohanty, Chandra Talpade. 2003. *Feminism without Borders: Decolonizing Theory, Practicing Solidarity*. Durham: Duke University Press.

———. 1997. "Women Workers and Capitalist Scripts: Ideologies of Domination, Common Interests, and the Politics of Solidarity." In *Feminist Genealogies, Colonial Legacies, Democratic Futures*, ed. M. Jacqui Alexander and Chandra Talpade Mohanty, 3–29. New York: Routledge.

National Women's Law Center. 2008 November. "Congress Must Act to Close the Wage Gap for Women: Facts on Women's Wages and Pending Legislation." Fact Sheet. Retrieved 8 April 2009, from www.nwlc.org/pdf/Pay_Equity_Fact_Sheet_Nov2008.pdf.

Parry, Janine A. 2001. "Family Leave Policies: Examining Choice and Contingency in Industrialized Nations." *NWSA Journal* 13(2): 70–94.

Purvis, Jennifer. 2004. "Grrrls and Women Together in the Third Wave: Embracing the Challenges of Intergenerational Feminism(s)." *NWSA Journal* 16(3): 93–123.

United Nations Commission on the Status of Women. 1979. "Convention on the Elimination of Discrimination against Women." Convention Text. Retrieved 27 February 2011 from www.un.org/womenwatch/daw/cedaw/cedaw.htm.

Wollstonecraft, Mary. 1988. *Vindication of the Rights of Woman*, 2nd ed. New York: Norton.

Wright, Melissa. 2000. "*Maquiladora Mestizas* and a Feminist Border Politics: Revisiting Anzaldua." In *Decentering the Center: Philosophy for a Multicultural, Postcolonial, and Feminist World*, ed. Uma Narayan and Sandra Harding, 208–225. Bloomington: Indiana University Press.

Zangana, Haifa. 2007. *City of Widows: An Iraqi Woman's Account of War and Resistance*. New York: Seven Stories Press.

PART I **Getting In Is Not Enough: The Limits of Women's Access to Public Work**

CHAPTER ONE

The Cost of Being a Girl: Gender Earning Differentials in the Early Labor Markets

YASEMIN BESEN-CASSINO

The gender wage gap is among the most persistent and durable facts about labor markets and women's lives in the United States. Due to widespread social and academic interest in the topic, much progress has been made in explaining the gender wage gap, though a substantial portion remains unexplained. Many social scientists have approached the problem of pay discrepancy between men and women from different perspectives ranging from economics to psychology to sociology. However, despite the differences in approach almost every study on the gender wage gap focuses on adult employment. Whether it is part-time or full-time work, as Paula England summarizes (1992; see also Blau, Ferber, and Winkler 2006), most studies on the topic focus on the adult labor market. However, in the United States almost every teenager works while still in school (Entwisle, Alexander, and Olson 2000; Manning 1990). Therefore, employment—and hence, possibly, the gender wage gap—actually begins well before adulthood.

The gender wage gap is typically measured by annual earnings of either full-time workers (England 1992) or part-time employees (Corcoran and Duncan 1979; see also Polachek 1981). Despite the variance in measurement, this sort of analysis can fully explain the gender wage gap only if we agree that the experience of work begins with adult employment. On the contrary, men and women in the United States rarely enter the labor market for the first time after the completion of their education. According to the United States Department of Labor's *Report on the Youth Labor Force,* almost every American high-school student works at some time (Herman 2000; see also Finch et al. 1991; Greenberger and Steinberg 1986; Mortimer and Finch 1986; Paternoster, Bushway, Brame, and Apel 2003; Schoenhals, Tienda, and Schneider 1998; Steinberg and Dornbusch 1991). Thus, in the United States, the labor market experience of both men and women begins well before adult employment. Explanations of the gender wage gap cannot be complete if only adult employment is considered; rather, an understanding of the gap requires that we also examine the pay patterns of teenagers in the labor market. Furthermore, as Barbara Reskin and Irene Padavic demonstrate, "the younger the workers are, the more equal women's and men's pay"

Originally published in the Spring 2008 issue of the *NWSA Journal* (20.1).

(1994, 107). Therefore, a study focusing on early employment patterns not only offers a more comprehensive understanding of the gender-based wage differentials by including a previously excluded—yet substantial—portion of the labor force, but also provides the opportunity to trace the origins of the gender wage gap while allowing us to control for individual characteristics such as domestic and maternal duties.

Prior Research

A substantial body of research attempts to explain the difference in pay for men and women. Prior inquiries operate under two distinct strands: studies that focus on individual differences between men and women, and studies that focus on occupational differences between men and women.

The human capital/productivity approach focuses predominantly on the individual differences between men and women and attempts to explain the gender wage gap through individual differences which might result in lower productivity (Becker 1985, 1993; Bielby and Bielby 1988; Mincer 1962; Schultz 1960). In such explanations, the lower earnings of women are argued to be the result of lower productivity among women and are often associated with their domestic duties and childcare responsibilities or with interruptions in employment due to these duties (Berk and Berk 1979; Hersch and Stratton 1997; Hochschild 1989; Mincer and Ofek 1982; Ross 1987; Waldfogel 1998).

Lower productivity of women has been associated with proposed differences in education and experience between men and women. Earlier studies have argued that different levels of formal education between men and women account for the gender wage gap, but this explanation has failed to explain fully the gender-based differences in earnings (England 1992; Tomaskovic-Devey 1993; Treiman and Hartmann 1981). However, many similar studies have shown that years of experience on the job account for a substantial portion of the gender wage gap. Due to women's traditional domestic duties, such as child rearing and housekeeping, the average woman on the labor market has fewer years of experience than the average man, which contributes to the difference in pay between men and women (Light and Ureta 1995; Mincer and Polachek 1974; Reskin and Padavic 1994; Sandell and Shapiro 1978).

Some scholars have also focused on differential preferences of men and women. Filer (1983) argues that different tastes and personality characteristics predict differential earnings for men and women. However, the hypothesized effect is an indirect one, where values and preferences predict different types of jobs, which result in unequal pay; the mechanisms through which these values lead to a wage disparity remain unaddressed. A more direct association between values and the wage gap can be observed in a number of studies that examine the relative importance men and women place on earnings and other occupational characteristics. These findings indicate that men place more importance on earnings than women do, and, therefore, men end up in higher-paying jobs (Brenner and Tomkiewicz 1979; Herzog 1982; Lueptow 1980; Major and Konar 1984; Peng, Fetters, and Kolstad 1981), though some studies fail to find such a difference in attitudes toward earnings (Walker, Tausky, and Oliver 1984). More recently, however, the field has accepted as conclusive the Jacobs and Steinberg (1990) argument and rejected this line of reasoning based on different preferences and values. Jacobs and Steinberg show that men and women's attitudes toward earnings do not explain the gender wage gap.

A second set of explanations, instead of focusing on the characteristics of the employees, focuses on structural and occupational differences between men and women. This view argues that the pay differential between men and women is predominantly due to occupational characteristics. First, this strand of research argues that the difference in pay between men and women is due to employment in different industries (Bayard, Hellerstein, Neumark, and Troske 2003; Blau, 1977; Daymont and Andrisani 1984; Groshen 1991). Earlier studies show that women are more likely than men to be employed in traditionally feminine occupations which require nurturing social skills and which are generally associated with lower pay (Jacobs and Steinberg 1990; Kanter 1977; Kilbourne et al. 1990; Steinberg 1990). In addition to sex segregation by occupation, there is also sex segregation by firm. The disproportional employment of women in lower-wage firms only adds to the gap created by occupational sex segregation (Aldrich and Buchele 1989; Beck, Horan, and Tolbert 1980; Blau 1977; Coverdill 1988; Ferber and Spaeth 1984; Hodson and England 1986). More importantly, for men and women, there is a difference in the types of jobs they hold: Where men tend to pursue managerial positions, women typically occupy nonmanagerial jobs (Blau, Ferber, and Winkler 2006).

In addition to these explanations, the gender wage gap has been explored based on characteristics of women—such as race, ethnicity, and age—which exacerbate the gender wage gap, showing that women of different racial and ethnic backgrounds experienced the gender wage gap differently (Goldin 1990; Jones 1985; Kessler-Harris 1986). Finally, instead of explaining pay discrepancy in terms of demand and supply, many feminist scholars have explored the organizational setting (Acker 1990; Feldberg and Glenn 1979; Ferguson 1984; Kanter 1977; MacKinnon 1979; Smith 1979). These scholars argue that the gendered nature of the workplace contribute to the gender wage gap.

All these explanations focus on different aspects of employment that contribute to the gender wage gap, but even when all of these explanations are considered, a substantial part of the gender wage gap remains unexplained. Given that a substantial portion of the labor force experienced the labor market before adulthood, it is possible that the gender wage gap originates from early employment. Hence, studying early employment patterns not only complements the current literature on the gender wage gap by offering an analysis of a substantial portion of the youth labor force, but also provides an opportunity to trace the origins of the gender wage gap. For the first time, we will be able to see how early labor market experiences contribute to the gender wage gap.

In the youth employment literature, research on youth wages is extensive in two major areas: structural and individual factors affecting wages. The first, and more dominant, wave of studies—structural factors that determine youth wages—considers governmental policies and restrictions, parental cash transfers (Pabilonia 2001), training programs (Andrews, Bradley, and Upward 1999; Grossberg and Sicilian 1999; Lynch 1989, 1992; Schiller 1994; Sweet 1995; Umana 1992), minimum hour requirements (Chen 1991), labor unions (Oklan 1987), neighborhood characteristics (Vartanian 1999), and, most importantly, changes in the minimum wage (Abowd, Kramarz, Lemieux, and Margolis 1999; Currie and Fallick 1993; Mangan and Johnston 1999; Meyer and Wise 1983; Neumark 1995; Neumark and Wascher 1999; Welch and Cunningham 1978).

While the literature on youth wages is dominated by such structural explanations and emphasizes the role of external factors on wages, the personal differences among young workers have received relatively scant attention. Partially because of data limitations and partially because all youths were assumed to make approximately the same amount of money (i.e., minimum wage), wage disparity in the youth labor market was rarely noted until recent years. Now, however, there is burgeoning literature on the role of individual or personal factors in determining youth wages. Because all youths were assumed to make similar wages, the most dominant wave of research in this new literature focused on "deviant" youth and attempted to identify factors that resulted in lower wages for some teenagers. Extensive inquiries explored the effects of smoking (Levine, Gustafson, and Velenchik 1997), alcohol consumption (Kenkel, et al. 1994), drug use (Gill and Michaels 1992; Kaestner 1991), arrests (Grogger 1995), teenage pregnancy (Klepinger, Lundberg, and Plotnick 1999), obesity (Register and Williams 1990), and interrupted schooling (Light 1995) on wages. In addition to deviant behavior, more recent studies have also explored the effects of nondeviant activities, such as extracurricular activities (Ewing 1995) and academic majors (Weinberger 1999) on wages. Finally, demographic factors have been included in the study of youth wages, with the most important demographic factor being race (Shapiro 1984; Weinberger 1998).

In the youth employment literature, almost no work exists on the effects of gender on youth earnings. Typical studies of the gender wage gap often portray the youth labor market as a "gender utopia," where there is no marked difference between what boys and girls earn. A limited number of studies do, however, point to different earnings of boys and girls, the most definitive one being by Greenberger and Steinberg (1983). But even these analyses have various shortcomings: First, the gender wage differential is noted only on the descriptive level—the discrepancies in pay are not explained; second, these youth employment patterns are not linked to the adult labor market; finally, due to data restrictions, an accurate difference from a nationally representative sample has not been offered. Because there have been so few studies of gender inequality in the youth labor market, this chapter focuses on that understudied part of youth employment—youth wages and different pay by gender—and reveals that the youth labor market does not, in fact, offer a gender utopia.

The Gender Utopia of Youth Work

The main source of data in this line of inquiry is the *National Longitudinal Study of Youth* 1997, *NLSY97* (Bureau of Labor Statistics, 1997). *NLSY97* provides ample data on income and employment variables along with demographic information on youths. To enable analysis and to explore changes over time, the data have been clustered into three age groups: 12- to 13-year-olds, 14- to 15-year-olds, and 16- to 19-year-olds. These data are particularly valuable not only in terms of the detailed, nationally representative information provided on the employment characteristics of youths, but also because of the inclusion of 12- to 15-year-olds, most of whom are traditionally omitted from analyses of youth labor. Typical accounts portray youth labor force participation rates among boys and girls as nearly equal, creating what seems to be a type of "gender utopia."

If we focus solely on labor force participation rates, in fact, we observe no significant differences in any of the three age groups. Among the 12- to 13-year-olds, 36 percent of girls and 37 percent of boys work; among the 14- to 15-year-olds, 47 percent of girls and 51 percent of boys work; and among the 16- to 19-year-olds, 66 percent of girls and 65 percent of boys are employed. Such marginal differences mean that we can treat the labor participation rates, at least, as being approximately equal. This well-known finding, perhaps, leads to the perception of the youth labor market as a place of gender equality.

However, a lack of differences in the likelihood of youths working does not imply equality in all aspects of youth employment. Simply because boys and girls of a certain age are equally likely to work does not mean that they receive the same pay for their work or hold the same types of jobs.

The Emergence of the Wage Gap

Based on median annual earnings of dependent youths, we observe approximately equal annual median earnings for both genders during their early employment years. Among the 12- to 13-year-olds, boys, on average, make $120, while girls make only slightly more, $125. If for no other reason this is important because it is the first instance of gender equality in earnings in the American labor force. As a further analysis shows, by the time that the youths in the study are in the second age group, 14- to 15-year-olds, boys' earnings surpass girls' wages substantially, with boys earning an average of $400 a year and girls earning only $266. Thus, we observe the beginnings of the gender wage gap, and it only widens with older groups. Within the third group, 16- to 19-year-old boys, on average, make $950, while their female counterparts earn only $750.

Although comparing yearly wages is the conventional and more reliable method of measurement, the low hourly pay and relatively fewer hours worked at earlier ages makes it important to consider the hourly pay rate. Interestingly, parallel with the above findings, we observe that, for the 14- to 15-year-olds, boys have higher hourly wages than girls. However, at these early ages, most working youths are engaged in freelance, non-hourly employment that is often paid on the basis of a completed task. Because of this, calculating hourly rates of pay leads to high standard deviations in the estimates of hourly earnings. Thus, annual earnings are a more reliable measure of earning power, but it is important to note that an analysis of hourly wages yields similar results as that of the median annual wages.

The mechanism behind the increasing gap in pay among genders is not immediately clear. Most of the traditional explanations of the gender wage gap fail when brought to bear on youth employment. Explanations of the gender wage gap based on individual differences in productivity or years of education would not be applicable in the case of youth employment. Girls, especially suburban girls as a group, in these early age groups would presumably not be less productive because they are having children.

Similarly, explanations based on differences in human capital between boys and girls are not applicable. For youth in the specified time bracket, difference in education, skills, credentials, or experience would not be relevant factors leading to different pay. All of them have the same education—less than high school—and the same experience—none.

Despite the fact that almost all individual explanations fail to account for the gender wage gap, the only applicable individual difference is the number of hours the youth works per week. When we look at the data, girls and boys, on average, work almost equal hours, with girls working slightly more than boys. Based on the *NLSY97* data, we can see that girls, on average, work 7.9 hours per week, with a standard deviation of 9.9, while boys work 7.2 hours per week, with a standard deviation of 9.9. Comparing similar standard deviations, we can see that girls work slightly more hours than boys do; therefore, there is no reason to suspect that different hours of employment contribute to the gender wage gap. Since the gender wage gap in youth jobs cannot be explained by individual differences such as differences in productivity, education, and experience, especially due to domestic or maternal duties, we must look for alternative explanations.

The second set of explanations in the literature focuses on structural factors such as the type of job. One potential explanation is that boys and girls, while having equal labor force participation rates, may work in different types of jobs. The types of jobs in which youths are employed do seem to differ by gender. Among the 14- to 15-year-olds, girls are more likely to be employed in freelance jobs such as babysitting while boys tend to hold traditional employee-type positions such as those in retail stores or fast-food restaurants, which offer more regular hours and set rates of pay (Herman 2000).

We observe the gendering of jobs within both employee-type and freelance jobs (which will be discussed later at length) as early as age 12. However, it seems that teenagers also adopt traditional gender roles quickly upon entering the workforce, largely by concentrating either in employee-type or freelance jobs.

The Making of the Gender Wage Gap: Type of Job

The overall analysis of the data shows a difference in the types of jobs girls and boys hold and particularly exhibits a marked concentration of girls in freelance jobs and boys in employee-type jobs. However, we have yet to show that this is the cause of the gender wage gap. The data do show that there is a disproportionate concentration of girls in freelance jobs, as opposed to employee-type jobs, and points to the gendered nature of both broad categories. However, we cannot be immediately certain that the gender wage gap arises from these differences. First, there is no evidence to suggest different pay for different types of jobs among youths. The vast majority of youths employed in employee-type jobs receive the minimum wage, while there is no evidence to support that freelance jobs pay more to one gender than the other.

Second, the disproportionate employment of girls in freelance jobs cannot alone be the cause of the gender wage gap, as child labor restrictions prohibit youths under 16 from employment. Therefore, the 12- to 13-year-olds and 14- to 15-year-olds are predominantly employed in freelance jobs. If the disproportionate employment of girls in freelance jobs explained the gender wage gap, we would not observe the degree of difference in pay for 14- to 15-year-olds that we do, as relatively few of these teenagers work in employee-type jobs. In fact, the wage gap is significant even among this group. Moreover, while the concentration of girls and boys in traditionally gendered jobs increases, this does not map onto the earliest signs of the gender wage gap. Even among the 12- to 13-year-olds, where girls actually earn slightly more than their male counterparts, girls and boys tend to concentrate in traditionally gendered jobs. However, the extent to which job choice results in the discrepancy in pay needs to be tested.

To examine the effect of gender on income, I perform a multivariate regression analysis that will assess the effect of gender on income while controlling for other likely influences on income. Because structural explanations for the wage gap among youths suggest that the type of job can contribute to differences in wages, I include in this analysis a variable that measures whether the job is a freelance position or an employee-type position. In addition to gender, I also include a number of demographic control variables traditionally included in similar wage analyses such as race (coded white or Asian versus nonwhite), age (older youths typically earn more than younger youths), and the socioeconomic status of the household (measured as household income, as a percentage of the local poverty level). I also control for the number of hours worked, as this will clearly influence overall pay across individuals. The results of this analysis will allow us to assess whether gender is significantly associated with pay, above and beyond the effects of race, age, socioeconomic status, hours worked, and type of jobs.

The results of the model show that this is the case. Accounting for all of the explanations applicable to the youths in our sample, including the number of hours worked and the nature of the job, girls can expect to earn about $93 less per year solely because of their gender. While this may not seem like a great deal, it is very large relative to the average earnings of a girl in the sample, which come out to only $606.76 per year. Thus, at these young ages, girls are making almost 13 percent less than boys.

Other factors in the model were used for control purposes not only to identify the pure effect of gender but also provide interesting comparisons to better comprehend the magnitude of the effects of gender on income. It is interesting to see that the effects of race result in an average of $63 per year, while the pure effect of gender is $93.

In addition to the standard regression results, the heteroskedastic maximum likelihood regression also allows us to substantively interpret the causes of the variance in our model. As predicted, the variance in the model increases with age and income—the latter bolstering our assertion of depressed model fit due to reporting errors in the dependent variable—but decreases with the interaction of the two, a striking result, especially given the relative strengths of the coefficients. We can interpret this result to mean that as youths become more like adults, older and earning more money, the relationship of their demographic characteristics to their earnings becomes more predictable. It may be only this variance that allows for the equality of pay in the youngest groups, and it fades away rapidly with increases in age and earnings. A further analysis of the heteroskedasticity patterns shows an interesting clustering of higher age and higher income youths—most of whom are boys, with the marked omission of girls.

Thus far, I have identified the pure effect of gender on the earnings of youths by controlling for all possible explanations and demographic characteristics. However, it is important to show how these factors translate into the gender wage gap. While the maximum likelihood estimation identified the direct effect of gender, it also revealed unequal earnings through the high concentration of girls in freelance jobs. The total average gender wage gap in the youth sample is $130, of which 71 percent, or $93, is attributable purely to gender. In addition to this, 10 percent of this difference is accounted for by the higher concentration of girls in freelance jobs. Therefore, overall, the model accounts for 81 percent of the gender wage gap.

In our attempt to unravel the factors that contribute to the making of the gender wage gap, we have reviewed the two major approaches in explaining the pay differences between men and women. The first set of explanations, or the individualist approach, is not applicable to the youth labor market. Girls in these age groups do not show any differences from boys in education, skills, experience, and the number of hours they work. Furthermore, they are neither married nor typically have maternal or domestic duties.

The final set of explanations, which explains the pay differences because of the types of jobs, however, provides a partial explanation for why boys make more than girls. When youths approach the ages of 14 and 15, girls tend to concentrate in freelance jobs, while boys seek employee-type jobs. This polarization explains an important portion of the gender wage gap but offers only a partial explanation. While only 10 percent of the gender wage gap is explained by the difference in jobs, the most important portion of the gender wage gap is explained purely by gender. Over 80 percent of the gender pay discrepancy is "the cost of being a girl."

While our model explains a substantial portion of the gender wage gap, there is still a minor, unexplained, portion of this gap. This portion cannot be attributed to either individual or value differences, but it is possible to consider further inner differences, such as personal value placed on income, within the types of jobs boys and girls hold. In our sample, the main and the most pronounced difference is between the kinds of jobs—freelance or employee-type. Despite the small extent of such effects and the limitations of the data, it is important to acknowledge the inner differences within all categories. Such differences in the minor job assignments often are obscured through the data collection process. However, it is important to test for such effects for future research, especially after more detailed data collections enable us to observe the nuances in job selection.

Conclusion and Direction for Future Research

The youth labor force, like a social laboratory, offers a time when most traditional explanations of the gender wage gap are not applicable and almost every individual characteristic, like education and experience, is equal. The absence of these potentially confounding variables makes youth labor the ideal laboratory for the study of the gender wage gap.

Previous explanations of the gender wage gap have attempted to account for the gap through differences in individual characteristics between men and women such as education, experience, skills, domestic obligations, or childcare practices. None of these explanations apply to youth labor, yet the gender wage gap remains. While a cursory examination of youth employment patterns shows almost no difference in labor force participation rates and even seems to favor girls, a detailed analysis of the data shows the origins of the gender wage gap. In this chapter, we have traced the creation of the gender gap through youth employment and the contribution of early market experiences of youths to the pay disparity. Our findings show that demographic variables such as race, age, and income significantly increase the gender wage gap and that the type of work explains the pay disparity between boys and girls. However, despite controlling for all possible explanations and testing for differences in values, the gender wage gap persists.

While our analysis of youth labor eliminated a number of the frequently used explanations of the wage gap, further research needs to unravel the mechanisms through which this gap is created, internalized, and translated into the gender wage gap in full-time employment. Many feminist scholars argue that organizations are gendered in full-time work. The next step would be to unravel the mechanisms, with detailed ethnographic work, through which the early labor market experiences translate and contribute to the adult gender wage gap and subsequently to unravel the everyday experience of the gender wage gap for youths.

References

Abowd, J. M., F. Kramarz, T. Lemieux, and D. Margolis. 1999. "Minimum Wage and Youth Employment in France and the United States." In *Youth Employment and Joblessness in Advanced Countries*, ed. D. Blanchflower and R. Freeman, 427–472. Chicago: University of Chicago Press.

Acker, J. 1990. "Hierarchies, Jobs, Bodies: A Theory of Gendered Organizations." *Gender and Society* 4(2): 139–158.

Aldrich, M., and R. Buchele. 1989. "Where to Look for Comparable Worth: The Implications of Efficiency Wages." In *Comparable Worth Analyses and Evidence*, ed. M.A. Hill and M. Killingsworth, 11–28. Ithaca, NY: ILR Press.

Andrews, M., S. Bradley, and R. Upward. 1999. "Estimating Youth Training Wage Differentials during and after Training." *Oxford Economic Papers* 51(3): 517–544.

Bayard, K., J. Hellerstein, D. Neumark, and K. Troske. 2003. "New Evidence on Segregation and Sex Difference in Wages from Matched Employee-Employer Data." *Journal of Labor Economics* 21(4): 887–922.

Beck, E. M., P. M. Horan, and C. M. Tolbert II. 1980. "Industrial Segmentation and Labor Market Discrimination." *Social Problems* 28(2): 113–130.

Becker, G. 1985. "Human Capital, Effort, and Sexual Division of Labor." *Journal of Labor Economics* 3(1.2): S33–S58.

Becker, G. S. 1993. *Human Capital: A Theoretical and Empirical Analysis with Special Reference to Education*, 3rd ed. Chicago: University of Chicago Press.

Berk, R. A. and S. F. Berk. 1979. *Labor and Leisure at Home: Content and Organization of the Household Day*. Newbury Park, CA: Sage Publications.

Bielby, D. D., and W. T. Bielby. 1988. "She Works Hard for the Money." *American Journal of Sociology* 93(5): 1031–1059.

Blau, F. D. 1977. *Equal Pay in the Office*. Lexington, MA: Lexington Books.

Blau, F. D., M. A. Ferber, and A. E. Winkler. 2006. *The Economics of Women, Men and Work*, 5th ed. Upper Saddle River, NJ: Pearson Prentice Hall.

Brenner, O. C., and J. Tomkiewicz. 1979. "Job Orientation of Males and Females: Are Sex Differences Declining?" *Personnel Psychology* 32(4): 741–750.

Chen, Y. H. 1991. "Youth Labour Supply and the Minimum Hour Constraint: The Case of Single Males." *Applied Economics* 23(1B): 229–235.

Corcoran, M., and G. J. Duncan. 1979. "Work History, Labor Force Attachments, and Earning Differences between the Races and Sexes." *Journal of Human Resources* 14(3): 3–20.

Coverdill, J. E. 1988. "The Dual Economy and Sex Differences in Earnings." *Social Forces* 66(4): 970–993.

Currie, J., and B. Fallick. 1996. "The Minimum Wage and the Employment of Youth: Evidence from the NLSY." *Journal of Human Resources* 31(2): 404–428.

Daymont, T., and P. Andrisani. 1984. "Job Preferences, College Major, and the Gender Gap in Earnings." *Journal of Human Resources* 19(3): 408–428.

England, P. 1992. *Comparable Worth: Theories in Evidence*. New York: Aldine.

Entwisle, D. R., K. L. Alexander, and L. S. Olson. 2000. "Early Work Histories of Urban Youth." *American Sociological Review* 65(2): 279–297.
Ewing, B. T. 1995. "High School Athletics and the Wages of Black Males." *Review of Black Political Economy* 24 (Summer): 65–78.
Feldberg, R. L., and N. Glenn. 1979. "Male and Female: Job versus Gender Models in the Sociology of Work." *Social Problems* 26(5): 524–538.
Ferber, M. A., and J. L. Spaeth. 1984. "Work Characteristics and the Male-Female Earnings Gap." *American Economic Review* 74(2): 260–264.
Ferguson, K. E. 1984. *The Feminist Case against Bureaucracy*. Philadelphia: Temple University Press.
Filer, R. 1983. "Sexual Differences in Earnings: The Role of Individual Personalities and Tastes." *Journal of Human Resources* 18(1): 82–99.
Finch, M. D., M. J. Shanahan, J. T., Mortimer, and R. Seongryeol. 1991. "Work Experience and Control Orientation in Adolescence." *American Sociological Review* 56(5): 597–611.
Gill, A. M., and R. J. Michaels. 1992. "Does Drug Use Lower Wages?" *Industrial and Labor Relations Review* 45(April): 419–434.
Goldin, C. 1990. *Understanding the Gender Gap: An Economic History of American Women*. New York: Oxford University Press.
Greenberger, E., and L. D. Steinberg. 1983. "Sex Differences in Early Labor Force Experience." *Social Forces* 62(2): 467–486.
Greenberger, E., and L. Steinberg. 1986. *When Teenagers Work: The Psychological and Social Costs of Adolescent Employment*. New York: Basic Books.
Grogger, J. 1995. "The Effect of Arrests on the Employment and Earnings of Young Men." *Quarterly Journal of Economics* 110(February): 51–71.
Groshen, E. L. 1991. "The Structure of Female/Male Wage Differential: Is It Who You Are, What You Do, or Where You Work?" *Journal of Human Resources* 26(3): 457–472.
Grossberg, A. J., and P. Sicilian. 1999. "Minimum Wages, On-the-Job Training, and Wage Growth." *Southern Economic Journal* 65(3): 539–556.
Herman, Alexis. 2000. *Report on the Youth Labor Force*. Washington DC: United States Department of Labor.
Hersch, J., and L. S. Stratton. 1997. "Housework, Fixed Effects, and Wages of Married Workers." *Journal of Human Resources* 32(2): 285–307.
Herzog, A. R. 1982. "High School Students' Occupational Plans and Values: Trends in Sex Differences 1976 through 1980." *Sociology of Education* 55(1): 1–13.
Hochschild, A. R. 1989. *The Second Shift*. New York: Viking Penguin.
Hodson, R., and P. England., 1986. "Industrial Structure and Sex Differences in Earnings." *Industrial Relations* 25: 16–32.
Jacobs, J. A., and R. J. Steinberg. 1990. "Compensating Differentials and the Male-Female Wage Gap: Evidence from the New York State Comparable Worth Study." *Social Forces* 69(2): 439–468.
Jones, J. 1985. *Labor of Love, Labor of Sorrow*. New York: Vintage.
Kaestner, R. 1991. "The Effect of Illicit Drug Use on the Wages of Young Adults." *Journal of Labor Economics* 9(October): 381–412.
Kanter, R. M. 1977. *Men and Women of the Corporation*. New York: Basic Books.

Kenkel, D. S., D. C. Ribar, P. J. Cook, and S. Peltzman. 1994. "Alcohol Consumption and Young Adults' Socioeconomic Status." *Brookings Papers on Economic Activity, Microeconomics* 119–175.

Kessler-Harris, A. 1986. "Women's History Goes to Trial: EEOC vs. Sears, Roebuck, and Co." *Signs* 11 (Summer): 767–779.

Kilbourne, B. S., P. England, G. Farkas, and K. Beron. 1990. "Skill, Compensating Differentials, and Gender Bias in Occupational Wage Determination." Paper presented at the annual meeting of the American Sociological Association.

Klepinger, D., S. Lundberg, and R. Plotnick. 1999. "How Does Adolescent Fertility Affect the Human Capital and Wages of Young Women." *Journal of Human Resources* 34(3): 421–448.

Levine, P. B., T. A. Gustafson, and A. D. Velenchik. 1997. "More Bad News for Smokers? The Effects of Cigarette Smoking on Wages." *Industrial and Labor Relations Review* 50(3): 493–509.

Light, A. 1995. "The Effects of Interrupted Schooling on Wages." *Journal of Human Resources* 30(3): 472–502.

Light, A., and M. Ureta. 1995. "Early-Career Work Experience and Gender Wage Differentials." *Journal of Labor Economics* 13(1): 121–154.

Lueptow, L. B. 1980. "Social Change and Sex-Role Change in Adolescent Orientations toward Life, Work and Achievement: 1964–1975." *Social Psychology Quarterly* 43(1): 48–59.

Lynch, L. M. 1989. *Private Sector Training and Its Impact on the Earnings of Young Workers*. Working Paper No. 2872, National Bureau of Economic Research.

———. 1992. "Private-Sector Training and the Earnings of Young Workers." *American Economic Review* 82(1): 299–312.

MacKinnon, C. 1979. *Sexual Harassment of Working Women: A Case of Sex Discrimination*. New Haven: Yale University Press.

Major, B., and E. Konar. 1984. "An Investigation of Sex Differences in Pay Expectations and Their Possible Causes." *Academy of Management Journal* 27(4): 777–792.

Mangan, J., and J. Johnston. 1999. "Minimum Wages, Training Wages, and Youth Employment." *International Journal of Social Economics* 26(1): 415–429.

Manning, W. D. 1990. "Parenting Employed Teenagers." *Youth and Society* 22: 184–200.

Meyer, Robert, and David Wise. 1983. "The Effects of the Minimum Wage on the Employment and Earnings of Youth." *Journal of Labor Economics* 1(1): 66–100.

Mincer, J. 1962. "On the Job Training: Costs, Returns and Some Implications." *Journal of Political Economy* 70(5): 50–79.

Mincer, J., and H. Ofek. 1982. "Interrupted Work Careers: Depreciation and Restoration of Human Capital." *Journal of Human Resources* 17(1): 3–24.

Mincer, J., and S. Polachek. 1974. "Family Investments in Human Capital: Earnings of Women." *Journal of Political Economy* 82(2):76–108.

Mortimer, J. T., and M. D. Finch. 1986. "The Effects of Part-Time Work on Self-Concept and Achievement." In *Becoming a Worker*, ed. K. Borman and J. Reisman, 66–89. Norwood, NJ: Ablex.

National Longitudinal Study of Youth (NLSY97). 1997. Washington DC: Bureau of Labor Statistics, U.S. Department of Labor.

Neumark, D. 1995. *The Effects of Minimum Wages on Teenage Employment, Enrollment, and Idleness.* ERIC Document No. ED397241; Clearinghouse No. CE072034.

Neumark, D., and W. Wascher. 1999. "A Cross-National Analysis of the Effects of Minimum Wage on Youth Employment." *NBER Working Paper.*

Oklan, M. J. 1987.*The Effects of Labor Unions on the Wages of Youth.* Ph.D. dissertation, University of Oklahoma.

Pabilonia, S. W. 2001. "Evidence on Youth Employment, Earnings, and Parental Transfers in the NLSY 1997." *Journal of Human Resources* 36(4): 795–822.

Parent, D. 2000. "Industry-Specific Capital and the Wage Profile: Evidence from the NLSY and the PSID." *Journal of Labor Economics* 18(2): 306–323.

Paternoster, R., S. Bushway, R. Brame, and R. Apel. 2003. "The Effect of Teenage Employment on Delinquency and Problem Behaviors." *Social Forces* 82(1): 297–335.

Peng, S. S., W. B. Fetters, and A. J. Kolstad. 1981. *High School and Beyond: A Capsule Description of High School Students.* Washington DC: National Center for Education Statistics.

Polachek, S. W. 1981. "Occupational Self-Selection: A Human Capital Approach to Sex Differences in Occupational Structure." *Review of Economics and Statistics* 63(1): 60–69.

Register, C. A., and D. R. Williams. 1990. "Wage Effects of Obesity among Young Workers." *Social Science Quarterly* 71(1): 130–141.

Reskin, B., and Padavic, I. 1994. *Women and Men at Work.* London: Pine Forge Press.

Ross, C. E. 1987. "The Division of Labor at Home." *Social Forces* 65: 816–833.

Sandell, S. H., and D. Shapiro. 1978. "A Re-examination of the Evidence." *Journal of Human Resources* 13(Winter): 103–117.

Schiller, B. R. 1994. "Moving Up: The Training and Wage Gains of Minimum-Wage Entrants." *Social Science Quarterly* 75(September): 622–636.

Schoenhals, M., M. Tienda, and B. Schneider. 1998. "The Educational and Personal Consequences of Adolescent Employment." *Social Forces* 77(2): 723–761.

Schultz, T. W. 1960. "Investment in Human Capital." *American Economic Review* 51(1): 1–17.

Shapiro, D. 1984. "Wage Differentials among Black, Hispanic, and White Male Youth."*Industrial and Labor Relations Review* 37(4): 570–581.

Smith, C. B. 1979. "Influence of Internal Opportunity Structure and Sex Worker on Turnover Patterns." *Administrative Science Quarterly* 24(3): 362–381.

Steinberg, L., and S. M. Dornbusch. 1991. "Negative Correlates of Part-Time Employment during Adolescence: Replication and Elaboration." *Developmental Psychology* 27(2): 304–313.

Steinberg, R. 1990. "Social Construction of Skill: Gender, Power and Comparable Worth." *Work and Occupations* 17(4): 449–482.

Sweet, R. 1995. "The Naked Emperor: Training Reform, Initial Vocational Preparation and Youth Wages." *Australian Economic Review* 2(110): 101–108

Tomaskovic-Derey, D. 1993. *Gender and Racial Inequality at Work.* Ithaca, NY: ILR Press.

Treiman, D. J., and H. I. Hartmann. 1981. *Women, Work, and Wages.* Washington, DC: National Academy Press.

Waldfogel, J. 1998. "The Family Gap for Young Women in the United States and Britain: Can Maternity Leave Make a Difference?" *Journal of Labor Economics* 16(3): 505–545.

Walker, J., C. Tautsky, and D. Oliver.1982. "Men and Women at Work: Similarities and Differences in Work Values within Occupational Groupings." *Journal of Vocational Behavior* 21(1): 17–36.

Weinberger, C. J. 1998. "Race and Gender Wage Gaps in the Market for Recent College Graduates." *Industrial Relations* 37(1): 67–84.

———. 1999. "Mathematical College Majors and the Gender Gap in Wages." *Industrial Relations* 38(3): 407–413.

Welch, F., and J. Cunningham. 1978. "Effects of Minimum Wages on the Level and Age of Youth Employment." *Review of Economics and Statistics* 60(1): 140–145.

CHAPTER TWO

Retail on the "Dole": Parasitic Employers and Women Workers

LYNN S. DUGGAN

The retail sales industry is one of the lowest paying and fastest growing industries in the United States today, employing 18 percent of the country's workforce, or 22.1 million people (Mishel, Bernstein, and Schmitt 1999).[1] The occupation of *cashier* which has fueled the growth of employment in this industry is remarkable for what it demonstrates about rising trends of female employment ("Occupational Employment Projections to 2008" 1999).[2] Eighty percent of cashiers are women, and their average wage was $6.29 per hour in the mid-1990s, usually with no health insurance or pension benefits. Consequently, a large number of cashiers and other retail employees rely on government poverty assistance to make ends meet. Increasingly in recent years, retail businesses themselves also receive public assistance in the form of tax credits to encourage employment of welfare recipients.

This article examines the expansion of United States retail employment within the context of the growth of primarily female part-time work, the trend toward *de-skilling* of work in this industry, and the increasing use of wage subsidies to employers. I begin by drawing on Beatrice Webb and Sidney Webb's turn-of-the-century analysis of *parasitic trades* and then turn to an analysis of retail employees' compensation, working conditions, and receipt of public assistance. Finally, I examine the tax credits introduced in the wake of the welfare reform of 1996, which are measured against the goal of jobs with higher wages and better employee benefits. Using the Webbs' notion of parasitic trades, I argue that the proportion of low-wage jobs in this country is higher due to these employers' subsidies than it would be in their absence.

Parasitic Industries

Economic theory of labor markets and employee compensation can be roughly divided into two approaches: neoclassical (or mainstream) economics, which holds that market forces of supply and demand are neutral and, when unimpeded, foster efficient uses of resources; and political economy, which directs attention to power relationships and historical changes in these relationships and holds that economic actors'

Originally published in the Fall 2001 issue of the *NWSA Journal* (13.3).

power and status shape supply and demand for resources, goods, and services.

In applied economics, each of these two frameworks is useful in its own right. For example, while neoclassical models best explain the dynamism of markets, political economy analyzes differences in access to capital among demographic groups and nations. Overlap in the use of these two schools of thought would be greater if not for the fact that economists are usually trained in just one of them. A neoclassical lens tends to "filter out" power relationships, while a political economy lens accentuates them. This is a recent development, however. In the nineteenth century, the field of economics was a "moral science" in which theorists and economists practiced political economy.

The Fabian social theorists Beatrice and Sidney Webb, founders of England's Labour Party, belong to this classical political economy tradition. Their 1897 treatise, *Industrial Democracy*, analyzes the tendency of certain parasitic industries to impose some of their costs of doing business onto society, taking away from workers more than their wages restore to them.[3] They differentiated between parasitic and *self-supporting* industries as follows: "if the employers in a particular trade are able to take such advantage of their workpeople as to hire them for wages actually insufficient to provide enough food, clothing, and shelter to maintain them in average health ... that trade is clearly obtaining a supply of labor-force which it does not pay for" (Webb and Webb 1965, 751). Such parasitism has serious implications for a society:

> [I]n thus deteriorating the physique, intelligence, and character of their operatives, [such trades] are drawing on the capital stock of the nation. And even if the using up is not actually so rapid as to prevent the "sweated" workers from producing a new generation to replace them, the trade is none the less [sic] parasitic. In persistently deteriorating the stock it employs it is subtly draining away the vital energy of the community. (Webb and Webb 1965, 751-2)

The Webbs note, for example, that mill owners were tempted to replace mules with cheaper "well-nurtured and respectable young women" as cotton ring-spinners. Purchased draft animals required "in addition to the daily modicum of food, shelter, and rest, the whole cost of breeding and training, the successive relays to keep up their establishments" (1965, 751). In the case of free human beings not purchased by their employer, however, "this capital value of the new generation of workers is placed gratuitously at his disposal, on payment merely of subsistence from day to day" (1965, 751).

Profit rates need not be higher in parasitic than in other industries, but because their lower labor costs are passed on to consumers in lower prices, these industries expand further than they would if employers had to pay a wage that covered workers' social and physiological costs.

Writing in 1897, the Webbs could not know that their critique of industrial revolution exploitation would provide insight into the expansion of the retail industry and other service jobs a century later in the United States.[4] Amid widespread social activism on both sides of the Atlantic, their efforts helped to bring about national minimum wage and collective bargaining legislation, social security programs, poverty relief, and safety standards in the early decades of this century.

Today, inequality, as measured by the ratio of income between rich and poor, has again reached the extremes that prevailed in the Webbs' time. In the last 25 years, the entire U.S. wage structure has shifted downward, leaving a smaller fraction of the workforce in middle-income brackets.[5] Many of those working at the low end of the wage scale, disproportionately women and children, have sunk into poverty or deeper poverty.

Beatrice and Sidney Webbs' theory of parasitic industries is compatible with, and has been deepened by, 1970s–1990s feminist economic theory of the devaluation of caring occupations, those "in which the worker provides a service to someone with whom he or she is in personal (usually face-to-face) contact" (England and Folbre 1999, 39). Hartmann (1985) and England and Folbre, among others, argue that workers in jobs in which women predominate receive lower wages than those in other occupations due to cultural sexism and women's historical subordination.[6] Empirical research in the 1970s through the 1990s provides support for this thesis, and many job reevaluation initiatives have taken place within the U.S. public sector to promote pay equity in the last two decades (see England 1999). The vast majority of American women work in the private sector, however, where employers have made no efforts to redress the devaluation of caring work.

The New American Economy: Growing Inequality

Between 1979 and 1995, hourly earnings fell for the bottom two-thirds of U.S. employees (Mishel, Bernstein, and Schmitt 1997, 143–4). Low unemployment and tight labor markets raised wages slightly in the late 1990s, but the occupational and wage structures on which earnings are based foster deeper poverty. For example, while in 1979, 4 percent of full-time workers earned wages insufficient to support a family of four at a living standard amounting to 75 percent of the poverty threshold (wages less than $5.78 per hour in 1997 dollars), by 1997, 12 percent earned wages below this level (see table 2.1). Within these figures, the percentage of women earning poverty wages rose from 7 percent to 16 percent (Mishel, Bernstein, and Schmitt 1999, 135–8).

TABLE 2.1
Percentage of Full-Time Workers Earning Wages Less than 75 Percent of Poverty Wages

	1979	1997
All	4.2%	12.1%
Men	2.4%	8.8%
Women	6.7%	15.7%

SOURCE: Mishel, Bernstein, and Schmitt 1999

TABLE 2.2
Percentage of Full-Time Workers Earning Wages Less than 75 Percent of Poverty Wages, by Race

	1979	1997
Whites		
All	3.9%	10.0%
Men	2.0	6.6
Women	6.3	13.7
African Americans		
All	6.3	16.3
Men	4.3	12.8
Women	8.5	19.4
Hispanics		
All	5.3	21.9
Men	3.5	18.2
Women	8.2	27.5

SOURCE: Mishel, Bernstein, and Schmitt 1999

Over this period, racial and ethnic earnings gaps have also widened. As Table 2.2 shows, the percentage of "white" full-time workers who earned less than 75 percent of the poverty wage rate increased from 3.9 to 10 percent, while the percentage of such African American full-time workers rose from 6.3 percent to 16.3 percent and the percentage of such Hispanic American workers rose from 5.3 percent to 22 percent (Mishel, Bernstein, and Schmitt 1999, 140–2).

As noted, job security and benefits have also declined in recent decades. Workers who lost jobs in 1993 earned 15 percent less at their new jobs, and 25 percent of those who formerly had health insurance benefits received no coverage in their new jobs. The proportion of full-time workers in medium and large firms with health insurance paid partially by their employers dropped from 92 percent to 82 percent from 1989 to 1996 (Wessel 1996). Among private-sector employees working 20 or more hours per week, health insurance coverage fell from 70 percent to 63 percent from 1979 to 1996 (Mishel, Bernstein, and Schmitt 1999).[7]

Young parents, especially those without college degrees, have been the hardest hit by these changes. From 1973 to 1990, the median earnings of U.S. household heads under age 30 and living with children fell 44 percent. Even children living with married parents under 30 were 2.5 times more likely to be poor in 1992 than in 1973 (Edelman 1992, 13–19). One in five U.S. children is poor today; among African American and Hispanic children, 37 percent are poor (Mishel, Bernstein, and Schmitt 1999, 281).

Although today's young workers have more education, they are poorer than their parents were at the same age (Mishel, Bernstein, and Schmitt 1999, 156).[8] Entry-level wages for high school graduates fell 28 percent for men and 18 percent for women between 1979 and 1997. College graduates' beginning pay fell 8 percent for men and, after an initial 11 percent increase from 1979–1989, fell 7 percent for women from 1989 to 1997 (161–2).

In contrast to the lean wages at the bottom of the pay scale, positions at or near the top have become more lucrative in the last quarter century. In 1973, the top 5 percent of the U.S. population received 11.3 times the income of the bottom 20 percent; by 1997, the top 5 percent received 19.5 times as much as the bottom 20 percent (Mishel, Bernstein, and Schmitt 1999, 50). Although productivity growth has slowed since 1973, national output per hour increased 29 percent from 1973 to 1997 (153–5). The vast majority of this income growth, however, went to the top 20 percent of the population and, increasingly over this period, to the top 10 percent (Mishel, Bernstein, and Schmitt 1997, 57). Since the mid-1990s, earnings inequality in the United States has outpaced that of any other industrial country. According to Mishel, Bernstein, and Schmitt, the typical low-wage worker in an advanced European country earns 44 percent more (measured by purchasing power) than such a worker in the United States, a result of lower earnings dispersion (1999, 365–8). No sound economic rationale underlies this large-scale redistribution of income and wealth (1999, 21).

> The factors causing the pain of greater dislocation, economic vulnerability, and the long-term erosion of wages have not made the economy into a "better" economy, nor has the large-scale redistribution of income and wealth . . . been associated with improved economic efficiency, compensation, or income growth. (1999, 30)

Krugman attributes the "spiral of inequality" to unions' declining strength from the early 1970s to the present (1996). In 1973, when 24 percent of the private sector workforce was unionized, organized labor acted as a political counterweight to corporate power; now, at only 10 percent of the private sector, the labor movement wields less power (1996, 44–9; Hirsch and Macpherson 1996, 10). As unions lost numbers, they lost political power, and corporate assaults on workers' rights, incomes, and dignity grew more successful. The fall in union density can be traced to the shift from manufacturing to service sector jobs, in part caused by growing international competition.[9]

The tendency of labor leaders to devote little time and few resources to organizing in the service sector, where most women worked, also contributed to unions' declining density.[10] More recently, under the leadership of John Sweeney (former president of the Service Employees International Union), the AFL-CIO (American Federation of Labor–Congress of Industrial Organizations) has made organizing a priority and service sector union density has begun to swell; still, yearly membership declines due to manufacturing job losses usually outnumber new union memberships.

Part-Time Work and the Retail Industry

The proliferation of low-skill jobs in recent years has been a large factor behind falling U.S. wages. From 1957 to 1997, part-time employment grew from 13 percent of the U.S. workforce to 18 percent (Tilly 1996, 13; Hirsch and Macpherson 1996, 24).[11] When all else is equal, employers tend to prefer part-time employees because their compensation rates are lower and hours can be increased without paying time-and-a-half for overtime. Lower wages without health, vacation, and pension benefits result in higher employee quit rates, which in turn reduce productivity. Nonetheless, economically rational employers may continue to convert full-time to part-time jobs if the savings in wages and benefits outweighs the cost of hiring, training, and lost productivity.[12]

This long-term trend of replacing full-time workers with part-time ones resulted, between 1973 and 1989, in a significant growth in *involuntary* part-time employment: workers looking for full-time jobs were only able to find part-time jobs (Mishel, Bernstein, and Schmitt 1999, 247–8).[13] By 1997 the rate of involuntary part-time work had fallen to slightly above its 1973 level, but by then more than 6 percent of the workforce (8.2 million Americans) held two or more jobs, with most multiple job holders working over 40 hours per week.[14]

Frequently, today's *voluntary* part-time employment reflects parents' need for more flexible work, and only one in five part-time workers in retail say that they would prefer full-time work.[15] Because working parents in low-wage occupations often cannot afford high-quality childcare, they tend to choose part-time employment in order to care for their own children as much as possible, with assistance from trusted friends and relatives. Since the vast majority of part-time jobs are in the retail industry, especially evening and night jobs (when friends, relatives, or spouses are less likely to be at work), parents with low-paying job skills can often be found working in stores and fast-food establishments.

The retail industry holds the dubious distinction of offering the largest percentage of part-time work in the U.S. economy. Since 1966, the average workweek in this industry has fallen steadily, from 36 hours to 29 hours, the shortest workweek of any industry (*Employment and Earnings* 1996, 49). From 1979 to 1997, employment in the retail industry grew 47 percent, and retail jobs accounted for 22 percent of the 32.4 million jobs created from 1979 to 1997 (Mishel, Bernstein, and Schmitt 1999, 173). Based on 1994–1996 Current Population Survey data, 48 percent of all non-managerial and non-professional retail jobs are part-time (Duggan 1997). Fifty-eight percent of cashiers and 54 percent of baggers and stock clerks work part-time (Hirsch and Macpherson 1996, 100, 108).

Despite the increase in part-time retail jobs, the union density rate in this industry is only 6 percent, less than half the rate for the labor force as a whole. Among part-time workers in the United States, union density is only 7.5 percent, so there is little upward pressure on part-time wages (Hirsch and Macpherson 1996, 19, 77). Consequently, anyone needing part-time work to care for children or relatives must accept a lower hourly wage and forego benefits.

Based on 1994–1996 Current Population Survey data, over 76 percent of retail workers are not covered by employer-provided health insurance.[16] The lack of health insurance in part-time jobs means that, when a dependent child experiences a health crisis, employees may be forced to give up their jobs to qualify for public medical assistance, resulting in yet higher turnover and lower productivity in the industries that absorb part-time workers. Where present in the retail industry, unions have usually bargained to reduce the wage and benefit differential between full- and part-time workers, giving employers less incentive to convert full-time to part-time jobs.[17] But from 1977 to 1995, the unionized percentage of retail workers fell from 11 percent to 6 percent (Hirsch and Macpherson 1996, 77).

The De-Skilling of Retail Jobs

Driving the explosion of jobs in this industry is the trend toward de-skilling of work to create jobs that can be filled with *cheaper* workers. As Chris Tilly writes, retailers have broken complex jobs into units which involve little skill or responsibility. The new de-skilled workforce "need not be especially stable or committed, but it must be cheap.... In fact, creating part-time jobs is a way to attract a secondary workforce and to legitimize a lower standard of pay" (Tilly 1996, 9).

This trend is only the latest symptom of a century-long process of deskilling and devaluing retail work, which until the early twentieth century was usually restricted to U.S.-born white men. In 1910, 71 percent of sales clerks in stores were men, 29 percent women, and less than 1 percent African American (U.S. Bureau of the Census 1914, 422–23). To reduce wages, and in response to union militancy and wartime labor shortages, retailers began to employ increasing numbers of white women, later adding non-white men and women as salesclerks and cashiers. By 1950, women comprised 44 percent of U.S. retail workers, and by the mid-1990s, 53 percent (Hirsch and Macpherson 1996, 100).

As retail occupations were transformed from men's to women's and minorities' work, employers redefined these jobs as unskilled, converting some of the services and information formerly provided by clerks to *self-service* and making ever greater use of advertising to transmit information to customers.[18] Despite such reorganization and redefinition, Katherine Newman argues that retail jobs are complex, involving greater skills than employers and society are willing to acknowledge and compensate workers for (1999, 139–49).

Women workers, as noted earlier, landed disproportionately in the lowest paying jobs. Nona Glazer notes that gender segregation has replaced gender exclusion. Today 80 percent of cashiers are women; *front-end* jobs in stores are low-wage *women's jobs* (1995, 73). Cashiers' hourly earnings fell a steep 12 percent from 1983 to 1995. The average wage in this occupation was $6.29 per hour in the mid-1990s (a figure that includes the wages of cashiers with many years of experience) (Hirsch and Macpherson 1994, 120; 1996, 100). A cashier working 29 hours per week—the average number of hours for retail employees (including managers and supervisors)—and earning the average wage of $6.29 earns $9,485 in a year. Wages in the retail industry as a whole are slightly higher, averaging $8.04 per hour in 1995, or $12,166 annually for the average employee who works 29 hours per week (1996, 100).[19]

Mainstream economics teaches that a worker's skill level, motivation, and productivity determine the type of job he or she will find. However, the reverse is true as well: job characteristics and wages also determine workers' skills, motivation, and productivity. As retail employers have converted full-time jobs to part-time, in the process reducing wages, benefits, and training, workers' productivity has fallen due to rising quit rates among employees. Studies estimate turnover to be as high as 60 percent per year.[20]

Because employers' cost reductions are greater than the cost increase that comes with high turnover, a vicious cycle is set in motion: the lower the cost of labor, the less incentive employers have to increase the productivity of these workers through training, technical improvements, or work reorganization. Because they pay so little for labor, they can afford to use it inefficiently. In fact, it is economically rational to do so.

The vicious cycle of falling wages and high turnover described above contributes to a decline in workplace safety that can be seen in retail jobs, especially in grocery stores. Attempting to keep costs to a minimum despite the continual hiring of new workers, employers tend to provide too little training. If one storeowner reduces costs, and thus prices, by limiting workers' safety, other owners are compelled to do likewise, increasing the chance that an employee may be disabled for life. Without strong unions and active enforcement of government safety standards, workers' lives and health may be thrown away as employers compete to pay as little as possible for wages, safety, and training costs.

A recent study of all U.S. industries by the Bureau of Labor Statistics ranked the grocery store industry third in the United States in recorded injuries and illnesses, with about 250,000 cases in 1990 (Campany and Personick 1992).[21] Grocery store rates of 12.3 cases per 100 full-time workers, with back injuries and carpal tunnel syndrome accounting for the majority of injuries, can be compared to an average of 8.8 cases for private industry as a whole. Department stores also ranked among the industries with the highest recorded injuries and illnesses.[22]

When firms in a competitive industry are given the option of low-wage labor, if the wage differential between skilled and unskilled workers is sufficiently large, they will choose unskilled labor. As the Webbs explain:

> If [employers] can get the work done by parasitic labor they will have so much the less inducement to devise means of performing the same service with the aid of machinery and steam power, and so much the less interest in adopting mechanical inventions that are already open to them. Thus the parasitic trades not only abstract part of the earnings of other wage-earners, and use up the capital stock of national vigor: they actually stand in the way of the most advantageous distribution of the nation's industry, and thus prevent its capital, brains, and manual labor from being, in the aggregate, as productive as they would otherwise be. (1965, 754–5)

The savings of parasitic employers in the form of wages, benefits, and training costs not paid and in technical advancements and work reorganization not undertaken come at a loss not only to a large fraction of the U.S. workforce but also to society in general. Furthermore, as the number of low-skill, low-wage jobs grows, an ever-greater segment of the population suffers from lower standards of living and quality of life. Society is forced to absorb the costs of "reproducing" or caring for these workers in the form of poverty relief.

Aid to Dependent Industries

As discussed above, a large portion of the *costs* of low wages in retail jobs is absorbed by the workers in those jobs, and by these workers' children, in the form of missed health insurance, inadequate medical attention, low job security, low living standards, and high stress levels. If workers and their families receive public assistance, they are also likely to be burdened with social stigma, as the U.S. public tends to blame poor workers for their lack of marketable skills rather than employers for their predatory use of these (usually female) workers. But another part of the bill not paid by parasitic employers is absorbed by society in general—by taxpayers and other employers. The 76 percent of retail workers without employer-provided health insurance must rely on family members' health insurance if this is possible and, if not, must use Medicaid or hospital emergency rooms. Among households of U.S. cashiers over age nineteen living with children, 24 percent receive food stamps and 13 percent receive some kind of public assistance other than Medicaid or food stamps.[23]

According to Sidney and Beatrice Webb, when taxes are used to subsidize the cost of labor in an industry, employers are encouraged to expand this industry (in addition to discouraging training, as described above). As a result, the equilibrium number of low-skill, low-wage jobs in the economy is higher than it would be in the absence of subsidies:

> If the community chooses to give to all the employers in a particular industry an annual bounty out of the taxes ... it is obvious that this special privilege will, other things being equal, cause the favored industry to outstrip its rivals. The subsidy or bounty will enable the endowed manufacturers to bribe the public to consume their article, by ceding to them what they have not paid for. (1965, 749)

Moreover, the Webbs note, "the mere existence of any parasitic industry tends incidentally to check the expansion of the self-supporting trades, whether these are regulated or unregulated" (1965, 753). Their analysis of parasitic industries is painfully relevant to our time. During the 1980s and 1990s, federal poverty relief programs have extended public subsidies to employers in the form of tax credits to encourage employment of certain groups of workers.

A short detour is needed here to explain the origin and thrust of the 1996 welfare reform and the Temporary Assistance to Needy Families (TANF) program that it spawned. The federal poverty relief program that preceded TANF, Aid to Families with Dependent Children (AFDC), legislated as part of the 1935 Social Security Act, imposed a high penalty on paid work by the single parents who received welfare. Until the Civil Rights era, racial discrimination largely excluded non-white women from this program, designed by upper-class women who believed that individual mothers should care for their own children in their own homes, as long as these were deemed suitable by a caseworker. Childcare assistance was not provided and cash assistance was reduced dollar for dollar if a mother worked for pay, although the levels of assistance were never sufficient to cover families' subsistence. Predictably, AFDC recipients often failed to report income from other sources (such as relatives, boyfriends, and work) in an attempt to improve their and their children's lives (Edin and Lein 1997).

In the 1960s, welfare rights activists fought racial discrimination, making the AFDC program accessible to all who qualified for such assistance. As the program grew, it came under increasing attack due to one of the contradictions built into it from the start: strong disincentives against paid work despite welfare recipients' willingness to do such work. Legislation was passed in the early 1980s to allow states to experiment with programs that included incentives for paid work and provided support services such as childcare assistance. However, most of the critics of AFDC did not acknowledge another contradiction in policy: the stark dichotomy between the politically legitimate Social Security program that insured the retirement income of (mostly male) workers with lifetime labor force attachment (while wives raised children) and the stigmatized, meager AFDC assistance that insured women with children in the event of widowhood or desertion and, at the same time, *interfered* with their participation in labor force work (Gordon 1994).

The new approach to poverty assistance channels low-cost employees, subsidized by welfare programs, to employers who provide part-time jobs. The Personal Responsibility and Work Opportunity Reconciliation Act (PRWORA) of 1996 devolved administration of welfare (now called TANF) from the federal government to states. Today the focus of poverty assistance is to provide poor parents who receive welfare benefits with jobs at which they will "work off" their welfare checks.

To make sure private sector employers hire sufficient numbers of welfare workers, beginning in October 1996, the federal government has provided Work Opportunity Tax Credits (WOTC), amounting to a maximum of $2400, to employers of TANF recipients, Food Stamps clients, and other *hard-to-employ* workers. In January 1998, a second tax credit, termed Welfare-to-Work (W2W), for a maximum of $8500, was introduced to encourage employment of *long-term* welfare recipients, those who have received TANF for eighteen consecutive months prior to the date they begin work.[24] As of November 1999, employers in Michigan, a leader in *work first* programs (those which channel welfare recipients straight into the labor force with no training except in life skills), qualified for $91.2 million in tax savings through these programs. Illinois employers qualified for a potential tax savings of $127.6 million, and Wisconsin employers qualified for $52.6 million from these two programs.[25]

The 1996 reform of the AFDC program attempts to resolve its first contradiction—the conflict between disincentives to paid work and aid recipients' willingness to work. It is unsuccessful because the second conflict—the failure to acknowledge the imbalance of resources and power between those who work for pay and those who care for family members—remains unaddressed. In a market-based society, unpaid work historically performed by women in homes, such as childcare, is erroneously assumed to involve less skill and effort than other kinds of work. This assumption is particularly troublesome when it is applied to low-income families unable to purchase the many services that help average-income families care for their children.

The welfare reform defined by PRWORA imposes minimum work requirements on welfare receipt and decentralizes the implementation of these requirements to state governments. Within certain parameters states now decide which families will receive assistance, their exact benefit levels, and which types of support services will be made available to them. The federal maximum lifetime limit for welfare receipt is five years, but states are free to reduce this limit, and many have chosen two years as their maximum. Within this limit, PRWORA requires that any one period of TANF participation be no longer than two years.

The results of a recent test carried out by the National Campaign for Jobs and Income Support indicate that many poor people seeking federally subsidized services to which they are entitled (such as food stamps, Medicaid, and childcare) encounter a "culture of discouragement." This illustrates a trend that poverty researchers have regularly reported on since the 1996 reform: state and federal governments are unwilling to acknowledge that help is needed with costly services such as health care and childcare in order to move from welfare to work. The Urban Institute reports that roughly 1 million adults and 1.2 million children disappeared from Medicaid rolls from 1995 to 1998 (Rubin 2000). In 1998, states began an outreach effort to expand poor children's access to Medicaid, but not assistance to poor parents.

This approach to poverty relief is at best a short-term solution. With its work-first focus, this welfare reform strictly limits higher education or skills training (Schmidt 1998). The channeling of welfare workers into retail jobs and other low-skill jobs is also problematic for other reasons. First and most fundamentally, without a national health insurance system and plentiful high-quality, affordable childcare, employment in jobs that do not offer benefits will do little to move single parent families out of poverty (McCrate 1998). PRWORA provides for the continuation of

Medicaid coverage for only a limited time after a period of TANF assistance. Federally subsidized childcare is also only temporarily available, and the quality and affordability of this care varies from state to state.

The tax credits described above encourage the expansion of retail and other parasitic industries that do not provide private health insurance, training, or other forms of non-wage compensation. Because the WOTC and W2W credits are a wage subsidy, amounting to between 25 percent and 50 percent of the wage costs of employing a welfare recipient, their value is a greater fraction of employee compensation in jobs that do not include benefits such as health insurance. Most of the employers who participate in these programs are in the retail industry (including fast food), nursing homes, and temporary work agencies.[26] Results of the National Survey of America's Families, carried out by the Urban Institute, indicate that only 23 percent of former welfare recipients who were employed in 1997 had health insurance coverage through their employers (Loprest, Schidt, and Witte 1999, Table 4).

Second, employers will also have an incentive to dismiss employees after they have benefited from the tax credit, reinforcing the high turnover rate in this industry. Each of these credits contains an incentive for the employer to keep the subsidized employee working, a component of the program that has been added since the WOTC program was first introduced in 1996. WOTC consist of 25 percent of the employee's first $6000 in earnings if he or she works under 400 hours and 40 percent if work hours exceed 400. The W2W credit, for longer-term welfare recipients, encourages employers to keep the subsidized employee for two years, as the credit is increased in the second year, consisting of 35 percent of the first $10,000 in wages during the first tax year of employment and 50 percent during the second year (Davis 1998, 64). But after the first year of employment subsidized by a WOTC credit, and the second year in the case of a W2W credit, employers are subject to no disincentive or penalty for dismissing these workers. The wage cost to employers of a W2W subsidized employee doubles after her second year of employment, while that of a WOTC subsidized worker increases by 80 percent after her first year. An economically rational employer will weigh the cost of hiring and training replacements against the costs associated with single parent workers whose children sometimes interfere with their parents' schedules by getting sick or having other problems.

Third, single mothers on TANF, with little or no higher education, are in a tenuous financial position and, in effect, have two bosses: their employers and the agencies overseeing their public assistance. As a result, they are less likely than other employees to join in organizing efforts to improve pay, benefits, and working conditions or to challenge workplace discrimination. If TANF workers in Michigan, for example, lose their jobs *for cause*, they lose 25 percent of their public assistance. State governments determine the exact nature of cause and the exact form of welfare reform within their borders and are free to consult with employer associations regarding the type of control to exert over difficult (i.e., vulnerable) groups of workers. Similar to the way in which state governments bid against one another in offering tax abatements to businesses to locate within their borders, the "new federalism" in welfare may mean that states engage in subtle bidding wars to offer firms more strictly controlled workers at subsidized wage rates.

Last but by no means least, this tax credit program serves as an incentive for firms to expand part-time work in order to employ larger numbers of public assistance recipients, which in turn means these businesses will be less likely to provide full-time or sufficient hours of work with health benefits to workers who are not on welfare, because welfare workers are cheaper to employ. Moreover, as the Webbs explain, such employer subsidies lead not only to ever greater numbers of low-wage jobs within certain industries but also to the expansion of the industries in which such jobs proliferate.

In short, government encouragement of the creation of jobs with pay insufficient to meet the needs of workers' families only perpetuates, deepens, and multiplies the very poverty it purports to alleviate. A 1996 study by the Economic Policy Institute (Mishel and Schmitt) supports this reasoning, predicting that if one million welfare workers were to enter the low-wage labor market in that year (and nothing else were to change), the increased labor supply in this sector would drive wages down by an estimated 12 percent for the bottom 30 percent of workers in the nation as a whole.[27] According to this model, the current approach to welfare reform, by augmenting the overabundance of low-skilled U.S. workers, actually exacerbates the poverty of all low-wage workers.

Economic theory dictates that, in the absence of any other changes, when firms' labor demands increase, wages rise. The current business cycle expansion has led to a slight increase in workers' average pay. Theory also tells us, however, that if roughly a million workers had not been added via welfare reform to low-wage labor markets, earnings would have increased further in these markets. The wage subsidy can be said, however, to have increased the demand for labor in occupations in which wages are the bulk of compensation, so this has surely counteracted at least part of the downward pressure on wages that would have taken place if not for this subsidy. The question that remains, therefore, in a static model, is whether this use of taxes has resulted in enough labor demand (and job creation) in these markets to offset the dampening effect on wages of the additional low-wage workers.

But economies are dynamic, not static. Regardless of the effect of the wage subsidy on workers' pay at this point in this business cycle, the basic structure promoted by the welfare-to-work subsidies is one of an ever growing percentage of low-wage, low-skill jobs. If not for the subsidy of hard-to-employ workers, the ratio of poverty-wage jobs in comparison to living-wage jobs would be lower. Public subsidies of parasitic employers are an ineffective use of tax revenues.

But the problem is larger still. Capitalist economies are not only dynamic but also cyclical. In a recession income, tax receipts fall and unemployment rises, and no amount of tax credits will reverse falling real wages. The greater the fraction of the population depending on low-wage jobs for survival, the greater will be the destitution.

At a time when economic inequality has reached a new high, it stands to reason that social policy changes should be aimed at evening the jagged playing field and restoring balance among jobs and incomes. The subsidy of low-wage employment at such a time raises questions about government's commitment to single parents and children. Is the wage subsidy to retail employers in the interests of the working poor parents it purports to serve, or is it a response to more powerful actors? Will these subsidies reduce retail employers' parasitism and increase the likelihood that they will provide living wages, or do the opposite? Have wage subsidies to low-wage U.S. employers been put in place to protect those who do caring work in our society or to allow others to benefit from their lower bargaining position in labor markets?

There are many alternatives to this type of welfare reform, including entitlements taken for granted in other industrial countries. Legislation could make part-time work available to parents of young children across all occupations; pay and benefits for part-time work could be regulated to achieve proportionality to full-time work; pay equity legislation could be used to bring about equal pay for work of comparable value, not only between men's and women's jobs but among jobs in which different racial/ethnic groups predominate; health insurance reform could provide universal coverage; and labor law reform could support union organizing drives in low-wage occupations (non-union employees in the U.S. retail industry earned an average of $7.41 per hour in 1995, while unionized retail employees earned $10.16 per hour).[28]

Some additional welfare-related, labor market policy reforms have been proposed by the Women's Committee of 100, a group of feminist academics, professionals, and activists concerned with the relationships between women, economic survival, and the work of caregiving. These include, for example, a shortened standard workweek for both women and men so that both can meet their responsibilities for family caregiving; a living wage that allows a single adult to bring a family of three above the poverty line; affirmative action remedies that open up higher-paying jobs and redress gender, race, age, and ability discrimination; paid family and medical leave for all wage earners; an end to discrimination against workers because of their care-giving responsibilities and to employment conditions that unreasonably interfere with those responsibilities (such as overtime as a condition of employment); unemployment insurance for part-time, very low-waged, and intermittent as well as full-time workers; and universal access to higher education and skill-building programs that prepare women for better-paying occupations (2000).

Conclusion

As this chapter has demonstrated, the trend in recent decades toward de-skilled part-time employment in the U.S. retail industry has been characterized by falling pay rates, deepening poverty, deteriorating working conditions, lower skill levels, and fewer protections such as health insurance. Taxpayers are increasingly called upon to subsidize low-wage employers directly through tax credits, as well as indirectly via public assistance to employees. As I have shown, this approach to welfare reform is counterintuitive and counterproductive. Instead of providing a route out of poverty, it encourages a vicious cycle of further de-skilling and higher turnover among employees.

If Beatrice and Sidney Webbs' analysis provides insight into the future of industries and occupations in the United States, then in the absence of raised union density or government regulation as described above, parasitic employers will continue to reduce business costs below the social costs of employment. Parasitic industries will expand at the expense of their disproportionately female workers, of self-supporting industries, and of society in general.

If its goal is to correct market-driven inequities and inefficiencies and to reverse the trend of growing inequality, social policy should not include incentives that encourage the de-skilling of jobs. Instead, policymakers should seek to eliminate the compensation differential between part- and full-time work and the premiums and penalties attached to male- versus female-dominated work. Pay equity legislation, government regulation, labor law reform, and increased support for caring work are better policy tools toward this end.

Notes

1. The retail industry includes all private sector establishments in which the sale of goods (new or used) and/or services is the primary economic activity, including, for example, stores, hotels, gas stations, insurance, catalog sales,

and eating and drinking places of all kinds ("Occupational Employment Projections to 2008" 1999).

2. In addition to cashiers, the occupation of *retail salesperson* is forecast to generate the third largest number of jobs. The Bureau of Labor Statistics forecasts employment growth for 1998–2008 for the occupation systems analyst to be 577,000 jobs. The two occupations, cashiers and retail salespersons, together were forecast to total 1,119,000 jobs ("Occupational Employment Projections to 2008" 1999).

3. Marilyn Powers provides a fuller discussion of early twentieth-century arguments in England and the United States for a national minimum wage, as well as an analysis of their relevance to feminist wage theories and living-wage campaign activism of today (1999).

4. The concept of parasitic trades was, however, used in the United States in the early twentieth century in reference to women department store workers (Filene 1923).

5. Service sector employment grew from 70 percent of the workforce to 79 percent, while manufacturing employment fell from 29 percent to 21 percent (Hirsch and Macpherson 1996).

6. Barbara Ehrenreich also uses a socialist-feminist analysis to understand class differences and social divisions among women (2000).

7. Private sector, wage and salary workers, ages 18–64, working at least 20 hours per week, 26 weeks per year.

8. The percentage of the U.S. labor force without a high school diploma fell from 28 percent in 1973 to 14 percent in 1989. The percentage with some years of college rose from 15 percent in 1973 to 22 percent in 1989.

9. From 1979 to 1997, employment in *goods-producing* industries (mining, construction, and manufacturing) declined from 29.5 percent to only 20.2 percent of U.S. employment. Jobs in *service-producing* industries grew from 70.5 percent to 79.2 percent of the total workforce; within this, jobs expanded in the lowest paid industries (Mishel, Bernstein, and Schmitt 1999, 171–4). For a discussion of the effects of international trade on inequality, see Moran (1999) and Freeman (1999).

10. Women now account for 60 percent of new workers and of new union members, as traditionally female sectors of the labor market are growing fastest. They are making inroads into union leadership positions, despite obstacles including centralization, gender and racial stereotyping, and male union culture (24-hour unionism with wives' support) (Needleman 1998).

11. Part-time is defined here as less than 35 hours per week.

12. For the effect of low wages on employee turnover and employer costs, see Ahmed and Wilder (1995).

13. The number of involuntary part-time jobs fluctuates with the unemployment rate, but the general trend is increasing (Tilly 1996, 14–15).

14. From 1979 to 1989, the Current Population Survey (Hirsch and Macpherson 1996), from which this data is drawn, asked multiple jobholders why they held more than one job, but this question is no longer part of the survey. In 1989, half of these people gave economic hardship as their reason (Mishel, Bernstein, and Schmitt 1999, 251–2).

15. Based on analysis of 1994–1996 Current Population Survey data (Duggan 1997).

16. See Duggan 1997. Health insurance paid to any extent by employers is henceforth referred to as employer-paid.

17. This differential is much smaller or absent in certain countries, such as Canada and Germany.

18. "Employers brought women into paid employment at the same time that they were asking women customers to do self-service. The result is a new division of labor: women shoppers do *some* of the work that men once did as salesclerks; women paid workers do *some* of that work as cashiers" (Glazer 1995, 73).

19. Supervisors' and managers' earnings are not included in these averages.

20. Low hourly earnings are a major factor contributing to this high turnover rate (Ahmed and Wilder 1995, 36).

21. The grocery store industry includes food retailers such as convenience food stores, food markets, supermarkets, and their supporting operations, such as warehousing and transportation.

22. Only nine industries reported more than 100,000 cases. In 1990, grocery stores' average rate of 12.3 cases per 100 had increased from 11.5 cases per 100 in 1980. Department stores' average rate was 11.2 cases per 100 full-time workers in 1990. In first and second place for highest rate of workplace injuries and illnesses were eating and drinking places and hospitals. Ranking in fourth, fifth, and sixth place were trucking and courier services, except air, motor vehicles and equipment manufacturing, and nursing and personal care facilities. Grocery store workers lost 98 workdays per 100 workers per year, while the rate for private industry, as a whole, was 75 workdays per 100 workers. The grocery store industry is also among the top ten industries with the largest number of repeated trauma disorders in 1990—the only non-manufacturing industry on this list. Other injuries included knife cuts,

lacerations, punctures, contusions, and bruising. See Campany and Personick (1992, 9–10, 12).

23. See Duggan 1997.

24. *Harder-to-employ* categories include veterans, ex-felons, summer youth, and residents of empowerment zones. This program replaced the sixteen-year-old Targeted Jobs Tax Credit program, expanding the groups that are considered harder to employ (Davis 1998).

25. The Michigan Unemployment Agency issued 14,613 WOTC certifications in fiscal 1999, for a potential tax savings of $35.1 million to employers. Another 6,607 W2W certifications were also granted, which will save employers up to $56.2 million ("Tax Credit Programs Save Michigan Employers $91.2 Million Reports Unemployment Agency" 1999).

26. The federal program was authorized through 31 December 2001 (Isotalo 2000).

27. Mishel and Schmitt estimate that, if the economy were to absorb almost 1 million more workers, "Nationally, the wages of low-wage workers (defined here as the bottom 30 percent of workers—about 31 million men and women who earn less than $7.19 per hour) will have to fall by 11.9 percent" (1996, 1).

28. Within this average, non-unionized cashiers earned $6.03 per hour in 1995, while union cashiers earned $8.59 per hour. Non-union stock handlers and baggers earned $6.20 per hour, while union stock handlers and baggers earned $8.15 per hour. Among stevedores and freight, stock, or material handlers, those who did not belong to a union received $8.00 per hour, while those who were unionized received $11.95 per hour (Hirsch and Macpherson 1996, 100, 108).

References

Ahmed, Ziaul Z., and Patricia S. Wilder. 1995. "Productivity in Retail Miscellaneous Shopping Goods Stores." *Monthly Labor Review* October: 33–7.
Campany, Sarah O., and Martin E. Personick. 1992. "Profiles in Safety and Health: Retail Grocery Stores." *Monthly Labor Review* September: 9–16.
Davis, Elaine. 1998. "How to Get Tax Credits." *Corporate Report–Minnesota* 3(March): 64.
Duggan, Lynn. 1997. *The Crisis in Retail Employment: A Study of Working Conditions, Earnings, and Benefits in Michigan*. Local 951, United Food and Commercial Workers International Union, Grand Rapids, MI.
Edelman, Marion Wright. 1992. "Vanishing Dreams of America's Young Families." *Monthly Labor Review* (September): 9–10, 12. First published *Challenge* (May–June): 13–19.

Edin, Katherine, and Laura Lein. 1997. *Making Ends Meet: How Single Mothers Survive Welfare and Low-Wage Work.* New York: Russell Sage Foundation.

Ehrenreich, Barbara. 2000. "Maid to Order: The Politics of Other Women's Work." *Harpers Magazine* 300(1799): 59–71.

Employment and Earnings. 1996. Bureau of Labor Statistics, October.

England, Paula. 1999. "The Case for Comparable Worth." *Quarterly Review of Economics and Finance* 39:743–56.

England, Paula, and Nancy Folbre. 1999. "The Cost of Caring." *Annals of the American Academy of Political and Social Science* 562:39–52.

Filene, Edward. 1923. "The Minimum Wage and Efficiency." *American Economic Review* 13:411–15.

Fishlow, Albert, and Karen Parker, eds. 1999. *Growing Apart: The Causes and Consequences of Global Wage Inequality.* Washington DC: Council on Foreign Relations.

Freeman, Richard. 1999. "The New Inequality in the United States." In *Growing Apart: The Causes and Consequences of Global Wage Inequality*, ed. Albert Fishlow and Karen Parker, 21–66. Washington DC: Council on Foreign Relations.

Glazer, Nona. 1995. *Women's Paid and Unpaid Labor: The Work Transfer in Health Care and Retailing.* Philadelphia: Temple University Press.

Gordon, Linda. 1994. *Pitied But Not Entitled: Single Mothers and the History of Welfare.* New York: Free Press.

Hartmann, Heidi, ed. 1985. *Comparable Worth: New Directions for Research.* Washington DC: National Academy Press.

Hirsch, Barry, and David Macpherson. 1996. *Union Membership and Earnings Data Book 1995: Compilations from the Current Populations Survey.* Washington DC: Bureau of National Affairs.

———. 1994. *Union Membership and Earnings Data Book 1994: Compilations from the Current Populations Survey.* Washington DC: Bureau of National Affairs.

Isotalo, Norm (Michigan Unemployment Agency). 2000. Telephone interview with author, 11 July.

Krugman, Paul. 1996. "The Spiral of Inequality." *Mother Jones*, November–December: 44–9.

Loprest, Pamela, Stephanie Schidt, and Ann Dryden Witte. 1999. "Welfare Reform under PRWORA: Aid to Children with Working Families." Working Paper 99-12, Wellesley College, Wellesley, MA.

Mantsios, Gregory. 1998. *A New Labor Movement for a New Century.* New York: Monthly Review Press.

McCrate, Elaine. 1998. "When Work Doesn't Work: The Failure of Current Welfare Reform." *Gender and Society* 12(1): 61–81.

Mishel, Lawrence, Jerrod Bernstein, and John Schmitt. 1999. *The State of Working America 1998–99.* Armonk, NY: M.E. Sharpe.

———. 1997. *The State of Working America 1996–97.* Armonk, NY: M.E. Sharpe.

Mishel, Lawrence, and John Schmitt. 1996. "Cutting Wages by Cutting Welfare: The Impact of Reform on the Low-Wage Labor Market." A special report prepared at the Economic Policy Institute, Washington DC.

Moran, Theodore. 1999. "Foreign Direct Investment and Good Jobs/Bad Jobs: The Impact of Outward Investment and Inward Investment on Jobs and Wages." In *Growing Apart: The Causes and Consequences of Global Wage Inequality*, ed. Albert Fishlow and Karen Parker, 95–117. Washington DC: Council on Foreign Relations.

Needleman, Ruth. 1998. "Women Workers: Strategies for Inclusion and Rebuilding Unionism." In *A New Labor Movement for a New Century*, ed. Gregory Mantsios, 151–70. New York: Monthly Review Press.

Newman, Katherine. 1999. *No Shame in My Game: Working Poor in the Inner City*. New York: Knopf.

"Occupational Employment Projections to 2008." 1999. *Monthly Labor Review* November: 51–77.

Powers, Marilyn. 1999. *Feminist Economics* 5(1): 61–78.

Rubin, Alissa. 2000. "For Some, Welfare Reform Leaves Safety Net Tenuous." *Los Angeles Times*, 9 May. Retrieved 5 July 2000 from http://pqasb.pqarchiver.com/latimes/.

Schmidt, Peter. 1998. "States Discourage Welfare Recipients from Pursuing a Higher Education." *Chronicle of Higher Education* (23 January): 134.

"Tax Credit Programs Save Michigan Employers $91.2 Million Reports Unemployment Agency. Two Federal Tax Credits Encourage Employers to Hire 21,200 Hard to Employ." 1999. *PR Newswire*, 30 November. Retrieved 5 July 2000 from http://ehostvgw4.e . . . ork%20and%20tax%20and%20credit&fuzzyTerm=.

Tilly, Chris. 1996. *Half a Job: Bad and Good Part-Time Jobs in a Changing Labor Market*. Philadelphia: Temple University Press.

U.S. Bureau of the Census. 1914. *Population 1910, Occupation Statistics*, 422–23. Washington DC: Government Printing Office.

Webb, Beatrice, and Sidney Webb. (1897) 1965. *Industrial Democracy*. New York: Sentry Press.

Wessel, David. 1996. "Firms Cut Health Costs, Cover Fewer Workers." *Wall Street Journal*, 11 November.

Women's Committee of 100. 2000. "Welfarebeat: Immodest Proposal." *Sojourner: The Women's Forum*, May, 28.

CHAPTER THREE

Economic Development Policies and Women Workers: Filipina Workers in a Japanese Transplant

NIZA LICUANAN-GALELA

Economic globalization has resulted in the integration of economies and workers on a worldwide scale. Export industrialization is one of the key strategies that has made globalization possible; central to the success of export industrialization programs are transnational corporations (TNCs) that engage in offshore productions. Encouraged by the economic success of export industrialization, many developing countries have anchored their development programs on this economic strategy. To secure investment in their countries, governments offer inducements that often include export processing zones (EPZs) with no-strike policies, cheap but highly skilled labor, and tax holidays. In return, the host governments expect the TNCs to create employment opportunities and, through their investments, to boost the domestic economy.

Women are the major resources for the cheap but skilled labor force that are found in the EPZs. For example, in the Philippines, women compose more than 80 percent of workers involved in export industrialization and have formed the backbone of the country's economy (Chant 1996; Chant and McIlwaine 1995; Hutchinson 1992). Fuentes and Ehrenreich contend that, because of both biological and social reasons, women have been heavily recruited to do the labor-intensive jobs found on global assembly lines (1983). Boserup (1970) and others (Beneria and Sen 1981; Buvinic 1976; Ward 1988) contend that economic development strategies, especially those concerned with industrial development, more often led to further marginalization of women's status. Studies on women in global assembly lines indicate that women's work experiences, especially the way they are treated in these factories, have profound effects on their perception of their status (Chant and McIlwaine 1995; Nash and Fernandez-Kelly 1983; Ong 1987; Poster 1998; Tiano 1994; Ward 1990; Wolf 1992).

This study addresses two questions on women engaged in TNC global assembly-line work.[1] First, what type of labor-management policies are found on global assembly lines in the Philippines? Second, how have these labor managerial policies and practices affected Filipino women workers on the global assembly line? Beyond these questions, the chapter also explores the implications of these work experiences on rural women's social

Originally published in the Fall 2001 issue of the *NWSA Journal* (13.3).

position in the Philippines. If global assembly-line work emerges as the most dominant form of industrial work for rural women, would it lead to the enhancement or further marginalization of women workers' status?

This research is based on a case study using in-depth interviews with Filipino women workers in a Japanese automotive wiring-harness assembly plant. The data provide insights on how work is engendered on the global assembly lines. It helps us understand the workplace dynamics that underlie the experiences women workers have reported in earlier research (see Chant and McIlwaine 1995; Eviota 1992; Fuentes and Ehrenreich 1983; Grossman 1980; Ong 1987). This study also offers insights into how national development policies are transformed at the local level into labor-management policies which directly affect women's work experiences.

I argue that the working conditions in the local factories are a product of the interplay between the local culture's gender ideology and the work cultures' gender ideology. The detailed information presented here on how Japanese labor-management systems are transferred and adopted into Southeast Asian global assembly lines broadens our understanding of the degree and form of transference of Japanese labor managerial practices; it also delineates the unique ways in which gender is manipulated in the workplace. In global assembly lines not only are investments and technology transferred from the mother corporation to the offshore production factories, but systems of gendered labor management are transplanted as well.

Labor-Management Systems: Japanese Transnational Corporations and the Local Filipino Work Culture

In recent years, there has been a profusion of studies on Japanese labor systems (Amante 1992; Graham 1993; Kenney et al. 1998). The adoption of Japanese management policies, for example, in Japanese car subsidiaries in the United States has been hailed as an improvement over traditional Western labor-management systems. Japanese labor-management systems have been credited with greater employee participation (Brown and Reich 1989), emphasizing the importance of teamwork over individual performance, creating coordination and harmony (Lincoln and Nakata 1997), and enhancing quality control (Amante 1992). Despite these management achievements, Japanese organizations are also critiqued for their paternalism and sexism (Lincoln and Kalleberg 1990; Milkman 1991; Ouichi 1981). In the factory studied for this case study, managerial tactics in the factory included such strategies as traditional authoritarianism, scientific management, family metaphors, and group work teams.

Examples of how these managerial techniques are applied to the production floor will be discussed throughout the chapter.

Frank Lynch writes that one of the most important values Filipinos hold is the maintenance of "smooth interpersonal relations" (1973). Smooth interpersonal relationships may be defined as "the ability to get along with others in such a way as to avoid outside signs of conflict" (Andres 1981, 17). One of the ways in which Filipinos measure their success in getting along with others is through the achievement of *pakikisama* (from the root *sama*, "to accompany, go along with"). In the work culture, *pakikisama* refers to "giving in or yielding to the wish of the leader or majority, even when at times, it contradicts one's ideas or the common good" (Andres 1981, 17). It is a means to achieve harmony and consensus in the workplace, a condition desired greatly in Asian workplaces (see similar findings in Lincoln and Nakata's 1997 study on Japanese organizations).

Recognizing *utang na loob* (a debt of gratitude or moral indebtedness) is an essential component of *pakikisama*. Having *utang na loob* means that one acknowledges that she/he was a recipient of a voluntary offering of material or nonmaterial gift that was given without prior agreement and accepted without any reservation (Tiglao-Torres 1988). This gift is to be paid back in a culturally determined way. The recognition of an *utang na loob* only occurs when the involved individuals are already engaged in reciprocal obligations (Hollsteiner et al. 1975; Tiglao-Torres 1988).

An emotional component of *pakikisama* is *hiya*. *Hiya* refers to a "painful emotion" which is expressed in interpersonal situations perceived as "dangerous to one's ego" (Bulatao 1989). It is the fear of being treated like an object, of being analyzed or criticized and being found wanting. *Hiya* often occurs when one fails to perform his/her part of a reciprocal obligation. Thus, to avoid losing face or *mapahiya*, one has to strive as much as possible to follow culturally prescribed ways of relating to others.

Thus in Filipino workplaces, *pakikisama* can be used effectively to generate cohesive informal groups in the workplace. It can also be abused, since the group will tend to follow the wishes of the dominant member of the group, which can lead to rigid superior-inferior relations (Andres 1981). Andres argues that management by Filipino values tends to be authoritarian and particularistic. Relations in the workplace put more emphasis on being able to relate well on an interpersonal level than, for example, how efficient one was in doing his/her own work.

In summary, the women workers involved in this study are exposed to two different but complementing cultures: the Filipino culture and the Japanese corporate culture. Both carry ideologies that emphasize harmony and consensus and also women's lesser status. I will discuss how these two cultures act upon each other to create a hybrid form of labor-management systems. I will also argue that these hybrid systems have increased management's control over women, resulting in feelings of powerlessness among these workers.

Methodology

I conducted this study in a rural area in the Philippines from July to December, 1992.[2] The area of study was among the rural villages heavily involved in EPZ employment. I focused mainly on Filipino women workers employed in a Japanese-Filipino factory which manufactured wiring harnesses for both domestic and international markets. Workers studied in this research were living within the three surrounding villages. I interviewed a total of 45 women workers as well as the factory's personnel manager. Other sources of information included observations, especially during the factory tour, interviews in the villages, analysis of factory handouts to workers, and official documents collected in the local municipal hall.

The Fuji Women Workers

The transnational corporation Fuji employed 4500 workers, of whom almost 80 percent were women.[3] Women workers were assigned mainly to the assembly lines, while men were in either the packing or shipping departments. There was no evidence of female management officers. The conspicuous absence of female management supported the claim that women were often discriminated against in Japanese organizations.

The personnel manager explained that the disproportionate number of women in the factory was due to management's belief that women possess the natural dexterity and patience needed to perform assembly work. He said that assembly work was like crocheting, which women supposedly did very easily. Management assumed that this dexterity was inherent in women and thus did not administer dexterity skill tests for female applicants. Like women in other global assembly lines, women workers in Fuji were recruited for what a predominantly male management believed to be the *natural* skills women possessed that fit assembly-line work (Fuentes and Ehrenreich 1983).

Management Philosophy

Fuji managed its workers by incorporating Japanese work efficiency practices, familism, and local cultural values to control their work behaviors. The management strategy was to emphasize the importance of *pakikisama, utang na loob,* and *hiya* in the workplace. One of the ways in which Fuji ensured workers' loyalties was to convince the families of the workers that their daughters/wives were in good hands. Fuji achieved this mainly through sponsoring an annual factory tour for relatives of current workers. Interviews with the workers' parents or spouses revealed that family members "came to understand" what it meant to be a factory worker during these factory tours. They became more supportive of the workers and allowed their wives/daughters to prioritize factory work over their domestic responsibilities. Family members also pressured workers to work well for Fuji so as not to lose face. Parents and spouses became the most intimate enforcers of Fuji's control over their workers' attitudes and behaviors.

To emphasize further the need for *pakikisama* and kinship among its workers, Fuji adopted a factory motto, "One for All, All for One." The personnel manager described the work atmosphere as that of "one big happy family" where management treats the workers as "their children." As in most other Southeast Asian global assembly lines, Japanese labor-management systems relied on familism to control workers by creating intimate ties between the workers and the supervisors (Hong 1997). This familism was also illustrated by the way workers described their relationships with their supervisors. Supervisors were addressed as *ate* which was a Filipino word for older sister or *kuya* which was the term for older brother. As one assembly-line operator described these relationships:

> We think of our supervisors as older siblings, some, we see as our parents. You see, work is not everything in Fuji. Sometimes, they [the supervisors] give us advice especially on our attitudes and behavior. People have different personalities. What is important is that you learn to get along with them.

Although such personalism in the workplace may make the workers feel more at home, it also prevents them from developing the autonomy needed to succeed in other industrial work areas. By accepting the demands of *pakikisama*, both workers and supervisors fail to detach the meaning of their work from the interpersonal relations around them. Often, work performance is dependent on the achievement of smooth interpersonal relations. Personalism stunts professional growth among the workers and traps them in a system where getting along with others is the thing that matters most to the worker.

To further promote paternalism, Japanese corporations tend to discourage labor unions in their factories; the Fuji factory did not have a labor union. The absence of a formal labor union in the factory demonstrated the power of Fuji's familial approach to controlling the employees. Fuji had a *wardship* system where a ward leader, often a line supervisor, was in charge of ten workers. Ward leaders were supposed to resolve workers' grievances against management. If this did not work, then the ward leaders were to bring the grievance to the higher-level officials. According to the personnel manager, this system worked well since workers had not gone on strikes since the factory started.[4] As the manager reiterated, "anybody can talk to anybody directly" meaning that assembly line workers could approach the personnel manager whenever they had problems.

This ward system, however, did not look after the needs of the workers for it clearly was on the management side. Dissatisfactions among the workers were not truly addressed because there were no proper channels to give them voice. For most of the workers, it was better to remain silent and keep your job. On subsequent interviews with some of the workers, the workers expressed their desire to have a real labor union. However, they were afraid to organize one because union organizing had grave consequences to the organizers. The threat of being fired was a reality that workers had to face if they were to decide to fight for their rights. These workers' reactions to union organizing was apparently seen in other Southeast Asian countries where the labor union had been marginalized due to industrial restructuring (Deyo 1997) and the "hands-off" policies most governments practice with regard to multinational corporation export-oriented factories.

Recruitment and Apprenticeship

Recruitment of new workers was also based on *pakikisama* and familism. Workers were recruited either through people who were already working in the factory or because they were related to current workers. Fuji also often recruited new employees through the use of *barangay* captains (elected leaders of small villages). *Barangay* captains functioned as representatives of villages and had political clout in the area. When Fuji needed new employees, management requested the *barangay* captains to recommend potential workers from their *barangays*. Fuji did not administer aptitude tests to applicants, but only required that they bring with them certification of a high school education and that the applicants were not older than 20 years old. The most important requirement for applicants was the recommendation from either the *barangay* captain or by somebody who was already working for Fuji. Chances of getting hired were very slim for applicants who were not recommended this way.

The personnel manager asserted that this recruitment procedure was "in line with the culture," which implied that the workers could be controlled through *pakikisama*. The recruitment procedure assumed that an applicant's gratitude to the *barangay* captain or whoever recommended her was strong enough for her to feel *utang na loob*. Because of this cultural debt, she worked hard in order not to embarrass her recommender. The recommender, on the other hand, served as a parent for the newly recruited worker and guided her through the work in the assembly line. This reciprocity helped to ensure that the recommender would not lose face vis-à-vis the management, since it assured proper behavior on the part of the new worker and did not raise questions about the judgment of the *barangay* captain. Through these reciprocal obligations between the recruit and the recommender, Fuji was assured of workers being controlled by personal relationships with other workers in the factory.

Apprenticeship focused on practices of selection and self-selection that management designed to prevent deviance. The apprenticeship period was used to produce docile, hardworking workers. Since women were supposedly more patient and persevering than men, the expectation was that they were easier to train into workers with the "right attitude." Having the right attitude meant that the worker was a positive thinker, uncomplaining, and hardworking. An example of this right attitude can be seen from this statement made by a worker.

> No, I did not have a hard time adjusting [to the physical demands of factory work]. If you do not like it, the door is wide open for you to leave. Also, when you are new, you have to learn how to get along with your supervisor. There is a seniority system that exists in the factory. Since I was the new one I have to learn how to get along. You get used to things in the factory.

There are two important insights that can be inferred from this statement. First, the worker makes it clear that one has to be on good terms with the supervisors, and this means doing the work without complaints. Also, as the newest member of the line, one is expected to do most of the *pakikisama*. This raises the point that the major onus of performing *pakikisama* falls on the shoulder of the newcomer, who has the lowest status. In this manner, *pakikisama* reinforces the traditional authoritarianism found at the factory.

Secondly, through the apprenticeship, workers learn to rationalize that even if the work is hard at first, they eventually will get used to it. This learned behavior reinforces the management claim that women are patient and persevering and sustains the gendered assertion that women are the ideal workers for an assembly line. However, the vaunted female patience and perseverance may not have been *natural* but rather a reflection of women's awareness of their lack of better job alternatives. Women have low expectations about what constitutes a good job because of their lack of alternatives (Lincoln and Kalleberg 1990). Thus, women workers perceive that the tedious, physically demanding assembly-line work is still a good job compared to the alternatives—unpaid household work, farm work, or domestic service.

Termination of Contract

Employment in Fuji was relatively stable compared to high turnover rates reported in previous studies (see Fuentes and Ehrenreich 1983). In my sample, the average length of service was seven years, and most of the workers were in the factory for at least four years. The extreme specialization of task on the Fuji assembly line prevented any line worker from becoming highly attractive to other employers in the area. These were *de-skilled* jobs, which carried all the implications for low job power and easy replaceability (Braverman 1974). In this study, the factory hired women with little education, and the factory prevented them from learning any highly valued marketable skills while employed there. Each of these practices contributed to the workers' sense of having few attractive employment alternatives. Workers were aware of how vulnerable they were in the job market because they did not have the necessary qualifications for better paying jobs. Moreover, most of the jobs around the area were assembly-line jobs, which also offered only de-skilled work. Workers were trapped, and thus, no matter how difficult or unpleasant the work conditions, the women workers were forced to tolerate them for lack of better alternatives.

Implications for Women Workers' Status and Conclusions

This study attempted to answer two questions concerning women workers in global assembly lines: first, what types of labor management are found on a global assembly line in the Philippines, and second, how do these labor-management policies affect women workers' workplace experiences. This study demonstrated that there is indeed a hybrid form of managerial system in the factory studied. The factory management utilized a combination of Filipino values and the Japanese management system renowned for its industrial efficiency. These two approaches reinforced each other and resulted in policies that seemed very effective at controlling and containing workers' behaviors. The de-skilled jobs that women performed only further emphasized the women's lack of other, better job alternatives. Subjected to such normative structures, the women workers' daily experience reinforced their low status and powerlessness, not only within the factory but also in their communities.

Moreover, factory management expanded the patriarchal network surrounding the women workers by utilizing a male-dominated, local, political hierarchy. Fuji provided a predominantly male group of village captains a new source of power. This power enabled the captains, and indirectly the factory management, to control the economic opportunities for women by reserving to themselves the power to choose who to recommend. A power relation between the village captains and women workers that had not existed previously in the village became institutionalized as part of the village patriarchy. It is likely that this new power structure will remain embedded in the local culture long after the factory ceases to exist.

In conclusion, economic development policies such as export industrialization can and do affect women's social positions in their communities. The success of labor-management policies that seek to control workers in a global assembly line depends greatly on how management can work within the particular culture where the assembly lines are located. Unfortunately, these modified labor-management policies as well as the de-skilled work women experience every day in the global assembly lines constantly reinforce the subordinate positions of women workers in the factory and outside the factory. Their low status and lack of power to control their lives shape the social relations of these female assemblers. In reframing these relations as experienced in both their villages and their workplaces, the labor-management practices turn women into nothing more than workers with "nimble fingers and shy smiles."

Afterword

I last visited the study area in 1999 and found enormous changes in the villages. The village is now part of a larger economic zone, attracting thousands of migrant workers to the area. Through informal interviews, I was able to talk to ten of the original 45 women interviewed in 1992. Seven of these women are still working for Fuji while the rest quit their jobs after their second children. One of the seven who stayed on has been promoted to a junior assistant supervisor. Most of the workers told me that work is harder now since they are experiencing some competition from migrant workers. Also, since the Philippines is currently going through an economic crisis (in 1992 the dollar was worth 25 pesos, today it has plunged to 48 pesos), they stated that life is very hard and their salaries have not adjusted to the increasing prices of basic commodities.

Notes

1. Global assembly lines refer to the division of a production process into different special stages. The operation of each stage of production is carried out in a location where it will cost the companies the least amount of expense (i.e., comparative advantage of a certain location). Global assembly lines allow TNCs to be competitive in the world market by reducing the cost of labor for production.

2. I used interviews as the most appropriate method of data gathering in this case study in order to obtain detailed accounts of the workers' experiences inside the factory. The factory personnel manager provided me an employment roll and I used this initial roll to determine a core set of respondents. I created a purposive sample based on the following criteria: length of employment in Fuji (not the factory's real name) should have been more than two years; the worker should be on the production floor and not in the clerical department; she should be living in the village initially targeted as the area of study, and she should be between 20 and 35 years old. It was preferable, but not required, that her mother live nearby and agree to be interviewed. The core set of respondents

was fifteen women workers. From this core set, I created a snowball sample by asking the fifteen women to recommend other Fuji women. A research assistant and I conducted the interviews in Tagalog, the village's vernacular language.

3. The women workers fit the socioeconomic profile of most global assembly-line workers. They were generally well educated with at least ten years of formal education, in their middle twenties, and came from generally low-income groups. Fuji women workers, however, stayed longer in the factory and continued working even if they got married and had their first child, reflecting Lin's (1987) finding that paid work is no longer merely a pre-marriage phenomenon among Southeast Asian women.

4. Chant and McIlwaine (1995) documented cases in several Philippine-based MNCs where management practiced recruitment procedures that screened for "agitators," strikers, union organizers, activists, and so on.

References

Amante, Maragtas, S.V. 1992. "Japanese Industrial Relations Interface in the Philippines: Background to the Issues." In *Japanese Industrial Relations Interface in the Philippines*, 1–26. Research report by the School of Labor and Industrial Relations of the University of the Philippines U.P. SOLAIR in cooperation with the Japan Foundation. Quezon City, Philippines: U.P. SOLAIR.
Andres, Tomas. 1981. *Understanding Filipino Values: A Management Approach.* Quezon City, Philippines: New Day Publishers.
Beneria, Lourdes, and Gita Sen. 1981. "Accumulation, Reproduction and Women's Role in Economic Development: Theoretical and Practical Implications." *Feminist Studies* 8:157–76.
Boserup, Ester. 1970. *Women's Role in Economic Development.* New York: St. Martin.
Braverman, H. 1974. *Labour and Monopoly Capital: The Degradation of Work in the Twentieth Century.* New York: Monthly Review Press.
Brown, C., and Reich, M. 1989. "When Does Union-Management Cooperation Work? A Look at NUMMI and GM–Van Nuys." *California Management Review* (Summer): 24–6.
Bulatao, Jaime C. 1989. "Another Look at Philippine Values." In *Manila: History, People and Culture*, 321–30. Proceedings of the Manila Studies Conference held at the Barrio San Luis Complex, Intramuros, Manila. Manila, Philippines: De La Salle University Press.
Buvinic, Myra. 1976. "A Critical Review of Some Research Concepts and Concerns." In *Women and World Development*, ed. Irene Tinker, Michelle Bo Bramsen, and Myra Buvinic. New York: Praeger.
Chant, Sylvia. 1996. "Women's Roles in Recession and Economic Restructuring in Mexico and the Philippines." *Geoforum* 27(3): 297–327.

Chant, Sylvia, and C. McIlwaine. 1995. "Gender and Export Manufacturing in the Philippines: Continuity or Change in Female Employment? The Case of the Mactan Export Processing Zone." *Gender, Place and Culture* 2:147–76.

Deyo, Frederic. 1997. "Labor and Post-Fordist Industrial Restructuring in East and Southeast Asia." *Work and Occupations* 24(1): 97–118.

Eviota, Elizabeth. 1992. *The Political Economy of Gender: Women and the Sexual Division of Labour in the Philippines*. London: ZED Books.

Fuentes, Annette, and Barbara Ehrenreich. 1983. *Women in the Global Factory*. Boston: South End Press.

Graham, Laurie. 1993. "Inside a Japanese Transplant: A Critical Perspective." *Work and Occupations* 20:147–73.

Grossman, Rachel. 1980. "Women's Place in the Integrated Circuit." *Southeast Asia Chronicle–Pacific Research*. SRC No. 66/PSC 9(5).

Gutek, B., A. Stromberg, and L. Larwood, eds. 1988. *Women and Work*. Newbury Park, CA: Sage Publications.

Henderson, Jeffrey, and Manuel Castells, eds. 1987. *Global Restructuring and Territorial Development*. Newbury Park, CA: Sage Publications.

Hollsteiner, Mary Racelis, Maria Elena Chiong, Anicia Paglinauan, and Nora S. Villanueva, eds. 1975. *Society, Culture and the Filipino: Introductory Readings in Sociology and Anthropology*. Quezon City, Philippines: Ateneo de Manila University, Institute of Philippine Culture.

Hong, Doo-Seung. 1997. "Dynamics of Asian Workplaces: An Introductory Essay." *Work and Occupations* 24(1): 5–11.

Hutchinson, Jane. 1992. "Women in the Philippine Export Industry." *Journal of Contemporary Asia* 22:471–89.

Kenney, Martin, Goe, R.W., Contreras, O., Romero, J., and Bustos, M. 1998. "Learning Factories or Reproduction Factories." *Work and Occupations* 25: 269–304.

Koike, Kazuo, and Takenori Inoki. 1990. *Skill Formation in Japan and Southeast Asia*. Tokyo: University of Tokyo Press.

Lin, V. 1987. "Women Electronics Workers in Southeast Asia: The Emergence of a Working Class." In *Global Restructuring and Territorial Development*, ed. Jeffrey Henderson and Manuel Castells. Newbury Park, CA: Sage Publications.

Lincoln, James, and Arne Kalleberg. 1990. *Culture, Control and Commitment: A Study of Work Organizations and Work Attitudes in the United States and Japan*. Cambridge, UK: Cambridge University Press.

Lincoln, James, and Yoshifumi Nakata. 1997. "The Transformation of the Japanese Employment System." *Work and Occupation* 24(1): 33–55.

Lynch, Frank. 1973. *Four Readings on Filipino Values*. Quezon City, Philippines: Ateneo de Manila University, Institute of Philippine Culture.

Milkman, Ruth. 1991. *Japan's California Factories: Labor Relations and Economic Globalizations*. Los Angeles: University of California Institute of Industrial Relations.

Nash, June, and Maria P. Fernandez-Kelly. 1983. *Women, Men, and the International Division of Labor*. Albany: State University of New York Press.

Ong, Aihwa. 1987. *Spirits of Resistance and Capitalist Discipline: Factory Workers in Malaysia*. Albany: State University of New York Press.

Ouichi, William. 1981. *Theory Z: How American Business Can Meet the Japanese Challenge.* Reading, MA: Addison-Wesley.

Poster, Winifred. 1998. "Globalization, Gender and the Workplace: Women and Men in an American Multination Corporation in India." *Journal of Developing Societies* 14:40–65.

Tiano, Susan. 1994. *Patriarchy on the Line: Labor, Gender and Ideology in the Mexican Maquila Industry.* Philadelphia: Temple University Press.

Tiglao-Torres, Amaryllis. 1988. *The Urban Filipino Worker in an Industrializing Society.* Quezon City, Philippines: University of the Philippines Press.

Tinker, Irene, Michelle Bo Bramsen, and Myra Buvinic, eds. 1997. *Women and World Development.* New York: Praeger.

Ward, Kathryn. 1988. "Women in the Global Economy." In *Women and Work*, ed. B. Gutek, A. Stromberg, and L. Larwood, 17–48. Newbury Park, CA: Sage Publications.

———. 1990. *Women Workers and Global Restructuring.* Ithaca, NY: ILR Press.

Wolf, Diane. 1992. *Factory Daughters: Gender, Household Dynamics and Rural Industrialization in Java.* Berkeley: University of California Press.

CHAPTER FOUR

The Rise of the Bangladesh Garment Industry: Globalization, Women Workers, and Voice

FAUZIA ERFAN AHMED

If globalization provides the backdrop for drama, then the achievements of the garment industry in Bangladesh are indeed dramatic. In the short space of 15 years, Bangladesh emerged as the eighth largest garment exporter to the United States by 1991. Approximately 100 different types of garments are now exported to 50 countries around the globe. A major source of foreign exchange, the garment sector grew at a compound rate of 125 percent from 1977 to 1991 (Wahid and Weiss 1996, 167) and the garment industry provided jobs for women. Almost overnight a labor force of approximately 200,000 young women appeared in Dhaka city (Feldman 1992, 118), the capital of Bangladesh. Cited as evidence of a modern environment that allows talent to make it through sheer effort, the garment industry is now also hailed as the liberator of women.

In this chapter I examine the extent to which these statements, now so often repeated that they have become conventions, are true. Are the garment factory owners talented risk-takers and is their rise evidence that Bangladesh has become a more modern (i.e., a more meritocratic and egalitarian) society? Have these garment factories empowered women by giving them jobs? Empowerment is inextricably linked to choice; whether the garment industry has created possibilities of exit and voice (Hirschman 1970) must be examined through this perspective.[1] I have drawn on Hirschman's framework in its simplest form: *exit* means that workers can leave if conditions become unbearable, and *voice* signifies that workers can protest if there are problems. Because the workers are women, voice also means greater decision-making power within the household. Furthermore, in a globalized economy, firms can exit just as easily (or even more so) as workers. Can the women's garment factory workers exercise either option with impunity? It is also pertinent to ask whether the income gives these women greater voice or decision-making power at home. Given the forces of globalization, will these options, even if they can be used, change the way in which the garment factory is organized?[2] My investigation analyzes the historical context and political economy of "the entrepreneur" and the household gender dynamics of women employees by combining an analysis of gender roles and practices within a framework of exit and voice.

Originally published in the Summer 2004 issue of the *NWSA Journal* (16.2).

Rise of the Proto-Capitalist

Current analyses seem confined to how the market-oriented policies of the post-1975 government developed the industry and the new industrial class. In fact, it was the 1971 war that created the proto-industrialist.[3] Young, but not entirely without business talent, proto-industrialists were impervious to scruples. It was these proto-capitalists who germinated in the completely unfettered war environment.

In the feudal prewar society that was dominated by gentleman scholars, this proto-capitalist group had no status. They came from the lower middle class but did not belong to it as far as their aspirations were concerned. They were sons of school teachers who, not having developed a taste for the discipline of the classroom, could never hope to follow in their fathers' footsteps or sons of bank clerks, who could never aspire to the envisioned life of petit bourgeois mediocrity because they rejected the requisite belief in the legitimacy of bureaucratic authority. The proto-capitalists found the havoc of war convenient and thrived in the social vacuum that it created.

The landed gentry did not pose a rival threat in the war environment. Accustomed to a life of leisurely pursuit, which allowed him, among other things, to read poetry (and even to write it), the gentleman scholar recoiled from the business that the proto-capitalists found so opportune. Proclaiming revulsion, the aristocracy refrained from joining in the fray. The truth, however, was more matter-of-fact: unable to cope with the riposte of the often shady business deal, the aristocrats were quite ill-equipped for the shape of things to come. It required an effort and agility that was alien to their culture. Thus, the war compelled them to relinquish their supremacy and leave the arena open to, as they termed it, "all sorts of people." The old order had, quite literally, disintegrated. Having tasted what money could mean, the proto-capitalists envisioned the postwar period as a chance also to gain respect in a society that had previously scorned them and to pursue their accumulation of wealth without interruption.

Economic Policies of the Government of Bangladesh

The disaffection of the proto-capitalists can well be imagined when the government of newly independent Bangladesh introduced nationalization as the cornerstone of its economic program in 1972. The government thus acquired 85 percent of the capital assets of the industrial sector (Wahid and Weiss 1996, 168). Various restrictions further reduced the growth of the private textile industry. Import substitution was a keynote in the vision of "Golden Bangladesh" propounded by the then–Prime Minister Sheikh Mujibur Rahman.[4] Fears of land reform also alienated the landed gentry; the bureaucrats (who ran the country) felt upstaged by the "Whiz Kids," the group of left-leaning economists on whose advice the prime minister relied. With the inflexibility often peculiar to the high-minded, these advisers quickly alienated powerful national interests through a policy implementation process that was characterized by its zeal as much as it was by its lack of political imagination.

Sheikh Mujibur Rahman was killed in 1975, and the new military government lost no time in reassuring the Western powers, on whose support it relied, that henceforth Bangladesh would adhere to the path of the market. Privatization was now pursued with passion.[5] Liberalization was the means to attract foreign capital. Specifically, the export-oriented strategy involved currency devaluations, reduced trade barriers, and restrictions on repatriation for foreign investor profits. It gave tax holidays for foreign investors who established garment factories, created Export Promotion Zones (EPZs), and made it easier for foreigners to participate in Bangladesh business ventures, and even to own them.

Not surprisingly, these policies attracted foreign investment. Much has been written about General Ziaur Rahman's Western tilt, but more needs to be written about his connection with the proto-capitalists.[6] Restive and chafing at the bit, this group supported his government with alacrity. General Zia's policies set the foundation for a perspective that promoted those internal social forces that courted global capital. In 1977, Reaz and Jewel Garments shipped 40,000 shirts to France and Germany (Wahid and Weiss 1996, 169). Clearly, these were not the "pioneering entrepreneurs"; rather the changed policy environment had helped the proto-industrialist become the industrialist. This class had finally come into its own.

This emergence of the industrialist is a phenomenon that is entirely new and has profound implications for the national polity. It is not just that this class has acquired political power and connections;[7] their values, symbolized by a lavish lifestyle, the scale of which has not been seen before in Bangladesh, have come to dominate the sociocultural landscape. "Anyone can make it rich, and people who do must show off their wealth"—this, indeed, is the prevailing motto. As I have said before, these men were self-made only to the extent that they were able to take advantage of the chaos of the war. However, they have introduced, for the first time in Bangladesh, the myth of the self-made entrepreneur, a political ideology that is, perhaps, a necessary accompaniment to liberalization. In fact, a large number of low-cost and compliant women workers, stringent efforts to curb militant labor, tax breaks, government insurance for imported machinery, and, of course, foreign capital (provided again through state auspices) made the garment venture entirely feasible.

The feudal system, wherein the relationship between tenant and landlord was part of a complex web of reciprocity, custom, and exploitation, is being replaced. It is not true that a new element is being introduced within the rubric of feudalism, but an entirely new system, complete with its own set of values, is supplanting the feudal framework. Land defined the landed gentry; it was also their future. To the aristocrat, complacent with the pride of an inherited identity (and property), innovation was anathema.[8] The war created the proto-capitalists, but it is in global capital that their future lies. Innovation is essential to their survival.

Creation of the Compliant Workforce

Contrary to theory, a ready supply of appropriate workers does not always exist, in reserve, to fulfill the needs of global capital (Feldman 1992). International competition demands an educated and compliant workforce. The use of women as employees was an ingenious innovation of the nascent Bangladeshi industrialist. Initially, the recruits were not the poorest of the poor; they were women of the rural middle class.

An explanation of what "rural middle class" means in the context of a rural society is critical. These families may live in *pukka* (brick) houses and have land, but they are cash poor. Not necessarily sharecroppers but the managers of sharecroppers, they are only too conscious of the narrow boundary that separates them from the rural underclass. While they can never become aristocrats, the rural middle class feels that, at all costs, the social distance from the poorest peasants must be maintained.

Varying degrees of poverty exist within the family itself. The women are poorer. They have less control over finances (particularly if they are younger). Despite their lack of cash, social convention prevents them from seeking work as sharecroppers. It is not surprising, therefore, that these women are recruited as garment factory workers by industrialists, who have created "socially acceptable" work for them. In fact, many of these women are village kin. Belonging to the same village ensures trust and the industrialists were perceived as "village heroes" who had made good and would share by providing their kin with jobs. Thus, the industrialists were able to persuade reluctant male guardians that the honor and propriety of the women would be protected in the factory, which also allowed spatial segregation between the sexes. Initially, this sense of kinship was more important than prestige because it assured the women and their families that there would be no sexual exploitation.

The preference for hiring women is, in fact, an employer preference for a compliant and low-cost workforce. It is the "docility and dispensability" of these women that make them so attractive to employers (Kabeer 1994, 168). They are very cheap—being paid $0.25 an hour when American garment workers make $7.53 (Beatty 1999, 105). Resented by workers in the industrialized countries, vulnerable to protectionist legislation, these women and many others like them all over the world have become unwitting symbols of the new world order. What does working in the garment factory mean to them? Are they wage laborers in sweat shops, as leftist critiques assert, or exhilarated consumers able to enjoy for the first time the fruits of their labor and economic independence? For once, the truth does not lie between these extremes; its dimensions are more complex and it is found in overlapping circles of culture, class, and gender roles.

Voices of Women Garment Workers at Work and at Home

Does working in a garment factory give women a voice in the workplace and at home? Class issues prevent solidarity, as does the threat of imminent layoffs. Women are reluctant to unionize, having been excluded from the exclusively male trade union movement. Interviews with these workers (Kibria 1995) show how work means different things to women of different classes and how these perceptions influence gender roles and practices within households.

At Work

Compelled by the imperative of low labor costs, the garment factory owners are ever vigilant to the threat of unionization. To this end, certain village kin are selected as "informers who rat on workers engaged in worker actions in exchange for pay increases and promotion" (Feldman 1992, 123). There are reports that some workers use their lunch hour to train for improved speed, which significantly improves output and job performance. It is true that these workers can successfully bargain for improved wages because other garment factories are always willing to hire them at a higher wage. In this way they can, and do, exert choice. But they bargain as individuals. This negotiation, therefore, can only be an individual choice and not a collective one, since the women cannot unionize to demand even the national minimum wage.

Union organizers complain about their inability to organize garment workers. It is not only the threat of layoffs that makes these women reluctant to unionize. By creating a multiclass workforce, the industrialists have reduced the possibility of cohesion within it.

Few social groups are as conscious of degrees of status as the aspiring middle class to which many of these workers belong. Even though, as Agarwal says, "women's class position has always had an ambiguous character," these women did not come from families that had any sympathy with rural uprisings, much less with the urban trade union movement

(1994, 15). As women, they are socialized to be docile, and the rough and ready politics of the union movement frightens them.

Fractured by interunion rivalry, organized labor in Bangladesh lacks the collective bargaining culture that can include these women. Union disunity can be traced to the years of military rule, when even finding its voice, let alone experimenting with how to use it, was impossible. It is not surprising that, under martial law, many more debates were settled through "unconditional return to work" and not through employer-employee bargaining contracts (Mondal 1992). Nationalization may have limited trade union activity. Questions of wages and worker benefits were assigned to expert commissions who proved ineffective because they were made up of state representatives who were supposed to advocate for worker interests.

The spatial segregation of the sexes in the factory is an outward expression of gendered wage segregation, with the few men at the top having jobs with more control and higher wages. Women do not want to progress along the ladder for fear of sexual harassment. Unable and unwilling to unionize and locked in low-paying jobs by a gender hierarchy, these women have no voice on the factory floor.

At Home

Economic need compels most women to work in garment factories. An analysis of this somewhat bland statement is needed to understand the different meanings that income has for different groups of women in the household. Voice at home is related to the woman's circumstances and background. For those who came from poverty or were beset by a sudden catastrophe, the garment factory has increased their employment options. It is better than working as a domestic servant, prostitute, or home-based piece worker. For those women in a higher class bracket who were compelled to work outside the home for the first time, it was seen as a (perhaps, only) "respectable" form of employment. In the latter instance where the women were not the only breadwinners, they used their earnings to raise the standard of living for the household. A small percentage of women who came from well-off families said that they used this income entirely for personal needs.

Interestingly enough, the young unmarried girls from poor rural families who had left their villages had more control over money, like their affluent counterparts, but for reasons that were entirely different. They had made an exit from the parent-child obligation characteristic of Bengali culture:

> Father and mother can't feed me, my brothers can't feed me, and my uncles can't feed me. So that is why I am working in garments, to stand on my own

feet. Since I am taking care of my own expenses, I have no obligation to give to my family.

—*Unmarried garment worker, late teens*
(Kibria 1995, 289)

That the work in the garment factory has damaged their sexual reputation, making them considerably less eligible for marriage, did not deter them from speaking confidently of the future. "Because I am self-sufficient, I can go where I want and marry whom I want" (Kibria 1995, 304).

The causal link between earning income and having greater voice in the household is, at best, equivocal. Most of the garment workers lived in households with male-dominated budgets. They handed over all their income to the male of the household, who then gave them a monthly allowance. Fear of household disruption (violence, perhaps) and abandonment often compelled women like Ameena, a garment worker, to hand over all her earnings to her husband. She fought for one year with her husband when he discovered that she was withholding 20 percent of her pay as savings and then gave up, as she indicates:

> After that time, I stopped keeping money for myself; every time I get paid, I come home and give all my money to my husband. I see some of the marriages of women in the garment factory be ruined over money; they don't give all the money when he asks for it, the husband leaves her, and then she and her children will be struggling to find rice to eat. After all women have only one dream in life, to remain with their husbands forever.

—*Ameena, garment worker*
(Kibria 1995, 304)

This lack of control should not be analyzed by patriarchy alone; class is also important. The husband's employment situation and traditional breadwinner role influenced whether the woman's income was perceived as a threat or a gift. Wives worked hard to mute the suggestion that their earnings, in any way, reflected on their husbands' inadequacy to provide for the family. Male pride and class distinction were actively maintained by the women even when they routinely made their own earnings available for basic necessities during difficult months:

> My husband likes that my income is for luxuries, for the little things that catch my fancy. Although sometimes I pay for household things during difficult months. He tells me, it is his job to provide for food, clothing, rent, and other necessities. Why should he take my money like the lower class men?

—*Married garment worker*
(Kibria 1995, 302)

Other women, whose circumstances were not so strained, had more control over their income. Such lower-middle-class women hoped that their earnings would ensure a future for their children. The case of Simmi, who was able to keep a large share of earnings for her children's private school expenses (the realization of a middle-class dream), is illustrative (Kibria 1995, 301). In this class, men could indulge in the "honor and pride" of not taking the earnings of their female relatives.

Recommendations

The ultimate question is: are the garment workers better off with these jobs? This query has to be answered at two levels: individual and collective. As individuals, as members of families who rely on their support, as mothers who want a better standard of living for their children, as young unmarried women who want the status that economic independence sometimes brings, these women may be better off.

In a collective sense things have become worse for women's rights. Can a sweatshop ever be a vision of a way out for women? Becoming a garment worker and keeping your job is synonymous with losing collective voice and staying mute. The women of the garment factory are vulnerable for economic and social reasons. They are more insecure than their rural sisters because of their need to maintain class boundaries and the higher cost of living. Some can never go back to their families for social reasons. While their connections to the women's movement and political consciousness have been heightened after a fire on the factory floor killed 25 garment workers and their children in 1990 (Alam 1995, 201), innovation and ingenuity have to be exercised in order to give this multiclass group more voice. Detailed recommendations are beyond the scope of this chapter; what follows here is an attempt to discuss solutions. The secular, nonpartisan, and multiclass character of the Bangladesh women's movement is its signal achievement. It should include garment workers by approaching their families as a whole. Targeting them as objects of trade union activity has been the standard route, but it cannot be the only pathway.[9] Inviting their husbands and in-laws to the mass meetings that the women's groups often hold in Ramna Park, in the capital city, will at least give them exposure. Raising the consciousness of male relatives may give the women more voice at home.

Employers should begin a voluntary plan to allow women to deduct savings from their paychecks. Such a strategy would allow women to save some of their hard-earned money without arguments at home. Since industrialists will never voluntarily agree to a minimum wage, why not share at least some of the profits through year-end and Eid (Muslim religious holiday) bonuses? Another recommendation would be to ask NGOs to provide support for child care by building creches (day care centers). This issue remains conspicuously absent in the studies I reviewed, but no one should assume that the mother-in-law is taking care of the kids, given the breakdown of the extended family in urban areas. Another recommendation, since layoffs seem inevitable in the business, is to provide severance pay for one year or, more important, for NGOs to create alternative employment through micro credit (small loans for entrepreneurial ventures). Given current geopolitical realities, it is probably not possible for the state to enforce these recommendations; however, a coalition of activists, academics, and international organizations should start a dialogue with more approachable industrialists on these aspects of garment worker welfare.

International organizations like the International Labor Organization (ILO) have to be part of the solution because the Bangladesh garment industry, and the women who work in it, are not isolated from what happens to workers in industrialized countries. Globalization means that jobs move from north (expensive labor) to south (cheap labor).[10] Clearly, there is a need to advocate not only for local living wages but for global living wages and working standards. The ILO, with its mandate to protect the rights of workers worldwide, is the logical starting point for this movement.

Conclusion

The recruitment pattern of giving jobs to village kin fits the traditional patron-client feudal scenario. But the resemblance ends there. The vagaries of global capital are such that the industrialists do not (and cannot) guarantee job security. In 1985, more than 250 factories were compelled to shut down and 80,000 workers were laid off in response to a U.S. protectionist veto that restricted the import quotas for textiles (Kamaluddin 1986). The industrialists do not lose face when they lay off workers— even if they are village kin. This lack of accountability is a radical departure from the feudal relationship, which, though oppressive in many ways, also contained the expectation of reciprocity.

Globalization has produced the garment industry in Bangladesh. It has also fashioned a new millionaire class and provided new employment opportunities for women. While it can legitimately be argued that garment factory jobs do not give women more voice, this employment has become an essential component of family income. These jobs are desperately needed, but women workers also need voice and security. I have suggested ideas to humanize working conditions to provide some bulwark against the inevitable layoffs. But I am well aware that these women are exploited and the nature of the exploitation, unlike feudalism, is impersonal. Self-congratulatory statements about the garment industry boom hide the complex choices and avenues of exit that accompany the influx of global capital and mask the profound unease shared by millionaire and garment worker alike.

Notes

1. A challenge to the economic model, which assumes that economic actors always act with unchanging rationality in a world of perfect competition, Hirschman proposes that failing firms can be alerted to performance problems through the alternative pathways of exit and voice. *Exit* means that customers refuse to buy their products or workers leave. *Voice* indicates protest: customers or workers voice their unhappiness to the relevant authorities. According to Hirschman (1970), both these pathways can compel the firm to carry out corrective measures.

2. Globalization is defined as the process enabling financial and investment markets to operate internationally, largely as a result of deregulation and improved communications. But globalization is not just a way of managing markets; it is a process. A globalized market enables the French service sector to deal with its customers through a call center in India or for a garments manufacturer to design its products in Europe, make them in Asia, and then sell them in America (Jeffrey 2002).

3. Bangladesh was formerly the eastern wing of Pakistan. In March 1971, the West Pakistan army invaded East Pakistan. Bangladesh was liberated after a 9-month pogrom that left three million people dead.

4. In 1974, the Awami League announced a moratorium on nationalization and raised the ceiling on domestic private investment in an attempt to pacify this class (Alam 1995). But I argue that, despite these measures, the proto-capitalists did not believe that the Awami League would ultimately take care of their interests.

5. Approximately 650 enterprises were denationalized, with 27 textile mills and 33 jute mills being denationalized in a year. Even the World Bank termed it "one of the most extensive denationalization programs of the public sector enterprises in the world." (Cited in Development Studies Report, No. 142, 1996.)

6. For a detailed discussion see Alam 1995.

7. In 1996, approximately 25 percent of members of Parliament were industrialists. (*Daily Star*, 15 June 1996.)

8. This dependence on an age-old land tenure system has resulted in low cropping intensity and lack of agricultural innovation.

9. The *Sramik Karmachari Oikho Parishad* (The United Council of Workers and Office Personnel in Garments) is a trade union that came into being after the fire (Alam 1995).

10. In 1993, Smith Corona moved its plant from Cortland, New York, to Tijuana, Mexico. The workers in Cortland, of whom 58 percent were women, had few other employment opportunities. In Tijuana, Smith Corona downsized, but even then 75 percent of its employees were women. This has meant more jobs for women in Tijuana, but is this a benefit to women in the long run? There are fewer jobs in Mexico than there were in Cortland, and the workers receive lower wages. Mexican workers do not necessarily receive what the North American workers have lost (Lourdes and Lind 1995).

References

Alam, S. M. Shamshul. 1995. *The State, Class Formation, and Development in Bangladesh.* Lanham, MD: University Press of America.
Agarwal, Bina. 1994. *A Field of One's Own: Gender and Land Rights in South Asia.* Cambridge: Cambridge University Press.
Beatty, Jack. 1999. Book review *The Stakeholder Society*, by Bruce Ackerman and Anne Alstot. *Atlantic Monthly* 283(April): 4.
Chaudhury, Salma Zohir. 1996. "An Assessment of Industrial Policy in Bangladesh: What Policies Are We Talking About?" Bangladesh Institute of Development Studies, Report No. 142.
Donahue, John. 1997. "The Courtship of Capital." In *Disunited States.* New York: Basic Books Division of Harper Collins.
Feldman, Shelley. 1992. "Crisis, Islam, and Gender in Bangladesh: The Social Construction of a Female Labor Force." In *Unequal Burden*, edited by Lourdes Beneria and Shelley Feldman. Oxford: Westview Press.
Hirschman, Alan O. 1970. *Exit, Voice, and Loyalty.* Cambridge: Harvard University Press.
Jeffrey, Simon. 2002. "What Is Globalisation?" *Guardian Review*, October 31.
Islam, Anisul M., and Munir Quddus. 1996. "The Export Garment Industry in Bangladesh: A Potential Catalyst for Breakthrough." In *The Economy of Bangladesh: Problems and Prospects*, ed. Abu N. M. Wahid and Charles E. Weiss. Westport, CT: Praeger.
Jahan, Rounaq. 1995. *The Elusive Agenda: Mainstreaming Women in Development.* London: Zed Books.
Kabeer, Naila. 1994. "Women's Labour in the Bangladesh Garment Industry: Choices and Constraints" In *Muslim Women's Choices: Religious Beliefs and Social Reality*, ed. Camille Fawzi El Solh and Judy Mabro. Oxford: Berg Publishers.

Kamaluddin, Syed. 1986. "Jamming on the Brakes: U.S. Quotas Hit Thousands of Bangladesh Textile Workers." *Far Eastern Economic Review* January 30.

Kibria, Nazli. 1995. "Culture, Social Class, and Income Control in the Lives of Women Garment Workers in Bangladesh." *Gender and Society* 9(3): 289–309.

Lourdes, Beneria, and Amy Lind. 1995. "Global Markets: Threats to Sustainable Human Development." In *A Commitment to the World's Women: Perspectives on Development for Beijing and Beyond*, ed. Noeleen Heyzer, Sushman Kapoor, and Joanne Sandler. New York: UNIFEM.

Mondal, Abdul Hye. 1992. "Trade Unionism, Wages and Labour Productivity in the Manufacturing Sector of Bangladesh." Bangladesh Institute of Development Studies, Report No. 133.

Reich, Robert B. 1992. *The Work of Nations.* New York: First Vintage Books Edition.

Rodrik, Dani. 1997. *Has Globalization Gone Too Far?* Washington, DC: Institute for International Economics.

Wahid, Abu N. M., and Charles E. Weiss. 1996. *The Economy of Bangladesh: Problems and Prospects.* Westport, Conn.: Praeger.

CHAPTER FIVE

Wading through Treacle: Female Commercial School Graduates in Egypt's Informal Economy

MOUSHIRA ELGEZIRI

Reporting the findings of the 2006 Egyptian Labor Market Panel Survey, Assaad (2006) indicated that, despite the decline in unemployment rates for all educational groups in 2006, as compared to 1998, those pertaining to female technical school graduates remained extremely high.[1] He attributed this mainly to the dramatic decline in government hiring, which dropped from 30 percent in 1988, to 23 percent in 1998, to 15 percent in 2006 (20). Around the same time, other studies (for example, El-Kogali and Al-Bassusi 2001) investigated why young Egyptian women did not seek work options outside the government—why they did not, for example, find attractive the work in the newly built industrial zones on the outskirts of Cairo—and the reasons behind the lukewarm relationship in general between them and the private sector. Women attributed their reluctance to the nongovernmental sector's long and harsh working conditions which could be endured only for a short period of time and until they got married. Two articles appeared in the *International Journal of Middle East Studies* reviewing the "Arab Human Development Report 2005: Towards the Rise of Women in the Arab World." The respective authors of these two articles, Lila Abu-Lughod and Fida Adley, criticized the report for its "liberal, modernist discourse" (Adley 2009, 117) and the unquestioned assumptions it makes about the role of education and employment in empowering women and expanding their human capabilities and individual choices (Abu-Lughod 2009; Adley 2009).

This chapter is part of a larger project that examines, through in-depth interviews, the work experiences of sixty female commercial school graduates (CSGs) and their roles in their occupational and social mobility; like Abu-Lughod and Adley, I question the roles of education and employment in advancing the quality of women's lives. Here, I focus on CSGs' work experiences in Egypt's informal economy, in which women are expected to secure their own employment and fend for themselves—in clear contrast to previous decades when the public sector guaranteed their employment and status as members of the middle class, albeit on the periphery. With greatly increasing privatization and the retreat of the state from the role of provider of public services, female graduates of commercial schools have largely withdrawn from the labor force (Assaad

---

Originally Published in the Fall 2010 issue of *Feminist Formations* (22.3).

2006, 25). However, our knowledge of those women either seeking employment or who are already employed in the informal economy is deficient (an exception is Barsoum 2004). Therefore this article focuses on CSGs' search for work and their transitions and experiences on the job. While their experiences are not identical, as products of this type of education, they all face the same objective structures that produce the same social environment, with its "closed doors," "dead ends," and "limited prospects" (Bourdieu 1977, 86).

Grasping the gender and class dynamics in the labor market is essential for understanding the opportunities and constraints these women face and how they shape their options for upward occupational mobility. This chapter is based on interviews with a sample of sixty women between ages 20 and 40 who work in the informal labor market. I begin by reviewing the main stages in women's social histories, with an emphasis on their education and employment, and specifically on the development of commercial education as a feminized stream of education in which women are present in large numbers. In the following sections, I explain what is meant by the "informal" labor market and describe the theoretical currents that inform the main argument. Next, I discuss the job search process and present vignettes of women to highlight the types of work and available opportunities. Finally, the last section analyzes the study's principal conclusions.

Women's Education and Employment: An Overview

When the Egyptian officers launched the July 1952 revolution, they proclaimed social justice as one of their main goals, which included the elimination of class distinctions and mitigation of the strong bias against the poor that characterized Egyptian society (Abdel-Fadil 1980, 1–2). Ensuring the people's rights to health and educational services was among the objectives of the new regime. On the eve of the revolution, the nation's educational system was generally bleak, though more so for women than men, because the British occupation forces had an interest in educating only those who could work in the civil service. Essentially, this meant focusing on men to serve in the bureaucracy (Richards and Waterbury 1996, 122). Consequently, after the revolution, educational advances addressed both men and women, and the revolution's most significant contribution in this sphere was to foster a more positive attitude toward girls' education. Laws were passed that specified equal educational opportunities for boys and girls (Hyde 1978, 41). Because of free and universal education up to the university level, families no longer had to choose which of their children, sons or daughters, to educate.

Concerning employment, the state envisioned a role for women in its plans for industrialization and modernization by establishing "state feminism," whereby women's reproduction and work opportunities became its responsibility. Women were not only guaranteed equal standing in the labor force and equal access to job opportunities, but also they could now hold public office. At the same time, the family was affirmed as the main unit of society; the state assumed responsibility for safeguarding the family and protecting mothers and childbearing (Hatem 1996).

Abu-Lughod (1998) has written about how women are used by newly established governments in their projects of state-building and modernization, which on the one hand granted new freedoms and citizenship rights but on the other entailed high costs not only for the loss of independence by women's movements and organizations but also for the new forms of control instituted over women's minds and bodies (13). Other authors (for example, Hatem 1996, 2000; Hoodfar 1997; Moghadam 1998) take this a step further by asserting that states' encouraging women's entry into the labor force actually represents a first step in the *devaluation* of their work, particularly with the "feminization" of the public sector and the concentration of women in "flexible" jobs that better suit their domestic responsibilities and that were not too demanding. This, Moghadam (1998) emphasized, opened the door for the "deterioration of income and status associated with government employment" (109). Hatem (2000) also argued that despite state support, Egyptian women still faced "fraternal public resistance," as, for example, by some public enterprises making sure not to hire more than ninety-nine women employees in order to avoid the costs of child day-care centers stipulated by labor law (no. 91 [1959]) for firms employing one hundred or more women, which undermined women's full participation in paid employment (51).

While the above argument is basically sound, it must be qualified. Elsewhere I have argued that white-collar jobs in the public sector provided CSGs with the social status and dignity they needed to assert their newly acquired identities as members of the middle class, albeit on its periphery. I demonstrated, moreover, that the organizational rules and social homogeneity of the public sector did not spotlight women's gender and class identities in the way that the informal economy later did, as shall be demonstrated below. Once they had attained white-collar jobs and the prestige that came with them, the main objective of these female public-sector employees was to consolidate this recognition and status by attempting to ensure that the benefits of employment in the public sector passed on to their children.

By the late 1960s, however, it became clear that President Gamal Abdel Nasser's state-led "import-substitution" industrialization, which established the country's industrial infrastructure, was unable to continue at the same time both its excessive public-sector employment and the provision of low-cost commodities. During the ensuing years attempts were made to change import-substitution industrialization by introducing a more liberal economic open-door policy. The state backed away from its commitment to gender equality and the protection of working women, which harmed lower-middle- and middle-class women in particular, who had to work for financial reasons (Hatem 1996). As the economy continued to slacken and with rising unemployment, social unrest and increased religiosity followed, which opened the way for conservative Islamists to step in to remedy what they claimed was the immorality and westernization caused by the country's economic open-door policy (El-Guindy 1981).

State patriarchy works best when it mediates and mobilizes its resources in the interests of all actors of society (Walby 1986). As the Egyptian government continued to face employment problems, it called for women to stay at home as wives and mothers and began to encourage women to take leaves of absence to look after their homes and to raise children. It was no coincidence that during this period there were heated debates with Islamist overtones about the "desirability" of women's work. An Islamist discourse prevailed about the negative effects of women's work upon families and the psychological problems that befell children of working mothers. In addition, working women were blamed for the crowded streets and transportation system and for taking away men's jobs (Hatem 1996, 235). In clinics affiliated with mosques, personnel encouraged women to reject contraceptives because their use was considered to be un-Islamic, and the clinics also reinforced the division of labor by gender and women's domestic roles as mothers and wives (Karam 1998, 165).

Nasser's successors Anwar al-Sadat (1970–1981) and Hosni Mubarak (1981–2011) were caught between their desires to please their Western allies and to appease the Islamists at the same time. Therefore the regime adopted laws that, on the one hand, restricted women's economic opportunities and, on the other, sought to improve their personal lives. For example, public law no. 44 (1979) conferred upon the wife the right to retain the family domicile after divorce and the right of a wife to be informed of her husband's marriage to a second woman, in which case she could demand a divorce. But women were granted the right to work outside the home only if the family's economic circumstances made it necessary and provided that they were observing the rules and principles of the *Shari'ah* (Islamic divine law). Thus, the *Shari'ah* was invoked in a way that limited women's equality with men in the public sphere (Hatem 1996, 242).

With the deterioration of the economic situation at the end of the 1980s, the Economic Reform and Structural Adjustment Program (ERSAP) was launched in 1991 upon the recommendation of the International Monetary Fund and World Bank to stabilize the Egyptian economy. The state adopted a deregulated, private sector-dominated market economy, and by 2001, nearly half of all public enterprises were sold off and privatized (Hinnebusch 2003, 220). At the same time, Egypt's population continued to increase, reaching close to seventy million by the mid-1990s (with an active labor force of sixteen million, out of a total of thirty million over age 15). The state's traditional sectors for employing large numbers of workers—the government bureaucracy and public enterprises—were filled to capacity, and the official unemployment rate in 1993 was reported to be 10 percent (the World Bank claimed it was 13 percent) (Radwan 1998, 6). Public expenditures on health and education declined dramatically. Attendance fees state schools and universities were introduced by the government and for despite their relative low cost, have been cited as one of the factors leading to an increase in the dropout rate from primary schools, particularly in rural areas (Heba Nassar 1996, qtd. in Moghadam 1998, 107).

At the same time, the government was urged by international lending institutions to eliminate the structural rigidities that hindered private investments from contributing more significantly in the marketplace; therefore, it turned a blind eye to the private sector's violations of the labor code and disrespect for the contractual rights of workers. For example, inherent in the present labor law no. 12 (2003) is a great amount of flexibility concerning hiring and terminating workers' contracts. The law also allows repeated labor-contract renewals for finite periods (Posusney 2002, 53–54). In addition, the protections accorded to women in Egyptian labor laws, such as maternity leave, and the extra costs and restrictions involved have had the effect of discouraging employers from hiring them, especially given the abundant supply of male workers. Concurrently, women themselves have been reluctant to work in the private sector because of this trend toward short-term contracts instead of permanent employment and the long working hours involved (El-Kogali and Al-Bassusi 2001).

But how did the new economic situation in Egypt affect the work decisions of women from the lower classes? Some who had to work for financial reasons discovered that, with the dwindling role of the public sector and diminishing salaries, being employed was actually losing its rationale and cost-effectiveness because, after the costs of transportation, clothing, and other work-related expenses, not much was left to contribute to the household. In such a situation, women invoked the high value they attached to their traditional domestic role as mothers, which is a source of pride and status. As increasingly women decided to remain at home, the household consequently became dependent upon the husband as the sole income provider (Hoodfar 1997, 115). Other women, however, continued to work for the same financial reasons, either because the incomes of two were needed to make ends meet or for financial security in case of divorce or widowhood (Hatem 1996, 237). To avoid conflicts with husbands or their communities, women of the lower classes wore veils, which served to convey the message that they were bound by Islamic notions of gender roles despite their wage-earning activities and also that they respected Islamic values and traditions (Hoodfar 1997; Macleod 1992). It is now agreed that the Islamic attire has given women more freedom of movement and confidence in their ability to negotiate within both their families and the workplace.

Commercial Education: Historical Background

In modern industrial societies, schools mainly serve, aside from their educational role, to ensure a certain degree of permanence in the social structure and conformity with its objectives (Boudon and Bourricaud 1989). Commercial education is one of the three tracks of intermediate technical education that have functioned in the Egyptian educational context (the two others being industrial and agricultural technical education). Initially, technical education was designed to provide students with the advanced vocational, practical, and technical (as opposed to theoretical or academic training) knowledge and skills required for a labor force to promote the nation's economic and industrial development.

Selection of either a general secondary school (leading to the university) or a technical education (which theoretically offers the chance to attend a university and higher institutes, though in practice is a dead-end education) takes place at the end of the preparatory (middle school) stage. At this point, families, especially poor ones, have to decide if they are willing and able to keep their children in school, given that free education is no longer the reality in Egypt. Private schools with tuition, which offer a higher-quality education, have been growing in number. In addition, there has been an increased awareness that students' progress in the educational system cannot be ensured without private lessons to compensate for the deteriorating quality of classroom instruction, which, of course, makes it more expensive to keep children in school (Papanek 1985; Williamson 1987). Thus, if poor households managed to resist withdrawing their children from schools at the early primary stage so that they could enter the labor force, at the middle-school stage many of them opted to send their children to public technical schools. During 2005–2006, technical-education students constituted 56 percent of all secondary-school students, while public general-secondary-school students represented 33 percent, Al Azhar religious education was 8 percent, and private general-secondary-school students constituted 3 percent (Egypt Ministry of Education 2006, 77).

Notwithstanding that it has the largest number of Egypt's young people in secondary education, technical education has been called the "poor sister" of general education (Williamson 1987, 137). In addition to its chronic problems of poor-quality education due to outdated and theoretical curricula and poorly trained and paid teachers (European Training Foundation and World Bank 2005; Richards and Waterbury 1996), the objectives of technical education have been marred by a lack of planning and an inability to change along with the nation's economic priorities as the ambitious industrial plans of the 1960s and '70s faltered and the economy slackened. Although in recent years it became increasingly obvious that technical education was superfluous and no longer serving any need, the government continues to steer students toward it merely to limit demand on general secondary education and universities—to such an extent that technical education is now described as merely serving as the government's safety valve for young men and women of poor socioeconomic backgrounds (Antoninis 2001; Gill and Heyneman 2000).

Among the three intermediate technical education tracks, commercial education is particularly interesting because of its gendered history and the insights it brings to the debate in the literature on occupational and social mobility on the manual/nonmanual scale. Unlike industrial and agricultural education, commercial education has always been regarded as the closest to women's traditional interests in domestic chores and home economics and is a natural continuation of the "female cultural schools" that targeted women before the 1952 revolution and afterward, while males were encouraged to attend technical industrial and agricultural schools (Hyde 1978).[2] Gradually, however, in accordance with the 1952 revolutionary climate that emphasized the need for public mobilization to respond to the exigencies of nation building, women began to quietly enroll in industrial and agricultural schools, while at the same time their numbers continued to steadily increase in commercial schools. By 1979, the percentage of women enrolled (52.6 percent) was greater than that of males, and from then onward women comprised the majority of students in commercial schools (Metwalli 1989, 166). During the 2005–2006 school year, 54 percent of the women in technical schools were enrolled in commercial education, 41 percent in industrial, and 5 percent in agricultural education (Egypt Ministry of Education 2007–08, 105).

There are two troubling aspects in the discussions concerning commercial education. The first is that, unlike the industrial and agricultural schools, commercial schools do not likewise entail the high costs of equipment in workshops and laboratories. Therefore, successive governments have used this comparative advantage to expand the number of commercial schools and enroll more students, which served to meet the increasing demands of the lower classes to educate their children (Metwalli 1989). In addition, despite (or given) this public demand, among the three technical tracks, commercial education accepts those students with the lowest preparatory school grades. This combination of high demand, limited resources, and low status has resulted in a vicious circle of commercial schools teaching obsolete skills and offering a poor-quality education, which places their graduates at an immense disadvantage in the labor market.

The second troubling aspect is that commercial education has been of central importance in the lives of Egyptian women who come from modest working-class backgrounds and have illiterate parents. Even though for many of these families the dream of sending their children to college remained unattainable, the fact that they could give their daughters an education that prepared them to be clerks, accountants, and secretaries was still acceptable. As mentioned above, particularly when a commercial education guaranteed a job in the public sector within the context of the government's massive employment scheme that was in force during the 1960s, it was a significant mark of distinction for women of this socioeconomic background, as it promised a qualitative rise to the more prestigious white-collar domain and a higher social status on the periphery of the middle class.

The strong attraction to white-collar work in government among Egyptians and their concomitant aversion to manual labor had been observed by British officials since the occupation of the country in 1881 (Angliker 1935). After the 1952 revolution, despite the government's strong efforts to improve the image of and promote manual labor and to instill a sense of national pride in factory workers who bore the banner of industrialization, and although the 1960s marked a remarkable improvement in the standard of living and income of blue-collar workers, this group remained socially distinct from white-collar workers (Abdel-Fadil 1980). John Waterbury, in his *Egypt under Nasser and Sadat: The Political Economy of Two Regimes* (1985), reminds us of the subtle differences among different strata of the lower classes by emphasizing that it has always been the perceived social status, dignity, respect, and esteem the white-collar position conferred that was at stake, and not income.

Informality and Segmentation

A good part of the international literature on the growing informality of labor markets during the past decades has dealt with the impact of the relocation of manufacturing from high- to low-income countries, where production costs are lower and labor is cheaper. The rise of export-oriented industrialization and conditions of "deregulated employment" (Pearson 1998, 176) in many third world countries, especially in Asia, wrought the destabilization of labor markets, changing production processes at the factory level, and the increasing preference for women laborers because they were regarded as docile, dexterous, and cheap. To facilitate this, new work arrangements for women include part-time schedules and home-based labor (Beneria 2001, 39).

This focus on export-oriented industrialization and the consequent feminization of labor, however, does not apply to Egypt, which did not experience an increase in the manufacturing of exportable, labor-intensive textiles—a traditional domain for women—and owes the surge in its foreign-exchange revenues to increasing international tourism (Assaad 2004). In Egypt's case, the effect of the privatization policy of the 1990s is best reflected in the impoverishment of white-collar occupational categories, as a result of the large-scale layoffs of public-sector employees— close to 40 percent of whom were below 50 years of age—contributing 25 percent of the unemployed in Egypt (El-Issawi 2007, 519–20).

It was no coincidence that the continued decline of public-sector employment during the following years coincided with the rise of the informal sector. At a time when public-sector employment dropped to 25 percent in 1998, from 60–70 percent during the 1970s, the share of new entrants into the labor market whose employment was in the informal sector rose from less than 20 percent during the 1970s to 60 percent during the 1990s (Radwan 2007, 42). By 2006, first employment in the informal sector represented half the jobs obtained by female CSGs, a phenomenon that was virtually nonexistent three or four decades earlier (Amer 2007a).

Beneria (2001) argues that, with the introduction of neoliberal policies, the deregulation of markets blurred the boundaries between the formal and informal sectors, particularly as the former resorted to such informal-sector practices as outsourcing and subcontracting. More importantly, however, the informal sector was no longer viewed as the "anomaly that will eventually be absorbed by the 'modern' sector" and, in fact, has been rendered more attractive because of its low production costs and for becoming the source of livelihood for many families (37). Taking this a step further, Elyachar (2003) explains how in recent years the concept of "informality" has even acquired a positive meaning in Egypt as international organizations began to link it to micro-enterprises, which are acknowledged as the engines of production and economic growth, and when "survival strategies" began to be valued for their role in alleviating poverty (586–87). In this context, Elyachar (2002) explains that nongovernmental organizations (NGOs) have acquired a new role in the Egypt's new political economy by not only filling in for the state by providing welfare services but also becoming representatives of the people and the communities that the World Bank and other donors are now supporting. Nongovernmental organizations are now contributing to Egypt's new development agenda by helping people to survive without the help of the state (496–500). At the same time, however, questions are being raised about NGOs' true ability to create jobs and be genuine agents of social development, given their reliance on donor funds and project funding structures (Abdelrahman 2007; Bayat 2006, 150–51; Karshenas and Moghadam 2006, 20; Thomas 1992).

In all cases, I use "informal sector" here not in the sense of such micro-enterprises but to describe employment activities linked to industrial and service work in formal settings in which job-holders are not "recognized, supported, or regulated by the government and even when they are registered, and respect certain aspects of the law, they are almost invariably beyond social protection, labor legislation, and protective measures at the workplace" (Mokhtar and Wahba 2002, 133). This informal sector that now constitutes 55 percent of the Egyptian labor force has not been dynamic, lacking growth potential and unable to generate "decent work" for the young, the majority of whom being graduates of technical schools forced to take such jobs merely to survive (Radwan 2007; World Bank 2003, 81). More worrisome, however, is that this informal sector is not a temporary situation and that those whose first job after graduating is in this sector will be unable to transition into formal-sector employment; 95 percent of those who were employed in informal jobs in 1990 were still in those or similar jobs in 1998 (Mokhtar and Wahba 2002, cited in World Bank 2003, 83).

Although informal-sector jobs have grown swiftly among women due to the downsizing of their main employers in the public sector, these kinds of jobs have affected men even more.[3] The fact remains that women continue to be rather modestly represented in Egypt's labor market. Out of a total labor force of 19.3 million in 2001, women constitute 21 percent, and men 79 percent (El Mahdi and Amer 2005, 37). Factors to account for women's low employment numbers have ranged from patriarchal family-value systems, household dynamics, the effects of the oil boom on the masculinization of the work force, and the limited demand for female labor (see Assaad and Barsoum 2007 for a detailed discussion).[4] Recent studies have pointed to the segmentation of the Egyptian labor market, with gender identified as a central, albeit not sufficiently studied, feature of that segmentation (Assaad 2003; Moghadam 1998; Nassar 2003). Walby (1990) describes the shift in the public patriarchy of paid work from an "exclusion from" to "subordination within"—that is, "from attempting to exclude women from paid work to accepting their presence but confining them to jobs which were segregated from and graded lower than those of men" (179). Egyptian working women are generally squeezed into a gendered occupational ghetto, which is mostly in the lower levels of the service sector, with some job areas like construction and mining being completely closed off to them. Aside from construction and mining, men are also better represented in such fields as communications and manufacturing. Women face barriers to employment in the private sector, where their wages are lower than those of their male counterparts, as they also are in the public sector (Assaad 2003).

In general, labor-market segmentation theories, particularly the dual-market variety, are useful because they describe the labor-market situation in terms of there being two sectors: the primary and secondary markets, with the former monopolizing the good job opportunities and the latter the lower quality ones, whereby job-holders become trapped and unable to advance out of it. These theories, however, are merely descriptive, being unable to provide causal explanations for such segmentation and, more importantly, failing to explain the dynamics of segmentation and how it comes about (Fine 1992).

Using the case of female CSGs, I argue that gender and class are central to the segmentation of the Egyptian labor market, referring here to "class" not merely as a function of economic resources but also as including cultural distinctions such as status, lifestyles, and tastes, as well as significant social connections. Gender is viewed as an ideological construct but one that has material consequences "in terms of the production and allocation of socially valued resources of different types" and involves "hierarchical and inferiorising [sic] discourses and practices" leading to social inequality (Anthias 2001, 838; see also Anthias and Yuval-Davis 1983, 66).

Both class and gender determine women's marketable skills and value in the labor market. I examine from women's experiences how class and gender manifest in the everyday lives of working CSGs and how they reinforce and inform each other. While not denying the importance and uniqueness of individual experiences, it is useful to draw on Bourdieu's (1977) notion of a shared "class habitus" (85) based on the likelihood that individuals from the same class will confront situations more similar to members of their class than will others from outside of it. Female commercial education, with all its possibilities and limitations and the fact that it reflects a specific set of socioeconomic realities, has contributed in a major way to producing a "group reality [which] transcends individual experiences" to the extent that individual opportunities and constraints on a daily basis will resemble those confronting a group" (Collins 2004, 247). It is important to see how commercial education has created "a single standard" and set up a "single market" for its graduates, "guaranteeing the convertibility of cultural capital into money, at a determinate cost in labor and time" (Bourdieu 1977, 187). This "commonality of experiences" (Collins 2004, 248), which is based on a shared common location in relations of power, can be traced to the structures of gender and class and their dominant discourses (McNay 2004, 187).

Finally, I draw on the theoretical debate around the manual/nonmanual divide in differentiating between the class positions of the middle and working classes, which has been of central importance in the literature on stratification. While in general there has been some consensus on the importance of the movement along the manual/nonmanual line to account for social mobility, several authors have questioned the tendency of class convergence between lower nonmanual employees and manual, working-class employees, given the increasing proletarianization of white-collar workers and the embourgeoisement of the working class (Braverman 1974; Crompton and Jones 1984; Gallie 1996; Lockwood 1958). Braverman (1974) in particular argues that, with the increased mechanization of clerical work, it has become similar to factory work: deskilled, degrading, repetitive, and routine, offering few opportunities for career improvement. Examining the same divide in light of the class domination/subordination of the new lower middle class, Poulantzas (1974) recognizes its importance and also its complexity. Given his line of thought, he would probably agree that the commercial-education track is not "intellectual" in nature but is the type of education popular among the new lower middle class, which aspires to white-collar, intellectual employment (260–61).

With this theoretical debate as backdrop, in what follows I examine the rise of new forms of employment that are not well defined in terms of their clerical or manual nature and that also further blur this manual/nonmanual divide with its implicit gender issue. In contrast to Acker's (1990) abstract jobs that require "disembodied" workers that only men can fill, the jobs that CSGs acquire are embodied both in gender and class terms and also, in some cases, require "emotional labor" that feeds on gender ideologies and is typically performed by women in low-level positions (Wolkowitz 2006, 77).

In Search of a Job

In many cases, CSGs' searches for jobs are largely based on pragmatism of their chances, given the broader context of unemployment (unemployment was 11.7 percent in 1998 and dropped to 8.3 percent in 2006) (Assaad 2009, 20). Generally, the period of transition that follows graduation, which can reach up to a year, is spent in recuperating from what is believed were long and difficult school years and also in performing domestic chores, socializing, and basically exploring the options of marriage, education, and work. Choices are perforce made by elimination rather than by careful deliberation or calculation. CSGs discover that continuing their education by entering college, which has been a postponed project and dream, is, in fact, not possible because college is expensive and even the Egyptian Open University not only requires the passage of five years after graduation from commercial school before applying but also a prohibitively large fee, which new graduates of modest means and no job cannot afford.[5]

Also, for many young women, considerations of marriage are no longer urgent. Egypt, like several other Arab countries, has seen marriage being delayed. Between 1992 and 1997, those who were married by age 20 constituted 41.4 percent of Egyptian women, compared to 64.8 percent approximately twenty-five years ago, while during the same period, close to 4 percent between the ages 30–39 were unmarried, compared to 2.5 percent in 1960 (Rashad and Osman 2003, 25). Recent research has shown that the financial costs of marriage are increasing—a burden particularly heavy on poor households—and that more young women are paying their own expenses, in addition to any help from their families (Singerman and Ibrahim 2003).

If neither marriage nor further education is an option, and moreover if the family starts to impose restrictions on her freedom, a young woman will go out in search of employment, as CSG Naglaa, age 26, relates:

> After the diploma, I stayed at home for a year, then I thought about work. I had thought that I would be able to go out and do things as I used to do during the school days, but it turned out to be more difficult. At home they would ask where I was going and what time I would come back. So I thought to continue my education, but it was too late. The date of submitting my application had long gone. And the truth is, I did not want to study again. So I decided to work.[6]

For other women, the experience of boredom and not knowing what to do next or where to look for a job lasted much longer, as Safaa, age 36, says:

> I graduated in 1992 and worked in 1995. I was getting really bored. I would wake up late in the morning, eat breakfast, idle about at home, do crossword puzzles or play backgammon, go out around sunset and return in the evening to go to bed and do the same thing the next day. We were all like this except my younger brother who had an industrial diploma and Father arranged for him to get training in a nearby workshop.

Basi (2009) points out that two types of female workers in Indian call centers used the term "time-pass" to explain why they sought work there: women who lacked career ambitions and others who were economically secure and did not need to work. Egyptian CSGs used similar expressions of "alleviating boredom" and "entertaining oneself" to describe the same situation. However, for these women from poor socioeconomic backgrounds to describe their jobs as a time-pass is their way of dispelling any association with financial need or poverty and providing a fall-back position in case they failed to find work. Such "role distancing" (Goffman 2006, 105) allows them to save face and claim that they were neither very interested nor serious in their endeavors, should they fail to find appropriate jobs. My own interviews, however, have shown that often this was a veneer masking a great amount of uncertainty and lack of faith in the job market. When CSGs search for work they become dismayed by their prospects because the jobs offered are usually menial and have no career prospects. Considering the little confidence they have in their own skills and their ability to compete against others with higher education, a vicious cycle begins to operate: They are offered poor jobs and, because of their need, are not selective in accepting or rejecting them, which generally, in turn, prohibits them from ever investing in their own human capital or upgrading their skills. Essentially, they become trapped in a series of bad jobs.

During the mid-1980s, the Egyptian government stopped its employment program, which up till that time had guaranteed jobs to graduates of institutions of higher education and technical schools. With the advent of the state's neoliberal market ideology, the "ideal worker" then became the entrepreneurial individual who did not need the assistance of the state. By the mid-1990s, the responsibilities of the Ministry of Manpower were confined to collating information about job opportunities and issuing employment bulletins, in addition to helping young people acquire "soft" skills like the ability to work on computers, make presentations, and demonstrate proficiency in the English language.

While the phrase "the needs of the labor market" (Amer 2007b, 22) remained largely obscure in Egypt, the problem has been posed as a mismatch between the needs of its domestic labor market and the qualifications of its young people. The Ministry of Manpower's centralized employment services have since been replaced by several smaller employment bureaus—joint projects between the Egyptian government and bilateral donors like the Canadian International Development Agency (CIDA)—whose responsibilities have been to liaise between new graduates and private-sector employers. Although several of these bureaus are currently being evaluated to gauge their impacts in matching labor supply with demand, initial findings indicate that technical school graduates have not been among the main beneficiaries of their services (Khouzam 2007). In fact, a recent International Labor Organization (ILO) report indicated that these new employment bureaus have been underutilized, as only 10 percent of job applicants solicit their assistance, the vast majority of applicants searching for jobs by relying on the assistance of friends, family members and relatives, and acquaintances (El-Zanaty and Associates 2007, 20).

Given these daunting employment prospects, young people have learned not to approach the government directly for jobs. Although they still look for job advertisements for clerical positions in the public sector, they find them increasingly intimidating and have learned how to scrutinize them carefully and exercise self-exclusion. Many of the jobs being advertised require proficiency in English and computer skills, which often they do not possess, and the other jobs that do seem appropriate are, in fact, a test of their "social worth" and the power of their social and cultural capital, rather than being truly open opportunities or competitions. After repeatedly having their applications rejected, female CSGs have come to realize that most of these advertisements are merely a formality dictated by law and that often the appointment decisions have already been made. The need for influential personal connections (*wasta*) has severely curtailed the chances of employment for less advantaged younger people. When I met a young woman named Iman, she was working as a maid in the house of a middle-class family. She is an attractive single woman, age 30, who after obtaining her commercial diploma knew that she wanted to work in the field of television and film production:

> I have always been attracted to that field and am an avid magazine reader. I knew everything by heart. I knew who directed all the films and who produced them. This is what I had been doing all my life. I knew I could be successful.... I applied to work as a secretary in the radio and TV building. I wanted to begin as a secretary then find my way up to do programming.... There were 5,000 applicants and places for only 100. They sent me a letter and I went for the exam. There were lots of people but only those who had connections made it and I failed the exam.... I always felt that these exams were nothing but a formality and that those who were to work had already been chosen.... Some people had connections from members of Parliament.... There was a veiled woman who was asked to make a decision about her veil and whether she planned to keep it. She insisted on keeping it and was denied the job, but her strong connection brought her back because he was a powerful man.

Barsoum (2004) points out that *wasta* is indispensable in securing a government job. Because of the very large number of applicants to government employment, which is now a scarce commodity, the government has resorted to a "filtering mechanism" and to accept "recommendations" (85) for specific candidates to avoid a long and time-consuming selection process. And yet, despite the sense of bitterness Iman experienced when she was denied a job opportunity she believed she deserved because of *wasta*, she had no choice but to resort to the same expedient later on in order to secure a job, except that in her case, she was asked to compromise herself:

> And when I tried later to find a *wasta*, I went to see ... who had nominated himself for local elections but found out that he wanted me to go visit him every day at work and spend time with him chatting and drinking soda, so I decided to stop pursuing it. Earlier I had also submitted my papers to the data center at the Ministry of Electricity which was opening and wanted data-entry personnel but again, they only took those who had connections.... Now I have given up.

When *wasta* failed her, Iman made the decision to give up and stay at home, saying, "I know that in Egypt there is no proper system to find work. I have no trust in the system. Anywhere you go, if you do not have connections nothing will work. But even if you are not a good worker but have the right connections, you will find a job."

Iman could not abide by her decision for long, however, and live without any source of income. Both her parents had died and she was living in her family's house along with her four siblings, all of whom were unemployed and in a similar desperate situation. Therefore Iman's last resort was to work as a maid for the same family her mother used to work for. She was paid a decent wage of EP500 (Egyptian pounds, equivalent to approximately US$90), which is equal to the salary of a CSG after several years of service in the government.

In her ethnographic account of Egyptian women's job-search process, Barsoum (2004) describes in detail the separate worlds of employment agencies that cater to two distinct types of job applicants: Those agencies for the rich and those for the poor. Higher-level employment agencies function as gatekeepers to ensure that only applicants with the appropriate skills and characters are given a chance for placement. Their ideal candidate is a woman with proficiency in foreign languages and computer skills which invariably result from a background of some degree of wealth, but, most importantly, who also possesses the "valorized capital" and appearance of the *bint nass* ("who does not look poor") and is well-groomed, cultured, and stylish (42–59).

The lower classes, on the other hand, only have access to the numerous, run-down employment agencies that have arisen in poor areas. It is a remunerative business, as these agencies charge the numerous job applicants a few pounds each just to fill out an application. Despite their bleak appearances, these agencies do provide links between job seekers and private businesses, and several of the women I spoke with obtained their jobs through them. Other channels for the poor finding work include vehicles with speakers that cruise the streets announcing vacant positions, among other things. Finally, there are employment advertisements in free newspapers, some of which, it is believed, involve fraudulent or unethical practices. In the following, Samira, age 28, describes her experience with a job she came across through one of these free newspapers that had specifically called for CSGs and promised a salary that could be as high as EP1,000 (US$180):

> I went to the company and found it in a narrow and dark alley. I asked for directions and people started telling me to be careful but I had to find out for myself. I went upstairs and found a depressing room in a state of havoc; no place to sit; it did not look at all like a company. A man wearing pants with suspenders without a shirt appeared. As soon as I saw him, I opened the door and walked away. I went back to the newspaper and told them that they needed to follow up and make sure where they were sending job applicants.

Regarding a similar advertisement, another woman said:

First they told me it was a job in a factory, that I would learn hand embroidery, then they said I will sit at a machine and at the end it turned out to be a sales job, that I would go around carrying a heavy bag of things selling them to people in the streets and in cafes and going up to flats where sometimes you find single men and other times they kick you out and close the door in your face... it is all immoral and degrading.

As their dreams of clerical jobs in respectable office settings have become less attainable, CSGs are now recruited for fields that are considered appropriate for their middle-level education and numeracy skills, as well as for their very basic knowledge of foreign languages that their commercial education provided. They now work as assistant teachers in schools and kindergartens, bus supervisors, sellers in shops, waitresses, typists and secretaries in small businesses and local NGOs, attendants in clinics, and, increasingly, as domestic maids. The male counterparts of these female CSGs are active in sales that require physical mobility in order to market products; they also serve as office helpers and as waiters in cafés and fast-food restaurants and often can be seen on the streets making food deliveries.

Starting salaries of CSGs range from EP150 (US$27) to EP250 (US$45). Periodic raises are usually insignificant in terms of amount, besides being arbitrary and following no fixed rules. As one assistant teacher stated: "One year she [the school owner] gives us a raise, another year she does not. We do not know the rules and she always makes you feel that you are begging from her. Seven years ago I started out at EP150. Now I earn EP300 [US$54]." The upper end of the range—namely, EP250—is just below the minimum wage recommended by the National Wage Council in 2008; at the same time economists and other experts were calling for a minimum wage of EP450 (US$82) to EP600 (US$109), which would more realistically reflect inflation and the increase in prices (Farghali and Hamed 2008, 14). Moreover, most of these jobs offer neither medical insurance nor social security, although some offer these options.

Generally speaking, in the informal marketplace, insurance is not a subject that employers and employees discuss. To contribute to a security plan means to have deducted a specified amount from paychecks, usually constituting a substantive part of what is already low pay, which many young people are not willing to do. At the same time, an employer is required to contribute an even larger amount for that employee, which it is also reluctant to do unless pressured by the employee. There is also a common misunderstanding on the part of employees that social and medical security constrains their freedom and makes it difficult for them to leave their jobs if they so choose.

It is indeed true that young women often speak about their plans to stay at a bad job for only a short period of time until they are able to move on to a better one. But the fact is that such mobility does not happen often.

Amira, age 29, is a CSG who worked in a school for five years without insurance, thinking insurance was not worth it because she would soon be leaving. When she realized that quitting was not really an option for her, that she did not even have time to look for another job, and moreover that she was not psychologically ready to make a move ("what you know is better than what you do not know"), she decided to ask for insurance.

Working in a Shop

> "So your ladyship has an MBA from the American University?
> Why, the beggars in the street have commercial diplomas
> the same as you!"
>
> —Alaa El-Aswany (2006, 43)

These lines come from the novel *Yakoubian Building*, which provided a controversial glimpse into contemporary Egyptian society. The lead female character, Buthayna, is in her twenties and a graduate of a commercial school. After unsuccessfully searching for employment she asks her friend for advice, who realistically reminds her of the vast difference between herself and American University graduates and that her diploma has become worthless. Buthayna finally goes to work in a boutique and offers sexual favors to its owner in return for extra money that, in addition to her wages, allows her to support her family—a mother and many siblings. The boutique in downtown Cairo is owned by a womanizer and is the site of sexual harassment and moral dissipation. The novel's image of CSGs being slovenly and promiscuous has been a popular theme in other works as well. For women working in small shops and offices with few coworkers and staff members, sexual harassment is a genuine menace, which partly explains why they are reluctant to work in such places despite the limited availability of opportunities. The fact is, however, that often they do end up working in such places.

Women working in shops know that one of the main tasks is to keep the place clean and dust the merchandise daily. These requirements are not subject to negotiation and women cannot claim ignorance about the rules. However, given their general aversion to cleaning places that are not their own family's and meanwhile coming to realize that their education has been a waste of time and money because thus far it only reinforces their belonging to the lower classes, working in such a shop is a bleak experience that symbolizes their lack of alternatives. Naturally, there should be no conflict between taking up work for a livelihood and acquiring skills at the same time. But all the women interviewed agreed that working in shops offers no opportunities for learning or growth and is a dead end. When I asked CSGs to list and describe the jobs they have held, they often omitted to mention such positions in shops, regarding these as insignificant because, they believed, they added nothing to their knowledge and skills.

Unlike companies that occupy flats or have spaces in office buildings, shops are places "without doors," which implies informality and openness to the street. For many women, a street-level store is associated with social abasement; the idea is that as one descends to street level and mixes with the lower classes, one's own social status is also sacrificed. For example, Entessar, age 32, said that her current temporary government job in an office is much better than her previous job as a seller in a shop, where "it felt as though you were sitting in the street, getting all the vulgar language of passersby and listening to the low words of merchants and lay people."

Given this reputation of being one of the least popular workplaces, shops' turnovers are quite high and therefore shop owners are always in need of new workers. The process of recruitment is simple: Young women often walk into shops asking if there are any vacancies; in consequence, informal interviews take place with shop owners during which questions are asked about previous experience in similar positions, and if the working hours and pay are suitable, these applicants often begin working on the spot. No formal proof of education or legal documents are required, although for security reasons, shop owners retain photocopies of identification cards. Typically, the position involves a twelve-hour workday, from 10:00 in the morning to 10:00 at night, sometimes with a break for lunch that the women bring from home or buy from neighboring shops. The standard pay is about EP150, with no work contract and no insurance.

Female CSGs work in a variety of retail establishments, ranging from small shops in narrow streets that sell trinkets and may also have a photocopying machine to increase income to upscale department stores and boutiques in central commercial areas. Most shops place advertisements on shop windows for "Good-looking young women, holders of commercial diplomas." The usual requirements are an ability to read, write, and use simple arithmetic, as well as possessing good interpersonal skills. Because these requirements are not difficult to find in women with less than commercial school degrees, stores, depending on their size, hire a variety of women with different education levels, ranging from only a few years of education to commercial degrees. In recent years, some shop owners started to add "veiled" to the job requirements so that they would have employees who combined attractiveness with a respectable Islamic appearance, thus enhancing the shop's reputation. In fact, because formal employment regulations do not apply to them, shop owners have discretionary power to set rules and codes of dress, often becoming intrusive and interfering in the smallest details. For example, Dina's (age 25) first job was in a photocopying shop near her house. The owner made daily remarks about her appearance and dress and that of his other female employees. He dictated what they could wear and forbade them from wearing jewelry, makeup, and nail polish.

What bothers female CSGs most about their work in stores, however, is the actual interaction involved in buying and selling. Admittedly, service work and working with clients are understood to entail emotional pressures on employees, with the "inauthentic nature of service interactions" potentially producing alienation and leaving workers unhappy and uncertain about their true feelings (Hodson 2001, 228). Many women describe this situation in similar ways:

> My friend came to visit me in the shop where I worked and after watching me said she could never do these things like laughing with the clients and negotiating with them so they would buy. She said she did not have the patience or the skills for this kind of thing. The client kept on trying things and left without buying. My friend did not understand how I was able to endure that and also keep a smile on my face.

But rather than as a financial transaction that should end with a sale, shop workers also view interactions with clients and their efforts to conclude sales as an ongoing act of humiliation that compromises their dignity and respectability. Selling involves two sources of tension for shop workers. The first is their awareness that the job is about showing clients merchandise and helping them try out different items. In fact, shops' low wages are largely augmented by sales commissions. However, shop workers realize that this very act of selling is a social-class encounter that clients use to deliberately place them in an inferior position so as to make them appear as their "servants." Female CSGs working in shops find it especially frustrating that their education and certified diplomas make no difference whatsoever and do not bring them any respect in the workplace. As one woman said: "Some people come to boss you around and show you that you are of lower standard. They order you around and say get me this and get me that, let me try this or that . . . so you feel you are little. And they are not polite so they do not even say 'Please' or 'Thank you.' I feel like I am their servant—just to help them put on clothes, and at the end, they leave me and go without buying anything." Another female shop worker added:

> That a worthless, barely educated woman would walk in and ask you to bring everything down from the racks, then look at them and in the end leave you and you have to put everything back in place. . . . I go home every night boiling at the humiliating treatment and at the end, he [the owner] tells me it was my fault that I was not able to persuade them to buy. But who

do they think they are? A bunch of worthless, uneducated women who have some money.

Notwithstanding the experiences related above, for most CSGs, working in shops is an inevitable part of their work trajectories, particularly when transitioning from one job to another and as a quick fix to financial problems. The case of Gihan, age 28, is typical. She is a single parent and has returned to live with her parents and siblings in the small family apartment. She is a regular customer of the shops in her neighborhood, having worked intermittently in several of them for varying periods whenever she needed money to pay her daughter's school fees. Jokingly, Gihan said that local shop owners now knew when to expect her at their doors by monitoring when school fees were due.

On the other hand, Nashwa, age 29 and a CSG, had continued working in shops for six years, though not very happily, until she became an assistant teacher. As she and I were talking, Nashwa realized that she had spent an average of a year in each place, and that every time she left, there was a "strong reason," it being "no fault of hers." Nashwa's first job was in a telephone exchange that operated round-the-clock, which was divided into shifts. After six months, she was forced to quit when an amount of money disappeared from her drawer. Because of the informality of the establishment and its many employees, the owner was not able to discover who stole the money until much later. But Nashwa decided to leave after an argument with the owner in which she tried to convey the point that "being poor did not mean that she stole the money." Her next job was in a shop that sold women's garments but again she had to quit after a short period because the owner was a womanizer and gave the girls who worked for him such a hard time that they always dreaded being left alone with him. After that job, Nashwa worked in a shop that sold dairy products and was glad about finally acquiring a new and useful skill—learning how to make yogurt and cream—but when the owner took on a partner and the business started floundering, she was paid irregularly, so she quit. Similarly, her next job was in a shop that sold women's accessories, but when business declined the owner sold the shop to someone else, who decided to turn it into a car rental agency. Nashwa was angry when the original owner told her that she could be "part of the transaction" and be "sold" to the new one. She left after politely telling him that this new line of business was of no interest to her. Then for a year Nashwa stayed at home, because she didn't know how to look for the kinds of jobs she wanted. During this time she restarted her father's carpentry shop, which had closed after his death, but because of her lack of experience in this field she had to close it again. All these work experiences of hers lasted for six years, until she finally heard from a friend about vacancies for assistant teachers in a school south of Cairo, where I met her.

Assistant Teachers

Like all other stages of private schooling in Egypt, private kindergartens are now a lucrative business, particularly after the recent education reforms—"National Strategic Plan for Pre-university Education Reform in Egypt"—that regard preschooling as part of formal schooling (Egypt Ministry of Education 2006). Inexpensive public and NGO-sponsored kindergartens that government employees can afford and where children learn basic skills are abundant. However, preschooling in Egypt is also an area where class differentiation is conspicuous, with the middle and upper-middle classes sending their children to German, Irish, French, or English kindergartens so as to start learning the language of their intended education, thus already gaining an advantage for the later entrance exams and interviews preceding formal primary school admission. With this formative period of education in mind, middle-class parents are careful to choose good schools for their children. For these parents, a good kindergarten would be located in an upscale neighborhood and have foreign management and teachers who speak the mother tongue. These kindergartens charge an average of EP1,500 (US$300) per month.

The kindergarten I visited is located on a busy street in a residential, middle-class neighborhood of Cairo. Two Egyptian, female business partners with university degrees and proficiency in English established this modern, "American-style" kindergarten, where the monthly fee is EP800 (US$140). The teachers here, most of whom are female, are university graduates; they are helped in their tasks by CSGs—"assistant teachers." One of the two partners, an elegantly veiled woman in her thirties, was sitting in a large office with a closed-circuit television monitor, which she used to track the performances of her fifteen teachers. As we were chatting in her office, we could hear the voices of small children repeating verses of the Quran after listening to the male teacher, who comes for an hour each day to teach them the Scripture. This kindergarten is part of a new trend of nurturing "modern Muslims." Private Islamic schools are becoming increasingly popular, catering to parents who want their children to have an Islamic identity along with the credentials that will enable them to compete in the modern global marketplace.

These private, expensive kindergartens are the first stage in exclusive schooling that culminates in the upper levels of luxurious "investment schools and universities"—*Madaress Estesmariya* are private, profit-making schools established by business people—that have been established on extensive grounds on the outskirts of Cairo and that include such amenities as horse stables, swimming pools, and tennis courts (Herrera 2006).

Freeman (2000) explains how some "pink" professions have a certain image of femininity (and I add "class") and how clothing contributes to specific professional work identities. This image, in the case of Freeman's offshore clerks in the Caribbean, is observed to be in opposition to women's objective class positions. As the Egyptian kindergarten principal mentioned above chooses candidates for assistant-teacher positions, she is careful to select those who are "adjustable"—that is, those who can fit the image of the modern, veiled Muslim woman but who would also feel comfortable wearing jeans and sneakers and know how to use the simple though elegant makeup typical of Egyptian middle-class women.

For these positions, the principal recruits both older and younger women, the former being important in dealing with small children because "they have experienced what it is to be a mother and would be kind to the children"; however, it is also essential to have on staff younger women because of their physical energy in playing with the children. In one school, the principal was so outspoken about the "inflexibility" of married women that when she expressed her dissatisfaction with a young woman's work performance, she told her she hoped she would get married and have children so that she could get rid of her. A willingness to stay later until all children have been picked up by parents, doing extra work and spending longer hours, working on weekends, and performing personal domestic tasks and baby-sitting favors for the principal are all part of the job and generally do not entail additional remuneration.

Parents Day at such kindergartens is an occasion when space is organized in a Goffman-style "theater" that mirrors the occupational and class hierarchies involved which are visible in the way that all the women role-play in their face-to-face interactions within the institutional setting (Hacking 2004). On such special occasions, parents visit the school to spend a few hours meeting with teachers and watching their children perform activities like singing and dancing, after which everybody goes out to the school's playground for informal chats. *Dadas*, or female cleaners, who are mostly older, uneducated women, stand in the rear in their uniforms of checkered blue coats so that parents can spot them and exchange smiles of recognition; when the meeting is ended these parents give them money as tokens of appreciation for what they do for their children. Assistant teachers stand closer but still a little way off from where parents and teachers are in discussion. The rule is that assistant teachers be attentive and prompt to answer any question addressed to them but not interfere in the discussions unless specifically asked to do so. Like *dadas*, they also receive monetary gifts, but these are discreetly placed in envelopes with the assistant teachers' names handwritten on them and sometimes along with such phrases as "With thanks and love from [the child's name]." The university-educated teachers, who are the closest to parents in terms of social-class background and temperament, converse with them in Arabic, English, or French. Teachers do not receive gifts of money, but instead receive other tokens of appreciation such as handbags, jewelry, and flowers.

The duties of assistant teachers are to be present in the classrooms with the principal teachers, help with activities, supervise the children while they play on the playground, and generally watch over them. Assistant teachers believe that in many ways they are closer to the children than the principal teachers themselves because they spend more time with them and can therefore offer useful information to parents if allowed to join in the discussions and voice their opinions. Their professional role is curtailed, however, by management, which constantly monitors assistant teachers' performances. The schools' managers react to pressure from parents, who want their children to converse only in a foreign language so as to facilitate mastering it—hence the rule that assistant teachers have only minimal interactions with the children. In performing their work, they use a limited repertoire of essential words in English or French, such as playground, toilet, class, lunch, and so on. Assistant teachers are also taught how to assist principal teachers in reciting simple English or French songs to the children (after correcting their accents and monitoring their "Bs" and "Ps").[7] A kindergarten principal described the situation as follows: "Parents insist that their kids should speak in English all the time they are at school and I would be in trouble if it becomes obvious that the assistants cannot really converse in English. The maximum I can make use of is to teach them to sing with the kids in English and even then I get mothers who claim that their kids are not pronouncing the words right and the assistant teachers are passing on their bad English accent."

Essentially, assistant teachers hover between the worlds of teachers on the one hand and *dadas* on the other, although in many ways they are closer to the latter. The difference in pay between them is insignificant: EP100 (US$20) on average; the difference between these two and principal teachers is substantial, being at least US$100. A kindergarten principal explained that she had no problem at all finding assistant teachers and *dadas*; when there is a vacancy she places an advertisement in newspapers and always gets a large number of applicants, but also, at other times, quite often young women ask her if there are any vacancies without being solicited, and she finds that many CSGs are happy to work as *dadas.*

Assistant teachers also sympathize with *dadas* because the latter's difficult, menial work reminds CSGs of what they themselves would be doing if they didn't have their diplomas. Conversely, CSGs harbor a sense of envy toward the principal teachers, who they feel are privileged only by their higher, university education. And yet, for all their sympathy with *dadas*, assistant teachers feel that despite, though also because of, their own vulnerable situation, they are compelled to draw a clear distinction between themselves and *dadas*. As assistant teacher Safaa, age 25, said: "The rules are clear. Anything at the table level is my job as an assistant; anything that falls on the floor is the cleaners' job. If some food falls on the floor, I will insist that the cleaning woman comes to remove it. Also I do not take the kids to the bathroom. I can wash the children's hands and help them brush their teeth, but no toilets."

Secretaries

Our knowledge of the secretarial and clerical work experiences of CSGs has largely been shaped by and limited to that of an older generation of female public-sector employees: That such work is essentially of low productivity, boring, and unchallenging. In the formal private sector, the representation of CSGs in clerical positions is insignificant, due mainly to their lacking the appropriate skills to meet the demands of this competitive sector, including the knowledge of foreign languages and computer skills. In recent years, CSG employment in the formal private sector has been limited to males in such lower positions as office helpers and messengers. With the large supply of university graduates and rampant unemployment, there is no reason for the private sector to recruit technical school graduates when it can get university graduates with higher skills and on reasonable financial terms.

In the informal economy, the title of "secretary" is now applied to a broad spectrum of women which ranges from those who perform secretarial work in office settings, to others working in doctors' clinics, to those performing "paper-pushing" functions and a variety of other jobs of indeterminate character. None of these so-called secretaries I met while conducting this study had received any secretarial training or courses or followed a linear trajectory of performing secretarial work. Most of them have had irregular occupational paths and only came to their secretarial positions from such disparate backgrounds as sellers in shops, waitresses, and blue-collar factory workers. These women understand that they do not have the competence or skills required to make good secretaries and that what they do now has little resemblance to the ideal of the well-paid, -respected, and -skilled secretary they once had envisaged.

Secretarial work for CSGs occupies a vague gray area between manual and clerical. When Farida, age 22, was promoted to "secretary" from being a blue-collar factory worker, she did not notice any significant change in her work; in fact, some advantages, like her relatively high pay, vanished. As a factory worker, Farida was paid on the basis of her performance and output, which amounted to a lot more than the fixed salary she was now receiving as a secretary. Similar studies in Britain on women who managed to cross over the manual-/nonmanual-labor divide found out that often the move was an indication of the "less favorable context of nonmanual work . . . [rather] than an indication that working-class women . . . 'overcome' their origins" (Hayes and Miller 1993, 659). Since Farida was moved from the factory to the administrative floor, she realized that becoming a secretary was in reality not a promotion at all and that her job was a euphemism for "office helper." The work she now did required very little mental effort but a great deal of "light weight and agility" (*khafifa*—thin and can move easily and quickly): "Actually I do not even have a desk. Everyday in the morning, my supervisors give me tickets for work orders and my job *as a secretary* is to distribute them among workers in the factory. I also receive papers from the various departments and distribute them for signature and approval. I am always running around feeling like a complete jerk" (emphasis added).

Nagwa, age 29, on the other hand, did have the chance to sit at a desk and type. She worked as secretary to a middle-aged lawyer whose two-room office is located in a densely populated, popular area of Cairo. Her working hours were from 9:00 am to 10:00 pm and she earned EP120 (US$22) per month. Her job duties were to clean the office, serve tea and coffee to clients, type legal memoranda (on a typewriter, as the office has no computers), and go to court to pay young lawyers to appear before judges and request postponements of legal cases. Nagwa did not mind the job of cleaning the office when she arrived in the morning. To help make it bearable, she likened the task to her domestic role as a woman and the office to her home: "Cleaning is something I am used to as a woman and I do it in my own home and an office where one is comfortable and well-treated, is like home." However, when her employer formalized this degradation by asking her to wait until everyone was gone before cleaning the office again in the evening, thus adding to her gendered task a class dimension and reinforcing her image as an office helper, Nagwa decided to quit. The domestic and menial chores now thus outweighed her professional tasks and she could no longer justify her job as "secretary"—even to herself.

Female Office Helpers

Medium- and large-sized firms with departments that require specific technical specializations and skills apply dual-employment practices. Members of the technical, professional, and executive staffs who are "indispensable" for operations and who have been employed for a long time have long-term contracts, health and social insurance, and other benefits. New recruits, however, particularly those for lower-level positions like secretaries and janitors, are given contracts for only short or finite time-durations or no contracts at all and have no insurance benefits. The dubious call for "graduates of commercial schools required for a reputable firm" is typically understood to mean recruiting for "office helpers."

Office helpers in public and private establishments are predominantly men. As mentioned previously, there is a tacit understanding that women should perform domestic duties only within the confines of their homes, but also that men are physically stronger and, in this case, thus represent more flexible labor than women, since they are more capable of doing additional tasks that require muscular strength like moving furniture and lifting heavy loads. Lately, however, with the increase in female-headed households and the rising role of NGOs in the area of employment, more women are recruited as office helpers. In order to allay the possible stigma of "public domestic servant," office helpers are also asked to perform tasks such as photocopying and sending faxes, which gives them some sense of importance in their otherwise menial work. Making and serving coffee and tea to employees are part of the job, but young women office helpers have devised a slightly modified work arrangement, implemented discreetly, whereby they try to limit their serving of senior management, in addition to avoiding serving staff members of their own social standing or work hierarchy such as drivers and other low-level employees. Moreover, they also heed the age factor by trying to serve only older and senior individuals. In a nice way, these women office helpers try to encourage young people, regardless of their work positions, to serve themselves.

When they apply for these office helper jobs, which generally provide an acceptable work environment and good pay, young women hope that they will be able to move on to better positions. Often, however, they find that these jobs have no potential for growth and, once in them, the young women are trapped in battles for survival, eventually giving up on hopes of promotion, which have become increasingly unattainable.

For example, Doaa, age 24, saw a job with a large construction company advertised in a local newspaper and applied for it without knowing beforehand what it actually entailed. She was given a typing test and was interviewed by a staff member, so Doaa assumed that it was going to be a secretarial job. In any case, she did not want to jeopardize her prospects by asking questions about the position because she badly needed it in order to support her mother and younger brother after her father had abandoned them. A few weeks later, Doaa was summoned to the office together with four other young women and told that she could begin work as an "office helper" in the food buffet. She did not object, as she liked the idea of working with four other women, three of whom had commercial diplomas like herself and one who was a university graduate. Later, the university graduate was given a clerical position. Doaa had hopes to be given a secretarial position when a vacancy arose because she spoke some English and her typing was proficient.

Doaa's job required that she arrive at 7:00 am, before all other employees, to clean the office and stay till 6:00 pm, after everyone was gone, to clean up afterward. Throughout the workday, she and the four others made tea and coffee and photocopied documents until, one day, management decided to "masculinize" the buffet and "get rid of all the girls." There was no one to complain to—the girls had no binding contractual rights. What had happened was this: The relatively progressive management team that hired Doaa and her colleagues was replaced by one more conservative and male which thought that the kitchen was becoming dominated by women, hence making the male employees there feel uncomfortable and restricting their movements in and out of the kitchen. In addition, with the young women being "young and giggly," the office was deemed to be becoming "unprofessional." Doaa and her colleagues were devastated by management's decision. As she says,

> [t]his was my only source of livelihood. I begged them and I wept and said if I made any mistake I would correct it but they confirmed that all three of us had done nothing wrong and that it was just a managerial decision to change the team of girls to a team of boys. . . . It was a disaster for me and although my salary was already very low, I had adjusted myself and my family to the money. I knew how much I gave my family and how much I kept.

Interestingly, not long afterward, the same management team that had dismissed the young women began to discretely bring them back, though placing them separately. Only Doaa returned to work in the kitchen, though this time with a much older, illiterate male. Although she was relieved to have her job back she was disappointed because she had hoped that her position would be changed to a clerical one, which would be more compatible with her education and skills. Doaa was disheartened that, once again, management disregarded her education credentials and, worse, placed her to work with this man who also turned out to be a thief, stealing food and beverages from the kitchen. Although she distanced herself from him as much as possible, Doaa was always afraid that she also could become implicated.

In order to get herself out of this quagmire, Doaa began a "sandwich enterprise" within the firm whereby she made sandwiches for workers and sold them at prices that were not only reasonable but also provided a small profit. The enterprise was going well and she even expanded to other firms within the same building as hers until she was told by management that it was interfering with her original job in the kitchen. Doaa tried to explain, though to no avail, that this additional income was important for her family's survival. (She told me that because of her enterprise's success, she had been considering quitting her job with the firm so as to be able to devote herself full time to it.)

Crestfallen, Doaa was forced to stay with her original job in the firm and to give up her enterprise. Since she no longer had the extra income for her family, her colleagues collected EP5 (less than US$1) each month to help her out. At the same time, she received several offers from her managers to work as a domestic servant in their homes at double the salary she was making at the firm. But Doaa refused, saying that, had she accepted, she would have completely demeaned herself. The last time I saw Doaa, she was trying to convince management to start using her as a messenger by sending her out on errands, such as going to the bank and delivering mail to other companies. She was desperately trying to find a way to keep herself out of the kitchen. But in the end she said that "I am now convinced that even if there is a vacancy, they will never take a girl from the buffet and make her a secretary. The problem is I will never grow in this job. It has no future."

Working with Women's NGOs

Farida's (see "Secretaries" above) experience as secretary in a lawyer's office was especially unsatisfactory, given her previous work experience in a women's NGO and the aspirations it had inspired. She was introduced to this NGO when she solicited its help in filing for divorce from her husband. After this, Farida became a regular participant in the NGO's activities, particularly its weekly seminars organized for young women to enhance their reproductive-health knowledge and to educate them on issues of women's empowerment. As she continued to frequent the NGO and show interest in its work, she was recruited as an outreach volunteer to help raise women's awareness in other parts of the city, in return receiving a monthly honorarium of EP200 (US$36), which became a regular source of her income for about a year. With this income from her work as a volunteer, Farida earned as much as other CSGs did from their "regular" full-time jobs.

Female CSGs working for women's NGOs were happy that they finally had real opportunities for professional growth, as well as different possibilities to choose from. They learned to develop a sense of respect and dignity from their work. For example, Amina, age 27, describes how she interacted with a group of businessmen in the context of a study in which she participated as an interviewer for the NGO she was working for: "I felt my work was important and conveyed this sense to the man I was interviewing. I gave him the feeling that he was not condescending to me—he will help me but is not doing me a favor. People have to learn to respect you. I gave him the message that, *emphatically, I* was giving *him* the opportunity to participate in an important study and express his opinion, an opportunity that not everyone can have."

In addition to growth opportunities, female CSGs said that, despite their lower educational level, they were treated on an equal basis with the more educated middle-class staff and were listened to when they had something useful to contribute to discussions: "Here in the NGO, we all meet around the table to talk about our work; there is no hierarchy; each of us has something important to say and we all listen to each other. There are no social differences here. We know that our managers are from the upper class, but they do not make us feel different. It was as though it was in their nature to be simple."

Safaa, age 30, was struck by the informality in the women's NGO she worked for as a librarian and also by the general climate of equality that prevailed. Even though she believed that social divisions existed in Egyptian society at large, her experience in the women's NGO taught her that class did not matter and that its barriers could be broken; in her case, class and gender empowerment came together. Safaa's position on use of the veil (*hegab*) is illustrative of this, but before I move on to this point, some contextualization is in order.

The *hegab* has important symbolic value as an indicator of gender and class distinctions. Regarding it, Macleod (1992) identifies a unique lower-middle-class subculture that is not "merely part of a generalized dominant culture" (28) but is at the same time subordinate to the broader society and to its power and social relations. She states that lower-middle-class women have a gender ideology ensconced within the framework of Islamic traditions that attaches value and priority to their roles as mothers and wives; however, they are also torn between these loyalties and their regarding work as essential for providing material comfort to their families. When they go out to work they are careful to maintain the modest appearance of Muslim women, while at the same time are aware of the social differences separating them from professional women above and poor women below. They have no desire to emulate middle-class women, as they perceive them to be too liberal and not abiding by social norms, while at the same time they regard the poorer women beneath them as too traditional and unable to cope with modernity and fashion. Hence their desire to maintain their own identity is reflected even in the way they tie their scarves and the materials and colors they choose. On another level, though, the *hegab* dissolves differences between veiled lower-middle-class and middle-class women, because they all submit to the general code of Islamic dress and choose to appear as Muslim women.

Even though the veil has now become the norm among lower-middle-class women in Egypt (in my sample, of the fifty-five young Muslim women, all were veiled but one), young women associated with women's NGOs articulated a liberal and relaxed view about the veil.[8] This position was in line with that of their "reference group" (Turner 1964), the founders and senior staff of the NGOs—educated middle-class women who predominantly remained unveiled. In my interviews, the young women made it a point of letting me know that they were not bound by the veil as other women *in their class position* were, that they felt they could take it off at any time, and that for them it had a purely utilitarian function: To allow for more secure mobility in and out of their conservative neighborhoods. Once they were within the familiar and secure confines of their NGO offices, they had no qualms about uncovering their heads, even in the presence of male colleagues.

Like other young women who had work experience in NGOs, Farida, Amira, Safaa, and others felt let down when their tasks came to an end—mainly due to lack of funds—and they consequently were forced to join the ranks of the unemployed. The young women had expected the NGOs to become more involved in their lives and help them through the process of securing other jobs that matched the training and skills they had acquired. Safaa says that she "had high expectations because of my work with [the NGO]. I tried to be patient and look for a similar job or something of the same social standing. It was hard for me to go to a lower place."

Indeed, NGOs involved in women-empowerment issues face the moral dilemma of their inability to sustain their services to such young women in the long run. This, Desai (2002) explains, is related to the broader role that NGOs have been playing as a "shadow state" in providing welfare services and thus being caught in the dilemma of trying to respond to the different needs of women—needs that should not be separated from one another, which, when addressed separately, might even hinder the original goal of empowerment. Empowerment cannot be addressed independently from the problems of employment, health, and education. While women's NGOs certainly help in the short term and become involved in their beneficiaries' lives, they are unable to sustain such involvement in the long run because of the amount of financial and emotional support this entails.

The young women's frustrations and feelings that they have been abandoned resonate well among some women's NGO staff members, who acknowledge their disappointment and relate it to developments within NGOs, the general deterioration of education, and changes in the job market. As one such staff member related:

> When we first started, it was hard to find an employee. People didn't want to work or be involved with NGOs or the private sector. They were suspicious of them, plus there was an abundance of jobs in the public sector.... At the

beginning we saw ourselves as a manpower-development agency. Having more people on board and giving them intensive experience. We brought in more people than we actually needed so we could train them for other people to take. This was the whole idea behind participatory training which we upheld. Years ago I was looking for opportunities to bring people into the system. I never had job descriptions. It was more of what can you do to make your life easier and better. We had an obligation to hire some of these people, and for years we did not pay attention to educational qualifications. It was all based on their ability and willingness to sell themselves. But then the quality of education had gone down and we got to a point where they [the hired workers] could not move forward when we introduced machines and language skills had started to become important.

These women's NGOs were also finding it difficult to continue supporting young women due to precarious funding situations and their accountability to donors, who often wanted quantifiable targets and tangible impacts and were increasingly less interested in learning about the root causes of the problems (Desai 2002). As a senior NGO activist stated:

We had a vision in the past because the environment was conducive when it was much easier to incorporate these people into the system and convince donors of your ideas. Donors were more willing then to give you extra funds to develop different levels of people. Now they have become more focused on the results they wanted and don't address the constellation of factors behind a particular issue. For example, employment. They just want to get people in jobs but there are reasons why people do not work or do not know how to work and much of it has nothing to do with the skill itself. Sometimes it is the attitude towards work; lack of understanding of why they are there. The whole world of work is something not familiar to young people.

The young women had hoped it would be easy to find secretarial work in other NGOs once they demonstrated the relevance of their previous work experience. Most of them had learned how to draft impressive resumes in which they documented all the events and workshops they had participated in, but discovered instead that just because they were called NGOs did not necessarily mean that these organizations were concerned about them as persons and about their rights as employees. Like other informal organizations, NGOs often did not sign contracts with their employees or provide them with benefits, to say nothing about the low salaries they paid. These young women were critical that some NGOs did not live up to their reputations by not "practicing what they preached." For example, Mohga, age 25, explained to me why, when searching for a job, she did not approach the international NGO she had previously done some work for:

When I first went [to the NGO], I was intimidated and thought I was going to see something I have never seen before. But I found out that it was nothing but a good décor—a façade. There were good people sitting at their desks but they were not better than me in any way.... When I went to deliver the work, I felt that all they wanted was the work—the questionnaires. They did not care how much work I had put into it or the stories I brought back from the field. After delivering the questionnaires, they were not interested in me as a person any more. They did not even get me a cup of tea. "Here is the work—here is your money. Bye-bye!"

Both Desai (2002) and Goetz (1996) warn about the class and status cultures of some NGOs, which might include notions that challenge those of the constituencies they are trying to serve, and even the cultures of some of their own employees. They also emphasize the need to be aware of the distinctions among the aims of NGOs, the perceptions and capabilities of their staffs, and the issues facing the constituencies they are serving. For example, in actual practice, not all NGOs are in favor of gender and class equality. Describing the first job she obtained in an NGO for the handicapped after her previous job in a women's organization, Samira, age 28, said that

I liked my job as a secretary, but I had a hard time because I had assumed that as an NGO they knew better, but they really did not respect the rights of their employees or respect them as they were. They always wanted to change us the way they wanted. My boss, the chief administrator, had always worked in the area of physical training and tourism and did not understand what it meant to work for an NGO. He used to demand that I obey him without discussion, forgetting that in my previous work, I had learned how to debate and discuss. I used to stay after work and explain to him our rights as employees to dignified treatment. Really, the question is how people treat individuals with lower degrees. In our office, a person who has no education is different from a person who has [a] university degree and again different from the technical diploma holders. They could not shout at someone who had a university degree but thought that people with a lower degree could be shouted at. In fact, they thought that yelling was the only way that worked with people like us, and that we would not understand any other way. This was simply not acceptable to me.

Samira's statement was confirmed by a male NGO staff member who described his experiences working with young men and women with intermediate-education degrees. His task was to train them to become outreach officers. In the following, he refers in particular to the young women who came to him from women's NGOs with more empowering work cultures. He believed that these women needed to be disciplined and restrained:

Some of them came to us from other NGOs where they have been completely brainwashed. They speak when they want and want to tell you their opinion about everything. They started to call everybody informally on a first-name basis. I had to stop all that. This is not a way to work. They are not used to the notion of rights and duties and tend to forget the latter. . . . [What were] their duties? They have to remember that they do not have [a] university education. When you have a BA, this is a proof that you have acquired a certain respectable culture and certain life skills. The academic subjects you learn in the university are not the issue; it is the culture that you get there. These kids [CSGs] must take things gradually and you should not open the door for them very wide. They have to know how to grow but continue to respect others; they have to know that the "eye cannot rise above the eyebrows."

Conclusion

In the introduction, reference was made to criticism of the "Arab Human Development Report 2005: Towards the Rise of Women in the Arab World" and Abu-Lughod's (2009) and Adley's (2009) discomfort with its modernization and human-development tone, which uncritically blames patriarchal structures for constraining women's education and employment in the Arab world. In different ways, the two authors made plausible arguments that not all education problems have their roots in gender discrimination or that all types of employment are empowering for women. Despite the persuasiveness of this line of argument, Abu-Lughod's and Adley's exclusive focus on gender threatens the essentialism of Arab women when, for example, the authors seek to explain their low labor-force participation by the satisfaction women derive from their attachment to their families.

Above all, this line of reasoning preempts the opportunity to undertake—what the authors only allude to—a critical assessment of what education and employment, as the two principal elements of the modernization project in Egypt, truly contribute in terms of advancing women's professional and social lives. In other words, instead of attributing Arab women's reluctance to work to family attachments and obligations, in this chapter I attempted to reveal just *what* it was in the education and employment experience that makes staying at home an attractive option. In this context, I borrow Abu-Lughod's (1998) own words when she spoke about modernity: how to "appreciate the forms of energy, possibility, even power that aspects of [modernity] might have enabled" (12).

For a meaningful discussion, the research needed to go beyond the "urban middle-class perspective on women's lives" (Abu-Lughod 2009, 85), which assumes a middle-class notion of work that is remunerative, fulfilling, and empowering. Hatem (1993) persuasively argued that the education and employment opportunities created by modernization have focused on the middle class and diverted our attention away from the experiences of the lower social classes and the new power relations among women of different classes (121). By examining education and employment from the perspective of women from the lower classes, I have shown how their class interacts with their gender to effect limited opportunities in life. While recognizing that difficult transitions into the labor force are faced by all young entrants—in general, they suffer the highest rates of unemployment and lowest earnings, experience devaluation of their educational credentials, and are concentrated within the informal economy's poor-quality jobs and precarious working conditions (Assaad and Barsoum 2007)—there is no doubt that some young people are more disadvantaged than others. As we recognize that progression in one's career, in the sense of coherent upward mobility, is an experience that not many individuals enjoy, we also must understand what it means to be trapped in a variety of bad jobs, with only limited horizontal prospects. My hope is that the vignettes presented here of young female workers succeed in making this point.

Their education is key to understanding the predicament of CSGs and why their experiences in the labor market are unpleasant and precarious. Much of the problem has to do with the intermediacy of this type of technical education that, on the one hand, is an academic credential qualifying women to work but on the other does not really open new paths for growth and promotion. This situation has worsened in recent years as, in general, the value of education has declined and degrees from public institutions are no longer significant markers of social distinction as they were in the past (Amin 2009, 122). This development has further relegated CSGs, with their limited economic and social capital and educational credentials of dubious value, lower down in the Egyptian social hierarchy.

Although each woman had a unique experience, mechanisms of closure point to the effects of class and gender structures that followed the same logic in all cases. Public patriarchy of the labor market kept CSGs subordinated in gendered, low-level jobs, but even in their everyday lives, women were forced to adhere to specifically prescribed gender and class roles. In some workplaces, women's performances were regulated and their freedom of expression checked; they could lose their jobs simply by being regarded as sexual objects or supposedly threatening the masculine "orderly procedures" of their organizations and upsetting the gender hierarchy (Acker 1990, 151). Often, women were required to suppress their frustration over what they perceived was the humiliating treatment they received. In other cases, they were informed that the empowerment they learned in women's NGOs was an anomaly and that they had to abide by the enforced rules of social and gender hierarchies.

The manual-/nonmanual-labor divide was a central terrain upon which these issues were played out. A CSG could only become a secretary if she combined her clerical work with the additional tasks of a maid. And because a woman who cleans is a woman who performs a "traditional" and "natural" job, then it is not a skill for which she should expect to be remunerated (Enloe 1990, 162). Female CSGs bear to their workplaces the burden of the "unpaid family labor" legacy for which women are not rewarded. The women's vignettes presented here highlight the rigidity of status in the Egyptian social structure, which was dormant in the past, when the state's role as arbiter of occupational and social mobility was central. As it provided public-sector jobs to CSGs, the state not only conferred upon women financial means but also a middle-class status. But now, with the state no longer providing these types of jobs, women's experiences in the informal labor market amply demonstrate the extent to which class and status matter. There is now a tacit understanding that CSGs have a specific position in the social structure, in which they are expected to remain.

Dominant groups, mainly employers, have used direct and "elementary forms of domination to produce and reproduce conditions of domination," and through "socially recognized" symbolic violence have ensured submission (Bourdieu 1977, 190). This explains the reactions of workers in shops who perceive that when clients inspect merchandise, they (the shop workers) are being dominated, or the reactions of NGO staff members interpreting young women's desire to be heard and grow in their jobs as attempts to go beyond "natural" limits. Bourdieu elaborates that the struggle here is about "the imposition of the dominant systems of classification. The dominated classes have an interest in pushing back the limits of *doxa* [his term to denote what is taken for granted in any particular society] and exposing the arbitrariness of the taken for granted, the dominant classes have an interest in defending the integrity of *doxa*" (169).

We should also recognize, however, that because work relationships in the informal work sector do not function within the context of the prescribed rules that characterize the formal sector, they provide larger spaces for potential maneuverability, negotiations, and reflexivity. For example, in the case of Doaa (the vignette of the female office helper), the male management team that terminated her and her female colleagues was the same that reinstated her after making new work arrangements for her. It was also the same management team with whom she negotiated a different job description that would keep her from degrading work in the kitchen and away from a dishonest male colleague. In some of my interviews, school principals revealed that, when hiring women on an informal basis as assistant teachers, they often twisted bureaucratic rules to allow these women to benefit from the same financial and other benefits given to regular staff. These gestures remind us of the "gift" (in the sense used by Marcel Mauss in *The Gift* [2000]) that simultaneously represents an act of solidarity and the superiority of whoever gives the gift. They also remind us that, in the informal market economy, people are not always individualist and independent and calculating beings (Godelier 1999, 12).

Finally, Beneria (2001) and Pearson (1998) have cautioned that, although the neoliberal market has reinforced the precariousness of women's work conditions, the fact that women are now employed in various sectors might enhance their presence in the public sphere and increase their empowerment. The example of NGOs and their inability to sustain support for female CSGs indeed raises questions about their role in Egypt's new political economy, but the fact remains that it was through work in NGOs that some women learned to question their social position and used their positive experiences there to reflect on how to promote their case in other jobs and also to educate management of other NGOs about their rights and expectations. Similarly, the case studies of CSG assistant teachers and secretaries point to the negotiations between women and employers on the nature of work—the boundaries between *clerical* and *manual*—and CSG's attempts to set the rules and establish acceptable work conditions.

Notes

This article is based on a chapter in the author's doctoral dissertation from the International Institute of Social Studies, Erasmus University, Rotterdam. In various places in the article I make reference to different chapters of the dissertation, which was expected to be completed in December 2010.

1. Unemployment among university graduates also rose in 2006, compared to 1998; see Assaad (2009, 29).

2. Before the 1952 revolution, female cultural schools were established that ran parallel to the general academic and technical-education streams. These schools offered needlework, home economics, and domestic sciences to prepare girls for their future careers as housewives. In 1959, 65.7 percent of the graduates of these cultural schools indeed became housewives (Boktor 1963, 66). With improvements in general and technical education, the cultural schools were eventually discontinued.

3. Participation in informal work increased among females, but it is still lower than men's. Among females, it was 9 percent during 1974–78 and rose to 51 percent during 1994–98; among males, it rose from 20 percent during 1974–78 to 57 percent during 1994–98 (Assaad 2002, 8).

4. Assaad (2002, 2004), Karshenas and Moghadam (2006), and Moghadam (1998) speak about the effect of oil-related revenues and remittances of Egyptians

working in the Gulf States on preserving the patriarchal family structure, with the male as breadwinner and female as housewife. The argument is that, because of their husbands' high incomes from work in Arab countries, women did not seek employment and thus were financially dependent.

5. In 1990–91, branches of the Open University were established in Egyptian public universities to offer higher education to individuals with a secondary education who could not attend a public university.

6. All of the quotes in this article are from interviews I conducted with commercial school graduates during 2006.

7. Many Egyptians do not distinguish the "B" from the "P," and it is quite common to hear one say "beoble" instead of "people" and "prother" instead of "brother."

8. In my sample of sixty women, five were Christian Copts and fifty-five were Muslims.

References

Abdel-Fadil, Mahmoud. 1980. *The Political Economy of Nasserism*. Cambridge, UK: Cambridge University Press.
Abdelrahman, Maha. 2007. "NGOs and the Dynamics of the Egyptian Labor Market." *Development in Practice* 17(1): 78–84.
Abu-Lughod, Lila. 2009. "Dialects of Women's Empowerment: The International Circuitry of the Arab Human Development Report on Women 2005." *International Journal of Middle East Studies* 41: 83–103.
———, ed. 1998. "Feminist Longings and Postcolonial Condition." In *Remaking Women: Feminism and Modernity in the Middle East*, 1–31. Cairo: American University in Cairo Press.
Acker, Joan. 1990. "Hierarchies, Jobs, Bodies: A Theory of Gendered Organizations." *Gender and Society* 4(2): 139–58.
Adley, Fida. 2009. "Educating Women for Development: The Arab Human Development Report 2005 and the Problem with Women's Choices." *International Journal of Middle East Studies* 41: 105–22.
Amer, Mona. 2007a. "The Egyptian Youth Labor Market School to Work Transition, 1998–2006." Economic Research Forum, Working Paper no. 0702, September.
———. 2007b. "Transitions from School to Work: Egypt Country Report." European Training Foundation, January.
Amin, Galal. 2009. *Misr Wal Misrioun fi 'ahd Mubarak* (Egypt and the Egyptians under Mubarak). Cairo: Merit Publishing House (in Arabic).
Angliker, H. William. 1935. *Industrial and Commercial Education in Egypt*. Cairo: American University in Cairo Press.

Anthias, Floya. 2001. "The Concept of 'Social Division' and Theorising Social Stratification: Looking at Ethnicity and Class." *Sociology* 35(4): 835–54.

———, and Nira Yuval-Davis. 1983. "Contextualizing Feminism: Gender, Ethnic and Class Divisions." *Feminist Review* 15: 62–75.

Antoninis, Manos. 2001. "The Vocational School Fallacy Revisited: Technical Secondary Schools in Egypt." European University Institute, Robert Schumann Center, Mediterranean Program Series, EUI Working Paper no. 2001/22.

Assaad, Ragui, ed. 2009. "Labor Supply, Employment, and Unemployment in the Egyptian Economy, 1988–2006." In *The Egyptian Labor Market Revisited*, 1–52. Cairo: American University in Cairo Press.

———. 2006. "Unemployment and Youth Insertion in the Labor Market in Egypt." Egyptian Center for Economic Studies, Cairo, Working Paper no. 118, December.

———. 2004. "Why Did Economic Liberalization Lead to Feminization of the Labor Force in Morocco and De-feminization in Egypt?" Paper presented at the conference organized by the Center of Arab Women Training and Research (CAWTAR) and the Mediterranean Development Forum (MDF), November.

———. 2003. "Gender and Employment: Egypt in Comparative Perspective." In *Women and Globalization in the Arab Middle East: Gender, Economy, and Society*, ed. Eleanor Abdella Dumato and Marsha Pripstein Posusney, 119–43. Boulder, CO: Lynne Rienner Publishers.

———. 2002. "Informalization and De-feminization: Explaining the Unusual Pattern in Egypt." Paper presented at Rethinking Labor Market Informalization: Precarious Jobs, Poverty, and Social Protection Conference, 18–19 October, at Cornell University, Ithaca, New York.

———, and Ghada Barsoum. 2007. "Youth Exclusion in Egypt: In Search of 'Second Chances.'" The Middle East Youth Initiative, Wolfensohn Center for Development and Dubai School of Government, Working Paper no. 2, September.

Barsoum, Ghada F. 2004. "The Employment Crisis of Female Graduates in Egypt: An Ethnographic Account." *Cairo Papers in Social Science* 25(3).

Basi, J. K. Tina. 2009. *Women, Identity and India's Call Centre Industry*. Abingdon, Oxon, UK: Routledge.

Bayat, Asef. 2006. "The Political Economy of Social Policy in Egypt." In *Social Policy in the Middle East: Economic, Political, and Gender Dynamics*, ed. Massoud Karshenas and Valentine M. Moghadam, 135–55. Houndmills, Basingstoke, UK: Palgrave Macmillan.

Beneria, Lourdes. 2001. "Shifting the Risk: New Employment Patterns, Informalization and Women's Work." *International Journal of Politics, Culture and Society* 15(1): 27–53.

Boktor, Amir. 1963. *The Development and Expansion of Education in the United Arab Republic*. Cairo: American University in Cairo Press.

Boudon, Raymond, and Francois Bourricaud. 1989. *A Critical Dictionary of Sociology*. London: Routledge. Accessed 14 December 2008, at www.Questia.com.

Bourdieu, Pierre. 1977. *Outline of a Theory of Practice*. Cambridge, UK: Cambridge University Press.

Braverman, Harry. 1974. *Labor and Monopoly Capital: The Degradation of Work in the Twentieth Century*. New York: Monthly Review Press.

Collins, Patricia. 2004. "Comment on Hekman's 'Truth and Method: Feminist Standpoint Theory Revisited': Where's the Power?" In *The Feminist Standpoint: Theory Reader Intellectual and Political Controversies*, ed. Sandra Harding, 247–53. New York: Routledge.

Crompton, Rosemary, and Gareth Jones. 1984. *White-Collar Proletariat: Deskilling and Gender in Clerical Work*. London: Macmillan.

Desai, Vandana. 2002. "Informal Politics, Grassroots NGOs and Women's Empowerment in the Slums of Bombay." In *Rethinking Empowerment: Gender and Development in a Global/Local World*, ed. Jane L. Parpart, Shirin M. Rai, and Kathleen Staudt, 218–35. London: Routledge.

Egypt Ministry of Education. 2006. "National Strategic Plan for Pre-University Education Reform in Egypt, 2007/08-2011/12." Accessed 12 June 2009, at http://knowledge .moe.gov.eg/arabic about/strategicplan.

El-Aswany, Alaa. 2006. *Omaret Ya'koubian* (Yakoubian Building). Cairo: American University in Cairo Press (in Arabic).

El-Guindy, Fadwa. 1981. "Veiling Infitah with Muslim Ethics." *Social Problems* 28(4): 465–85.

El-Issawi, Ibrahim. 2007. *Al Iktissad al Masri fin Thalatheen Aman* (The Egyptian Economy in Thirty Years). Cairo: Academic Press.

El-Kogali, Safaa El-Tayeb, and Nagah Hassan Al-Bassusi. 2001. *Youth Livelihood Opportunities in Egypt*. Cairo: Population Council.

El-Mahdi, Alia, and Mona Amer. 2005. "Egypt: Growing Informality, 1990–2003." In *Good Jobs, Bad Jobs, No Jobs: Labor Markets and Informal Work in Egypt, El Salvador, India, Russia, and South Africa*, ed. Tony Avigran, L. Josh Bivens, and Sarah Gammage, 31–69. Washington, DC: Global Policy Network/Economic Policy Institute.

Elyachar, Julia. 2003. "Mappings of Power: The State, NGOs, and International Organizations in the Informal Economy of Cairo." *Comparative Studies in Society and History* 45(3): 571–605.

———. 2002. "Empowerment Money: The World Bank, Non-Governmental Organizations, and the Value of Culture in Egypt." *Public Culture* 14(3): 493–513.

El-Zanaty and Associates. 2007. "School to Work Transition: Evidence from Egypt. Final Report." International Labor Organization, Employment Policy Department, Employment Policy Paper no. 2007/2, Geneva.

Enloe, Cynthia. 1990. *Bananas, Beaches, and Bases: Making Feminist Sense of International Politics*. Berkeley: University of California Press.

European Training Foundation and the World Bank. 2005. *Integration TVET into the Knowledge Economy: Reform and Challenges in the Middle East and North Africa*. DFID-World Bank Collaboration on Knowledge and Skills in the New Economy, January. Washington, DC: World Bank.

Farghali, Taha, and Abdel-Latif Hamed. 2008. "Disagreement on Minimum Wage Level." *Al Mussawar* 4,350, 22 February: 14–17.

Fine, Ben. 1992. *Women's Employment and the Capitalist Family.* New York: Routledge.
Freeman, Carla. 2000. *High Tech and High Heels in the Global Economy.* Durham, NC: Duke University Press.
Gallie, Duncan. 1996. "New Technology and the Class Structure: The Blue Collar /White Collar Divide Revisited." *British Journal of Sociology* 47(3): 447–73.
Gill, Indermit S., and Stephen P. Heyneman. 2000. "Arab Republic of Egypt." In *Vocational Education and Training Reform,* ed. Indermit S. Gill, Fred Fluitman, and Amit Dar, 401–29. Oxford: Oxford University Press.
Godelier, Maurice. 1999. *The Enigma of the Gift.* Chicago: University of Chicago Press.
Goetz, Anne Marie. 1996. "Dis/Organizing Gender: Women Development Agents in State and NGO Poverty-Reduction Programs in Bangladesh." In *Women and the State: International Perspectives,* ed. Shirin Rai and Geraldine Lievelsey, 118–43. London: Taylor & Francis.
Goffman, Erving. 2006. "Role Distance." In *Life as a Theater: A Dramaturgical Sourcebook,* ed. Denis Bissett and Charles Edgley, 101–11. Piscataway, NJ: Transaction Publishers.
Hacking, Ian. 2004. "Between Michel Foucault and Erving Goffman: Between Discourse in the Abstract and Face-to-Face Interaction." *Economy and Society* 33(3): 277–302.
Hatem, Mervat. 2000. "The Pitfalls of the National Discourses on Citizenship in Egypt." In *Gender and Citizenship in the Middle East,* ed. Suad Joseph, 33–57. Syracuse, NY: Syracuse University Press.
———. 1996. "Economic and Political Liberalization in Egypt and the Demise of State Feminism." In *Arab Women: Between Defiance and Restraint,* ed. Suha Sabbagh, 171–94. Brooklyn, NY: Olive Branch Press.
———. 1993. "Towards a Critique of Modernization: Narrative in Middle East Women's History." *Arab Studies Quarterly* 15(2): 117–22.
Hayes, Bernadette C., and Robert L. Miller. 1993. "The Silenced Voice: Female Social Mobility Patterns with Particular Reference to the British Isles." *British Journal of Sociology* 44(4): 653–72.
Herrera, Linda. 2006. "Islamization and Education between Politics, Profit, and Pluralism." In *Cultures of Arab Schooling: Critical Ethnographies from Egypt,* ed. Linda Herrera and Carlos Alberto Torres, 25–52. Albany: State University of New York Press.
Hinnebusch, Raymond. 2003. "Conclusion." In *Egypt in the Twenty-First Century: Challenges for Development,* ed. Riad El-Ghonemy, 221–51. London: Routledge.
Hodson, Randy. 2001. *Dignity at Work.* Cambridge, UK: Cambridge University Press.
Hoodfar, Homa. 1997. *Between Marriage and the Market: Intimate Politics and Survival in Cairo.* Berkeley: University of California Press.
Hyde, Georgie D. M. 1978. *Education in Modern Egypt: Ideals and Realities.* London: Routledge/Kegan Paul.
Karam, Azza. 1998. *Women, Islamists and the State: Contemporary Feminisms in Egypt.* London: Macmillan.

Karshenas, Massoud, and Valentine M. Moghadam, eds. 2006. "Introduction." In *Social Policy in the Middle East: Economic, Political, and Gender Dynamics*, 1–31. Houndmills, Basingstoke, UK: Palgrave Macmillan.
Khouzam, Raouf. 2007. "Egypt Labor Market Service Reform Project (ELMSR): End of Project Monitoring Report." Canadian International Development Agency (CIDA), Cairo, March.
Lockwood, D. 1958. *The Black-Coated Workers*. London: Unwin University Books.
Macleod, Arlene. 1992. *Accommodating Protest: Working Women, the New Veiling and Change in Cairo*. Cairo: American University in Cairo Press.
Mauss, Marcel. [1925]2000. *The Gift: Forms and Functions of Exchange in Archaic Societies*. Trans. W. D. Halls. Reprint, New York: W. W. Norton.
McNay, Lois. 2004. "Retheorizing the Habitus." *Sociological Review* 52(S2): 173–90.
Metwalli, Fuad Bassiouni. 1989. *Al Ta'leem el Fani, Tarikho, Tashri'ato, Eslaho wa Mostaqbalo* (Technical Education: Its History, Legislation, Reform, and Future). Alexandria, Egypt: Dar Al Ma'refa al Game'ia (in Arabic).
Moghadam, Valentine M. 1998. *Women, Work, and Economic Reform in the Middle East and North Africa*. Boulder, CO: Lynne Rienner Publishers.
Mokhtar, May, and Jackline Wahba. 2002. "Informalization of Labor in Egypt." In *The Egyptian Labor Market in an Era of Reform*, ed. Ragui Assaad, 131–57. Cairo: American University in Cairo Press.
Nassar, Heba. 2003. "Egypt: Structural Adjustment and Women's Employment." In *Women and Globalization in the Arab Middle East: Gender, Economy, and Society*, ed. Eleanor Abdella Dumato and Marsha Pripstein Posusney, 95–118. Boulder, CO: Lynne Rienner Publishers.
———. 1996. "Structural Adjustment and Its Implications for Women." Faculty of Economics and Political Science, Cairo University, May.
Papanek, Hanna. 1985. "Class and Gender in Education-Employment Linkages." *Comparative Education Review* 29(3): 317–46.
Pearson, Ruth. 1998. "'Nimble Fingers' Revisited: Reflections on Women and Third World Industrialization in the Late Twentieth Century." In *Feminist Visions of Development: Gender Analysis and Policy*, ed. Cecile Jackson and Ruth Pearson, 171–88. New York: Routledge.
Posusney, Marsha Pripstein. 2002. "Egyptian Labor Struggles in the Era of Privatization: The Moral Economy Thesis Revisited." In *Privatization and Labor: Responses and Consequences in Global Perspectives*, ed. Marsha Pripstein Posusney and Linda Cook, 43–65. Cheltenham, UK: Edward Edgar.
Poulantzas, Nicos. 1974. *Classes in Contemporary Capitalism*. London: Verso.
Radwan, Samir. 2007. "Good Jobs, Bad Jobs and Economic Performance: The View from the Middle East and North Africa." In *Employment and Shared Growth: Rethinking the Role of Labor Mobility for Development*, ed. Pierella Paci and Pieter Serneels, 37–52. Washington, DC: World Bank.
———. 1998. "Towards Full Employment: Egypt into the 21st Century." Distinguished Lecture Series 10, Egyptian Center for Economic Studies.
Rashad, Hoda, and Magued Osman. 2003. "Nuptiality in Arab Countries: Changes and Implications." Special issue on "The New Arab Family." *Cairo Papers in Social Science* 24(1–2): 20–51.

Richards, Alan, and John Waterbury. 1996. *A Political Economy of the Middle East*. Boulder, CO: Westview Press.

Singerman, Diane, and Barbara Ibrahim. 2003. "The Costs of Marriage in Egypt: A Hidden Dimension in the New Arab Demography." Special issue on "The New Arab Family." *Cairo Papers in Social Science* 24(1–2): 80–117.

Thomas, Alan. 1992. "Non-Governmental Organizations and the Limits to Empowerment." In *Development Policy and Public Action*, ed. Marc Wuyts, Maureen Mackintosh, and Tom Hewitt, 117–47. Oxford: Oxford University Press.

Turner, Ralph. 1964. "Upward Social Mobility and Class Values." *Social Problems* 11(4): 359–71.

Walby, Sylvia. 1990. *Theorizing Patriarchy*. Oxford: Blackwell.

———. 1986. *Patriarchy at Work*. Cambridge, UK: Polity Press.

Waterbury, John. 1985. *Egypt under Nasser and Sadat: The Political Economy of Two Regimes*. Princeton, NJ: Princeton University Press.

Williamson, Bill. 1987. *Education and Social Change in Egypt and Turkey*. London: Macmillan.

Wolkowitz, Carol. 2006. *Bodies at Work*. London: Sage Publications.

World Bank. 2003. *Unlocking the Employment Potential in the Middle East and North Africa: Toward a New Social Contract*. Washington, DC: World Bank.

CHAPTER SIX

The Gender Gap in Patenting:
Is Technology Transfer a Feminist Issue?

SUE V. ROSSER

Both in the United States and internationally, the focus for scientific research has shifted from basic to applied research and innovation, for which one of the primary indicators is patents granted. If women scientists and engineers are not obtaining patents at rates comparable to their participation in the science, technology, engineering, and mathematics (STEM) workforce and at significantly lower rates than their male peers, then women are not equal participants in the new areas and directions for science and technology. This hurts women scientists and engineers who are left out of the leading-edge work in innovation. Women are then not seen as leaders in their field, which hurts women financially and in their professional advancement. Commercialization of science can be extremely lucrative if the patent results in a product that is developed, brought to market, and successful. Since patents "count" as a marker of success, are similar to publications, and may even be required for some bonuses and "fellow" status in some industries, women's small percentages of patents also inhibit their professional advancement. Very few women obtaining patents hurts scientific innovation, technology, and competitiveness overall.

Increasing Numbers of Women in Science and Technology

During the last three decades, the overall percentage of women receiving degrees in STEM has increased dramatically. In many of the social sciences and the life sciences, women have reached parity in the percentages of degrees received (see Table 6.1). In other areas such as the geosciences, as well as mathematics and physical sciences, the percentages of women continue to increase, although they have not approached parity. In contrast, in engineering and computer sciences, the percentages of women have reached a plateau or dropped during the last decade. Unfortunately, these STEM areas, particularly computer science and engineering, represent fast-growing areas with the greatest workforce demand in our increasingly technological society.

Aggregated data mask the attrition of women at every phase of the educational and career STEM pipeline. Despite grades and other academic attainments equal to or surpassing those of the men who remain

---

Originally published in the Summer 2009 issue of the *NWSA Journal* (21.2).

TABLE 6.1
Women as a Percentage of Degree Recipients in 2004 by Major Discipline and Group

	All Fields	All Science & Engineering	Psychology	Social Sciences	Biology	Physical Sciences	Geosciences	Math/Statistics	Engineering	Computer Science
Percentage of Bachelor degrees received by women	57.6	50.4	77.8	54.2	62.5	42.1	42.2	45.9	20.5	25.1
Percentage of MS degrees received by women	59.1	43.6	78.1	55.9	58.6	37.5	44.6	45.4	21.1	31.2
Percentage of PhD degrees received by women	45.3	44	67.3	44	46.3	25.9	33.9	28.4	17.6	20.5

SOURCE: NSF 2007 Table C-2 for BS, F2 for Masters, F2 for doctoral.

TABLE 6.2
Percentage of Women Doctoral Scientists and Engineers in Academic Institutions by Field and Rank in 2003

	All Science & Engineering	Psychology	Social Sciences	Biology/Life Sciences	Physical Sciences	Engineering	Math & Statistics	Computer Science
Assistant Professor	41.0	63.1	48.4	38.4	24.5	16.0	29.2	23.3
Associate Professor	31.1	52.5	35.5	29.4	19.2	11.9	15.9	19.9
Full Professor	17.6	30.8	21.4	19.0	6.8	3.8	9.2	12.3
Total (includes Instructor/Lecturer)	29.8	50.0	32.8	32.1	14.8	10.3	17.1	18.3

SOURCE: Commission on Professionals in Science and Technology (CPST) 2007.

in STEM, more women leave science and engineering compared to their male counterparts. This results in very few women in senior and leadership positions in the STEM workforce (see Table 6.2). For example, at the top fifty PhD-granting institutions in chemistry, women accounted for 21 percent of assistant professors, 22 percent of associate professors, and only 10 percent of full professors (Marasco 2006). These sorts of institutions are the ones where most innovation and patenting occur in academia, although industry emphasizes patenting much more than does academia.

Juxtaposing the increasing emphasis of global science and technology on innovation with the data on gender participation in the science and technology workforce reveals an additional issue of potential consequence both for women scientists and engineers as well as for the competitiveness of the United States. The percentage of women granted patents ranks significantly lower than that of their male peers. Not only is the percentage of women obtaining patents lower than that of men, but it also ranks very low relative to the percentage of women in the STEM disciplines.

Measures of Productivity: Patents and Publications Obtained by U.S. Women

Overall, the U.S. Patent and Trademark Office reports that the percentage of U.S. origin patents in all categories that include at least one woman inventor has increased from 3.7 percent (1977–1988) to 10.9 percent in 2002, and that the number of U.S. origin patents that include at least one woman inventor has also been increasing (U.S. Patent and Trademark Office 2003).

A 2007 study from the National Center for Women and Information Technology reported that, from 1980 to 2005, approximately 9 percent of U.S.-invented information technology (IT) patents had at least one female inventor (Ashcraft and Breitzman 2007). Others use fractional counts. When the fraction of the patent that can be counted as female is calculated, the overall percentage of female U.S.-invented patents drops to 4.7 percent, although the fractional percentage has increased from 1.7 percent in 1980 to 6.1 percent in 2005 (Ashcraft and Breitzman 2007). These data underline that 93.9 percent of U.S. origin patents come from men, who constitute around 70 percent of the U.S. IT workforce. The percentage of U.S. origin patents obtained by women in IT ranks well below their percentage in the IT workforce.

Although women are closer to parity in numbers and percentages in the life sciences, a similar gender gap pattern found in other fields with regard to patenting appears to occur in the life sciences (Ding et al. 2006). A study of over 1,000 recipients of National Institutes of Health training grants in cellular and molecular biology revealed that 30 percent of men compared to 14 percent of women recipients had patented (Bunker Whittington and Smith-Doerr 2005). In contrast, this same study revealed that women's patents are more frequently cited than those of the men, suggesting a similar pattern to that found in earlier studies of publication rates in which men published more than women but women's publications were cited more frequently (Long 1993). A study restricted to a sample of 4,227 life science faculty found that 5.65 percent of the women and 13 percent of the men held at least one patent, despite no significant differences in publication patterns (Thursby and Thursby 2005). The lower percentage of women obtaining patents appears to hold across sectors of government, academia, and industry (Stephan and El-Ganainy 2007; U.S. Patent and Trademark Office 2003), with the exception of science-based network firms in the biotechnology industry (Bunker Whittington and Smith-Doerr 2008) where women are equally as likely as men to become involved in initial phases of patenting but do not patent as frequently as men.

Murray and Graham (2007) found that men at the "Big School" (a pseudonym for a high-status, private, urban Northeastern institution that leads in obtaining patents and technology transfer) had higher total publication counts (82 versus 55) and higher publication counts per year (3.7 versus 2.6) than women, although these differences were not statistically significant; however, the citation counts per paper were very similar (42 for men versus 41 for women). The significant difference between men and women was that men published 16 percent of their publications jointly with industry partners, while women published only 6 percent jointly with industry partners (see table 1 in Murray and Graham 2007).

International Comparisons of Patents Obtained by Women

Unfortunately, the gender gap also appears to hold internationally. Using the Scopus database, which covers more than 15,000 peer-reviewed journals in the life sciences, health sciences, physical sciences, and social sciences, Freitsch and colleagues (2007) found that, although the share of female authors varied by country and discipline, generally women publish somewhat less than men in each field, but women's publication rates are significantly higher than their patenting rates in all countries and all fields.

International studies document that in all countries in all different areas, the percentage of women obtaining patents is significantly lower than that of their male counterparts (Ashcraft and Breitzman 2007; Frietsch et al. 2007; Naldi and Prenti 2002). Considerable variation exists among the technological fields, with pharmaceutical (24.1 percent) and basic chemicals (12.5 percent) tending to have higher percentages of patents obtained by women, and machine tools (2.3 percent) and energy machinery

(1.9 percent) having lower percentages in 2001 (Frietsch et al. 2007). Considerable differences in the percentage of women obtaining patents occur among countries. The study of patenting in fourteen countries (Frietsch et al. 2007) documented that, in general, the percentage of women's patenting has increased during the past decade in all countries, but the percentage of women obtaining patents in each country is less than the percentage of women in the STEM workforce.

Issues surrounding quantification, quality, and association of some names with a particular gender might raise doubts if the gender gap in patents were small or not evident in all sectors, disciplines, or countries. But the gap is substantial. In short, in all countries across all sectors and in all fields, the percentage of women obtaining patents is not only less than their male counterparts but that of is less than the percentage of women in STEM in the field in the country. This raises the question of why women are not obtaining patents at the same rate as their male counterparts.

Why Aren't Women Obtaining Patents at the Same Rates as Their Male Counterparts?

The gender gap in commercial science has relatively recently been identified (Ding et al. 2006; Bunker Whittington and Smith-Doerr 2005) and researchers are only beginning to explore the dimensions of the gap across different fields, sectors, and countries (Ashcraft and Breitzman 2007; Frietsch et al. 2007; Naldi and Prenti 2002). Some recent studies have begun to examine possible causes for the gap (Murray and Graham 2007; Stephan and El-Ganainy 2007; Bunker Whittington and Smith-Doerr 2008).

Since the commercialization of science only began to explode in academia in the 1970s and was particularly fueled by the passage of the Bayh-Dole Act in 1980, encouraging academics to claim intellectual property and work with universities to license these rights to firms, in some ways it is not surprising that the "gender gap" was only recently discovered (Youtie and Shapira 2008). However, the recent studies that attempt to explain the gender gap uncover parallels, correlates, and reasons well known to those who study gender inequality in occupations in general and women in science and technology in particular.

What Is the Impact of Gender Inequity in Patents?

Very few women obtaining patents hurts scientific innovation, technology, and competitiveness overall. As feminist critiques of science have revealed, science is gendered in ways that bind objectivity with masculinity so that a latent, diffuse assumption that scientists are working toward the common good permeates approaches and results of science, when in fact it may be working for the good of only some races, classes, and one gender (Keller 1983, 1985). When women entered science in larger numbers, they revealed androcentric approaches that had biased questions asked, approaches to data collection, and theories and conclusions drawn from data. Similarly, the predominance of men in patenting may mean that innovations useful for a broader population may not be developed.

Although men dominate patenting in all fields, some relative gender differences in fields of patents were alluded to earlier in this chapter. Since ideas for patents often arise in areas with which the innovators have experiences, it is not surprising that studies of the patents obtained by women and of women inventors document that women invent more technologies related to reproduction or children (Macdonald 1992). Women also have invented many technologies for the home (a patented house that cleans itself, using 68 separate devices) and for caretaking, particularly of children (disposable diapers and the pull-down-from-the-wall baby-changing stations found in public restrooms). If more women were involved in commercialization, imagine the new, useful products to benefit society that might be developed.

Focusing Feminist Theoretical Lenses on Reasons for the Gender Gap in Industry

Exclusion or self-exclusion of women from commercialization of science and patenting hurts both women and science, while also shortchanging society. It is an issue that can benefit from both feminist critiques and feminist participation.

Patenting has been integral to technical and scientific firms for more than two centuries and remains central and significant for the culture of most science and technology corporations. Those who patent reap significant financial rewards and recognition, and a track record in obtaining patents is required for individuals to reach certain positions, such as fellow or chief engineer. Since the gender gap in numbers of patents obtained by women remains in industry, where the rewards, incentives, and motivations for patenting are positive and clear, attempting to understand some of the reasons behind the gap in industry might prove useful for understanding the gap in academia, where the effect of patents on the academic career path may be mixed or not well understood. Using feminist theoretical frameworks to contextualize responses of interviewees provides some further insights into the gender gap in patenting in industry.

Interview Data and Methods

I conducted interviews with ten people, two men and eight women, who served as software engineers, vice presidents, chief executive officers, or presidents of technology companies in the metro New York City area and in California's Silicon Valley. Although two individuals had worked at the same company in different positions during their entire careers, most had worked at a variety of companies, both large and established and small and start-up. Interviewees were obtained using the snowball method; at the close of each interview, I asked who else in another company in the area could answer these same questions to help me better understand the gender gap in patenting. All names and other identifiers of interviewees have been changed.

Each interviewee was asked the following five questions:

1. What is the percentage of women, compared to men, obtaining patents at the company(ies) with which you have been associated? How does that compare with the overall percentage of women in the company?
2. What role do patents play in advancing one's career in the company? Are patents becoming more or less important than they were ten years ago?
3. Why don't women patent at the same rates as men? What are the barriers?
4. How can we increase opportunities for women to patent? What actions is your company taking to facilitate this?
5. What (else) should I have asked about women and patents?

Most interviewees did not explicitly articulate feminist positions or critiques. In fact, most interviewees appeared to lack awareness of these critiques and their importance for construction of gender inequality. However, I saw ways that different critiques might be used to frame both responses of interviewees and other studies on gender and patents. The quotations that follow from three interviews are representative of the broader set of data collected.

An Essentialist/Existentialist Feminist View

I conducted an interview with technology sector CEO Sharlane Levitan. Sharlane finds from her experience in both large and small technology companies that women have different motivations and interests that may make them less likely to patent. Sharlane has worked in very large technology companies in a variety of roles, mostly on the marketing and development sides, as well as serving as CEO of two small technology companies. She believes that one reason women patent at lower rates than their workforce numbers in the IT industry is that most women move to the marketing, development, and human resource sides of the company. Although they may start in engineering or software development, many women move into the operationally oriented roles less likely to be areas from which patents emanate.

> In general, women are less interested in technology and more interested in socially oriented areas. I believe that the way to motivate women and retain them in technology is to emphasize context, creativity, and the arts side of technology, for which women may be more hard-wired.

Simultaneously, Sharlane believes that most women do take a risk-averse approach to their career, which inhibits their ability to think boldly and persistently about one big idea that might be patentable:

> To overcome these differences in motivation and risk aversion, companies should make mentoring others in the process of patenting part of performance plans and develop R&D [research and development] training programs to teach women about the process of patenting. That would help to change the climate and motivation for women to patent.

In interviewing Levitan, I found that sometimes, especially when talking about women being more "hard-wired" for creativity and the arts, Sharlane appeared to come from an almost essentialist feminist perspective. Essentialist feminist theory posits not only that all women are united by their biology but also that women are different from men because of their biology, specifically their secondary sex characteristics and their reproductive systems. Frequently, essentialist feminism may extend to include gender differences in visuospatial and verbal ability, aggression and other behaviors, and physical and mental traits such as brain lateralization, based on prenatal or pubertal hormone exposure.

Levitan's notions of women's risk aversion also appeared to emanate from the fact that women are more interested in and occupied with children and family, which might lead them to develop more patentable ideas in these arenas than in IT. Indeed, her contention receives some support from evidence from the studies of inventions by women and surveys of patents obtained by women that suggest that many women develop technologies related to reproduction (for example, Nystatin to prevent vaginal yeast infections), secondary sex characteristics (backless bra), or babies/children (folding crib) (Macdonald 1992). An essentialist feminist theoretical approach to these invention and patent data studies implies that differences such as hormone levels, menstruation, giving birth, and ability to lactate to nourish offspring lead to women designing different technologies and using technologies differently from men.

When I pressed her a bit, Sharlane took more of an existentialist feminist approach. She admitted that it might not be the biological differences between men and women but the societal views of gender based on biological differences as suggested by existentialist Simone de Beauvoir (1947) that resulted in this gender gap in patenting in IT.

When I interviewed women in industry about the gender gap in patenting, they immediately knew what I was talking about and suggested reasons for why they think the gap persists. In contrast, when I spoke with men in industry, most of the interview was spent challenging the data that the gap exists at all. After they became convinced that the gap might be real, they stated that it might hold for other companies, but they were pretty sure it was not true for theirs, although they had never thought about it or checked, as the interview I conducted with Rick Foot reveals.

Rick currently serves as president and founder of a very successful IT innovation company. In the past he has started other companies and headed several research and development operations. Friendly and generous with his time for the interview, he began by explaining the patenting process. He told me that he did not think there was a gender gap in patenting in the industry but that it must result from the persistently low numbers of women in the industry. When I explained the NCWIT study and the data showing that women patented at much lower rates than their participation in the IT workforce, he challenged the data with other questions about sector, publication rates, incentives, and age. When he finally accepted that the data for the gender gap might be solid, he said:

> I'm pretty sure that the women in R&D in my company patent at the same rate as their many male counterparts.

He did admit, though, that he had never thought about gender or checked the data for his company, which now he was intrigued to examine. In quite a different way from that of Sharlane Levitan, Rick Foot's perspective is existentialist feminist. Existentialist Simone de Beauvoir (1947) described the phenomenon as follows: "Representation of the world, like the world itself, is the work of men; they describe it from their own point of view, which they confuse with the absolute truth" (51). As Webster (1995) points out, "The 'objectivity' which is aspired to in the design process is the viewpoint of the men who design" (149). Rick Foot was quite convinced that his view of the world—that there could not be a gender gap in patenting or, if a gap did exist, it was proportional to the low number of women in IT—was absolutely true.

A Liberal Feminist Approach, Modified by Postcolonial Feminism

I conducted the following interview with Sal Calfit, a software engineer who works at one of the largest global information technology companies in the world. Concerned about the dearth of women obtaining patents in the company, she formed a community to support them and help them learn the process. Sal had observed that very few women in the company where she worked obtained patents. When she did some research to determine whether her observations were correct, she learned that data are scarce on the number of women who patent both inside and outside her company. She discovered that about 10 percent of the women obtained patents at her company.

When her own patent came up for review, Sal realized that all of the reviewers were men. That stimulated her to start the support community for women. She sent an e-mail to about twenty women in the company; she immediately received responses from all around the globe. In two years, the community has grown to 600 women who represent all sectors and all countries where the company is located.

> Patents weigh heavily for some promotions and career advancement in the company, which considers itself a leader in innovation. Not only do individuals who patents receive financial rewards, but patenting can be a make or break difference for certain promotions. For example, it's impossible to become a Fellow or Distinguished Engineer without having patented at the company where I work.

Sal believes that a variety of factors account for the low numbers of patents obtained by women:

> Women look critically at themselves and their ideas, wondering whether they are meritorious. They need someone both to encourage and to guide them through the process. Women also tend to be the workhorses on the team; they are more focused on the getting the job done than on the external rewards.

Sal also believes that women had less access to networks, which is why the network she created provides a lifeline for these women:

> The women seem to love the community atmosphere; they appear to crave the brainstorming, support, and nurturing atmosphere. Communities of the company are now springing up in China and India with large memberships of women.

In setting up the online support community for women in her company, Sal Calfit appears to operate from what might be described as a liberal feminist framework. Liberal feminism is the belief that women are suppressed in contemporary society because they suffer unjust discrimination (Jaggar 1989). Liberal feminists seek no special privileges for women and simply demand equal treatment on the basis of sex in access, employment, and removal of barriers. The access to networks and support from female colleagues provided by the online community appear to provide equal access and removal of barriers that prevent women from patenting.

The underpinning assumption of liberal feminism is that, once these barriers are removed, women will patent at the same rate as men. Neither the objectivity and integrity of the scientific method nor the structure of the organization is fundamentally questioned by this liberal feminist approach. The liberal feminist approach undoubtedly makes good sense for Sal Calfit, since she has developed the online support community, using company time and machines, with the blessing of the corporation that includes attracting more women as one of its goals.

The interest of women in India and China working for the corporation in the online communities to support patenting raises possibilities of postcolonial feminist critiques. As I have written elsewhere about postcolonial feminism and technologies, not surprisingly, technologies reflect the varying complex aspects of the interrelationships among developed and developing countries in general and between the particular cultures of the colonized and colonizing country (Rosser 2006).

The particular forms and ways that these shape and play out varies, depending upon the history, culture, geography, and length of colonization for both the colonized and colonizing countries. For example, the IT industry uses subcontracted female labor in developing countries, particularly for software development.

This example clearly demonstrates aspects of postcolonialism in that control of the economy of developing countries remains in the hands of developed countries under patriarchal control since women, not men, in the developing countries become the sources of cheap labor. Language becomes an interesting feature which continues to tie former colony with colonizer. Theoretically, satellites and telecommunications transcend geographical barriers and permit any developed country to use labor in any developing country. Practically, the ties developed between colony and colonizer, as well as the language of the colonizer learned by the colonized during the period of colonization, means that former relationships continue in the neocolonial modern world (Rosser 2006, 15-16).

Some of the studies about the gender gap in patenting for academic women also point to liberal feminist issues of access and discrimination. For example, Murray and Graham (2007) conducted semi-structured interviews of 56 life science faculty about their experiences with commercial science at "Big School." Only 23 percent of women faculty had patented, while 74 percent of men faculty hold at least one patent. Women faculty reported fewer opportunities and referrals from collegial networks to participate in the commercial marketplace by being asked to consult, serve on science advisory boards, and interact with industry, resulting in women becoming less socialized to commercial science. This led to women having fewer chances, relative to their male colleagues, to resolve ambiguities that many life scientists held about commercial science.

Psychoanalytic Feminist Perspectives

Murray and Graham (2007) then appear to move beyond liberal feminism to take what might be described as almost a psychoanalytic approach, reminiscent of the work of Evelyn Fox Keller (1985). They state, "Partly because of the dearth of women, the practices of commercial science, including those surrounding money and competition, became constructed as male" (682).

Dinnerstein (1977) and Chodorow (1978) have used an aspect of psychoanalytic theory known as "object relations theory" to examine the construction of gender and sexuality during the Oedipal stage of psychosexual development which usually results in male dominance. They conclude that the gender differences resulting in male dominance can be traced to the fact that, in our society, women are the primary caretakers for most infants and children. Keller (1983, 1985) in particular applied the work of Chodorow and Dinnerstein to suggest how science, populated mostly by men, has become a masculine province, in its choice of experimental topics, use of male subjects for experimentation, interpretation and theorizing from data, and the practice and applications of science undertaken by the scientists. Keller (1983, 1985) suggests that, since the scientific method stresses objectivity, rationality, distance, and autonomy of the observer from the object of study (that is, the positivist neutral observer), individuals who feel comfortable with independence, autonomy, and distance will be more likely to become scientists. This objectivity and rationality of science have become synonymous with a male approach to the physical, natural world.

Murray and Graham (2007) found that male constructions of "these intersections were reinforced across generations by homophily in mentoring and networks, work-family issues, and broader societal stereotypes towards women in commercial roles" (678). Although the effects were more severe on senior women, in the "entire population of junior faculty, 44 percent of men have been granted patents compared to only 11 percent of women" (Murray and Graham 2007, 677). Although not stated explicitly, the presence of the continuing gap even among junior women implies that the liberal feminist approach of eliminating barriers will not be sufficient, as long as organizational and societal stereotypes remain unchallenged.

Socialist Feminist Views

Stephan and El-Ganainy (2007) suggest that one aspect of the organizational context argument—that more men than women are employed at higher ranks at Research I institutions where most patenting occurs—only partially accounts for the gender gap. Although they appear to recognize some of the structural and power issues surrounding why Research I institutions with high prestige and better salaries are dominated by men, they do not really critique these organizational structures from a socialist feminist or even Marxist perspective.

Socialist feminist critiques include women and place gender on equal footing with class in shaping technology. In this dual systems approach, capitalism and patriarchy function as mutually reinforcing parts of a system where the sexual division of labor stands with wage labor as a central feature of capitalism and where gender differences in wages, along with failing to count contributions of women to reproduction and child rearing as "productivity" in a capitalist economy, reinforce patriarchy and power differentials in the home (Hartmann 1981; Eisenstein 1984). The predominance of men employed at Research I institutions, where wages are higher and hours are longer, results partly from a culture that is less family-friendly than that found at many less elite higher education institutions.

Stephan and El-Ganainy (2007) border on socialist feminist critiques when they provide evidence from various studies to suggest the following explanations in addition to employment at Research I institutions for the gap:

- Women are more risk-averse than men regarding financial decisions and may have less interest in money and a lower comfort level with financial transactions.
- Women dislike competition more than men, and commercial science is perceived as competitive.
- Women are less comfortable selling themselves and their science in the entrepreneurial manner needed for commercialization.
- Women are less likely to seek out opportunities to participate in commercial science.
- Women may choose areas for research less compatible with commercialization.
- Women have fewer characteristics, such as high productivity and a "title," that venture capitalists like.
- Compared to men, women have more family constraints which they perceive as a trade-off with their entrepreneurial activities.
- Women faculty may be less likely to be located in one of the three commercialization geographic "hot spots" in California, Massachusetts, or North Carolina.
- Women tend to have fewer peers involved in commercialization, partly because their collegial networks are likely to include more women than

those of men. Women scientists may have fewer graduate students and postdoctorate students than men, as well as less diverse networks than men.

Some women, particularly those coming from a socialist feminist perspective, purposely avoid commercialization of their research, which they view as "selling their science" to pander to capitalism. Current intellectual property rights agreements and laws provide opportunities for choices in technology development that further exacerbate class differences by transferring technologies developed using public moneys to the private realm through patents. The decisions regarding which products are developed fall under the influence of capitalist interests in profit margins. Such intellectual property rights function as a form of privatization (Mohanty 1997). They allow decisions about which products will be developed to occur in the private, rather than the public, realm. This results in capitalist interests in the bottom line, rather than public needs and interests, dictating which "products" are developed. New technologies in computer science and engineering are often developed using federal grants (paid for by taxes). In the patenting of intellectual property, rights (and profits) get transferred from the public who paid for the research with their tax dollars, to the private company, institution, or individual who controls the patent. Socialist feminists might view this as a transfer from the pockets of the working class, who pay the taxes to underwrite federal research, to the patent holders in the private sector who will reap massive profits, serving the interests of bourgeois capitalists.

Understanding that middle- and upper-class men create and design most new technology, along with serving as the sources of money for design and creation, explains much about whose needs are met by current technology and its design. Imagining women as designers, as well as users, of technology suggests that more technologies might meet the needs of women and be adapted for the spaces where women spend time. Socialist feminism would suggest that the allocation of resources for technology development should be determined by greatest benefit for the common good.

Venture capitalists may have a higher comfort level with men than women since most venture capitalists are men (Murray and Graham 2007, 18). Gender discounting (viewing the accomplishments of women differently from those of men, when all else is equal) of women's work by industry may lead to fewer women being asked to participate in commercialization.

In brief, although more research on the reasons for the gender gap needs to be undertaken, it appears that a variety of factors concerning attitudes and socialization of women, balancing work and family, sexist attitudes of venture capitalists and industrial partners, and women's differing collegial networks and research focus may serve as major contributors. As Stephan and El-Ganainy (2007) suggest, "Entrepreneurial science opened the possibility of having a 'boys' club' when it emerged on campuses in the late 1970s" just at the time when larger numbers of women and underrepresented minorities were entering academic science (486).

What Can We Apply from Gender and Women's Studies to Close the Patenting Gender Gap?

These "explanations" parallel many of the "reasons" elaborated during the last quarter century for why women do not participate in science. Many scholars who study women in science and engineering have suggested solutions or policy initiatives that mentors, departments, and institutions can undertake to attract and retain women in science.

In 1990, I suggested ideas to make science more female-friendly (Rosser 1990). Considering this list makes me wonder if adapting some of these ideas to issues raised about gender and patenting could be useful in attracting more women to commercialization of science. Murray and Graham (2007) suggest policy interventions for faculty PhD advisors, for institutions and their institutional technology transfer offices, and for the industrial and investment communities to facilitate women's participation in commercial science to "ensure that those scientific ideas with important commercial relevance are not squandered" (583). These interventions include suggestions to make certain that commercially active PhD advisors provide women and men students with the same, appropriate mentoring experiences, including encouraging all students to look into commercial science, facilitating ties to industrial and other sponsors who want to "buy" their ideas, and demonstrating, especially to women, how to sell their science without violating their scientific integrity. They suggest that institutions appoint more qualified women to high-level administrative positions to encourage industry to look more carefully at their science and leadership capabilities and appoint them to scientific advisory boards. Technology transfer offices should provide legitimacy and support for women faculty to navigate the commercial science marketplace. After being made aware of the data documenting their leadership role in fostering old boy networks, the industrial and investment community should actively seek out and assess ideas from women, as well as men, scientists.

Using the policy interventions suggested by Murray and Graham (2007), the "explanations" for the gender gap provided by Stephan and El-Ganainy (2007), who offer no explicit policy interventions, coupled with evidence of different areas in which women have patented (MacDonald 1992; Frietsch 2007) as a basis, I modified my earlier ideas in ways to make patenting more female friendly. I divided them into suggestions for women scientists, for corporations and venture capitalists, and for male faculty, institutions, and their technology transfer offices.

Suggestions for women scientists:
1. Consider expanding your scientific research agenda to include commercialization. This may mean overcoming notions about the purity of what counts as good science.
2. Formulate hypotheses that focus on gender as a crucial part of the commercialization/patenting decision. For example, in initial experimental design, ask whether a particular drug works differently in males and females? Might a drug cure an illness in both men and women or just men? Might an invention be adapted for a new product especially useful to women?
3. Consider basic research problems that might lead to patents and commercialization of products to help with complex problems more commonly dealt with by women in the home such as child caregiving, housecleaning, and care for the elderly.
4. Make a conscious effort to broaden networks to include both older and younger men and women scientists.

Suggestions for corporations and venture capitalists:
1. Collect data, disaggregated by gender, on who patents.
2. Expand the scientific research agendas open to commercialization by seeking out the work of women scientists to explore its potential.
3. Explore science and ideas that have not traditionally been considered for commercialization because of gender discounting.
4. Focus on gender as a crucial part of the commercialization/patenting decision. Does a particular drug work differently in males and females or cure an illness in both men and women or just men? Could this invention be adapted for a new product, especially useful to women, children or the elderly?
5. Include women on scientific advisory boards of corporations.
6. Make a conscious effort to overcome the "boys' club" atmosphere of commercialization and to broaden networks to include both men and women scientists.
7. Expand recruitment for commercialization ideas beyond males who self-promote very aggressively to include women who may initially appear less entrepreneurial.
8. Move beyond the signal shock stage of only inviting women with very high-level titles such as dean, provost, vice president, or president of the university to serve on scientific advisory boards to seek out women scientists who have not chosen the administrative career path but who have excellent ideas for commercialization.

9. Use national and international conferences to seek out scientific research ideas ripe for commercialization, recognizing that this may be an excellent way to reach women scientists in particular, who are more likely than their male colleagues to live outside one of the geographic hotspots for commercialization.
10. Consider other ways to find ideas for commercialization that rely less on self-promotion and competition with others and more on understanding the potential based upon solid explanation of the science.
11. Make technology transfer and commercialization companies more family friendly through on-site day care, holding meetings during business hours, and use of conferencing technology to limit necessity for travel.
12. Articulate the goals for commercialization of science to link them directly with making society better and helping people to provide powerful incentives for women to patent.

Suggestions for male faculty, institutions, and their technology transfer offices:
1. Make transparent all stages of the commercialization process and provide both male and female students with equal access, mentoring, and connections to each stage of the process.
2. Incorporate discussion of how to build a business plan and how to understand financial risks in commercialization into scientific training for all students, both male and female, just as learning to write grants, build budgets, and manage a laboratory are now considered necessary constituents of graduate training in science and engineering.
3. Encourage all students to undertake research agendas that include some "high risk" ideas and experiments and some "lower risk" ideas and experiments. This ensures that women have experience with higher risk ideas and learn that it is okay to fail. In contrast, some risk-seeking male students may need to learn to balance their high risk research agenda with the benefits of some lower risk ideas.
4. Alternate discussion, experiments, and problems assigned between basic and applied science in the classroom and laboratory to help students perceive a less sharp dichotomy between science and technology transfer and to help them overcome their aversion to commercialization.
5. Include information from economics, business, and policy, along with science courses in training to socialize students to commercialization and how "big science" works.
6. Ensure that mentoring of students is gender-neutral by inviting all students, both male and female, to explore the commercialization potential of their ideas and by making all parts of the process transparent. Mentoring should also be gender appropriate, in recognizing that women

may be more risk averse, be less inclined to sell science, and have different constraints. Provide women and men with a variety of approaches to address their particular constraints.
7. Include women in significant administrative positions in the university. This not only provides leadership opportunities and role models for women in the institution but also sends the shock signal corporations use to identify women with outstanding credentials.
8. Provide courses and online training and apprenticeship models/mentors to teach scientists how to sell their ideas to venture capitalists, angel funders, and corporations.
9. Emphasize the social usefulness, especially to help human beings and the environment, of technology transfer and commercialization.

Conclusion

In sum, although the percentage of women obtaining patents is increasing, a substantial gender gap in patents exists in all fields, countries, and sectors. Since the focus of scientific research has shifted from basic to applied research and innovation, for which patents serve as a primary indicator, the dearth of women obtaining patents suggests that women have not made the shift to these new areas and directions, representing leading edges in science and technology. Failure to make the shift hurts women's career advancement and deprives society of unique and useful products and innovations, as well as possible feminist critiques of the commercialization of science.

More research would elucidate the reasons for the gender gap in patents, but the limited extant studies suggest that the same or parallel explanations given in the last three decades for why women do not participate in science and technology in general emerge as the particular explanations for why women do not patent at the same rate as their male counterparts. Interventions funded by federal agencies have led to a body of practices and policies successful in attracting and retaining women in science. A major thread that unites many of the findings is that women are particularly attracted to science and technology to help living beings, especially people. This implies that technology transfer should particularly appeal to women when they understand its social usefulness. Feminist critiques of commercialization may lead to shifts in the culture surrounding technology transfer to make it more appealing to women. Articulating the goals for commercialization of science to link them directly with making society better and helping people should provide powerful incentives for women to patent and participate in technology transfer.

References

Ashcraft, Catherine, and Anthony Breitzman. 2007. *Who Invents IT? An Analysis of Women's Participation in Information Technology Patenting.* Boulder, CO: National Center for Women in Technology (NCWIT).
Bunker Whittington, Kjersten, and Laurel Smith-Doerr. 2005. "Gender and Commercial Science: Women's Patenting in the Life Sciences." *Journal of Technology Transfer* 30: 355–70.
———, and Laurel Smith-Doerr. 2008. "Women Inventors in Context: Disparities in Patenting across Academia and Industry." *Gender and Society* 22: 194.
Chodorow, Nancy. 1978. *The Reproduction of Mothering.* Berkeley: University of California Press.
de Beauvoir, Simone. 1947. *The Second Sex.* Ed. and trans. H. M. Parshley. New York: Vintage Books.
Ding, Waverly, Fiona Murray, and Toby Stuart. 2006. "Gender Differences in Patenting in the Academic Life Sciences." *Science* 313(5787): 665–67.
Dinnerstein, Dorothy. 1977. *The Mermaid and the Minotaur: Sexual Arrangements and Human Malaise.* New York: Harper Colophon Books.
Eisenstein, Hester. 1984. *Contemporary Feminist Thought.* London: Allen and Unwin.
Frietsch, Rainer, Inna Haller, Melanie Vrohlings, and Hariolf Grupp. 2007. "Battle of the Sexes? Main Areas of Gender-Specific Technological and Scientific Activities in Industrialized Countries." Paper presented October 16, 2007, Georgia Tech, GA.
Hartmann, Heidi. 1981. "The Unhappy Marriage of Marxism and Feminism." In *Women and Revolution,* ed. Lydia Sargent, 1–41. Boston, MA: South End Press.
Jaggar, Alison. 1989. "Love and Knowledge: Emotion in Feminist Epistemology." In *Gender/Body/Knowledge: Feminist Reconstructions of Being and Knowing,* ed. Alison Jaggar and Susan Bordo, 145–71. New Brunswick, NJ: Rutgers University Press.
Keller, Evelyn. 1983. *A Feeling for the Organism.* San Francisco: Freeman.
———. 1985. *Reflections on Gender and Science.* New Haven, CT: Yale University Press.
Long, Scott. 1993. "Women in Science, Part 1: The Productivity Puzzle." *Essays of an Information Scientist* 15: 248.
Macdonald, Anne. 1992. *Feminine Ingenuity: Women and Invention in America.* New York: Ballantine Books.
Marasco, C. A. 2006. "Women Faculty Gain Little Ground." *Chemical and Engineering News* 84: 58–59.
Mohanty, Chandra. 1997. "Women Workers and Capitalist Scripts." In *Feminist Genealogies, Colonial Legacies, Democratic Futures,* ed. M. Jacqui Alexander and Chandra Mohanty, 3–29. New York: Routledge.
Murray, Fiona, and Leigh Graham. 2007. "Buying and Selling Science: Gender Stratification in Commercial Science." *Industrial and Corporate Change Special Issue on Technology Transfer* 16(4): 657–89.

Naldi, Fulvio, and Ilaria Vannini Prenti. 2002. *Scientific and Technological Performance by Gender.* Luxembourg: European Union Commission.
National Science Foundation. 2007. "Women, Minorities, and Persons with Disabilities." Accessed 15 May 2008, at www.nsf.gov/statistics/women.
Rosser, Sue V. 1990. *Female Friendly Science.* Elmsford, NY: Pergamon Press.
———. 2006. "Using the Lenses of Feminist Theories to Focus on Women and Technologies." In *Women, Gender, and Technology*, ed. Mary F. Fox, Deborah G. Johnson, and Sue V. Rosser, 13–46. Urbana: University of Illinois Press.
Stephan, Paula, and Asmaa El-Ganainy. 2007. "The Entrepreneurial Puzzle: Explaining the Gender Gap." *Journal of Technology Transfer* 32: 475–87.
Thursby, Jerry, and Marie Thursby. 2005. "Gender Patterns of Research and Licensing Activity of Science and Engineering Faculty." *Journal of Technology Transfer* 30: 343–53.
U.S. Patent and Trademark Office. 2003. *U.S. Patenting by Women.* Washington, DC: U.S. Patent and Trademark Office.
Webster, Juliet. 1995. *Shaping Women's Work: Gender, Employment and Information Technology.* New York: Longman.

CHAPTER SEVEN

Is Sisterhood Conditional?
White Women and the Rollback of
Affirmative Action

TIM WISE

In *We Won't Go Back: Making the Case for Affirmative Action*, Georgetown law professors Charles Lawrence and Mari Matsuda argue: "If all women supported affirmative action, no politician would dare oppose it. The political power of women united, combined with men of color and progressive white men, would render any challenge to affirmative action futile. The current backlash against affirmative action is made possible, in part, by women's ambivalence" (Lawrence and Matsuda 1997, 152). Although such a statement is substantively true, as will be seen, the reality is more complex; after all, for decades, women of color have consistently expressed high levels of support for affirmative action (Kinder and Sanders 1996; Zia 1992). In essence, the "women's ambivalence" toward affirmative action, about which Lawrence and Matsuda are so justifiably concerned, is *white* women's ambivalence.

Despite the benefits that have accrued to all—and particularly white—women as a result of affirmative action, there has been an alarming silence on the part of most white women even as reactionary forces have begun to chip away at these civil rights gains. In California, white women actually joined with white men in November 1996 to cast the decisive votes for Proposition 209, which ended affirmative action in state hiring, contracting, and college admissions. Despite attempts to target those white women with campaign ads and a voter education drive highlighting the gender-based benefits of affirmative action, white women largely ignored the overtures made by opponents of 209, voting in favor of the initiative by 58–42% (Chavez 1998, 239).

The important question is why? Why would white women increasingly come to view affirmative action in largely the same negative terms as the "angry white men" about whom the media has made such an issue in recent years? Are white women thinking and voting more like white men on this issue because they identify their interests as being largely tied to those of white men—perhaps their husbands or sons—and are afraid affirmative action might restrict opportunities for loved ones and family members (Ladowsky 1995)? Is their ambivalence due to a false sense of efficacy and opportunity? Since white women have made some impressive gains over the past 30 years, do they now feel affirma-

---

Originally published in the Fall 1998 issue of the *NWSA Journal* (10.3).

tive action is no longer needed (Burkett 1998)? Are white women essentially identifying more with their perceived racial interest, than gender or individual interest, and thus responding predictably to the "racialization" of affirmative action in mainstream discourse? In other words, are white women hostile to affirmative action largely because of their own racial biases and desire to maintain racial privileges (Frankenberg 1993)? Or was the failure to convince a majority of white women to vote against 209 simply a failure of resource mobilization? Not enough money? Not enough time? In other words, the message was right, the strategy sound—to target white women and emphasize the gender aspect of affirmative action—but the "good guys" were simply outgunned and outspent?[1]

Tracking the Benefits of Affirmative Action

The reluctance of white women to stand up for affirmative action, a subject to which we will return, seems particularly surprising, given the measurable dividends such policies have paid over three decades. Although the Civil Rights Act of 1964 was a substantial step toward equity for women and people of color,[2] it became obvious after the act's passage that passive non-discrimination would be insufficient to alter the nation's opportunity structure. The development of affirmative action, and its essential rationale, was summarized in the 1995 Review of Federal Affirmative Action Programs, prepared by the president's staff, with the help of various government agencies. According to the review:

> Even after passage of the civil rights laws . . . judicial and legislative victories were not enough to overcome long-entrenched discrimination. . . . Formal litigation-related strategies [were] often dependent upon clear "smoking gun" evidence of overt bias or bigotry, whereas prejudice can take on myriad subtle, yet effective forms. Thus, private and public institutions alike too often seemed impervious to the winds of change, remaining all-white or all-male long after court decisions or statutes formally ended discrimination. As a result, both the courts and Republican and Democratic administrations turned to race- and gender-conscious remedies . . . developed after experimentation had shown that other means too often failed to correct the problems. (Review of Federal Affirmative Action Programs 1995)

President Johnson's initial Executive Order mandating that "affirmative action" be taken to remedy and prevent racial discrimination by government contractors was expanded to include women in 1968. By the early 1970s, any company meeting a particular threshold for number of employees and amount of business with the federal government was subject to affirmative action requirements. In cases where a "manifest imbalance" existed between the number of available, qualified women or people of color in a given location and the number of such persons actually hired by entities in those locations, the federal government was empowered to intervene, requiring that goals and timetables for more equitable representation be set and that good faith efforts for meeting these goals be made. Educational institutions were added to the list of covered parties beginning in 1972.

That such straightforward requirements have worked to the benefit of women—particularly white women—is hardly disputable. Thanks in large measure to affirmative action and civil rights protections that opened up previously restricted opportunities to women of all colors, from 1972 to 1993:

- The percentage of women architects increased from 3% to nearly 19% of the total;
- The percentage of women doctors more than doubled from 10% to 22% of all doctors;
- The percentage of women lawyers grew from 4% to 23% of the national total;
- The percentage of female engineers went from less than 1% to nearly 9%;
- The percentage of female chemists grew from 10% to 30% of all chemists; and,
- The percentage of female college faculty went from 28% to 42% of all faculty. (Moseley-Braun 1995, 8)

Furthermore, since only 1983, the percentage of women business managers and professionals grew from 41% of all such persons, to 48%, while the number of female police officers more than doubled, from 6% to 13% (U.S. Department of Commerce, Bureau of the Census 1995, Table 649). According to a 1995 study, there are at least six million women—the overwhelming majority of them white—who simply wouldn't have the jobs they have today, but for the inroads made by affirmative action (Cose 1997, 171).

The gender benefits of affirmative action have extended beyond economically privileged women, expanding opportunity for working-class women as well. The 1985 Perkins Act, which requires states to set aside 10.5% of federal vocational-education funds for girls and women—such as displaced homemakers and single mothers—has helped these women find new jobs to support themselves and their families. In Florida, thanks to this program, more than 70% of women receiving voc-ed funds found new jobs, at pay levels averaging twice their prior salaries (National Coalition for Women and Girls in Education 1995).

Often, the setting of fairly rigid goals and timetables has been necessary before significant gains for women have come about. For example, in 1979, women represented only 4% of entry-level officers in the San Francisco Police Department. By 1985, after the Department of Justice forced the SFPD to adopt an aggressive affirmative action plan, the number of women in entry-level positions increased to 14.5% of the total (Review of Federal Affirmative Action Programs 1995). Thanks in part to affirmative action in higher education, the number of women receiving PhD degrees grew from 14.4% of all PhDs in 1971 to 37% by 1991, many of these in fields like science and engineering, which were for so long effectively the exclusive domain of men (National Research Council 1993, 11).

There is also little doubt that affirmative action has promoted the proliferation of women-owned businesses, by expanding the work opportunities for women that then often led to entrepreneurship and by increasing the ability of such businesses to receive government contracts, capital, and small business loans. Prior to the passage of civil rights and other protective laws, women faced often insurmountable obstacles to starting their own businesses. Until the Equal Credit Opportunity Act of 1974, discrimination against women in lending was ubiquitous: single women were often considered unworthy of credit; married women often had difficulty establishing credit, since their financial records were in their husbands' names; and sources of income like alimony and child support were regularly excluded from consideration when women applied for bank loans (Review of Federal Affirmative Action Programs 1995).

Since the early 1970s, however, the percentage of U.S. businesses owned by women—again, the vast majority of them white—has exploded from only 5% of all businesses to more than 37% (Taylor 1997, 2). There are now eight million women-owned businesses in the United States, with nearly $3 trillion in combined sales, employing approximately 18.5 million employees. One in four workers employed by companies in this country now work for women-owned firms (National Association of Women Business Owners 1998). That the strength of such companies—not to mention their ability to compete fairly against their white male counterparts—is of vital importance to the economic health of the nation, is made plain by these and similar figures.

Although the gains to American women from affirmative action have extended in varying degrees to women of all colors, white women find themselves today in significantly better economic shape than do women of color. In 1993, for example, the median income for white women was 16% higher than for black women, and the median white family income was 45% higher than that for black families (Bennett

1995). In states like Washington—currently facing a voter initiative similar to Proposition 209—affirmative action has apparently aided white women more than people of color, be they male or female. According to state data, white women hold 35% of top administrative jobs in Washington, compared to 5.8% for women of color; furthermore, white women receive about 5% of state government contracts, which, although it is a paltry percentage of the total, is still larger than the 4% received by all people of color combined (Washington State Commission on African American Affairs 1995).

The benefits of affirmative action to women extend throughout society. Higher wages for women—due in large part to affirmative action raising, albeit not eliminating, the glass ceiling—are of substantial benefit to millions of families. More than 80% of married first-time home-buyers must rely on both spouses' income to make their mortgage payments, according to a 1995 survey by Chicago Title and Trust Insurers (Lawrence and Matsuda 1997, 159–60). Even the cause of public health has been advanced thanks to affirmative action for women. Since the number of women entering medicine has expanded, research on women's health concerns has progressed dramatically, helping to lessen the historic imbalance whereby most medical research was conducted on male subjects, often to the detriment of scientific knowledge generally and women's health in particular (Bergmann 1996, 107).

Ongoing Gender Bias in the United States

In addition to the measurable good that affirmative action has done for women's social and economic position, one might expect awareness of ongoing gender discrimination to mitigate against women's ambivalence toward the elimination of affirmative action. The progress symbolized by affirmative action has, after all, been incomplete and uneven. Discrimination against women has hardly been uprooted and reminds us that much is left to be done.

The 1995 Report of the Federal Glass Ceiling Commission noted that only 3–5% of senior management are women—almost all of these white—due, not to a lack of qualifications, aptitude, or ambition, but thanks to "fear, rampant stereotyping and prejudice," on the part of male personnel directors and middle managers (Report of the Federal Glass Ceiling Commission 1995). According to the report, women are regularly characterized as "not wanting to work," "not as committed to their careers as men," "not tough enough," "less flexible with their hours," "less relocatable," "too emotional," "not aggressive enough," or, paradoxically, "too aggressive" (148).

As an indication of how this glass ceiling plays out in practice, consider the following:

- Women are 30–40% of associate attorneys in private firms, but only 11% of law partners.
- Women are 50% of entry level accountants, but less than 20% of accounting firm partners.
- Women are 48% of journalists, but hold only 6% of top editorial jobs.
- Women are 42% of college professors, but only 11% of professors with tenure.
- Women are 72% of elementary school teachers, but only 29% of school principals. (Lawrence and Matsuda 1997, 250)

One of the biggest barriers to the professional advancement of women is the subtle bias that often creeps into otherwise "objective" evaluations of one's qualifications. Studies demonstrate that men typically evaluate the resumes, scholarly articles, and other indicators of merit differently, and less favorably, when they know them to be those of women (Heilman and Stopeck 1985, 202; Sturm and Guinier 1996). When evaluating men and women competing for positions, men tend to assign the most importance to whichever indicator of merit will work to the benefit of a man in a given competition—say, seniority—even though when faced with a different set of competitors, the same merit indicator that previously had been deemed paramount may be downplayed if a woman in the instant case would seem to benefit from its elevated significance (Clayton and Crosby 1992, 73–78).

Even when women avoid hiring discrimination, pay disparities remain a problem. Women who work full-time, year-round, earn nearly 30% less than their male counterparts; even after controlling for mitigating factors like educational attainment, seniority, experience, and age, full-time, year-round women workers still earn only 85% as much as similarly situated men (Blau and Ferber 1992, 129).[3] Women with master's degrees earn, on average, the same as men with associate's degrees (Review of Federal Affirmative Action Programs 1995), and even in female-dominated professions, disparities in earnings persist, with male nurses, for example, earning 10% more on average than female nurses, and male bookkeepers earning 16% more on average than female bookkeepers (Lawrence and Matsuda 1997, 251).

There appear to be considerable barriers to the advancement of women, even for those who are "career-oriented" and for whom work patterns largely mirror those of their male counterparts.[4] For example, women who receive their MBAs from Stanford earn only about 73% as much as their male classmates and are one-eighth as likely to be corporate CEOs a decade after graduation (Report of the Federal Glass Ceiling Commission

1995, 13–14). Similarly, a study of law school graduates at the University of Michigan found that after fifteen years of legal practice, female graduates were earning, on average, only 61% of their male counterparts. Even after controlling for grade differences, hours of work, family responsibility differentials, labor market experience, and the type of law career into which one entered, men still had a thirteen percentage-point earnings advantage (Wood, Corcoran, and Courant 1993).

Although there has been some narrowing of wage differentials among younger men and women in recent years, this has been more the result of declining male wages—due largely to the loss of high-paying manufacturing jobs since 1973—and far less the result of substantial wage gains for women. Young male high school graduates in 1993 earned about the same in inflation-adjusted dollars as young male dropouts had earned twenty years earlier, and young men with four-year college degrees in 1993 were earning only slightly more than their high school counterparts in 1973 (Sum, Fogg, and Taggart 1996, 84).

It is estimated that the costs of gender discrimination, in terms of opportunities denied and abilities undercompensated, come to around $5,000 annually for the average white woman, significantly affecting not only the well-being of those individuals on the receiving end of such discrimination but also the well-being of many millions of families and the nation as a whole (Bergmann 1996, 41).

Even with affirmative action in place for more than two decades, women are only now beginning to make inroads into federal and state contracting in areas like construction and professional services, indicating how difficult breaking into the "old-boys' network" so vital to procuring these contracts can be. Although women own 37% of American businesses, they receive only 2% of federal contracts (Belsky and Berger 1995), and it is apparent that in the absence of formal requirements that such companies receive consideration, the situation would be worse (Review of Federal Affirmative Action Programs 1995). Even before the passage of Proposition 209, California Governor Pete Wilson had issued an executive order eliminating affirmative action for contracting with state agencies. The result? Women-owned firms that had previously received thirty or more calls weekly asking them to submit subcontracting bids for various services, now receive nearly none. When female contractors have inquired about the falloff in bid requests, many of the male contractors have indicated their unwillingness to work with women-owned firms since they "don't have to anymore" (Stop Prop 209 1996b). This state of affairs will likely worsen, given that Wilson has now ordered an end even to the collection of data regarding how many women and people of color receive contracts from state government, making it harder if not impossible to track subtle or even overt bias in contracting (Rojas 1998, A21).

Backlash against Affirmative Action: "Racialization" and White Women's Ambivalence

It is with the above-mentioned facts in mind that the growing anti-affirmative action movement has sought to remove women as women from the affirmative action picture and instead emphasize the racial benefits to people of color and supposed white racial victims of these policies. Hoping to create in white men and women a shared sense of victimization at the hands of people of color, conservatives have made sure to ignore whatever gains have come to women through affirmative action and have sought to "racialize" the debate and its attendant imagery. As many as twenty-six states are now considering following California by eliminating race- and gender-based affirmative action, and in every case, the focus has been squarely on the supposed unfairness of "racial preferences"—the ideologically loaded term that has replaced the more benign-sounding (and popular) "affirmative action" in the parlance of right-wing attacks.

As the political manipulation of the affirmative action issue by far-right figures took hold in the early 1990s, it was clear the attacks would be exclusively race-based. In Louisiana, where white supremacist David Duke received 50–60% of the white vote in his bids to become a U.S. senator and the state's governor—with no major differences between white men and women—affirmative action was presented as a racial zero-sum game, with whites the aggrieved victims.[5] In North Carolina, when Jesse Helms found himself trailing in polls to challenger Harvey Gantt—the African American former mayor of Charlotte—in his 1990 bid for reelection to the U.S. Senate, he began airing a television commercial emphasizing the harm to whites from "having to hire a minority because of a quota" (Feagin and Vera 1995, 113). After successfully pressuring the University of California Board of Regents to abolish affirmative action in 1995, Pete Wilson announced that the vote "was the beginning of the end of racial preferences" (Wise 1995, 15), neglecting to mention that gender-based affirmative action at the schools had also been eliminated and would remain in the crosshairs of Proposition 209 a year later.

Assisting in the racialization process has been a steady shift in the presentation of affirmative action's "victims" by the right; thus, while most, if not all of the early public victims were "angry white men"—Bakke, DeFunis, Weber, or the white men at the Ward's Cove Packing Plant[6]—increasingly, conservative legal advocates have latched on to cases with white women in the forefront. The highest profile cases recently have been those of Cheryl Hopwood, at the University of Texas, who claimed she was denied admission to the Texas School of Law because of race-based affirmative action, and the case—recently settled while awaiting a Supreme Court ruling—of Sharon Taxman, a white public school teacher laid off in order to retain a black woman in the same department at a school in Piscataway, New Jersey.[7] In the case of Hopwood, and in a pending suit brought by the same lawyers against the University of Michigan, male plaintiffs were and are involved, but the "public face" of the suits has been that of a white woman, her dreams supposedly dashed by racial preferences (Marklein 1997, 4A). White women are also emerging, at least publicly, as the new victims of affirmative action in Washington State, where Katuria Smith is suing the University of Washington because its law school supposedly admitted "less qualified" people of color ahead of her, and in Boston, where a young white woman's father brought suit against Boston Latin school—an academic magnet institution—because of affirmative action preventing her admission there. By shifting the public's attention from angry white men to "aggrieved white women," the opponents of affirmative action are no doubt hoping to cast the debate in stark racial terms, ignoring the degree to which white women have generally reaped benefits from these policies far beyond whatever individual victimization may or may not have occurred in a specific instance.[8]

Of course, it is not surprising that men opposed to affirmative action would prefer to focus on the racial rather than the gender component of the issue. However, the fact that white women have proven so willing to accept this version of reality, rather than the contrasting one offered earlier here, is testimony either to the amazing persuasive powers of conservative white male commentators or to something else altogether, which cries out for explanation.

Consider that according to many commentators on the left, women are desperately concerned about gender inequities and "rank their own inequality, at work and at home, among their most urgent concerns" (Faludi 1991, xv; also see Feminist Majority Foundation 1996c). If such claims are to be taken seriously, one must then wonder, how can such persons be both knowledgeable and concerned about their own oppression and still so uninformed or unconcerned that they think nothing of passively accepting or even actively supporting the elimination of affirmative action? How and why this process plays itself out will be discussed below, but first, it is necessary to document the attitudes of white women with regard to affirmative action and the degree to which they seem increasingly hesitant to endorse the concept.

Ultimately, white women's views on affirmative action are hardly different from those of their male counterparts, particularly when the issue is framed as one of "preferences." Since the preference framework is the likely one to which affirmative action proponents will be responding in coming years, it is white women's attitudes on this issue that must concern us. According to national studies since 1986, white women are not substantially different from white men when it comes to their feelings on this issue. Opposition to "preferential hiring and promotion" has grown from 86% for white men and 79% for white women in 1986, to 90% for white men and 88% for white women in 1994. Similarly, opposition to admissions preferences in colleges stands at around 76% for white men and 70% for white women (Citrin 1996, 43).

Although only about a third of whites wish to eliminate all affirmative action programs when discussed without the preference framework, the differences between white men and white women, although present, are hardly massive. In effect, both are more or less equally hostile or supportive, although both are far less hostile and far more supportive, when preferences are not mentioned or are explained in context, so that voters know what they are voting for or against (Chavez 1998, 99). As mentioned previously, 58% of white women voted for Proposition 209, as opposed to 66% of white men. This is a gender gap, to be sure, but hardly the kind hoped for, expected, and needed to defeat the initiative.

White women's ambivalence to affirmative action is evidenced even among many feminists. A 1992 survey of *Ms.* magazine readers found that, while most supported affirmative action, high levels of concern were apparently absent, owing perhaps to the fact that only one in five white women thought they had benefited from affirmative action, while over half said they had not; this, compared to the one-half of black women and Latinas who said they had personally benefited from affirmative action, as opposed to only one-quarter who said they had not (Zia 1992, 2).

Apart from progressive women and women's organizations, many groups claiming to represent women show no indication of understanding or wanting to acknowledge the importance of affirmative action to the people they claim as constituents. For example, there is no mention at all in the recent materials of the National Association of Women Business Owners (NAWBO), or the National Association of Women in Construction (NAWIC), or the National Association of Female Executives (NAFE) as to the importance of affirmative action for opening up opportunities and making possible many of the individual successes that these organizations regularly trumpet in their publications and on their websites.

NAWBO, for example, discusses female business gains as if they took place entirely in a meritocratic vacuum (National Association of Women Business Owners 1998), while NAWIC, which claims to "promote and support the advancement and employment of women in the construction industry," says nothing about the importance of affirmative action in opening up such opportunities, nor do they seem concerned with the impact that affirmative action rollbacks might have on women in the industry (National Association of Women in Construction 1997), despite the fact that even with affirmative action and NAWIC's efforts, women are less than 2% of construction workers in the United States (Feminist Majority Foundation 1996b). NAFE's website and printed materials emphasize the importance of women knowing how to respond to job criticisms like "you're an idiot" from male superiors and how to get a NAFE Gold Card "at low interest rates," but make no mention of the importance of civil rights laws or affirmative action; nor do they show concern for the assaults on affirmative action that, if successful, would make the advancement of women as executives—ostensibly their mission—more difficult (National Association of Female Executives 1997). So long as groups such as these refuse to speak out publicly about the importance of affirmative action, it will be difficult to mobilize white women into a pro–affirmative action coalition, since most are not connected to feminist organizations and may even be hostile to the overtures of such groups, thanks to the steady backlash against feminism in recent years.[9]

Furthermore, polls indicate that whatever differences do exist between white women and white men on this issue apparently have little to do with differences in perceived personal interest, either in maintaining or eliminating affirmative action. Few white women think themselves beneficiaries of affirmative action, and most are simply not open to the idea that they have been; few if any expect it to help them in the future; and most share the same concerns as white men regarding "reverse discrimination," or the perceived hiring of unqualified minorities. The one factor that seems to explain virtually all the slightly greater support for affirmative action evinced by white women is their higher level of agreement with the notion that people of color still face substantial barriers and discrimination, and thus, it is simply too soon to abandon these programs (Garin and Molyneaux 1996). These facts are highly significant for supporters of affirmative action, as they indicate that, in order to gain support for affirmative action, appealing directly to these women as women may be fruitless, while emphasizing the ongoing problem of racial discrimination may prove more effective.

Lessons from California: What Went Wrong and Why

The difficulty of building substantial support for affirmative action among white women was never more apparent than in California, where, despite constant repetition by anti-209 organizations of the gender-based benefits to be had or lost, there was virtually no change in white women's feelings on the measure from May 1995 until the vote in November 1996

(Citrin 1996, 44–45). The primary opposition groups chose to focus on gender and to "de-racialize" the debate from 1995 on, prompted to do so in part by pollsters like Lou Harris, Democratic Party consultants like Celinda Lake, and even President Clinton (Chavez 1998, 153, 204). The opposition to 209 operated on the assumption they would need—and could receive—60% of the white female vote, 70% of the black vote, 60% of the Latino/a vote, and only 25% of the white male vote. As it turned out, they substantially overestimated the degree to which they could sway white women—seeing as how only 42% voted to retain affirmative action—while underestimating the degree to which people of color and white men could be swayed: 74% of African Americans voted against 209; 76% of Latinos/as did so; as did 34% of white men (Chavez 1998, 136). Sixty-one percent of Asians also opposed 209, despite attempts by its backers to woo them with arguments that they were losing out in college admissions to less qualified blacks and Latinos/as (Chavez 1998, 236).

Once the opposition to 209 decided on a gender-based strategy to target white women, its every public move reflected this thrust. Early educational and media efforts focused on discussing Clause C of the Proposition, which, it was explained, would actually lower the current legal standard for evaluating gender discrimination claims, making certain types of gender discrimination legal, in areas where it had never been before (Feminist Majority Foundation 1995b). Virtually all the public statements made by 209 opponents throughout 1996 attempted to focus attention on the potential consequences of Proposition 209 to women. When 209 opponents launched "Freedom Summer 1996," bringing students from fifty-two college campuses across the nation to California to educate voters, their message was uniformly tailored to stress the harms to women and girls (Feminist Majority Foundation 1996a). As the election drew near, and the campaign became a war of radio and television commercials, gender was once again the focus, with race and racism largely pushed to the side. No On 209 ran a series of gender-focused radio advertisements featuring prominent entertainers like Candace Bergen, Alfre Woodard, and Ellen DeGeneres (Chavez 1998, 230–32). The main opposition television spot, released in the final days of the campaign, showed a woman being stripped of a stethoscope, medical lab coat, hard hat, police cap, and then business suit—representing the gains to women because of affirmative action—while lecherous men chanted "take it off, take it all off" (Stop Prop 209 1996a).

There were signs early on, however, that the gender strategy was having problems. Early focus groups showed that many white women were convinced affirmative action was preventing their husbands and sons from getting jobs (Chavez 1998, 98). In addition, the six months of steady repetition regarding Clause C appears to have been fruitless, prompting no movement among white women in the polls, largely because of the complexity of explaining legal issues like "standards of review" to laypersons (Chavez 1998, 137, 152). Finally, the anti-209 gender-focused advertisements were undercut completely by radio and television spots run by 209 supporters. These ads featured Janice Camarena, a white, widowed, low-income single mother of three discussing how she had been told by an instructor at San Bernadino Valley Community College that she couldn't enroll in an English 101 class because it was reserved for blacks. Although her version of the "reverse discrimination" tale was questionable—she hadn't preregistered for the class, nor had she taken prerequisite classes, and there was an additional section of English 101 being taught at the same time with slots available—the truth hardly mattered. The anti-209 arguments about gender were simply too abstract and hypothetical when compared to the tangible, albeit flawed, image of Camarena, a flesh and blood human, more sympathetic than statistics about glass ceilings and comparable worth (Chavez 1998, 215–16).[10]

The decision to target white women in opposing 209 made sense, stemming as it did from a logical belief that, since there were not enough people of color to sway the vote, some whites would be needed, and women were more likely targets than men. The problem seems to have come in the fashioning of the message so as to capture the votes of those white women. Evidence indicating that the most effective message might have been one reminding voters of the ongoing problem of racial discrimination and that "ending racial and gender preferences" really meant eliminating all affirmative action,[11] was discounted in favor of telling women and anyone who would listen that mentoring programs for teenage girls and women's centers on college campuses might be closed if 209 passed (Chavez 1998). As history has shown, something prevented this strategy from succeeding.[12]

There are several theories as to why attempts to pare white women away from white men in their opposition to "racial and gender preferences" failed specifically in California and why convincing a majority of them to support affirmative action in general has proven difficult. First is the problem of overcoming the "preference" language. White women are just as likely as white men to think "preferences" unfair; thus, if affirmative action's supporters can't succeed in keeping such loaded words off initiative ballots—unlikely given the current trend—they will have to fully explain the ramifications to likely voters. This is not impossible, but does take time.

Second is the difficulty of de-racializing an issue that has been so thoroughly racialized in the public imagination. Most white women in California and elsewhere simply refuse to believe that affirmative action is about them. National focus groups as early as January 1996 seemed to indicate this problem. In many cases, even after group moderators would initiate a lengthy discussion among white women about the gender element of affirmative action, as soon as conversation wasn't specifically steered in that direction, participants would shift their discussion, and anger, back to race (Garin and Molyneaux 1996). Thus, even if it had been possible in the abstract to change the paradigm under which white women, like men, were apparently operating with regard to affirmative action, doing so in the short period of time called for by an electoral campaign would have been highly unlikely.

A third problem, closely related to the problem created by racialization, is the identification it forces between the interests of white women and white men. If white women perceive affirmative action in racial terms, they will be just as likely as white men—if they are heterosexual—to think they would be harmed by affirmative action, thanks to supposedly reduced opportunities for their husbands or partners (Ladowsky 1995). In this way, years of racialization have encouraged many white women to identify their own interests with those of the larger patriarchal structure that has kept them disempowered. As Lawrence and Matsuda argue (1997, 161–62), if angry white men are perceived as victims, any white woman who "defines self-fulfillment as loving that man" may be reluctant to support affirmative action.

But even women who are the most independent professionally and least tied to traditional patriarchal family structures are far from sufficiently supportive of affirmative action.

The fourth problem for those seeking to enlist the support of white women in an affirmative action coalition is pointed to by Madeline Heilman, professor of psychology at New York University, who has found that many women feel uncomfortable with the thought they may have benefited or could benefit from affirmative action, since to do so may call their own abilities and accomplishments into question (DeAngelis 1995). As white women have made substantial gains in the workplace, it is not at all surprising that many would be reluctant to embrace affirmative action as having been largely implicated in their personal achievements. The popular meritocratic explanation is after all more comforting in a culture where success is largely believed to be solely dependent upon one's personal characteristics, effort, and ambition. Ironically, thanks to the successes of the women's movement, millions of white women now find themselves intellectually able to eschew the very policies that have fundamentally improved their professional life chances. Indeed, targeting white women in a pro–affirmative action effort by focusing on gender bias and its likely intensification in the absence of such programs probably seems disempowering to many white women. It reminds them of their potential victimization by sexist structures, a subject about which they would rather not be reminded, particularly since they have a significant stake in believing the system is fair—namely, their racial stake, which guarantees them opportunities generally off limits to most people of color.

Finally, and perhaps most importantly, is the salience of white racial attitudes and the fact that perceived personal interest seems to have little or no effect on these attitudes. According to Kinder and Sanders (1996, 62), there is no statistically significant difference between whites on racial issues, including affirmative action, owing to perceived personal self-interest, nor from the degree to which one perceives a threat to one's own job or education, nor from differences in income or occupational status. Thus, attempts to gain support from white women on the basis of what they have gained and stand to lose personally, because they are women, were questionable given what is known about white racial attitudes. The only form of self-interest that does seem to affect white racial attitudes is perceived *racial group interest*: in other words, whites—male and female—perceive their racial interests as threatened by affirmative action. Unless this perception can be undone, reducing what Kinder and Sanders refer to as "white racial resentment" and subsequently increasing white support for affirmative action will prove problematic.

White Women and Racism: Invisible Realities, Visible Consequences

Although progressives are hesitant to acknowledge it, the fact remains that white women are not significantly more liberal on racial attitudes than are white men, obviously complicating attempts to get them to think positively about a topic like affirmative action. According to survey data, white women's racial attitudes are something of a mixed bag. While white women are more willing than white men to accept structural explanations for racial inequity and generally more accepting of affirmative action—so long as the issue isn't presented as one of "preferences"—many of the racial attitudes of white women are no better and perhaps actually worse than those of white men. For example, when asked if the federal government should intervene to create jobs and opportunities for blacks, there is no statistically significant difference between the responses of white men and white women. Similarly, there is no gender gap between white men and white women in response to the question: "Would you be willing to send your child to a school where half the students were black?" When asked if they would be willing to send their child(ren) to a school in which the majority of students were black, white women are actually more likely to object than their male counterparts, and white women are more disapproving of interracial marriage between whites and blacks than are white men (Schuman, Steeh, Bobo and Krysan 1997, 235).

These data indicate that white women are slightly more prone to giving a racially hostile response when the situation calls for more intimate contact between whites and people of color. So although women may be less racist in some abstract sense, it appears that if they perceive policies or gains for African Americans as requiring closer contact with themselves, white women are no different than white men, and perhaps even more racially hostile. Since affirmative action serves increasingly to integrate the workforce and schools, these concerns over close contact could spill over to a generalized anxiety, ambivalence, or even hostility with regard to affirmative action. Given the tendency for racial prejudices to cluster and operate as free-floating anxieties (Allport 1954), such a relationship between attitudes on seemingly unrelated aspects of racial thinking is all the more possible.

The degree to which "average, everyday" white women may be burdened with their own substantial racial prejudices can be anticipated by the significant extent to which even committed feminists and progressive white women are seen to model racially prejudiced attitudes and behavior. According to a 1992 survey by *Ms.* magazine, a third of their white female readers admit being uncomfortable talking to people of color about racial issues, and only 16% have "many" friends of another race, compared to 75% of Asian Pacific Americans, 74% of Latinas, 67% of Native Americans, and 53% of African Americans. Over one-third of white women say they have few if any friends of color (Malveaux 1992, 25–26). Although one can hardly measure racial prejudice by looking at friendships, the level of interracial isolation that seems to burden white women alone signals a degree to which white women, like white men, are largely cut off from the life experiences of people of color. Such isolation can lead to a less sympathetic outlook regarding issues of importance to people of color, like affirmative action.

As with most Americans, white feminists also deny in large measure that they suffer from significant racial prejudice, let alone racism. Only one in five in the *Ms.* survey admitted to prejudice, while only 18% claimed to be racist. Interestingly, white lesbians were the least likely to suffer from denial of their own racism problem: 42% admitted they were racist on some level (Malveaux 1992, 27). Such disparities between white heterosexual women and white lesbians are hard to explain, short of acknowledging that at least to some degree, so long as white women are intimately linked with white men—a problem which, by definition, is less of an issue for lesbians—they have a harder time perceiving the effects of their own racial conditioning. White male privilege operates as a veil, clouding the ability of many white women—even committed progressives—to perceive the degree to which they too are implicated in the system of racism.

It should come as no surprise that convincing white women of their shared interest with people of color—with regard to affirmative action or any other issue—would be challenging. After all, centuries of racist propaganda, particularly concerning the physical "danger" posed to white women by people of color (especially black men) was bound to have some residual effects. For white women to identify with these men of color now would require them to cast off the psychological detritus of anti-miscegenation laws, as well as the historical discourse that has posited white women as the victims of people of color and white men as their "defenders and rescuers" (Frankenberg 1993, 237). This psychosexual dynamic has been well established in discursive history and continues to have measurable results in the present. Consider that the contemporary discourse on black crime and violence—from Willie Horton, to Susan Smith, to the "Central Park Jogger"—has sought to recreate and reinforce this victim/victimizer dichotomy, with white women seen as at risk from racialized others. Such discourse makes it difficult for white women to identify with these racial "others," particularly when those others are typified as the black men whose mere presence in an elevator seems to regularly make white women clutch their purses or briefcases more tightly. Popular books, like Charles Murray and Richard Herrnstein's *The Bell Curve* and Dinesh D'Souza's *The End of Racism*, even attempt to excuse the white fear responses to blacks under the guise of "rationality." Blacks according to these authors really are more dangerous and violent, either due to bad genes or a "civilizational deficit."[13] In light of the persistent onslaught of such racist invective masquerading as social science, it will no doubt prove difficult to create in whites, male or female, a shared sense of destiny and interest with their fellow citizens of color.[14]

What Works: Framing the Affirmative Action Message

At this point, the reader may conclude that all is hopeless. If white women are too bound in racial privilege, or patriarchy, or false efficacy, to see how they have gained from affirmative action and what they stand to lose in its absence, then what in the world can be done? Luckily, there are arguments made by the supporters of affirmative action that seem to work with white women, and even with some white men. That these arguments are not apparently the ones stressing the particular benefits of affirmative action for women, or even stressing gender at all, may be surprising but should hardly be troubling.

According to recent focus groups, surveys, and available polling data, the points that appear most effective in convincing whites of both sexes to support affirmative action—or at least be hesitant about voting to abolish it—are the following:

- The problem of racial discrimination—particularly the closed nature of the "old boys' network"—makes it too soon to eliminate affirmative action. Although polls show most whites reluctant to acknowledge that racism is still a large problem, once evidence is provided on this score, movement is possible, particularly among white women.
- The persons pushing to eliminate affirmative action have questionable motives: In an attempt to divert people's attention from real economic and social problems, politicians are trying to scapegoat and pit the races against one another for their own political gain. Given the general distrust of political figures, this point has become increasingly important.
- The consequences of "backsliding" on discrimination would be particularly terrible given the changing demographics of the American population, with whites becoming less and people of color more of the nation's citizenry. In an increasingly non-white United States, anything that would lock out the new majority of the population from equal opportunity is seen as unfair and economically and politically suicidal.
- Affirmative action does not mean the hiring of unqualified people. It is particularly important to make this point, since popular perception assumes the opposite is true. Recent evidence from a study at Michigan State, indicating that persons hired under affirmative action actually have higher performance ratings than white men hired under traditional mechanisms, makes the point effectively (Feminist Majority Foundation 1997).
- Affirmative action and quotas are not the same thing. Both white men and women typically perceive "quotas" as the problem that abolishing "preferences" will solve. Pointing out the distinction between affirmative action—largely recruitment and outreach programs, flexible goals, and "taking a second look" to make sure women and people of color aren't excluded unfairly from consideration—and quotas, can make a significant difference. (Garin and Molyneaux 1996; Southern Regional Council 1996)

Despite the recent setbacks to affirmative action, there is still an opportunity to build a working coalition to defend against further erosion. This coalition can, and ultimately must, include white women. That building support for affirmative action among white women has proven difficult thus far, speaks more to the ways in which attempts to build this support have taken shape than to the inherent unwillingness of white women to join such a coalition. By emphasizing the gender benefits of affirmative action, along with the potentially devastating consequences of its elimination for women *as women*, supporters have hoped to persuade enough white women that their interests lie in voting against initiatives like the one in California.

Unfortunately, this strategy has failed. In part, it has failed because still not enough white women fully understand what they have gained and what they stand to lose, but there is something else going on as well. The successes of the women's movement have put white women in a position where it is harder for them to see—or more painful to acknowledge—the ongoing and potential problem of gender bias limiting their opportunities. Furthermore, the racialization of affirmative action has proven so complete that dislodging this paradigm from the minds of voters is largely impossible, especially in the short run, and probably counterproductive in the long run, due to the effect "deracialization" would have on solidifying white denial of the problem of racism. Finally, many white women suffer from the same racial prejudices as white men; thus, attempting to attract their support for affirmative action without directly confronting their misperceived racial interests and subtle but real racial hostility is all but guaranteed to fall flat.

Ironically, perhaps, much of what can work to gain support for affirmative action from white women can also work for some white men. Universal arguments about the benefits to the larger society as a whole and concerns over the ongoing problem of racial discrimination seem to be more effective than narrow gender arguments. If the right seeks to paint affirmative action as divisive because it "pits one group against another," the last thing proponents should seek to do is confirm this faulty analysis by papering over real racial divisions and creating in the minds of listeners and voters a new set of divisions based on gender.

Notes

1. This has essentially been the position of organized women's groups in the wake of the 209 setback. Those who emphasized gender over race in trying to defeat 209 have expressed, on a number of occasions, the belief that their strategies were basically sound, but that due to inadequate resources and getting a late start in the campaign, they were unable to convince enough white women in time for the November vote. Similarly, Kelli Evans, the director of the No on Initiative 200 campaign in Washington State (the group trying to prevent a 209 copycat from passing there), has expressed her confidence that the gender focus is appropriate, "the only way to win," and that the only reason the effort failed in California was due to organizational incompetence and lack of money. [*Author's Note*, added November 2005: As predicted in this piece, the gender focus in Washington, as in California, failed miserably.

Now, mainline civil rights groups are once again pushing for a gender focus in the campaign to preserve affirmative action in Michigan, the next state where the anti-affirmative action forces are trying to secure victory. It appears as though some people, especially mainstream liberal white folks, like consultant Celinda Lake, and Democratic Party types, never learn.]

2. Please note that use of the phrase "women and people of color" is a stylistic choice and is not meant to imply that women may not also be people of color or that people of color are synonymous with men. I realize this dichotomy is often perpetuated by commentators on race and gender, and I have no intention of joining in this unfortunate practice, as it has been aptly criticized by feminists of color for years. When lecturing, I typically refer to "women of all colors and people of color, male and female," but such phraseology could become unwieldy for a journal article. Let it suffice to say that when I refer to opportunity for, or discrimination against "women and people of color," I mean women as women and people of color as people of color.

3. Even those factors that some consider "independent" of gender bias and which explain about half of the gap in male/female earnings are far from what could fairly be considered truly independent variables. For example, while some of the wage gap is explained less by overt discrimination than by seniority, education, or experience in the workforce, all of these factors are themselves influenced by entrenched gender bias or institutional sexism. If women have less seniority, because, like people of color, they were largely excluded from certain types of jobs for many years, we should hardly consider that to be an independent source of wage disparities. In effect, virtually all the difference in male/female or white/non-white earnings reflects the reality of discrimination, either present or past, and its attendant consequences in terms of accumulated "credentials," which are themselves largely contingent upon one's place in the opportunity structure.

4. This is in direct conflict with the claims of conservative groups like the Independent Women's Forum in Washington, DC, which blames demographic and "human capital" factors for most of the existing wage disparities, like absenteeism, workforce participation rates, etc. (Furchtgott-Roth and Stolba 1996).

5. The author served as assistant director of the Louisiana Coalition Against Racism and Nazism, the organization that, in 1990 and 1991, was given much of the credit for defeating Duke in those races. For more information on Duke's political ascent, and fall, see Rose 1992.

6. For detailed information on the cases involving these men, see Ezorsky 1991 and Fiscus 1992.

7. The Piscataway School Board acknowledged it laid off Taxman so as to keep Debra Williams, a black teacher, for the sake of diversity in the Business Education Department of the high school. However, it should be noted that the decision to do so—which came about because of budget cuts—illustrates how

difficult it is for whites to evaluate people of color fairly against their white counterparts, even when it appears by objective measures that the person of color is more qualified. Taxman and Williams had identical seniority, having started teaching the same day, and, according to the board, were identical in their qualifications in every other way. Thus, the reason they ultimately kept Williams was because there were no other black teachers in her department, and the board felt an obligation to support diversity. This rationale is ultimately what became controversial and helped create in Taxman the perfect victim: injured solely because she was white. Interestingly enough, the case would never have come to court at all had the Board simply made the same decision based on a non-racial factor that was readily available to them, namely, merit. As it turns out, Williams held a master's degree in business education, while Taxman did not. Although such academic credentials may or may not mean that Williams was actually a better teacher, it goes without saying that whites with advanced degrees are regularly considered more qualified than people of color without them. Such a rationale is often used to explain why it is so difficult to attract more faculty of color on college campuses or in public school systems (Hampson 1997, 14A).

8. Claims by Hopwood that she was victimized by racial affirmative action are dubious, despite her victory at the appellate level, left intact by a Supreme Court decision to deny certiorari on appeal. Hopwood (and co-plaintiffs) claimed they had scored higher on the LSAT than many of the black and Latino students ultimately admitted to the first year law class. On this point there was no dispute. But what the court ignored in finding for the plaintiffs was that there were also 109 whites with lower scores than Hopwood (and 67 with lower scores than her co-plaintiffs) who were offered a slot at the Law School. Furthermore, the plaintiffs in this case were—with the exception of their LSATs—arguably no better qualified than those admitted under affirmative action. Hopwood herself filed no recommendation letters, no personal statement, despite being asked to do so, and her answers to application questions were rated by school officials as "vague," "brief," and "unimpressive." Plaintiff Doug Carvell had ranked 98 out of 247 graduates at low-prestige Hendrix College, in Conway, Arkansas, and was referred to in one recommendation letter as being a "mediocre" student. Co-plaintiff David Rogers had actually been kicked out of the University of Texas' undergraduate Honors program years earlier because of bad grades. After all but failing out of UT, Rogers got a professional writing degree from a branch of the University of Houston and filed no letters of recommendation with the UT Law School (Kauffman and Gonzalez, in Garcia 1997, 234).

9. According to recent surveys, two-thirds of American women refuse to call themselves feminists, and only one in five college women expresses willingness to identify with the women's movement (Burkett 1998).

10. This effective use of Camarena in California should serve as caution for those seeking to defend against 209's carbon copy in Washington. Since Katuria Smith—also a working-class white woman—is suing the University of Wash-

ington over its race-based affirmative action, there is little doubt that supporters of Initiative 200, as the effort there is called, will seek to utilize her to undercut any gender focus by the No On 200 forces. Unfortunately, as of this writing, No On 200 has shown no signs of learning from what happened in California and is, in fact, following much of the same playbook with regard to the gender focus (No Initiative 200 1998; Lake et al. 1998).

11. Focus groups since early 1995 had shown that, if voters understood the true implications of 209—the elimination of affirmative action—the overwhelming majority, in every demographic group, including white men, would vote against it. Throughout the campaign, however, it was difficult to convince voters of this outcome, and whatever resources could have been put into doing so went toward discussing narrow harms to women. Harris polls in mid-1996 found that nearly 60% didn't believe that 209 would end affirmative action. Confusion on this simple issue proved to be the most important factor in determining the outcome, since, according to exit polls by the *Los Angeles Times*, when voters were asked whether they supported affirmative action "to help women and minorities get better jobs and educations" 54% said yes, while 46% said no, exactly the opposite of the results on 209 that day (Chavez 1998, 237). Other polls indicated that nearly 30% of those voting for 209 thought they had cast a vote *in favor of* affirmative action.

12. Groups that invested considerable time and energy in pursuing a gender-focused strategy continue to advocate it and claim their grassroots efforts worked, but were short of money and thus incapable of stopping 209 (Chavez 1998, 239). In early 1997, NOW claimed grassroots efforts had closed the gap on 209 from twenty-five points to only eight by election day (Toledo 1997). This position ignored some salient caveats, including the fact that most of the grassroots work was performed by Californians for Justice (CFJ)—an organization which operated primarily in communities of color and focused on long-term movement building, stressing race instead of gender in the process. In fact, CFJ's efforts drove down support for 209 principally by increasing opposition, then turnout, among people of color, the majority of whom actually supported it before being reached by the grassroots mobilization efforts (Chavez 1998, 152). Although the opposition to 209 was outspent—thanks largely to the refusal by the Democratic Party to invest funds comparable to the Republicans—the combined funds of the various opposition groups surpassed $3 million (Chavez 1998, 252; Coleman 1998, 33), probably enough to do considerable grassroots work, if not the more expensive (and ultimately ineffective) media buys.

13. For more information on the attempts to normalize and rationalize white racism, see Armour 1997.

14. Not only will attempts to shift attention from race to gender likely fail—particularly in the short run as dictated by a political campaign—it is also likely that attempting to do so could have harmful repercussions for the long-term interests of racial equity. If the problem that gave rise to the need for

affirmative action in the first place was white privilege, white racism, and its attendant oppression of people of color, and if the corollary problem is the unwillingness on the part of most whites to acknowledge and confront that system of privilege and oppression, then how can it be helpful to further mask that system by refocusing our attention away from race and racism and pretending that explicitly racial issues are really about something else? In fact, doing so could ultimately strengthen white denial about institutional racism and privilege, thereby making systemic change more difficult. As Frankenberg (1993) explains, "Focusing on one's membership in a bounded group may mean failing to fully examine what it means to be part of a cultural and racial group that is dominant and normative" (230). To the extent affirmative action's proponents insist on "deracializing" the issue and choose to focus on talking to women as members of a bounded group—women under patriarchy—they run the risk of further making white racism invisible to the very white women they will need in order to build a working civil rights coalition.

References

Allport, Gordon. 1954. *The Nature of Prejudice*. Cambridge, MA: Addison-Wesley.

Armour, Jody David. 1997. *Negrophobia and Reasonable Racism: The Hidden Costs of Being Black in America*. New York: New York University Press.

Belsky, Gary, and Susan Berger. 1995. "Women Could Be Big Loser if Affirmative Action Fails." *Money* 24(8): 20–22.

Bennett, Claudette E. 1995. "The Black Population in the United States: March, 1994 and 1993." United States Department of Commerce, Bureau of the Census. Current Population Reports. P-20-480. Washington, DC: Government Printing Office.

Bergmann, Barbara. 1996. *In Defense of Affirmative Action*. NY: Basic Books / New Republic.

Blau, Francine, and Marianne Ferber. 1992. *The Economics of Women, Men and Work*. Englewood Cliffs, NJ: Prentice-Hall.

Burkett, Elinor. 1998. *The Right Women: A Journey through the Heart of Conservative America*. New York: Scribner.

Chavez, Lydia. 1998. *The Color-Bind: California's Battle to End Affirmative Action*. Berkeley: University of California.

Citrin, Jack. 1996. "Affirmative Action in the People's Court." *Public Interest* 125(Winter): 39–48.

Clayton, Susan D., and Faye J. Crosby. 1992. *Justice, Gender and Affirmative Action*. Ann Arbor: University of Michigan Press.

Coleman, Trevor W. 1998. "Affirmative Action Wars." *Emerge*, March: 30–37.

Cose, Ellis. 1997. *Color-Blind: Seeing beyond Race in a Race-Obsessed World*. New York: Harper-Collins.

DeAngelis, Tori. 1995. "Ignorance Plagues Affirmative Action." *APA Monitor* 26(5): 1, 8.

Ezorsky, Gertrude. 1991. *Racism and Justice: The Case for Affirmative Action*. Ithaca, NY: Cornell University.

Faludi, Susan. 1991. *Backlash: The Undeclared War against American Women.* New York: Crown.
Feagin, Joe, and Hernan Vera. 1995. *White Racism.* New York: Routledge.
Feminist Majority Foundation. 1997. "Affirmative Action Hires Are as or More Qualified than White Male Counterparts, Study Finds." *Feminist News,* January 13. Available at www.feminist.org.
———. 1996a. "Freedom Summer '96 Kicks Off." Press release, June 1. At www.feminist.org.
———. 1996b. "Affirmative Action: Expanding Employment Opportunities for Women." At www.feminist.org.
———. 1996c. "The Glass Ceiling." Online. Available at www.feminist.org.
———. 1995a. "Myths about Women in Business." Online. Available at www.feminist.org.
———. 1995b. "Women's Campaign to Defeat 'CCRI' Launched: Campaign Exposes 'No Women Need Apply' Clause." Press release. Online. Available at www.feminist.org.
Fiscus, Ronald J. 1992. *The Constitutional Logic of Affirmative Action: Making the Case for Quotas.* Durham, NC: Duke University Press.
Frankenberg, Ruth. 1993. *White Women, Race Matters: The Social Construction of Whiteness.* Minneapolis: University of Minnesota.
Furchtgott-Roth, Diana, and Christina Stolba. 1996. *Women's Figures: The Economic Progress of Women in America.* Washington, D.C.: Independent Women's Forum.
Garin, Geoffrey, and Guy Molyneaux. 1996. "Defending Affirmative Action: Communicating a Winning Message." Washington, DC: Peter D. Hart Research Associates. Internal report.
Hampson, Rick. 1997. "Can Race Decide Who Keeps a Job?" *USA Today,* 6 October, 14A.
Heilman, Madeline E., and Melanie H. Stopeck. 1985. "Being Attractive, Advantage or Disadvantage? Performance Based Evaluations and Recommended Personnel Action as a Function of Appearance, Sex and Job Type." Organizational Behavior and Human Decision Processes 35(2): 202–215.
Kaufmann, Albert H., and Roger Gonzalez. 1997. "The Hopwood Case: What It Says and What It Doesn't." In *Affirmative Action's Testament of Hope,* ed. Mildred Garcia, 227–247. Albany: State University of New York Press.
Kinder, Donald R., and Lynn M. Sanders. 1996. *Divided by Color: Racial Politics and Democratic Ideals.* Chicago: University of Chicago Press.
Ladowsky, Ellen. 1995. "That's No White Man, That's My Husband." *Women's Quarterly,* Spring (3): 1, 22.
Lake, Celinda, Alysia Snell, and Victoria Sneed. 1998. "Framing the Affirmative Action Debate." Memo to No On Initiative 200 Campaign, April 10. Washington, DC: Lake, Sosin, Snell, Perry and Associates, Inc.
Lawrence, Charles R., III, and Mari J. Matsuda. 1997. *We Won't Go Back: Making the Case for Affirmative Action.* New York: Houghton-Mifflin.
Macklin, Mary Beth. 1997. "Two White Students Sue over Entry Policies." *USA Today,* October 15, 14A.
Malveaux, Julianne. 1992. "What You Said about Race." *Ms.,* May/June, 20–23.

Moseley-Braun, Carol. 1995. "Affirmative Action and the Glass Ceiling." *Black Scholar* 25(3): 7–15.
National Association of Female Executives. 1997. "Hot Off the Presses." December. Online. Available at www.nafe.com.
National Association of Women Business Owners. 1998. "Some Facts about U.S. Women Business Owners." March. Online. Available at www2.nawbo.org.
National Association of Women in Construction. 1998. "About NAWIC." Online. Available at www.nawic.org.
National Coalition for Women and Girls in Education. 1995. *Empowering America's Families: Documenting the Success of Vocational Equity Programs for Women and Girls.* March. Washington, DC: National Coalition for Women and Girls in Education, Vocational Education Taskforce.
National Research Council, Office of Science and Engineering Personnel. 1993. *Doctorate Recipients from United States Universities.* Washington, DC: National Academy Press.
No on Initiative 200. 1998. "What Is Initiative 200?" Seattle: No on Initiative 200.
Report of the Federal Glass Ceiling Commission. 1995. *Good for Business: Making Full Use of the Nation's Human Capital.* March. Washington, DC: Bureau of National Affairs.
Review of Federal Affirmative Action Programs: Report to the President. 1995.
Rojas, Aurelia. 1998. "Minority Contractor Statistics Ban Fought." *San Francisco Chronicle,* April 3, A21.
Rose, Douglas, ed. 1992. *The Emergence of David Duke and the Politics of Race.* Chapel Hill: University of North Carolina Press.
Schuman, Howard, Charlotte Steeh, Lawrence Bobo, and Maria Krysan. 1997. *Racial Attitudes in America: Trends and Interpretations.* Cambridge, MA: Harvard University Press.
Southern Regional Council. 1996. "SRC Releases Executive Summary Results of Nationwide Racial Attitudes Survey." Online. Available at www.src.w1.com.
Stop Prop 209. 1996a. "Stop Prop 209 Releases TV Ad in a Final Push." Press release. November 1.
———. 1996b. "State Contractors Fund Prop 209 to Limit Competition and Scrutiny: Co-Chairs Connerly and Lewis Tied to Contractors." Press release. October 7.
Sturm, Susan, and Lani Guinier. 1996. "The Future of Affirmative Action: Reclaiming the Innovative Ideal." *California Law Review* 84(4): 953–1036.
Sum, Andrew M., Neal Fogg, and Robert Taggart. 1996. "The Economics of Despair." *American Prospect* 27 (July/August): 83.
Taylor, Charlotte. 1997. "Musings from the Entrepreneurial Edge: Getting the Banker to Say Yes to Your Small Business Loan." National Association of Female Executives. December. Online. Available at www.nafe.com.
Toledo, Elizabeth. 1997. "California Repeals Affirmative Action, Sets Stage for Copycat Attempts." NOW Update. National Organization for Women. January. Online. Available at www.now.org.
United States Department of Commerce, Bureau of the Census. 1995. *Statistical Abstracts of the United States,* Table 649. Washington, DC: Government Printing Office.

Washington State Commission on African American Affairs. 1995/1996. *Affirmative Action, Who's Really Benefitting? Part I: State Employment; Part III: State Contracting.* Olympia, WA: Washington State Commission on African American Affairs.

Wise, Tim. 1995. "White Privilege, Uber Alles." *Z Magazine*, September: 15–17.

Wood, Robert, Mary Corcoran, and Paul Courant. 1993. "Pay Differentials among the Highly Paid: The Male-Female Earnings Gap in Lawyer's Salaries." *Journal of Labor Economics* 11(3): 417–441.

Zia, Helen. 1992. "How You Feel about Race: The *Ms.* Survey Results." *Ms.*, May/June, 24–30.

PART II **Beyond Getting a Foot in the Door: Women Workers Accessing Power**

CHAPTER EIGHT

Progressive or Neo-Traditional? Policewomen in Gulf Cooperation Council Countries

STACI STROBL

Women in positions of authority in the Arab/Muslim world are often celebrated in the West as unique examples of feminist imaginings in a cultural space where stereotypes would indicate otherwise. The Western construct of the subjugation of Arab/Muslim women speaks to a cultural arrogance that is arguably a hangover from the colonial era—that problematic gender relations are *over there*. The legacy of this dichotomy continues to prevent identification of the full variation of women's lives and experiences in the Gulf region.

One of the most glaring examples of what has been overlooked is the long tradition of women in policing in most of the Gulf Cooperation Council (GCC) countries. Bahrain can boast a nearly forty-year tradition of women working as sworn officers, with Oman not far behind. Even as journalists reported about these policewomen, scholars in women's studies, Middle Eastern studies, and criminal justice barely noticed. These policewomen instead acted as subaltern subjects within the larger discourse about women and authority.

Theoretical models of how policewomen have emerged in modern nation-states were built without theoretical or empirical contributions from the experiences of policewomen in Arab/Muslim countries. As Abu-Lughod (2009) points out, the politics of the production of knowledge cannot be ignored in the post-Saidian era, in which the unpacking of cultural concepts becomes critical to legitimate scholarship. And, under the logic of Derrida's (1978) deconstructionist project, the marginal, overlooked cases provide important information about the politicized nature of what is typically explored in the "center" of things.

The emergence of modern policewomen in the Gulf region has important cultural and social meanings that challenge the dominant notions of women and policing in academic discourse. Meaningful analytics for how societies allow for a particular phenomenon, in this case the existence of female police units, cannot be divorced from a description of cultural process. Using postcolonial and comparative feminist theory, this article challenges dominant theories within the discourse on policewomen.

In Western literature on policewomen, the increased deployment of women in policing is universally construed as occurring in the context

---

Originally published in the Fall 2010 issue of the *Feminist Formations* (22.3).

of a secular democracy; contrastingly, in the GCC context, their burgeoning deployment has occurred alongside regional trends of neo-traditionalism and Islamism. Like Mahmood's (2005) study of women in Cairo mosques, the gender segregation associated with the Islamist movement may actually create opportunities for women in various occupations and roles that may expand their power, influence, and authority. Such Islamic feminist discourse encourages scholars to go beyond "the presumed passivity of women under the weight of Islamic tradition and the cultural hegemony of Islamism and examine how women are redefining their relationship to both" (Hatem 2002, 44).

This theoretical re-imagining employs what Silvestri (2003) has described as sensitivities to the attitudes and perceptions of women, particularly those concerned with developing and maintaining national policies around gender and policing. This approach, the "comparative feminist studies" model, seeks to simultaneously show how the local and the global constitute each other (Mohanty 2003, 242). I also draw on notions of transnational feminism (Jarmakani 2008) by situating the critique in the context of the GCC on its own terms, before exploring linkages to the world beyond. This chapter will approach the larger debate on women in Muslim societies through the lens of the deployment of women police within GCC states. As Kandiyoti (1998) observed regarding Muslim societies, there are "unresolved tensions around establishing workable codes of heterosocial modernity" (284) and, as such, gender policies often take confused or conflicting forms reflecting a wide range of influences, from modern to traditional.

Social institutions, such as the police, do not just reflect a patriarchal society but are the sites through which conflicting notions of gender are both produced and challenged (Kandiyoti 1996; Martin and Jurik 1996; Messer-schmidt 1993). Thus, the social construction of gender cannot be separated from logic operating in the cultural contexts in which it is found. Geertz (1973) describes culture as "an historically transmitted pattern of meaning embodied in symbols, a system of inherited conceptions expressed in symbolic forms by means of which men communicate, perpetuate, and develop their knowledge about and attitudes toward life" (89). This perspective defines culture as shared, public meaning. Social institutions like policing are not themselves culture but are "culturally-constituted phenomena" (Ross 1997, 45); they are not impervious to social attitudes that have deemed women as the "designated cultural carriers," the embodiment and protectors of Arab and Muslim identity that was subjugated by colonialists (Freeman 2004, 20; Kandiyoti 1997; Salhi 2003).

In a postcolonial context, such as in the Gulf states, there is a cultural hybrid and "the elements of borrowed, imported, or imposed 'culture' are susceptible to disaggregation for political purposes" (Abu-Lughod 2005, 192), with some Western-derived social trends derided while others are not. The nostalgia for pre-colonial traditions acts as a source of opposition for Islamists, who have actively reinforced notions of women as the designated cultural carriers. Any study of women's roles in Middle Eastern contexts suggests a retrospective process by which historical and cultural specificities are explored.

The GCC Countries and Female Penetration of National Police Forces

The six GCC countries—Bahrain, Kuwait, Qatar, Oman, Saudi Arabia, and the United Arab Emirates (UAE)—are on the coast of the Arabian/Persian Gulf and are bound by trade and security agreements. These countries share a common language and religious and cultural heritage, although there are distinctions that can be made among them. With the exception of Saudi Arabia, the countries are constitutional monarchies; women achieved the right to vote in Bahrain in the early 1970s, in Oman and Qatar in 2003, and in Kuwait in 2005. The UAE monarchy hand picks voters for elections.

In GCC countries' national police forces, policewomen are primarily in segregated units that focus on women and juveniles as victims, witnesses, and offenders. Women make up approximately 5 percent of the police forces in Oman, the UAE, and Qatar (Strobl 2007) and 10 percent of the force in Bahrain (Strobl 2008). They work as security screeners in airports and as investigators in cases involving child and female offenders, and they provide assistance to women and children victims and witnesses (Bjorken 2005; Cullen and McDonald 2005; Ren and Zhao 2005; Strobl 2008). In 2009, Kuwait graduated its first policewomen from its training academy, though in media accounts, it is not clear how many of them were recruited nor how they will be utilized ("First Kuwaiti Policewomen Graduate" 2009). Table 8.1 provides an overview of the percentage of women among police officers in the GCC countries, as well as the approximate year of the advent of women in ranked position within these forces.

The levels of penetration are fairly comparable to those in Western countries. For example, only 14 percent of police officers and less than 1 percent of police chiefs in the United States are women (Schultz 2003). In Israel and many Eastern European countries, which boast the highest rates of female penetration into the occupation, the level is approximately 20 percent (Strobl 2007). However, the duties of policewomen in GCC countries are generally more limited than those of their Western counterparts.

TABLE 8.1
Women's Penetration into GCC National Police Forces

Country	% female of sworn personnel	Year of women's entry into policing
Bahrain	10%	1970
Kuwait	unknown	2009
Qatar	4.7%	1980s
Oman	4.5%	1974
Saudi Arabia	none	—
UAE	unknown	early 1990s

GCC countries can be divided into three types of approaches to gender and law enforcement: The complete lack of women as sworn police officers (Saudi Arabia); a significant penetration of women into the force with a moderate range of duties (Bahrain, Oman, and Qatar); and a significant rate of penetration into the force with a wide scope of duties for policewomen (UAE). Kuwait only recently (April 2009) introduced native-born policewomen into its force, so it is too early to tell how they will fare relative to the larger force (prior to this, some expatriate women were deployed as police at the country's border stations). Notably, Kuwait also has women working alongside men in the inspection department of the Ministry of Commerce. In 2007, the ministry reported hiring ten such female inspectors whose duty was to ensure that Kuwaiti businesses were complying with regulatory laws. The impetus for this development was the growing number of female businesses that provide female-related products and services ("Kuwait's Female Inspectors" 2007).

In the Gulf region, policewomen primarily work in gender-segregated units that focus on women and juveniles. For example, in Bahrain, work in the various police stations throughout the country consists of a variety of tasks, the most important of which is taking statements from female and juvenile complainants, victims, witnesses, and offenders pursuant to investigation. Policewomen also accompany female offenders to medical exams, court proceedings, and meetings with prosecutors. Some specially trained policewomen cooperate with policemen on search teams concerning possessions belonging to women; they also are requested by policemen to make arrests of female offenders (Strobl 2007).

Typically, in Bahrain, cases begin at the women's section directly from complainants visiting the station. In addition, policemen initiate cases either while on patrol or responding to calls, which are then referred to the women's section if they involve female or juvenile offenders. In each station, a policewoman is always on call during off-hours in cases of emergency; for example, if an alleged female rape victim is brought to the attention of police during off-hours, a policewoman is called in to process the complaint, arrange for a forensic medical exam, and provide for the victim's needs (ibid.).

In constructing a theory about the development of policewomen in GCC countries, care must be taken to present the dialectical relationship between a progressive, modern imagining and a traditional notion of gender segregation that necessitates specialized, gender-based units. This complementary opposition challenges the dominant theory of policewomen's development previously set forth—a universalist-style theory based primarily on the experiences in Western societies. The tension between cultural relativism and universalism undercuts any comparative endeavor: The pragmatic desire to reduce phenomena to meaningful categories of comparison across all cases (universalism) inevitably blurs the uniqueness of various contexts with their interrelated and complicated social, cultural, and political influences (cultural relativism). Nelken (2009), in discussing comparativist approaches, calls for "a careful mix of explanatory and interpretive strategies" (292) and an engagement in the phenomenon in its own right and an understanding of meanings and unpacking of assumptions. Only through the interpretive process is it then appropriate to extrapolate relationships across differing contexts. The following section offers a critique of the universalist approach to the deployment of policewomen across countries, followed by a discussion of alternatives that incorporate more cultural relativism suggested by the experiences of policewomen in the Gulf region.

The Universalist Approach

Gender integration of a police force consists of women achieving formal access to the same job tasks, ranks, and promotional opportunities as policemen. Policies about employment and deployment must be gender nondiscriminatory for the force to be considered integrated. Formal gender integration does not preclude levels of informal resistance within an organization. Integration, therefore, involves the technical capacity for women to partake in all the jobs, ranks, and tasks of policing but does not directly address the *degree* of implementation. The universalist theoretical model has two assumptions that may be drawn into question by the experience in GCC countries: The inevitability of gender integration and that such integration develops linearly. In devising a cross-national model of the development of women in policing in Europe, Brown (1997) indicates that all forces with policewomen are progressing toward gender integration and that the rates of integration reflect the variation in developmental stages of policewomen within their respective forces.

At the time of the debut of the universalist model, research about policewomen generally compared the experiences of North American and European police and had yet to include cross-national analyses of other regions. Despite the European and Western cultural specificity of the data used to conceive of the model, it has been utilized and tested in other cultural contexts and thus has taken on a veneer of universal applicability (Brown, Hazenburg, and Ormiston 1999; Natarajan 1996, 2001). Brown's (1997; see also Natarajan 2001) model involves six stages:

1. Entry of women into policing.
2. Segregated units, in which women develop their policing skills in special women-only units.
3. Gender integration through legislation.
4. Take-off, where women solidify their integration through litigation.
5. Reform, in which research begins to document the experiences of policewomen as they cope with the backlash from the take-off stage.
6. Tip-over, when women gain a presence in the force.

The model can be represented as follows:

*entry → segregated units → gender integration →
take-off → reform → tip-over*

In a later version of the model, Brown and colleagues (1999) provide a matrix that would permit cultural variation of the above linear development along three dimensions: European, colonial, and Anglo-American. According to them, these categories allow for flexibility in terms of historical time-frames and the possibility of regression, as well as for progression along the trajectory toward integration. The categories were delineated as such, because these are often considered dominant traditions within modern policing; however, it should be noted that these traditions are all Western, with non-Western contexts falling into a "colonial" gloss.

Of particular note is the notion that reaching the integration stage involves the willingness of a group of "courageous individuals" in policing to litigate and publicize their desire for the integration of their forces (Brown et al. 1999, 221). This occurs in the context of a secular feminist consciousness in which the policewomen seek "reform and redress for women against exploitation by men" in the workplace (220). Many of the early women in Western police forces became famous "pioneers," including Mary Allen (UK), Lillian Wyles (Australia), and Alice Stebbins Wells (United States) (207): "Restrictions of women's role in policing is frequently not lifted without the intervention of equal opportunity legislation. It is not just the legislation per se which is important but the willingness of a few courageous individuals who are prepared to litigate in order to establish precedent for change" (221). Outside public support from feminist groups is also crucial to achieving integration, relying again on overt resistance, at least by some of the policewomen; otherwise policewomen are stalled at the segregation stage, enamored by their own separated success within segregated units—a phenomenon Brown (1997) calls being caught in a "crab basket" (13).

Whereas the above descriptions of women's integration into policing fits the historical experience of developed Western countries and some non-Western countries, it has rarely been explored in Arab/Muslim contexts, where manifestations of women's courage may not be litigious or public. As Butler (2007) argues, resistance is the exercising of human agency within certain cultural and structural constraints. Just as traditional gender roles are performed in a given social context, they can be recast on the micro-level through the subtle subversion of these roles. In this way, such poststructuralist theories provide a space for actions that are more subtle than litigation, though not necessarily less powerful or effective, and that make sense within the cultural imaginations of a given society. Given the social pressure to conform to patriarchal centralized leadership within Gulf countries that is derived from traditional tribal culture (Al-Mughni 2001), certain displays of resistance like litigation may create more confusion and conflict because of the socially aberrant nature of such public and political protests. In cultures where overt dissent is particularly deviant (ibid.), people participating in public life on lower political levels often feel too far out on a limb and facing social and political ostracism to want to be publicly cast as innovators. Because innovation has indeed occurred in the entry and deployment of women in policing in GCC countries, differential forms of resistance and change must be considered. As Said (1993) has argued, the forms and meanings of cultural practice must be analyzed in order to understand power and resistance.

Brown's (1997) universalist model is glaringly deficient in accounting for the variety of ways policewomen are imagined across societies. While the modified model of Brown, Hazenburg, and Ormiston (1999) attempts to address this deficiency, it retains a core that does not conform to the reality in GCC countries. The GCC context suggests that policewomen in some cultural milieus do not exhibit an overt, internal drive toward integration and do not take their battles to court or other public arenas, but nonetheless position themselves politically to continue to increase their participation in traditionally male-dominated fields like policing. An examination of where and how policewomen agitate for change in GCC countries reveals a resistance to integration that runs counter to the expectations built into the two Brown models.

Policewomen in the Gulf Region: Reluctance and Resistance

One of the most striking challenges to the two Brown models appears in Bahrain. Despite some support for facets of gender integration, a recent ethnography of Bahraini policewomen (Strobl 2008) suggests that any move toward gender integration is unlikely to be demanded from the policewomen themselves. This lack of internal drive, however, should not be interpreted as apathy on their part to press for changes in police policy.

Bahraini Policewomen

The Hijab *Initiative*

An example of policewomen organizing for change involves the recent effort in Bahrain to seek governmental permission to wear the *hijab*, or headscarf, with their police uniforms. Before 2003, policewomen were barred from wearing them on the job. Since 1971, the Bahraini uniform has included a policewoman's hat modeled on the British policewomen's uniform. However, in 2003, 135 policewomen signed a petition to King Hamad and the Minister of the Interior demanding that they be allowed to wear the *hijab*, because it was an important part of expressing their Muslim and Arab identity. The petition was debated in Parliament and ultimately supported. The then-interior minister Sheikh Mohammed bin Khalifa Al-Khalifa indicated that, in fact, there was no specific law against the wearing of the *hijab* by policewomen (A'ali 2003). Thereafter a green headscarf to match the policewomen's uniform was made available.

Based on field observations, a majority of Bahraini policewomen wear the regulation *hijab* within police stations, but outside, the policewoman's hat is worn atop the *hijab*. A minority of the women do not wear the *hijab* with their uniform; these were primarily older policewomen in their late thirties and forties who came of age during Arab nationalist times when many women stopped wearing the *hijab*. The fact that younger policewomen now want to wear it is related to Islamic revivalism and trends regarding highlighting Muslim identity through wearing the *hijab* and *abaya* (black outer garment) (Seikaly 1994, 1998). According to all the policewomen interviewed, the decision to wear the headscarf or not was one that was truly a matter of personal choice; none reported knowing of anyone experiencing any career repercussions for their choice (Strobl 2008). Wearing the *hijab* by Bahraini policewomen, therefore, represents an important and workable compromise that was made between progressive and neo-traditional political and social forces. It also quite explicitly shows how multiple identities are negotiated into a complementary hybrid: These women are simultaneously policewomen and Arab/Muslim women.

The *hijab* initiative also reveals the likely direction that Gulf-country policewomen's activism will take in the future. It suggests a greater will to push for policies that they believe reinforce cultural and religious values. Contrastingly, respondents often framed the dimensions of gender integration typically associated with policing, such as mixed-gender patrols and mixed-gender office environments, as Western constructs of how policing should operate, thus representing a potential value conflict if imported to Bahrain (ibid.).

Community Policing and Nametags in Bahrain

Another cultural flashpoint in Bahrain was evinced by an informal debate during October/November 2005 among policewomen about the initiation of community policing. Some members of the Women's Police Directorate were alarmed that the new female community-police officers in another unit wore nametags on their uniforms. Regular police uniforms do not have nametags, but rather a number that identifies the wearer. For some of the policewomen, nametags on the community-policing uniforms were problematic: Namely, use of the nametag exhibited a dishonorable forwardness because strangers would then know who a policewoman was and the family to which she belonged. In essence, the anonymity of the uniform had been serving as a layer of protection against social/cultural objections to women intermingling with strangers outside the home. By not being identifiable by name, plausible deniability was maintained in the event a policewoman's honor was called into question by virtue of her job. Community policewomen, in contrast, did not face the same pressures because traditionally they were permitted to work in public spaces and thus did not risk their family's reputation by encountering strangers and acting as authority figures outside the home.

Importantly, many policewomen who complained about the nametags believed that they were another example of Western cultural practices being imposed by the leadership without taking into consideration the will of the policewomen themselves. Some mentioned that advisors from Europe and Japan influenced the creation of community policing within the country, which was lauded by Bahraini police leadership as part of a "modernization phase to ensure better services" (Hamada 2005) and "a qualitative change to keep pace with developments in security measures in the developed world" (Fakhri 2005b). According to one Bahraini police officer, human rights, transparency, and accountability all characterize the new unit (Fakhri 2005a). Consequently, Bahraini women are markers in the government's drive toward modernizing, even at the expense of more traditional, local values.

Kuwait's New Women Police

Similarly, in Kuwait, the advent of Kuwaiti policewomen in 2009 was heralded as a modernizing mission. Ambassador to Bahrain Sheikh Azzam Mubarak Al-Sabah told the media that policewomen in Kuwait represent "a significant development and quantum leap that favorably reflects the performance of all security organs" and is part of the Kuwaiti emir's focus on women's rights, as well as being a "new nucleus for women's empowerment." According to the ambassador, Kuwait policewomen's work "had to take place in a protected environment among socially acceptable people" ("First Kuwaiti Policewomen Graduate" 2009). This echoes Longva's (1993) notion of female morality in Kuwait as connected to protected space; as women became more mobile in society and entered the workplace, the notion of protected spaces was redefined and reconstituted. Moreover, the larger societal debate over women and authority plays itself out in the daily contexts of policing. The ambiguity surrounding policewomen in Kuwait surfaced in May 2007 when the *Kuwait Times* asked several college students how they felt about the prospect of having women in the police force ("Sound Off" 2007). Among the few respondents no consistent position was apparent, the respondents instead positioning themselves across the entire spectrum of possibilities from support to rejection. In April 2009, the newspaper *Al Dar* reported that a female officer in Kuwait filed a complaint after a male officer of lower rank failed to salute her ("Can't Salute a Woman" 2009).

The UAE: Ajman and Mixed-Gender Traffic Patrols

The UAE provides another notable illustration of the dynamics surrounding the integration of policewomen within the Arab/Muslim context. In Ajman, which is one of the seven emirates composing the UAE, policewomen were deployed alongside their male colleagues on traffic patrols in 1999, only two years after they first joined the traffic department (Al-Jandaly 2001). This historic change in deployment policy involved top police officials deciding to deploy the mixed patrols even though such patrols were contrary to popular sentiment. Ajman has the largest number of policewomen within the UAE, and, according to the director of the Ajman traffic police, the policy is part of an overall strategy to help women in society acquire self-confidence and participate in decision making (UAE 2003). Importantly, the impetus to liberalize gender policies in traffic patrols did not stem from policewomen demanding to participate in policing alongside men; indeed, many policewomen protested being assigned to the patrols because it placed them in potential opposition to locally acceptable cultural and religious norms (Al-Jandaly 2003). But these protestations subsequently subsided and ultimately policewomen became a regular part of traffic patrols in Ajman, even stopping male drivers when they violated the law. These patrols started with five women officers, but the number grew to twenty within three months. As one policewoman said: "I have not had any harassment on the job. Sometimes young men who are fined for violating traffic rules start muttering angry words. But they must understand that we are only doing our job. Many older men wish us success in our work" ("Policewomen Keep Male Drivers in Line" 1999).

The story of Ajman policewomen and mixed-gender traffic patrols reflects the logic of honor. Indeed, as in other Gulf countries, popular sentiments about women and their roles in society are influenced by Islamic trends. In this region, citizens are more conservative as a whole (though there are notable exceptions) in their vision for women than is the government. Overt pressure to integrate policing comes from ruling families and top officials and not from the policewomen themselves, who tend to reflect the attitudes within their societies. Although, at the same time, policewomen's attitudes are more nuanced than would superficially appear to be the case, and the women are willing to integrate with their male colleagues as long as it can be done in a way that does not jeopardize or threaten Arab/Muslim cultural values and preserves their dignity and honor within their social and cultural milieu.

Western observers may superficially view Ajman as an example of women being disinterested in becoming full members in their own profession and instead embracing the neo-traditional notion of gender segregation and the preservation of women's subordinate roles. However, a deeper look at the dynamic suggests a very important alternative to this reading: Because Ajman policewomen have largely accepted mixed-gender patrols, particularly for training purposes, it suggests that the mandate to integrate despite the women's subsequent protests is part of a larger, culturally specific dynamic that ultimately invites and does not shun some level of gender integration. Such integration is thus accomplished as reluctant compliance to a hegemonic order that allows the policewomen to avoid the uncomfortable position of violating gender-appropriate roles. By protesting, policewomen preserve their honor within the society in which they are a part.

As detailed by ethnographers of Arab societies (Abu-Lughod 1986; Lienhardt 2001), women's honor stems from deference to the patriarchal system performed as a voluntary act. Overtly desiring to patrol with men, therefore, and seeming too enthusiastic to do so, would place women in the untenable position of being viewed by others as rejecting their Arab/Muslim identity and forsaking their feminine identities within this cultural framework. Furthermore, it would place them in a position of social deviation (*inhiraf*), often condemned as (Western) selfish individualism.

Because of an orientation toward social roles and maintaining a collective balance (within tribes or within an emirate, as in this case), policewomen's approach to gender-policy issues may be more subtly negotiated than in the West and performed differently given the cultural context. Scholars who have delved deeply into the world of Arab/Muslim women have shown that female initiative in the region operates from within a social framework of family-oriented feminist identity (Fernea 1998; Hijab 1988) and within the framework of Islam (Abouzeid 1990; Ahmed 1992; Badran 2002; Fernea 1998) or Arab tribal identity (Abu-Lughod 1986). Mahmood (2005) suggests that Western feminist preoccupation with the binary of resistance/subjugation has failed to provide a theoretical framework with which to view the true range of possibilities in Arab/Muslim societies and has, in fact, continued to impose a teleological model of development that may be inappropriate. Likewise, Abu-Lughod's (1990) "diagnostic of power" explores resistance even in its more subtle form, therefore empowering scholars to heed strategies that make sense in particular cultural environments.

Natarajan's Model: Equity and Equality

Natarajan (2008), recognizing the cultural limitations of the Brown model, proposes a modified version based on the experience of policewomen in Tamil Nadu, India. Her theory begins with the notion that economic development has created opportunities for women in policing but that the patriarchal structure of South Indian society hinders some of the progress toward integration. She suggests that a completely integrated force in the way Western academics may imagine is improbable; an "equal but different" (151) doctrine that runs counter to the predicted pathway of the Brown model is possible. In essence, Natarajan links the development of policewomen to the overall movement toward community policing in which the police work creatively together to solve problems through a more inclusive, service-oriented approach. Among the principles of community policing is the aspiration to be fully integrated in terms of race, class, ethnicity, and gender. In this way, Natarajan envisions equity as a steppingstone to equality.

Introducing equity to a model for policewomen in non-Western countries is an important step forward in building theory and represents the primary problem when trying to reconcile Brown's model to the experiences in non-Western countries. A telling example of the tension between *equity* and *equality* in the Arab world is the Arab Human Development Report (UNDP) of 2005 which states: "[A]s human beings, women and men have an innate and equal right to achieve a life of material and moral dignity, the ultimate goal of human development ... [and] the rise of women in the joint framework of human rights and human development. In terms of human rights, the advancement of women is to be achieved as part of society's advancement to freedom, in its most comprehensive definition" (5). The report goes on to discuss what equality means in the context of competing notions of equity, including the assertion that, although there are differences between the sexes, that "in no way implies deficiency" of one over the other (ibid.). The report indicates that repressive regimes, in order to bolster their images in the global human-rights arena, have encouraged women's rights in ways that would not have happened as quickly if left to the natural progression of these societies.

Similarly, all GCC countries except Qatar signed the "Convention on the Elimination of All Forms of Discrimination against Women" (CEDAW) (UNDAW 1979), the second article of which establishes the principle of equality between men and women. Both the UAE and Bahrain are signatories, though with reservations about article 2, stating that the *Shari'ah* trumps this notion of equality with its focus on men and women as having different though complementary roles. Signatories Saudi Arabia and Oman also have reservations, saying generally that *Shari'ah* takes precedence in their interpretation and implementation of the convention. This notion of *Shari'ah* as an alternative to full equality is an important point of dissent that the Gulf countries offer on the larger discourse of the role of women. As Weiss (2003) found in a study of the implementation of CEDAW in Pakistan, within the Muslim world, equality is considered a Western construct whereas equity has cultural resonance. Religious scholars have also emphasized gender equity as the preferred approach, given the dictates of the Quran. According to Badawi (1995), "[t]he full equality of human beings before Allah is beyond doubt. This equality should not be confused, however, with role differentiation in the spirit of cooperation and complementarity. This is why equity is a more accurate term than equality" (13–14). Badawi explains that equity allows for overall equality and justice in a particular situation without equality on a line-by-line basis. Fernea's (1998) exploration of feminism in the Muslim world—as it is defined by Muslim women—found that the Western notion of strict equality between the genders was not the feminism most prevalent in the region; after interviewing women in a broad range of careers in eight countries, including the Gulf countries of Kuwait and Saudi Arabia, she concludes that "family feminism" reigns, in which "Islamic feminists strive to create equality, not for the woman as individual but for the woman as part of the family, a social institution still seen as central to the organization and maintenance of any society" (416). Rather than the Western notion of individual autonomy, the "contextual self" emerges as an identity that may be tied to family, tribe, and religion. Although borrowing from Western feminists in their pursuit of greater employment opportunities, Muslim feminist strategies differ significantly from those of the West because of the desire to work within the structure of Islam.

Linearity and Inevitability

Natarajan's approach is helpful in that it opens up the culturally specific discourse around equity in non-Western contexts; however, it ultimately does not alter the fundamental Western presumption that integration is an inherent good and part of the inevitable, linear trajectory of women in police forces. The latent implication of both the Brown and Natarajan models is the possibility of stimulating and even subtly socially engineering similar trajectories in "problematic" cultural spaces, perhaps through a human rights–oriented approach. Although this approach appears laudable on the surface, it does not confront the larger question of whether the existence of policewomen represents a continual process of subjugation of the region by Western powers—the powers that created these police forces in the first place, and, in the cases of Bahrain and Oman, actively installed policewomen in the late stages of colonialism as a legacy of secular, liberal influences (Strobl 2007).

The notion of integrated policewomen will ultimately never gain full cultural and social legitimacy in certain postcolonial contexts and will long remain a suspicious cultural import. As Spivak (1999) claims, such colonial encounters have spurred "a repeated tearing of time that cannot be sutured" (208). We also cannot ignore the double bind that we find ourselves in when it comes to cross-cultural theories on gender policies in which there is ultimately no safe space to place oneself as an objective observer outside the competing cultural processes. Even the notion that gender integration is the primary question one asks in the discourse on policewomen and their development, wherever they are found, represents a Western preoccupation with women as markers of secular liberalism. In an ironic cultural dialectic, it is precisely this marker and the construction of policewomen as also engaged in shoring up traditional gender segregation that makes this theoretical discourse attractive in the first place as a contested site in which to engage an understanding of gender.

Ultimately, as seen in GCC and other Arab countries, gender as it relates to policing is negotiated in ways that are inconsistent with a secular, liberal feminist agenda, contradicting the seeming inevitable march toward gender equality posited by the Brown and Natarajan models. To consider non-Western policewomen in secular or Western developmental models continues to relegate the real work of Arab/Muslim policewomen to the margins. In actuality, even nonsecular regimes, which do not enjoy the favor of the West and do not necessarily have a human rights or democratic agenda, have found their own ways of opening the doors for policewomen within their societies. For example, Hamas instituted opportunities for policewomen in 2008 but, because of traditional Palestinian sex segregation, these opportunities are mainly limited to work on drug and prostitution cases involving women (El-Khodary 2009). The very existence of patterns of gender segregation in society ironically give rise to opportunities for women to work in policing pursuant to maintaining protected spaces for women involved as witnesses, victims, or offenders in the criminal justice system (Strobl 2008).

The inclusion of women in the new community-policing unit in Bahrain and the expanding role of women in gender-integrated operations, such as traffic patrols, in the UAE and Bahrain are important harbingers of the expanding opportunities for policewomen in the region. These vectors of integration are primarily driven by the governments themselves. Ambitious plans to involve women in policing, as well as in government ministries and the workforce in general, comprise the strategies of various royal families to appear progressive to foreign (Western) investors and also to respond to external pressure from human-rights organizations. As part of their grand liberalization plans, policewomen are key players in softening the images of police forces as they shift away from a more dictatorial orientation to one that exhibits greater transparency and operates as a service to their communities (personal communications [Strobl 2007] with a Bahraini male police colonel [6 December 2005] and a Bahraini male police major [2 May 2005]).

Interestingly, leaders of Gulf countries may be more willing to support women in positions of leadership and authority than is the society in general, a situation that can be defined as a type of "state feminism" (Silvestri 2003; Stetson and Mazur 1995). Socially and culturally important critiques of gender liberalization remain formidable in more conservative Sunni and Shiite political blocks, representing competing possibilities for retreat into more restrictive policewomen deployments. The political context surrounding the deployment of policewomen projects "what is possible for women in policing" in particular nations (Silvestri 2003, 167). Greater attention to the nuances of state feminism and its dissent can better predict at any given moment whether policewomen will become more prevalent in the ranks and ultimately at higher levels of authority.

In addition, one notices that, when considering police organizations throughout the world, the idea that full gender integration is a linear inevitability remains unproven empirically. Women make up less than a third of the police in any given force, and they are largely kept in lower ranks in gender-segregated or gender-related deployments (Brown and Heidensohn 2000). As such, the endpoint of full integration remains a future, utopian possibility. Although it may be dubious to envision not having arrived linearly at this point in policewomen's history—embedded as this discourse is in linear thinking—a review of the GCC context suggests that the creation of this juncture in policewomen's history might not be linear and neat but instead reflect a negotiation and renegotiation of the cultural and political limits of having women in positions of public authority.

Performing Gender in Police Stations

The differential performance of gender integration within the Arab/Muslim context presents the greatest challenge to existing models of such integration. Starting with structural anthropology, the logic operating in particular contexts has been highlighted as an important variable in any comparative research. Lévi-Strauss's (1961) famous exploration of cousin marriage initiated the development of social-exchange theory in which the Western academic fixation on self-interested, individualistic motivations was questioned. Social exchanges, like the exchange of women in cousin marriage, were analyzed as ritual and not merely self-interested economic behavior (Befu 1977; Cutler 2001). Starting from the group rather than the individual, Lévi-Strauss showed that compliance to structural rules within particular cultural milieus can explain individual behavior that may superficially appear to be illogical or irrational. In essence, he called on researchers to take seriously the logic operating in the particular settings they encounter, emphasizing that, in such contexts, principles of reciprocity take on central importance.

On the other hand, structuralism suffers from certain fixed assumptions, such as the notion that cultural systems have internal coherence and external autonomy. This has been deemed dubious in light of subsequent poststructuralist analyses (Sperber 1979) that confront the increased interplay of a variety of cultural, social, and political forces at work in contemporary people's lives in a globalized age, in which the external and internal causes and effects of any power dynamic blur in a de-centered world of seemingly infinite independent variables (see Hardt and Negri 2000). Yet, understanding social and cultural systems on their own terms remains an important lesson learned, for it is a non-Western notion of social identity and social reciprocity that may account for Ajman policewomen's initial reluctance to work in mixed-gender patrols and Bahraini policewomen's seeming lack of enthusiasm for gender integration.

Problematizing the notion of cultural performance around police gender integration, however, is the fact that such a performance relies on male-dominated social institutions to participate in gender integration in the public sphere. In other words, integration relies on men to be complicit in granting women access to policing and gives men control as to the timing and the scope and nature of any gender-integrating initiative. For secular or national feminists, such a situation may seem disempowering because women find themselves waiting for male institutions to invite them in, rather than women themselves demanding entrance. But this only obscures the fact that regardless of how women resist patriarchy—whether overtly through legalistic means and even violence or more subtly—integration in all contexts, barring an Amazonian retreat to another world, must have support from existing patriarchal political entities, particularly in contexts in which women have yet to be present in the upper echelons of police organizations.

At the same time, some policewomen in GCC countries have articulated more overt modes of resistance toward male domination in policing. This reflects the postcolonial hybridization of positions—important nuances that must be acknowledged and disaggregated in order to present the mosaic of forces operating within a particular context (Abu-Lughod 1998; Said 1993; Spivak 1999), though most may adopt more subtle modes of resistance. Because of the long influence of the West in the region and the liberalization of society, individual calls for change will be made by a minority of women who feel comfortable operating in a way that more overtly resists. As one Bahraini policewoman said, "I like being a policewoman and helping people, but I think it's better in America. I want to carry a gun and patrol and be in the streets. I think I would be good at it" (Strobl 2007).

It is no mistake that the policewoman who articulated the above radical statement drew a direct connection with American policewomen and idealized Western notions of gender integration in police deployment. This is how notions of gender integration are often framed within GCC countries—as an imported concept. Even more importantly, such articulations were not accompanied by any plans to push police leadership toward integration. Unlike the *hijab* initiative, in which policewomen organized to have the right to wear the headscarf at work, there was no such evidence that an initiative is in the works around gender integration from within policewomen's ranks. This calls into question just how overt a resistance to gender segregation these women can be considered to be showing when no action on their part is planned. Nonetheless, when asked, their discourse is overt. Overall, this reveals that both the overt and subtle (traditional) modes of imagining gender integration of policewomen are present in Gulf-region societies simultaneously, ultimately reflecting in general the larger sociocultural ambiguity in Arab/Muslim societies about women's roles. As argued here, the more subtle approach appears to have a wider range of support and ultimately is more likely to be the vehicle for actual changes in police forces.

This chapter analysis of integration as a social performance of honor and political will is not to suggest an "otherization" of Arabs and Muslims or to suggest that Arab/Muslim policewomen's logic is somehow less than the logic operating in another (Western) context. Concerns around promotions and rank, the desire to have access to interesting, fulfilling, and challenging work, and an orientation toward confronting social problems unite these policewomen with their counterparts throughout the world. However, scholars looking for certain (Western) patterns of feminist resistance, such as cultural constructs of courage and the pioneering spirit (Brown 1997), may miss the entire story in non-Western contexts.

Policewomen and Patriarchy

Further problematizing the deployment of women police is a deeper reading of their relationship to other women within their society. The deployment of policewomen in the Gulf context can be viewed as a reification of patriarchal social control. Because policewomen are largely used to control the behavior of women and to enforce laws that are patriarchal in nature, the notion that women in policing operate as an inherent good is also drawn into question. In GCC countries, policewomen can both be markers of liberalizing policies designed to win over the hearts and minds of the global community, and be deployed in ways that further reinforce customary patriarchal notions about the roles of women, such as being used to handle cases of women offenders, children, and expatriate housemaids.

Are policewomen an example of feminism in the societies in which they appear when, ironically, they are empowered in ways that *disempower* other women? Strobl (2009) shows that the majority of cases faced by policewomen in Bahraini police stations involve expatriate housemaids accused of transgressions against their employers. Because of the lack of legal protection for foreign domestic workers, policewomen end up handling the problems, such as criminal charges, incarceration, or deportation, resulting from unregulated and often exploitative labor that subjugates foreign women, primarily those from South Asia. Ethnographic observations revealed that Bahraini policewomen do not identify with housemaids nor seek to protect them from exploitative sponsors but instead view them in the same way that the larger society does: That these foreign women are willing participants in the global labor market who by virtue of their class position should count themselves lucky to have any type of job.

Theoretical notions that assume that policewomen are an inherent good may privilege particular cultures, classes, and identities. Imagining police systems that are responsive to all the diverse members of a given society is part of the larger global trend to democratize policing (Haberfeld and Gideon 2008); policewomen may fit this representative, service-oriented approach by working in specialized units that can respond to the unique needs of women by acting as "an innovation in accessibility" (Nelson Reames 2008). Yet, when the policewomen themselves, embedded as they are in their social contexts, harbor nationalist, secularist, or otherwise potentially discriminatory orientations, their presence may offer advantage to some but not to all. Theories that assume that the mere presence of policewomen means that *all* women within their respective societies are better served or protected are failing to engage critically. Scholars of policewomen must begin to work within cultural spaces, while simultaneously maintaining critical approaches to identity politics and discriminatory policing that fuels the "devastating rhetoric of 'us vs. them'" (Suleri 1992, 756).

Ultimately, the construct of policewomen needs to be reconstituted to reflect the tension between their cultural context and a more utopian desire for a "planetary" feminism that embraces all women (Spivak 2006, 107), approached through Spivak's "politics of the imagination" (Sharpe and Spivak 2002). Because connecting capitalism, patriarchy, and criminal justice in late modernity is part of the imaginative power of the politics of corporate globalization, "it requires an equally forceful appeal to the imagination for contestation" (610). It means that critically engaging what is possible for women in the global age is an imaginative project but one that starts at the local level of countering the paternalist, postcolonial relationship between third world women and first world social science. For Spivak (1999), thick, qualitative engagement with subjects and an imaginative discourse can grow a radical opening through which self-reflexivity can counter human societies' otherizing by way of their own particular cultural forms. This presupposes a kind of cultural capital on the part of scholars who engage in a dialogue with subjects on their own terms.

An Alternative Model of Gender Integration and Policewomen

An alternative, regional model can address some of the unique aspects of gender policy and politics within the Gulf context, while also suggesting ways of maintaining women in policing through simultaneous gendered and integrated police units, constantly shored up and renegotiated through tangible accommodations for traditional practices demonstrating modesty and maintaining honor (see Figure 8.1). Any new, culturally specific model should not exhibit a zero-sum game of either segregation or integration; instead, both can be operating simultaneously in the same historical moment as legitimate and coherent policy given particular social, political, and cultural contexts.

This model reflects the contested notions of the role of women in positions of authority in the Gulf region and provides for specialized women police units in order to meet the needs of women and children in the community. In this regional model, using the GCC experience to extrapolate to an Arab/Muslim social and political environment, the

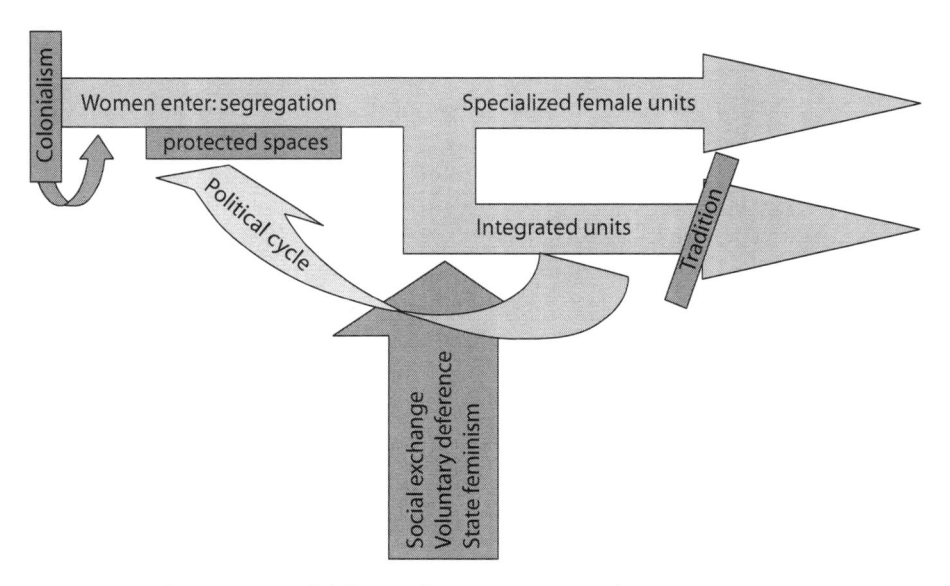

Figure 8.1. Alternative model for gender integration in the GCC context.

simultaneous operation of segregation and integration can backslide given political calls for neo-traditionalism or Islamic revivalism. Integrated units are established not because of courageous pioneers or overt resistance but instead through a variety of less transparent backroom politicking based on notions of bottom-up voluntary deference and social exchange, as well as on top-down state feminism. In addition, the model shows that integrated units may also tap out the social and political feasibility (indicated as "tradition" in the model) of women in certain roles—for example, in paramilitary units. The model suggests that the deployment of policewomen is a contested and dynamic site where constructions of women as police continue to be reconfigured and renegotiated.

The model also confronts potential outliers, such as the unwillingness in some countries to permit women to enter policing as sworn officers, as is the case in Saudi Arabia. Understanding gender in police organizations globally also involves exploring national contexts in which women cannot choose to become sworn officers. In these cases, we often find that women are working in the criminal justice system in positions that would earn them officer status in other countries, their deployment locked in a segregated status that exists in support of policing. In fact, the discourse in Saudi Arabia around the possibility of having women in sworn, ranked positions has faced a circular argument that reflects the general dialectic of the alternative model, in that the tension between traditional gender roles and policing is circular. For example, in 1999, Saudi Crown Prince Abdullah made a public statement that women should have expanded rights and that the prohibition on women driving automobiles in the country is merely a technical problem of not having female police officers (Khashoggi 1991). At the same time, other Saudi officials have outright rejected the idea of policewomen; a female police unit was "ruled out" in Saudi Arabia in 2007 for reasons unspecified, reflecting an interior ministry leadership that does not believe that women are a necessary part of their national police force ("Women-Only Police Force" 2007).

Conclusion

As Said (1993) articulates, Western scholars exploring postcolonial societies have often erred, in that they "assume the silence, willing or otherwise, of the non-European world" (58) rather than evaluating the situation on its own terms, under the logic operating in the particular context. Pushed further, Spivak (1999) has shown, in her analysis of the cultural modes of postcolonial resistance, that the subaltern, or those who occupy spaces outside or beyond a given post-colonial, dominant system, may actually be "speaking" their resistance to the patriarchal social order but are not heard. Hegemonic observers are positioned to detect only particular words, attitudes, situations, and constructs deemed as resistance, feministic, or revolutionary.

In hopes of better noticing policewomen in the Gulf countries and taking seriously the historical and cultural moment they occupy, this chapter proposes an alternative, culturally specific means of understanding contested gender policies around the deployment of policewomen in a postcolonial milieu. It explains and interprets the internal and external forces that account for the variety of ways in which policewomen are deployed in the region and what this means for the continuing contest among a continuum of forces, from neo-traditional to progressive. As such, hybridity is embraced and notions of full gender integration of the police as always and necessarily the goal of policing are interrogated in favor of culturally appropriate notions of complementarity and equity—important avenues for understanding the future trajectory of policewomen. Ultimately, policewomen in GCC countries are both progressive and neo-traditional, a position that is not merely hedging, but instead reflects a deeper understanding of the nature of gender and policing in these countries.

References

A'ali, Mohammed. 2003. "Scarf Ban on Bahrain Policewomen Lifted." *Gulf Daily News*, 4 July. Retrieved from *Gulf Daily News* archives in Isa Town, Bahrain.

Abouzeid, Leila. 1990. *Year of the Elephant: A Moroccan Woman's Journey.* Austin: University of Texas Press.
Abu-Lughod, Lila. 2009. "Overview: Engaging the Arab Human Development Report 2005 on Women." *International Journal of Middle East Studies* 41: 59–60.
———. 2005. "The Marriage of Feminism and Islamism in Egypt: Selective Repudiation as a Dynamic of Post-colonial Politics." In *Internationalizing Cultural Studies: An Anthology*, ed. M. Ackbar Abbas and John Nguyet Erni, 181–95. Malder, MA: Blackwell Publishing.
———. 1998. "Feminist Longings and Post-Colonial Conditions." In *Remaking Women: Feminism and Modernity in the Middle East*, ed. Lila Abu-Lughod, 3–31. Princeton, NJ: Princeton University Press.
———. 1990. "The Romance of Resistance: Tracing Transformations of Power through Bedouin Women." *American Ethnologist* 17(1): 41–55.
———. 1986. *Veiled Sentiments: Honor and Poetry in a Bedouin Society.* Berkeley: University of California Press.
Ahmed, Leila. 1992. *Women and Gender in Islam.* New Haven, CT: Yale University Press.
Al-Jandaly, Bassma. 2003. "Improving Image, Crushing Crime." *Gulf News*, 27 July. Accessed 19 April 2006, at www.gulf-daily-news.com.
———. 2001. "Policewomen Come in for Praise." *Gulf News*, 12 October. Accessed 19 April 2006, at www.gulf-daily-news.com.
Al-Mughni, Haya. 2001. *Women in Kuwait: The Politics of Gender.* London: Saqi Books.
Badawi, Jamal A. 1995. *Gender Equity in Islam: Basic Principles.* Plainfield, IN: American Trust Publications.
Badran, Margot. 2002. "Islamic Feminism: What's in a Name?" *Al-Ahram*, 17–23 January. Accessed 9 May 2006, at http://weekly.ahram.org/2002/569/cu1.htm.
Befu, Harumi. 1977. "Social Exchange." *Annual Review of Anthropology* 6: 255–81.
Bjorken, Johanna. 2005. "United Arab Emirates." In *Encyclopedia of Law Enforcement*, vol. 3, ed. Larry E. Sullivan and Maki Haberfeld, 1357. Thousand Oaks, CA: Sage Publications.
Brown, Jennifer. 1997. "European Policewomen: A Comparative Research Perspective." *International Journal of Sociology of Law* 25: 1–19.
Brown, Jennifer, Anita Hazenburg, and Carol Ormiston. 1999. "Policewomen: An International Comparison." In *Policing across the World: Issues for the Twenty-First Century*, ed. R. I. Mawby, 204–25. London: UCL Press Ltd.
Brown, Jennifer, and Frances Heidensohn. 2000. *Gender and Policing: Comparative Perspectives.* New York: St. Martin's Press.
Butler, Judith. [1990]2007. *Gender Trouble.* Reprint, New York: Routledge.
"Can't Salute a Woman, Policeman Tells Female Officer in Kuwait." 2009. *Gulf News*, 22 April. Accessed 22 April 2009, at www.gulfnews.com/news/gulf/kuwait/10306673.html.
Cullen, Stuart, and William H. McDonald. 2005. "Oman." In *Encyclopedia of Law Enforcement*, vol. 3, ed. Larry E. Sullivan and Maki R. Haberfeld, 1219–20. Thousand Oaks, CA: Sage Publications.

Cutler, Anthony. 2001. "Gifts and Gift Exchange." *Dumbarton Oak Papers* 55: 247–78.
Derrida, Jacques. 1978. *Limited Inc*. Trans. Samuel Weber. Baltimore, MD: Johns Hopkins University Press, 162–254.
El-Khodary, Tagheed. 2009. "Gaza City Journal: Under Robe and Veil, Crossing Boundaries as Policewomen." *New York Times*, 18 January: 18. Accessed 24 April 2009, at http://query.nytimes.com/gst/fullpage.html?res=9502E3D610 3EF93BA25752C0A 96E9C8B63.
Fakhri, A. 2005a. "New Unit 'Will Be a Model for the Nation.'" *Gulf Daily News*, 13 April. Retrieved from *Gulf Daily News* archives in Isa Town, Bahrain.
———. 2005b. "A New Force for Bahrain." *Gulf Daily News*, 22 September: 4. Retrieved from *Gulf Daily News* archives in Isa Town, Bahrain.
Fernea, Elizabeth Warnock. 1998. *In Search of Islamic Feminism: One Woman's Global Journey*. New York: Anchor Books.
"First Kuwaiti Policewomen Graduate." 2009. *Al-Watan*, 26 March: 1.
Freeman, Amy. 2004. "Re-Locating Moroccan Women's Identities in a Transnational World: The 'Woman Question' in Question." *Gender, Place and Culture* 11(1): 17–41.
Geertz, Clifford. 1973. *The Interpretation of Cultures*. New York: Basic Books.
Haberfeld, Maki R., and Lior Gideon. 2008. "Policing Is Hard on Democracy, or Democracy Is Hard on Policing?" In *Comparative Policing: The Struggle for Democratization*, ed. Maki R. Haberfeld and Ibrahim Cerrah, 1–12. Thousand Oaks, CA: Sage Publications.
Hamada, S. 2005. "First Batch of 190 Community Police Personnel Graduates." *Bahrain Tribune*, 22 September: 3.
Hardt, Michael, and Antonio Negri. 2000. *Empire*. Cambridge, MA: Harvard University Press.
Hatem, Mervat, 2002. "Gender and Islamism in the 1990s." *Middle East Report* 222: 44–47.
Hijab, Nadia. 1988. *Womanpower: The Arab Debate on Women at Work*. Cambridge, MA: Cambridge University Press.
Jarmakani, Amira. 2008. *Imagining Arab Womanhood: The Cultural Mythology of Veils, Harems, and Belly Dancers in the U.S.* New York: Palgrave Macmillan.
Kandiyoti, Denis. 1998. "Some Awkward Questions on Women and Modernity in Turkey." In *Remaking Women: Feminism and Modernity in the Middle East*, ed. Lila Abu-Lughod, 270–87. Princeton, NJ: Princeton University Press.
———. 1997. "Beyond Beijing: Obstacles and Prospects for the Middle East." In *Muslim Women and the Politics of Participation: Implementing the Beijing Platform*, ed. M. Afkhami and E. Friedl, 3–10. Syracuse, NY: Syracuse University Press.
———. 1996. "Contemporary Feminist Scholarship and Middle East Studies." In *Gendering the Middle East: Emerging Perspectives*, ed. Denis Kandiyoti, 1–28. Syracuse, NY: Syracuse University Press.
Khashoggi, Jamal. 1991. "Dialogue on Women's Role Urged." *Arab News*, 21 April. Accessed 23 June 2009.
"Kuwait's Female Inspectors Work Hand-in-Hand with Colleagues." 2007. Kuwait News Agency (KUNA), 21 September. Accessed 23 June 2009.

Lévi-Strauss, Claude. 1961. *A World on the Wane*. New York: Criterion Books.
Lienhardt, Peter. 2001. *Shaikhdoms of Eastern Arabia*. New York: Palgrave Macmillan.
Longva, Anh Nga. 1993. "Kuwaiti Women at a Crossroads: Privileged Development and the Constraints of Ethnic Stratification." *International Journal of Middle East Studies* 25(3): 443–56.
Mahmood, Saba. 2005. *The Politics of Piety: The Islamic Revival and the Feminist Subject*. Princeton, NJ: Princeton University Press.
Martin, Susan, and Nancy C. Jurik. 1996. *Doing Justice, Doing Gender*. Thousand Oaks, CA: Sage Publications.
Messerschmidt, James. 1993. *Masculinities and Crime: Critique and Reconceptualization of Theory*. Lanham, MD: Rowan & Littlefield.
Mohanty, Chandra. 2003. *Feminism without Borders: Decolonizing Theory, Practicing Solidarity*. Durham, NC: Duke University Press.
Natarajan, Mangai. 2008. *Women Police in a Changing Society: Back Door to Equality*. Farmhand, Surrey, UK: Ashgate Publishing.
———. 2001. "Women Police in a Traditional Society: Test of a Western Model of Integration." *International Journal of Comparative Sociology* 42(1): 211–33.
———. 1996. "Towards Equality: A Report on Women Policing in India." *Journal of Women and Criminal Justice* 8: 1–18.
Nelken, David. 2009. "Comparative Criminal Justice: Beyond Ethnocentrism and Relativism." *European Journal of Criminology* 6(4): 291–312.
Nelson Reames, Benjamin, 2008. "Neofeudal Aspects of Brazil's Public Security." In *Comparative Policing: The Struggle for Democratization*, ed. Maki R. Haberfeld and Ibrahim Cerrah, 61–95. Thousand Oaks, CA: Sage Publications.
"Policewomen Keep Male Drivers in Line: A Policewoman Checks a Motorist." 1999. *Gulf News*, 12 September. Accessed 24 May 2006, at www.gulf-daily-news.com.
Ren, Ling, and Ruohui Zhao. 2005. "Qatar." In *Encyclopedia of Law Enforcement*, vol. 3, ed. Larry E. Sullivan and Maki R. Haberfeld, 1269–70. Thousand Oaks, CA: Sage Publications.
Ross, Marc. 1997. "Culture and Identity in Comparative Political Analysis." In *Comparative Politics: Rationality, Culture and Structure*, ed. M. Lichbach and A. Zuckerman, 42–80. Cambridge, UK: Cambridge University Press.
Said, Edward. 1993. *Culture and Imperialism*. London: Vintage.
Salhi, Zahia. 2003. "Algerian Women, Citizenship, and the 'Family Code.'" *Gender and Development* 11(3): 27–35.
Schultz, Dorothy. 2003. "Women Police Chiefs: A Statistical Profile." *Police Quarterly* 6(3): 330–45.
Seikaly, May. 1998. "Women and Religion in Bahrain: An Emerging Identity." In *Islam, Gender, and Social Change*, ed. Y. Haddad and J. Esposito, 169–89. New York: Oxford University Press.
———. 1994. "Women and Social Change in Bahrain." *International Journal of Middle East Studies* 26(3): 415–26.
Sharpe, Jenny, and Gayatri Chakravorty Spivak. 2002. "A Conversation with Gayatri Chakravorty Spivak: Politics and the Imagination." *Signs: Journal of Women in Culture and Society* 28(2): 609–24.

Silvestri, Marisa. 2003. *Women in Charge: Policing, Gender, and Leadership.* Abingdon, Oxfordshire, UK: Willan Publishing.

"Sound Off: Here Are the Views of Some Students on 'Women Police.'" 2007. *Kuwait Times*, 2 May: 8.

Sperber, Dan. 1979. "Claude Lévi-Strauss." In *Structuralism and Since*, ed. J. Sturrock, 19–51. Oxford: Oxford University Press.

Spivak, Gayatri Chakravorty. 2006. "World Systems and the Creole." *Narrative* 14(6): 102–12.

———. 1999. *A History of Postcolonial Reason*. Cambridge, MA: Harvard University Press.

Stetson, Diane McBride, and Amy Mazur, eds. 1995. *Comparative State Feminism*. Thousand Oaks, CA: Sage Publications.

Strobl, Staci. 2009. "Policing Housemaids: The Criminalization of Domestic Workers in Bahrain." *British Journal of Criminology* 49(2): 165–83.

———. 2008. "The Women's Police Directorate in Bahrain: An Ethnographic Exploration of Gender Segregation and the Likelihood of Future Integration." *International Criminal Justice Review* 18: 39–58.

———. 2007. "Women and Policing in Bahrain." PhD diss., City University of New York/Graduate Center.

Suleri, Sara. 1992. "Woman Skin Deep: Feminism and the Postcolonial Condition." *Critical Inquiry* 18: 756–69.

"UAE: Ajman Has Largest Police Force in the Country." 2003. *Khaleej Times*, 11 August. Accessed 19 April 2006.

United Nations Development Programme (UNDP). 2005. "Arab Human Development Report (AHDR), 2005." Accessed 23 June 2009, at http://arabstates.undp.org/contents/file/ArabHumanDevelopRep2005En.pdf.

United Nations Division for the Advancement of Women (DAW), Department of Economic and Social Affairs. 1979. "Convention on the Elimination of All Forms of Discrimination Against Women" (CEDAW). Accessed 23 June 2009, at http://www.un.org/womenwatch/daw/cedaw/.

Weiss, Anita M. 2003. "Interpreting Islam and Women's Rights: Implementing CEDAW in Pakistan." *International Sociology* 18(3): 581–601.

"Women-Only Police Force Ruled Out in Saudi Arabia." 2007. *Arab News*, 7 March. Accessed 23 June 2009, at www.arabnews.com.

CHAPTER NINE

Motivational and Attitudinal Factors among Latinas in U.S. Electoral Politics

SONIA R. GARCÍA AND MARISELA MÁRQUEZ

Chicanas and Latinas have a long history of being political actors, dating as far back as the Mexican Revolution.[1] Yet scholarly research has only recently begun to address their contributions to American politics. In this essay, we delineate the increasing presence of Latinas and Chicanas in electoral politics as activists, candidates, and officeholders. Drawing from some of the more recent literature on gender and Latinas in politics, as well as our own study of 51 Latinas and Chicanas active in party or grassroots politics, we look specifically at the intersection of gender and ethnicity to explore why this group pursues political involvement and how it perceives its own political leadership. It is our contention that Chicanas and Latinas approach mainstream political participation differently than do their white female counterparts because of their unique experiences and political history as minority women. Studies such as Melville's and Cordova's underscore the complexity of the experiences of Chicanas in the United States (Cordova et al. 1980; Melville 1986). In particular, we argue that Chicanas and Latinas are much more likely to have community-oriented motivations for their political involvement and to manifest their political participation largely in relation to themselves, their families, and their particular ethnic communities.

Events prompting this research started in the late 1980s when Latinas and Chicanas began to reach a new level of visibility in the national political arena. Ileana Ros-Lehtinen, a Cuban American Republican from Florida, gained national attention in 1982 with her election as the first Latina to win a congressional seat. Gloria Molina, Los Angeles' first Mexican American of either sex to hold a county supervisory position in one of the largest metropolitan cities, came to national attention in the late 1980s. In addition, much-publicized elections for Congress, such as Anita Perez Ferguson's close bid in California, helped establish a new Latina presence in national politics in 1990. In 1992, two additional Latinas were elected to the U.S. House of Representatives: Lucille Roybal-Allard (D-CA), the first Mexican American assemblywoman from California, and Lydia Velazquez (D-NY), the first Puerto Rican assemblywoman from New York. More recent campaign successes include Loretta Sanchez (D-CA) and Grace Napolitano (D-CA). There are also a number of prominent Latinas within state legislatures, including Hilda Solis

---

Originally published in the Summer 2001 issue of the *NWSA Journal* (13.2).

(D-CA) from the Los Angeles area and Irma Rangel (D-TX). Equally important, recent hotly-contested mayoral elections and school board races in prominent cities such as San Francisco and Pasadena, California; Phoenix, Arizona; San Antonio, Texas; and Santa Fe, New Mexico have also brought attention to Latinas at a national level. With reference to the latter category, Latina elected officials, like their female counterparts in other race-ethnic groups, still appear most prominently on local school boards and in municipal government. Nevertheless, they make up a sizeable percentage of the total number of Latino-elected officials, surpassing the proportion of women in U.S. politics overall. Pachon and DeSipio, for instance, reported that in 1992, Latinas made up 30.1 percent of all Latino elected officials (1992). In that same year, women constituted only 17.2 percent of elected officials in the United States.

One factor contributing to the increased political representation of Latinas and Chicanas is the early involvement and support of Latina and Chicana organizations. In effect, Latinas and Chicanas are creating their own paths of leadership development. Organizations such as Comision Femenil Mexicana Nacional, which is a nonpartisan women's leadership organization based in Los Angeles, help prepare Latina women for political office. Other organizations, such as the National Hispana Leadership Institute and the Mexican-American Legal Defense Fund, offer leadership training for Latinos and Latinas in politics. Similarly, the National Women's Political Caucus (NWPC), specifically the Hispanic Steering Committee, sponsors candidate development conferences for Latinas. Regional organizations, such as Las Adelitas in New Mexico, target and assist potential political candidates.

Political action committees have also been established to foster Latinas running for office. The Latina Political Action Committee (LPAC), based in Sacramento, California, and established in 1990, was the first Latina political action committee to come into existence. Others, such as the Florida Hispanic Women's Pact and the Texas Women's Political Pact, followed suit. These organizations seek to raise money for Latina candidates and others who support their issues. In addition, the Center for American Women and Politics (CAWP) unveiled a Latina website titled Elección Latina that can be found at www.rci.Rutgers.edu/~cawp/Eleccion/home.htm.

Although Latinas have gained visibility in the national political arena and have clearly demonstrated leadership in American national politics, very few studies document their accomplishments. Two works by Sierra and Sosa-Riddell (1994) and Montoya, Hardy-Fanta, and García (2000) have begun to fill this void in this body of literature. Of the existing scholarship on Latinas and/or Chicanas in politics, three works stand out: Mary Pardo's research on the Mothers of East Los Angeles (1990), Paule Cruz Takash's research on Latina political officeholders in California (1993), and Carol Hardy-Fanta's research on Latinas in the Boston community (1993). These three works focus largely on how Latinas transform their networks, resources, and experiences into political assets; how differently Latinas, as political actors, behave in comparison to Latinos; and how differently Latinas view politics in comparison to Latinos.

Hardy-Fanta, for instance, concludes that Latinas have a vision of politics and political participation "as making connections" (1993, 25). These connections involve connections between people, connections between private troubles and public issues, and connections that lead to political awareness and political action. It is through these connections that Latinas reflect a more participatory vision of politics that incorporates cultural needs and expectations.

Similarly, Pardo concludes that Chicanas are able to transform traditional networks and resources based on family and culture into political assets and action (1990, 1998), while Takash concludes that Latina political officeholders are able to overcome barriers of race, class, gender, and culture largely because they are able to draw from their experiences as long-time community activists (1993). In short, these studies confirm Baca Zinn's observation that entering politics allows Chicanas and Latinas to alter their traditional sex roles and, at the same time, promote Chicano and Latino culture (1980).

The general literature on gender and politics—especially that dealing with attitudinal and perceptual differences between men and women as a whole—is also helpful in understanding Chicana/Latina involvement in politics and how Chicanas and Latinas are able to overcome the constraints that exist for them in the political arena. Burt-Way and Kelly, for instance, present a provocative theory that taps into the different calculations women use in deciding to run for office (1992). By delving into an attitudinal dimension of political ambition, Burt-Way and Kelly assess the relationship between women's beliefs about success and the constraints they perceive in the opportunity structure—specifically attitudes that affect women and men differently. They found that on every measure of success attributes, women were more likely than men to agree that "hard work, ability and reliance on an extensive system of political, professional and social connections" helped them overcome any barriers they perceived to their success (23). Bledsoe and Herring also find gender differences based on attitudes that have significant meaning for women but not men (1990). They contend that "circumstances that potential candidates and officeholders find themselves in" are of more importance to women than to men (213). Most intriguing, men are more likely to run for office, regardless of their perceptions of electoral success. Women, in contrast, are more likely to consider their political vulnerability and their perceptions of electoral success before deciding to run for (higher) office. Women also tend to be caught by internal factors, mainly feelings about the appropriateness of high female ambitions—or being politically active, for that matter. Additionally, studies such as Sapiro and Farah's (1980) and Carroll's (1989) demonstrate how women are more likely than men to experience conflict between political motivations and other personal commitments, such as family.

The following study builds upon the general literature regarding gender and politics, as well as the more specific studies regarding Latina and Chicana officeholders. In particular, it examines the combined influence (intersection) of gender and ethnicity on decisions to pursue political involvement and perceptions of political leadership on the part of Chicanas and Latinas. Studies such as this one are necessary to dispel the notion that Latinas are not serious political actors, are inexperienced in the political game, or are naïve to the necessary calculations when running for office. Most often, Latinas in the media either are simply not highlighted or are stereotyped as passive, meek, and not politically astute. As cited in Witt, Paget, and Matthews, former NWPC President Irene Natividad points out, "minority women must establish themselves as 'credible candidates'; they must be able to raise money and encourage candidates" (1995, 119). Similarly, California candidate, Anita Perez Ferguson, a former president of the NWPC, in assessing her own candidacy for Congress in 1990, felt that her gender and ethnicity affected her candidacy because minority women must establish their credibility. She was cited as stating that the general perception is "not one of competency and leadership" (118). This study attempts to dispel this perception and to set the record straight regarding the viability of Chicana and Latina candidacies for elected office.

The Study

This study addresses two central issues: (1) reasons that Chicanas and Latinas become politically involved and (2) the impact of risk assessment and self-confidence on the political development of Latinas and Chicanas. A total of 51 study participants was drawn from two sources: (1) a Latina Candidate Development Conference, sponsored by the LPAC in collaboration with the National Hispana Leadership Institute in Los Angeles in 1990, and (2) national convention delegates attending the 1992 Democratic Convention in New York. Participants were asked a series of questions pertaining to their reasons for becoming involved in politics, as well as their perceptions of the landscape of political opportunities, the risks associated with their participation, and the necessary confidence to overcome those risks. Specific questions pertaining to motivation and to risk and confidence assessments are located under the "Findings" sections of this chapter.

Participant Profiles

The participants in the Latina Candidate Development Conference came from Arizona, New Mexico, Illinois, and (primarily) California. The national delegates were from Texas, California, Arizona, New Mexico, and Colorado. Their political experiences varied; they were public officeholders, first-time political officeholders, candidates, party officeholders, convention delegates, party activists, campaign workers, community activists, and newcomers to the political arena. Most, in fact, had been active participants in party politics and grassroots politics for several years, with the average number of politically active years being roughly sixteen. They also belonged to a number of organizations, including occupation-related organizations, politically related women's groups, Chicana/Latina-based organizations (such as the ones already mentioned), and Chicano/Latino organizations. In other words, this group represented long-time political actors.

In addition, the participants in our study came from a pool of highly educated, mostly professional women with high incomes. Their educational backgrounds varied from some high school to professional degrees, with most of them indicating that they had a college or professional degree. Their personal incomes ranged from $15,000 to $90,000 per year and rose as high as $125,000 when family incomes were combined.

The majority of our study participants came of age during the Chicano movement in the 1970s, meaning their average age was 40. We believe that this partly explains their unique approach to, and level of involvement in, mainstream politics.

Only five participants identified themselves as immigrants. Most of them were either first- or second-generation U.S. citizens. The majority of them identified the country from which they or their parents had emigrated as Mexico, and most were bilingual in English and Spanish.

In terms of ethnic self-identification, participants chose from a variety of terms. Most preferred to be identified as either Mexican American or Latina/o, while some preferred Hispanic, Chicana/o, American of Mexican descent, or Mexicana/o. Interestingly, while most did not choose to be called Chicana/o, the majority did not view the term negatively. Most defined Chicana/o as either a political term chosen by people of Mexican descent or as meaning an American-born Mexican. One possible explanation is that participants had internalized the intentions of the Chicano movement, yet had moved away from the actual use of the term to define themselves. There was less consensus regarding the term Hispanic. Of the two terms, there was more expressed rejection of the term Hispanic than of the term Chicana/o.

Findings Regarding Motivation for Chicana/Latina Political Involvement

Participants were provided a list of seventeen reasons for being involved in politics. They were also asked to indicate the level of importance for each of the reasons. The list of reasons included their concern to elect particular candidates, the desire to make business, social, and political contacts, their commitment to the party, support for party policies or representing certain groups in the party, fulfilling civic responsibility, an interest in running for office or wanting a personal career in politics, a concern to contribute to their community and specifically to the Chicano/Latino community, to see others like themselves involved in politics, for fun or visibility, or simply because their friends and families were involved. They were also asked to provide any other reasons that were not listed to explain their political participation.

Participant responses to this question suggest that there is a great deal of variation in their motivation for political involvement. Of the seventeen reasons, five appear to be the most important: (1) to elect particular candidates; (2) to see people like themselves involved in politics; (3) commitment to their community; (4) to give something back to the Chicano/Latino community; and (5) to get the party and its candidates to support the policies in which they believe.

Most revealing about these findings is the combination of traditionally relevant political motivations with specific community-oriented motivations. That is, participants exhibited a commitment to getting particular candidates elected and certain policies addressed, as well as a commitment to both their own communities and the Chicano/Latino community at large. Participants *bridged* both traditional and community-oriented motivations for their political involvement. In effect, Latinas are entering traditional mainstream politics and bringing with them their experiences from grassroots politics and from their cultural networks and resources. Moreover, participants voiced a concern to "see others like themselves involved in politics." These dimensions make Latinas and Chicanas unique in mainstream politics and point to a more robust and complex understanding of the reasons that people become involved in politics.

Equally important are the reasons that were of least importance to participants in our study. These reasons were (1) having a personal interest in running for public office; (2) wanting a personal political career; and (3) participating in a political party to gain visibility, political contacts, and/or professional business contacts. A possible explanation is that these reasons reflect an individualistic, hierarchical view of politics. Although participants were generally professionals and highly educated, they, nevertheless, seemed to shy away from the material and self-interested gains that are typically associated with mainstream politics.

The open-ended responses also lend support for the premise that Latinas bring with them a unique vision of politics—a bridging of both traditional and community-oriented motivations. This bridging suggests that Latinas and Chicanas bring their community with them, rather than "leave it behind" or "forget where they come from." One theme that emerged in response to the open-ended question was "the need for change." As found in our study, two participants actually placed themselves at the center of that change—as "catalysts for change to focus public policy on human needs" and "to change unfair policies and regulations." Three participants made more of a connection to the tenets of democracy. One, for instance, indicated that she is involved in politics "to make democracy work." Another indicated that "participation is at the core of a democracy . . . if a system is to work, we must make it work for us." Still another participant tied her political involvement to her commitment to family, community, and a democratic process. She stated that she participates in politics "to involve my son and his friends in developing consciousness . . . I am his role model . . . he is my future." (García 1997; Márquez 1997; García and Márquez 1992).

Findings Regarding Perceptions of Risks

As mentioned earlier, participants comprised a cohort of political elites. As found in García, however, their level of experience did not make them impervious to certain barriers to participation in electoral politics (1998). In order to assess their role as political actors, participants were asked a series of questions that tapped into their perceptions of the landscape of political opportunities, the risks associated with their participation, and the necessary confidence to overcome those risks. Participants were asked to consider different types of risks for Latinas and Chicanas running for office, such as financial burdens, withstanding public scrutiny, invasion of family and personal life, risk of compromising personal values, and risk of compromising group values.

When asked to identify the top three risks for Latinas and Chicanas running for office, participants overall selected financial burdens, invasion of family and personal life, and the risk of compromising personal values. Variation among age groups or level of personal interest in running for office yielded no changes in this pattern. In other words, irrespective of age or interest in running for office, participants ranked these risks the same.

Findings Regarding Perceived Confidence Levels

Being involved in politics—and, in particular, running for office—requires an enormous amount of confidence. To gauge confidence levels, we asked participants whether they felt confident (1) to seek information and train others for political campaigns and running for office; (2) to serve as a resource and role model for others seeking political office; (3) to seek encouragement and support from others in consideration of running for public office; (4) to identify and contact individuals who could positively impact their political career path, financially or otherwise; and (5) to be the first and only Chicana/Latina running for public office in their community. These measures were designed to tap into an array of activities in politics from the resources that are necessary to run for office, to serving as *connectors* and role models for others, to being in the precarious situation of being *a first and only* to run for office in one's community.

In addition to determining participant confidence levels, this study examined the relationship between age cohorts and personal interest in running for office. Therefore, participants were divided into three groups: (1) those born before 1944, (2) those born between 1944 and 1962, and (3) those born after 1962. To gauge the effect of personal self-interest in their running for public office, participants were again divided into those who identified running for office as an important motivation for their involvement in politics versus those who did not. There were 28 women who considered running for office as either extremely or quite important and 23 who did not think it was very important or important at all.

In response to the confidence questions, the Latinas were extremely confident in pursuing everything from securing resources to serving as a resource and role model for others. On these measures the age cohorts vary in their confidence levels, and they vary in fairly predictable ways. What was most interesting was that their confidence levels reflected a structured role among the generations. For example, the first age group, those born before 1944, identified themselves as being most confident in serving as a resource for others seeking office. The second age group, those born after 1944 to 1962 (the so-called baby boomers), felt confident about seeking information and training others as well as being the first and only Latina running for public office in their community. Last, the youngest group, those born after 1962, felt most comfortable seeking encouragement as well as identifying people who could influence their political careers. With respect to their interest in running for office and confidence levels, the patterns described above essentially remained unchanged.

Prospects for Chicanas and Latinas into the Next Century

It should be pointed out again that this sample of Latinas represents a group of highly participatory political actors. They have been involved in both community-based and mainstream politics for a number of years. So, in some respects, they symbolize a small slice of Latinas within the Latino community. Clearly, the Latinas in this study do not represent Latinas nationwide, and most studies, such as Garcia, Garcia, Falcon, and de la Garza (1989) and de la Garza, Menchaca, and DeSipio (1994), have shown that there are vivid regional and ideological differences among Latinos, especially between Texas and California. These women also depict a small group of Latinas that are both educated and professional, despite the variation of socioeconomic backgrounds. So, a word of caution is necessary as to the generalizability of these findings. Nevertheless, this study gives readers insights into a group of women who reflect representational politics. Similar to the findings of previous research on women, Latinas in elite politics demonstrate their own approach to political participation.

Our study finds that Latinas share a common set of motivations for being politically involved. They are entering traditional mainstream politics and bringing with them their experiences from community-based politics, their cultural networks and resources, as well as their unique vision of politics. Additionally, these Latinas bridge both traditionally relevant political motivations and specific community-oriented motivations.

In sum, this study illustrates how these Latinas offer insight to their communities as role models and agents of change. As do most political actors, Latinas do identify themselves in a political landscape filled with certain risks. The risks that matter to Latinas are financial burdens, invasion of family and personal life, and the compromising of one's personal values. But they also demonstrated a high degree of confidence in overcoming these risks. Specifically, they felt they were skilled enough and motivated enough to seek resources, to be a resource for others, and to stand up as a first and only. Furthermore, that this level of confidence was found among various generations is an encouraging sign; there is a distinct *pipeline* of political candidates and officeholders.

Our study contributes to a growing body of literature that addresses the intersection of gender, ethnicity, and culture in the study of political participation. Further research, however, is necessary. The Latinas in this study point to a more robust and complex understanding as to what people are involved in politics and why. An area requiring further study is the influence of Latina-based organizations on developing the necessary skills, resources, and networking that are essential in politics. Equally important, case studies, such as Siem's work on Loretta Sanchez, are needed to address the increasing presence of Latina candidates and officeholders (1999). We also suggest research that examines the ethnic identification and ethnic labeling among Chicanas and Latinas, their view on various issues, as well as their political aspirations. Indeed, the Latinas and Chicanas in this study suggest a promising cadre of candidates and officeholders in national politics into the twenty-first century.

Note

1. The terms Latinas and Chicanas are used interchangeably to connote women identified with a wide coalition of women who are of Mexican descent.

References

Baca Zinn, Maxine. 1980. "Gender and Ethnic Identity among Chicanos." *Frontiers* 5: 18–23.
Bledsoe, Timothy, and Mary Herring. 1990. "Victims of Circumstances: Women in Pursuit of Political Office." *American Political Science Review* 84: 213–23.
Burt-Way, Barbara, and Rita Mae Kelly. 1992. "Gender and Sustaining Political Ambition: A Study of Arizona Elected Officials." *Western Political Quarterly* 45(1): 11–26.
Carroll, Susan. 1989. "The Personal Is Political: The Intersection of Private Lives and Public Roles among Women and Men in Elective and Appointed Office." *Women & Politics* 9: 51–67.
Cordova, Teresa, Norma Cantu, Gilberto Cardenas, Juan Garcia, and Christine M. Sierra, eds. 1986. *Chicana Voices: Intersections of Class, Race and Gender.* Austin, TX: Center for Mexican American Studies.
de la Garza, Rodolfo, Martha Menchaca, and Louis DeSipio, eds. 1994. *Barrio Ballots: Latino Politics in the 1990 Election.* Boulder, CO: Westview Press.
Garcia, John, F. Chris Garcia, Angelo Falcon, and Rodolfo de la Garza. 1989. "Studying Latino Politics: The Development of the Latino National Political Survey." *PS: Political Science and Politics* 22(4): 848–52.
García, Sonia. 1998. "Running as a Latina: Building a Campaign." Presented at the Annual Conference of the Western Political Science Association, 20 March, Los Angeles, CA.
———. 1997. "Motivational Factors for Latinas in Electoral Politics." Roundtable at the Annual Conference of the Western Political Science Association, 14 March, Tucson, AZ.
García, Sonia, and Marisela Márquez. 1992. "Political Ambition and Aspirations among Latinas." Roundtable on Latinas in Politics. Presented at the Annual Conference of the National Association for Chicano Studies, 27 March, San Antonio, TX.
Hardy-Fanta, Carol. 1993. *Latina Politics, Latino Politics: Gender, Culture, and Political Participation in Boston.* Philadelphia: Temple University Press.
Márquez, Marisela. 1997. "Redefining Politics: Survey on Chicana and Latina Political Actors." Roundtable at the Annual Conference of the Western Political Science Association, 14 March, Tucson, AZ.
Melville, Margarita B., ed. 1980. *Twice a Minority: Mexican American Women.* St. Louis, MO: C.V. Mosby.
Montoya, Lisa, Carol Hardy-Fanta, and Sonia García. 2000. "Latina Politics: Gender, Participation and Leadership." *PS: Political Science and Politics* 23(3): 555–62.

Pachon, Harry, and Louis DeSipio. 1992. "Latino Elected Officials in the 1990s." *PS: Political Science and Politics* 25(2): 212–17.
Pardo, Mary. 1990. "Mexican American Grassroots Community Activists: 'Mothers of East Los Angeles.'" *Frontiers* 11(1): 1–7.
———. 1998. *Mexican American Women Activists: Identity and Resistance in Two Los Angeles Communities.* Philadelphia: Temple University Press.
Sapiro, Virgina, and Barbara Farah. 1980. "New Pride & Old Prejudice: Political Ambition and Role Orientations among Female Partisan Elites." *Women & Politics* 1: 13–37.
Siems, Larry. 1999. "Loretta Sanchez and the Virgin." *Aztlán: A Journal of Chicano Studies* 24(1): 151–74.
Sierra, Christine M., and Adaljiza Sosa-Riddell. 1994. "Chicanas as Political Actors: Rare Literature Complex Practice." *National Political Science Review* 4:297–317.
Takash, Paule Cruz. 1993. "Breaking Barriers to Representation: Chicana/Latina Elected Officials in California." *Urban Anthropology* 22: 325–60.
Witt, Linda, M. Paget, and Glenna Matthews. 1995. *Running as a Woman: Gender and Power in American Politics.* New York: Free Press.

CHAPTER TEN

Feminists and the Welfare State: Aboriginal Health Care Workers and U.S. Community Workers of Color

NANCY A. NAPLES AND MARNIE DOBSON

As a result of the mandate to hire local community residents during the War on Poverty (1964–1971) in the United States, women residing in low-income communities in many cities across the United States were employed by the state as community workers. During the 1970s and 1980s, the Australian state began funding Aboriginal community-based programs in conjunction with the newly emerging land councils and within mainstream services. The U.S. and Australian states drew on different frames to justify employment of women of color and Aboriginal women. In the United States, the goal was to encourage *maximum feasible participation* of residents in these communities in the implementation of local community action programs (see Naples 1998a, 1998b). In contrast, the employment of Aboriginal health care workers can be understood in the context of Australia's prevailing ideology of *multiculturalism* that underpinned the implementation of more *culturally appropriate* services. Akhil Gupta and James Ferguson demonstrate the limits of multiculturalism and define it as "both a feeble acknowledgment of the fact that cultures have lost their moorings in definite places and an attempt to subsume this plurality of cultures within the framework of a national identity" (1992, 7). In the Australian context, the top-down and bureaucratic push for multiculturalism illustrates their critique (also see Clarence 1999). In contrast, we view *multicultural feminist praxis* as a grassroots strategy and an ongoing achievement based in the philosophy and practice of participatory democracy and situated knowledges (also see Hurtado 1999; Sandoval 1991; Zinn and Dill 1996).

In this chapter, we continue the feminist project of challenging the conceptual distinction between the so-called public sphere and the private sphere of the family and household (see Prokhovnik 1998) by incorporating community caretaking and *activist mothering* (Naples 1998a, 11). Activist mothering not only involves nurturing work for those outside one's kinship group but also encompasses a broad definition of activities including political activism. Rather than an expression of some essentialized gender identity, activist mothering is achieved through the process of reflection on experiences of and the actions taken to contest racism, sexism, and poverty in their daily lives. Women as well as men, with

---

Originally published in the Fall 2001 issue of the *NWSA Journal* (13.3).

or without children, engage in activist mothering when the work within their communities is self-consciously designed to counter the effects of racism, sexism, and poverty. The conceptualization of activist mothering draws attention to the historically specific context in which women of different racial-ethnic backgrounds develop their political analyses and citizenship practices.

Along with Mary Dietz, we believe that "feminists must first transform their own democratic practices into a more comprehensive theory of citizenship before they can arrive at an alternative to the non-democratic liberal theory" (1992, 78; also see Naples 1998b; Sarvasy 1997). Our analysis of the community work of low-income, American women of color and Aboriginal women provides different vantage points for exploring social democratic practice that remains sensitive to the intersection of race, class, gender, sexuality, culture, and political context among other differences in women's positionality vis-à-vis the state. Our approach highlights the rich political analyses and activist strategies developed by women who are often less visible in accounts of women's movements, civil rights, and indigenous rights movements.

In the next section, we describe the methodology used for the comparative study. We then briefly outline the specific political context in which the U.S. and Australian governments provided community-based, state-sponsored employment for women of color and Aboriginal women. We explore the women's relationship to women's movements, civil rights, and indigenous rights movements and discuss the dynamics of gender, race, class, culture, and community work. Last, we analyze how community workers resisted bureaucratic practices that were not responsive to the needs of their indigenous communities and challenged from within the patriarchal and racist state.

Activist Mothering in Comparative Perspective

Due to the gender division of labor that assigns women to caretaking and service work to a greater extent than their male counterparts, women form a majority of community workers and community health care providers in both the United States and Australia.[1] Our comparative study of women explicates the relationship between social movement organizing, social policy innovation, and women's community-based work. Research on the community activism of women of color in the United States highlights the ways that racism and a commitment to fight for social justice infuse their political analyses, political practices, and mothering practices (Glenn, Chang, and Forcey 1994; Gluck et al. 1998; Green 1990; L. Smith 1999). Women of color as activist mothers, especially those living in poor neighborhoods, must fight against discrimination and the oppressive institutions that shape their daily lives and, consequently, they model strategies of resistance for others in their communities. In describing her struggles on behalf of her own children in the East Harlem public schools, African American community worker Vera Green learned to negotiate with school officials and expanded her work to help empower other women. She offered the following advice to other parents: "You are considered troublemakers [but] we have to fight together, because all of our children are having the problems, and whatever we do that might not benefit our own children, it will in time benefit somebody else's."

Aboriginal women must also confront the legacy of colonialism that contours the personal and political terrain of their everyday lives. Calling attention to the continuing disparity between Aboriginal and Anglo-Australian health statistics, Australian activists advocated for funding of separate health services for Aboriginal people, especially in rural areas. In response to these concerns, both the Liberal and the Labour Party in the 1970s and 1980s worked to establish special representation rights and some self-determination rights for Aboriginal people, resulting in the formation of the Aboriginal and Torres Strait Islander Commission (ATSIC) in 1990.[2] ATSIC is a decentralized agency with elected representatives from 35 regional Aboriginal and Torres Strait Islander councils. However, Aboriginal political organizations such as ATSIC have a predominantly male leadership. According to Jan Pettman, Aboriginal women's organizing efforts have been "hampered by the variety of situations and backgrounds in which they live, and the urgency of survival and immediate family and community demands" (1992, 92).

Methodological Considerations

The two samples of community workers are relatively small in comparison to the number of non-white and Aboriginal women who found employment in state-sponsored community work positions in the United States and Australia, respectively. From these accounts, we are interested in developing a comparative framework for analysis that remains sensitive to women's racial and cultural diversity as a central feature of feminist-social-democratic praxis, as well as to explore the contradictions of the state for women who have historically been marginalized as citizens and political actors.

Naples interviewed 42 community workers employed in New York City and Philadelphia CAPs (Community Action Programs) using an open-ended, unstructured interview schedule. Of the 42 resident women community workers (e.g., those working in the low-income communities in which they lived) identified for this study, 26 were African American, 11 were Puerto Rican, 4 were European American, and 1 was Japanese

American. The first round of interviews was held in the mid-1980s. Follow-up interviews were conducted with a subset of the sample in the mid-1990s. Adapting Naples's interview themes to the Australian context, Dobson analyzed the experiences of Aboriginal women working in health care provision, community activism, and health care education in one region of southeast Australia.[3] She conducted interviews with a total of sixteen Aboriginal women and categorized the women into three groups based on work location. There were six women in the first group, referred to as mainstream workers because they were employed in *identified* Aboriginal positions in the state-funded area health service or in health care programs at the local university. Responding to federal and state equity initiatives, they directly implemented Aboriginal programs and/or acted as Aboriginal liaisons between their organization and the community. Dobson also interviewed six of eight women who were training to be nursing assistants in Aboriginal health care programs. The third group comprised four women employed by Aboriginal-controlled community organizations; two were public health workers at the local Aboriginal Medical Service and two were coordinators of other Aboriginal-controlled community organizations in the area.

Historical and Social Movement Context for State-Sponsored Community Work

Low-income and working-class women continue to struggle against the legacies of colonialism, racism, sexism, and poverty. In their fight against these interlocking systems of oppression, they develop activist strategies to contest their political and economic marginalization. In both the United States and Australia, the social movements in which many of these women participated were responsible for the policy innovations that led to their incorporation as employees and community-based policymakers. State-sponsored community work illustrates the link between social and political citizenship.[4] However, in both the United States and Australia, this form of employment provides a contradictory site from which to contest oppressive features of the state. In this section, we provide a very brief overview of the historical and social movement context through which these policy innovations occurred.

The Civil Rights Movement and the War on Poverty in the United States

Historically, the lives of African American and Latino women differed dramatically from those of white women in the United States. For example, a total of 38.9 percent of African American women and 25 percent of Puerto Rican women were in the workforce in 1920, while only

17.2 percent of white women were working for pay (Amott and Matthaei 1991). Many African American and Puerto Rican women were employed as domestic servants in the homes of upper-class white women. Black women were denied access to family supports available through the government agency, Aid to Families with Dependent Children, as well as forms of public assistance (see Abramovitz 1988). *De jure* discrimination in employment, welfare policy, education, and housing, among other arenas, continued at all economic levels until the 1960s (see Boris 1995). Neither the labor movement, nor social welfare organizations, nor ultimately the radical political parties of the first half of the twentieth century were especially responsive to the needs of African American and Puerto Rican workers and the urban poor. As jobs were eliminated following World War I, racial unrest grew among residents in urban communities. African American women played a crucial role in all political struggles from the time of slavery to the most recent civil rights movement (Giddings 1984; Robnett 1997).

The political relationship between the "mainland" and Puerto Rico continues to reflect the legacy of colonialism and the structural inequalities of racial formation in the United States (Rodriquez 1991). In the early 1900s, Puerto Ricans' economic lives were profoundly changed because of the reorganization of the island's agricultural economy under the U.S. colonial government. Consequently, approximately one-seventh of Puerto Rico's labor force migrated to the United States between 1909 and 1940. While many returned to the island during the Great Depression, those remaining, especially in New York, contributed much to the labor movement. For example, Puerto Rican women helped form the Unemployed Women Workers Association and contributed to the effective organizing of the Needleworkers' Union (Amott and Matthaei 1991). Puerto Ricans who migrated to the mainland faced much the same discrimination that affected African Americans living in large cities. Puerto Ricans organized to contest discrimination, police harassment, and educational and economic inequalities. Women were central participants in the Young Lords, the Puerto Rican Socialist Party, and the Puerto Rican Students' Union, among others, as well as founders of local and national Puerto Rican and Latina women's organizations.

Citizen participation and participatory democracy were important themes in the civil rights movements in the late 1960s and early 1970s and shaped the political environment that gave rise to the War on Poverty (Quadagno 1994). For example, the Student Nonviolent Coordinating Committee, initiated because of African American activist Ella Baker's organizing efforts, developed a practice of "group centeredness" and anti-authoritarianism. It created the opportunity for more people to take an active and visible role in the efforts of the organization and shaped the formulation of the Economic Opportunity Act, among other policies designed during the War on Poverty (see Marris and Rein 1972). The War on Poverty was the first U.S. state effort to involve the poor in decision-making, advocacy, and service provision in their own communities and to provide them pay for the work that many already performed on behalf of those communities.

The U.S. state justified the employment of women residing in low-income neighborhoods through the New Careers program, which was premised on the claim that non-credentialed resident workers had a greater commitment to their communities than did professional social service providers (Pearl and Riessman 1965). The New Careers program provided an alternative career path for those who had situated knowledge about their communities because of their daily life as residents of poor neighborhoods. New Careers legitimated the workers' efforts on behalf of their communities while simultaneously circumscribing their employment mobility. Since their expertise was based on knowledge of their specific communities, New Careers offered a somewhat limited career path for many community workers, especially those who refused to separate their paid work from their commitment to serve particular communities. As the community action programs came under more centralized bureaucratic scrutiny, more constraints were placed on their political activism. However, since many of the community workers hired during the War on Poverty viewed *maximum feasible participation* through the lens of these movements, they continued to view their employment as an opportunity to increase the political efficacy of low-income residents of their communities and racial-ethnic minorities (Naples 1998a).

The Aboriginal Rights Movement and Health Care Policy in Australia

The colonial Australian state sought to control and subjugate Aboriginal people through policies of protectionism, segregation, and eventually assimilation. Aboriginal tribal groups were removed from ancestral lands to government or church missions to make way for, or be absorbed into, Australia's pastoral economy. Dispossession of land meant the decimation of traditional hunting and gathering and other sociocultural practices that then forced dependency on a foreign and racist state for basic services (Hunter 1993; Kunitz and Brady 1995). Evolutionary ideologies of racial and cultural inferiority can be traced in the political and legal discourse as justification of this dispossession. These discursive practices continue to shape the social, political, and economic status of Australia's Aboriginal people (Cowlishaw and Morris 1997). The marginalization of the Aboriginal people resulted in exclusion from the basic services associated with social citizenship (see Saggers and Gray 1991).[5] In fact, as Maori researcher Linda Tuhiwai Smith (1999, 109) points out, Aboriginal people were not counted in the Australian census until 1967, following a national referendum to alter the constitution (see

Rowley 1970). In a policy of removal similar to the one utilized in the United States against American Indians, Aboriginal children were taken from their families and placed in government-run homes (see Jaimes 1997).

The liberal democratic welfare state in Australia has come under pressure from both the Aboriginal self-determination movement and the women's movement since the 1960s. The outcome of the women's movement and indigenous rights movement in Australia has been an institutionalization of women's rights by the state (Sawer 1999; Watson 1990) and the development of a "second welfare state" to meet Aboriginal rights activists' demands for indigenous self-determination (Pettman 1992). While there has been some overlap between the two movements, they have largely represented separate interests. The Aboriginal rights movement mobilized around liberal claims of political and social citizenship rights and garnered both international and domestic pressure for social change. The Australian state responded with a series of so-called multicultural policies that sought to reform the publicly funded mainstream services for minorities in Australia, including immigrant groups from Europe, Asia, and the Pacific Islands, as well as Aborigines. Appealing to the liberal discourse of full citizenship rights during this period brought increased access for Aboriginal people to social services, education, and health care as both clients and state employees.

Many Aboriginal activists were critical of these policies, arguing that they did not go far enough to address economic, cultural, and geographic (i.e., urban/rural) factors which circumscribed access and felt determination for Aboriginal people. These policies failed to confront the effects of a long history of government interference in the lives of Aboriginal people (see Cowlishaw and Morris 1997), and the distrust of Australian bureaucracies. Thus, many Aboriginal people were distrustful of the Australian state bureaucracy. Aboriginal community-controlled health services were initially funded during the 1970s as a temporary strategy; however, the long-term goal was to integrate Aboriginal people into publicly funded mainstream health services. These policies also failed to adjudicate between the conflicting models of curative Western biomedicine and traditional cultural holistic conceptualizations of health, nor did they adequately address the needs of Aboriginal people because of institutionalized racism and culturally inappropriate services. According to Stephen Kunitz and Maggie Brady, the assimilationist thrust of federal policy and budget allocation has been countered by "Aboriginal health activists who asserted that the community-controlled services were the only means by which to bring about long term health improvements" (1995, 554).

In addition to processes of racialization manifest in Australian state policies and practices, there are strong gendered patterns embedded in policy design and implementation. Pettman points out that Aboriginal men have stronger representation within government structures than do Aboriginal women, and Aboriginal women are over-represented as recipients of welfare services (1992). Gendered processes both internal and external to Aboriginal communities also lead women into community caretaking positions to a greater extent than Aboriginal men. According to Diane Bell, Aboriginal women are called on to resolve conflicts between indigenous groups and to act as a bridge between the white Australian and Aboriginal cultures (1993, 153; also see Collman 1988). Aboriginal women are described as "the ritual nurturers of relationships" and are therefore responsible for promoting the "harmony, happiness and thus health" of their communities (Bell 1993, 146).[6] As a consequence, Aboriginal women predominate as social and health service providers for their communities (Collman 1988). With the expansion of state support for Aboriginal community health and welfare services, Aboriginal women have gained a point of entry into the state. The *difference* of a gendered Aboriginal cultural identity became a form of cultural capital under the auspices of self-determination (also see Smith 1999). Analysis of Aboriginal women's paid work for the state provides an important context for elaborating the hidden activist contributions of these women to the Aboriginal rights movement and to the development of a multiracial feminist analysis of women's community work.

Community Workers' Relationship to Women's Movements and Feminism

The health care and community workers interviewed held diverse views about the women's movements in their countries and about feminism more generally. Most of the Aboriginal women did not find their concerns addressed by the dominant women's movement organizations and, furthermore, did not see a need for organizing separately as women. In contrast, the Puerto Rican and African American community workers emphasized how they contributed to woman-centered and feminist organizations organized by women of color during the 1970s and 1980s.[7] Many women-specific and feminist organizations were organized by Puerto Rican and African American women around the same time that white and middle-class organizations associated with the U.S. women's movement were established.

The U.S. community workers extolled the role women played in fighting for justice and equality for their communities. They also spoke out against the sexism they found in the civil rights movement organizations. Due to the centrality of race and class in their analyses, their women-centered organizing strategies and political analyses differed from what they saw as the approach and agenda of the dominant white women's movements. A result of the effective critiques developed by women of color and working-class women, contemporary women's movement and civil rights organizations have broadened their political agendas to incorporate intersectional analyses and political strategies.

The Aboriginal women rarely discussed experiences of sexism. Instead, they emphasized their experiences living with and opposing racism and cultural discrimination and detailed how they organized around issues pertinent to Aboriginal people in general, not just Aboriginal women. Australian scholars Diane Bell (1993), Meredith Burgmann (1984), and Aboriginal lawyer Pat O'Shane (1976) write of the mistrust and skepticism Aboriginal women display toward the women's movement in Australia. They argue that the Australian women's movement has had little bearing on the concerns of Aboriginal women, such as land rights, indigenous self-determination, poverty, and racism. The Aboriginal health care workers who expressed an opinion about the women's movement in Australia were critical of what they defined as a *white* women's movement. Aboriginal women's distrust of feminism and their alienation from the women's movement derives from the racism of Anglo-feminists as well as a lack of understanding of the different gender dynamics in Aboriginal communities as a result of colonialism (Bell 1993; Burgmann 1984). Several women interviewed in our study evoked a historical image of a "strong" Aboriginal woman who wielded her own power alongside Aboriginal men until colonial racialized gender relations eroded that place by privileging Aboriginal men over Aboriginal women. As Aboriginal community worker Jane Wallace explains:

> Still to be nurturers, to be gatherers, to be that strong woman that we were in traditional times, men had the power but so did women. Western people still look at it and they still don't understand our culture; they still think just because we followed behind the men, that we were treated like slaves—just because we carried water containers on our heads and our kids on our hips. We weren't treated that way at all in traditional times. We were treated better than we are today. I want to say: "Hey, just because we've been modernized, it doesn't mean that these men can put us down."

The Aboriginal health care workers resisted identifying as feminists, but most noted the important efforts of Aboriginal women and women's groups in Aboriginal rights struggles. While Aboriginal women have been less involved in conventional political action than Aboriginal men, during the 1980s and 1990s, Aboriginal women from diverse backgrounds have organized at the state and national levels and have joined other indigenous women as co-organizers and participants in international conferences (see Eisenstein 1996; Bell 1993; Pettman 1992).

Only some of the Aboriginal women were employed in positions that dealt with the traditionally separate cultural sphere "women's business" (i.e., childbirth, pediatrics, and women's sexual health). These women acted as liaisons between the bureaucratic concerns of the Western medical establishment and the cultural concerns of traditional Aboriginal women using medical services. In this sense, their goals were similar to many of the concerns articulated by the Australian women's movement (Broom 1991). The Aboriginal community workers dealing with "women's business"—in particular, those confronting domestic violence in their own lives and in the lives of their *clients*—also spoke about sexism within the Aboriginal community and noted the predominance of Aboriginal men in leadership positions, particularly in ATSIC. However, they attributed these forms of male dominance to the negative influence of the Anglo culture and not to intrinsic sexism in Aboriginal culture. The idea that colonial race relations subordinated Aboriginal men to Anglo-Australian men while privileging them over Aboriginal women resembles other critiques of the Western feminisms homogenous conceptualization of patriarchy (Grewal and Kaplan 1994). Their approach to community work and health care emphasized the diversity of issues facing Aboriginal people. Their situated knowledge of the impact of colonialism on the social problems and health of the community, coupled with the legitimacy they were granted as Aboriginals, contributed to their effectiveness as community workers. The U.S. community workers also stressed the dynamic relationship between their social identity as community members and their effectiveness as service providers and advocates. More importantly for this analysis, both groups of women understood their positions within the state as an opportunity to expand citizenship rights and social services for their communities.

Low-income women of color and indigenous women activists offer a political vision that emphasizes a collective model of organizing and a social democratic view of citizenship. In their study of Latina and American Indian women environmental activists, Diane-Michele Prindevill and John G. Bretting describe the women's "indigenous feminist" approach as communitarian since "[t]heir support of equality and access to opportunities encompasses all members of the community, not just women" (1998, 50). Like the community workers and health care workers we interviewed, the indigenous feminist environmental activists were committed to participatory democracy and sought community empowerment rather than individual advancement.[8]

Hester Eisenstein's analysis of Australian *femocrats* demonstrates how the demands of the women's movement were carried into the state by feminists turned bureaucrats (1996).[9] Eisenstein explains that the term *femocrats* was coined "when members of the Australian women's movement first developed the strategy of entering federal and state bureaucracies as a way of bringing feminist concerns onto the public policy arena" (67). She argues that femocrats helped place feminist issues on the political agenda and established "a range of feminist institutions funded by governments" in Australia during the 1970s and 1980s—the period she analyzes (70). Such feminist interventions are not a natural outgrowth of women's social location as employees of the state, nor are they limited to high-level administrators or public officials as this comparative analysis demonstrates. Eisenstein's analysis of the Australian femocrats illustrates how their social location as middle-class Anglo-Australians dictated their liberal concerns with equal opportunity and their narrow focus on sexism as the primary concern confronting all women.

In response to the concerns expressed by women of color and Aboriginal women and in the context of a growing critique of earlier feminist constructions that essentialized women, multiracial and multicultural organizing projects are appearing in both the United States and Australia, especially in struggles to fight violence against women. In the United States, women of color and white women activists have joined forces to fight for improved health care in poor communities, especially in early diagnosis and treatment of breast cancer and AIDS prevention. In Australia, some Anglo-Australian women have joined to support Aboriginal women in their struggle for land rights and more recently in confronting violence against women in indigenous communities. However, divisions among Anglo and Aboriginal women persist. For example, according to the Aboriginal women interviewed, little coalition building occurred between femocrats and Aboriginal women whose concerns were rarely incorporated into the state-sponsored women's programs.

Challenging the State from Within

The Puerto Rican, African American, and Aboriginal women interviewed all stressed their motivations for community work and health care as stemming from a commitment to work on behalf of their families and communities. Their biographical accounts indicated different pathways into their present work positions: through informal community work, through education in nursing or social work, or through the civil rights or indigenous rights movements. However, despite different trajectories, almost all the women interviewed described their paid work as a natural progression from the roles in informal care taking and political work and their social identities as members of their communities. Illustrating one trajectory from informal to formal community work, Tanya MacHale, coordinator of an Aboriginal family service organization, explained:

> Actually, I was probably doing welfare work before I started getting paid for it. There were a few of us who were friends, and the place I came from there were heaps of relatives and we all had little problems like with people drinking around us, like really drinking excessively, and we used to meet regularly as family and friends to just talk about issues and what sort of things we did and how we were going to try and solve things. So we'd been doing that for a lot of years and eventually a job came around and we thought well, why not get paid for it?

For the African American women, the church provided a significant context through which they first began informal community work. Josephine Card of East Harlem described how her "whole family ... were all in some part of [the Baptist] church" and believed that "the church was a catalyst for a lot of the things I do now." Her parents used to take her and her five siblings to church each week and then they would all go to the hospital to visit patients. She connected her church work and her community work because, she explained, "It was through the church that I understood the importance of working with people.... And if you have this talent, or this skill, or information, then you share it. And that's basically what it's all about."

State-sponsored community work involves negotiating between accountability to one's communities and accountability to managerial practices within the bureaucracy. As minorities in white-dominated institutions, the community workers also encountered racist attitudes and policies. Workers whose employment became increasingly bureaucratic and therefore further from direct community engagement were sometimes considered *sell-outs* by others in their communities. However racialized as members of a minority group, the community workers brought to their work a concern with gaining for their communities the rights accorded to all citizens in their countries.

The Aboriginal women reported "living in two worlds," one characterized by their work as a professional health care or community service provider and the other characterized by their membership in the Aboriginal community. State funding of Aboriginal units within mainstream services continues at the same time that Aboriginal-controlled organizations attempt to receive direct funding from the federal government via ATSIC. The Aboriginal women who were employed within the Aboriginal units of these mainstream organizations became entangled in the discourse and practice of mainstreaming while also disparagingly being referred to as *Abocrats* by some who worked in community-controlled organizations. As a consequence, the six indigenous women employed in the mainstream health care organizations as coordinators of Aboriginal programs or liaisons described a different set of challenges than those reported by the indigenous women in Aboriginal organizations with more direct community contact. This mirrors the accounts given by the

African American and Puerto Rican community workers. Workers who moved from community-based service delivery and advocacy positions to citywide administrative positions were especially frustrated by the demands of organizational maintenance and bureaucratic requirements that circumscribed their political activism. They also reported focusing on fighting the institutionalized racism within their workplaces rather than continuing the more difficult struggle against racism and poverty in their communities.

How women develop feminist and antiracist political analyses that differ from dominant perspectives to form what has been termed *oppositional consciousness* is a central question raised in literature on women's political activism, especially as articulated by Third-World feminists. The *oppositional consciousness* they developed by living in two worlds allowed the Abocrats to challenge fundamentally racist policies within the institutions in which they worked. Samantha Williams, coordinator of the Aboriginal health unit within the regional health care system, describes the dynamic:

> I had a meeting yesterday, I was with the general managers of the sectors, and we were talking about mainstream service positions, etc. And this person said: "It's about mainstream service and getting people into mainstream service." And I said: "Yes, providing it's appropriate for the person. You cannot again generalize that what's going to be right for the mob here in X is going to be right for the mob [over there] and if you're going to generically say across the board 'it's about getting people into the mainstream,' what you're saying to me is that you're going to enforce a policy of assimilation." And he said: "I get your point now." I said: "That's exactly what you're saying, 'mainstream them, make them all the same but we'll be sensitive to them.'" I said: "No, that's not good enough, sorry." But I've really got to be very sensitive and aware, because this goes on all the time. This is part of this institutional racism. That's part of the policy. It's part of the practice that you do day in and day out. And people do that and don't realize they're doing it.

Identifying the complexity of the issues facing Aboriginal health care provision and challenging the homogenizing tendency in racist policies were key objectives for Samantha Williams and other Aboriginal bureaucrats in these institutions. They worked to make visible the attitudes of non-Aboriginal bureaucrats who subscribed to the dominant ideologies of mainstreaming and assimilation that may have remained hidden without an Aboriginal presence and situated critique.

The Aboriginal women interviewed also expressed their frustration about the limited funding available for creating programs that would enhance community access to resources. Although the regional health service had implemented plans to increase the number of identified Aboriginal positions, that had yet to happen at the time of the interviews, and some of the women complained of the difficulty, if not impossibility, of carrying out effective programs single-handed and with limited resources. One woman, who was head of a new Aboriginal adolescent mental health unit, expressed her frustration and fears that the program had been set up to fail. In addition, talks underway between the state-funded area health service and the local, federally-funded Aboriginal medical service to share resources may indicate an attempt to mainstream community-controlled organizations.

With the withdrawal of funds for community action and social services beginning in the early 1970s in the United States and the increase in unemployment, homelessness, and poverty in many of the neighborhoods targeted for the War on Poverty, the community workers interviewed by Naples faced pressure to expand their social service functions. Many felt they had to limit the time they spent as advocates and political activists as well as place limits on the type of support they could provide community members living in poverty. Philadelphia community worker, Alice Porter pointed out that the increased economic needs and decreased supports for the poor further limited the type of activities she could perform. Interviewed in 1995, Porter described how, because of the increased poverty in her community and diminished resources available to deal with the related problems, she found it increasingly difficult to respond effectively to problems her neighbors faced.

> When I first started with the agency, if I couldn't persuade the landlord to repair a home, I would relocate [the family] to public housing. There was plenty of it. Now, there's a waiting list of three years and you are reluctant to tell a tenant to not pay the rent, because if the landlord boards the house up, they're going to be street people. So that has changed a lot. . . . Housing is worse. Employment is worse.

While the community workers criticized the limitations placed on participation of the poor, most also believed the programs contributed positively to the low-income communities and continued to provide vital services and advocacy.

Kunitz and Brady assert that direct federal funding of community organizations is the most effective way to forward Aboriginal self-determination efforts and to improve Aboriginal health (1995). However, some Aboriginal health care workers fear that the partnership between the state-funded regional health service and the ATSIC-funded Aboriginal medical service may result in decreased funding for community-based and community-controlled services. The fate of the CAPs in Philadelphia and New York as locations for community empowerment and alternatives to insensitive welfare state bureaucracies has already been decided. By 1971, the community action and participatory emphases of the initial legislation had eroded under growing city government officials' control of the program design and implementation. The U.S. community workers of color also understood the potential co-optation they faced as employees of the state and discussed creative ways they could resist this. Aboriginal women occupying positions in the state-funded bureaucratic organizations also discussed various strategies of resistance. Their personal experiences, social identities, and commitment to support the Aboriginal community provided the grounds from which the Aboriginal women interviewed contested dominant ideologies such as assimilation and tokenism.

Since they situated their work within the broader struggle for indigenous rights, which, in turn, is part of an international movement, the continuity of Aboriginal community-based programs seems more secure than were the participatory CAPs in the United States. However, employment in state-sponsored institutions also constrained the Aboriginal women's political activism in significant ways that deserve fuller exploration in the context of the indigenous rights movement in Australia.

In both the United States and Australia, the community-based programs provided new resources and employment opportunities to low-income, non-white, or Aboriginal communities, thus expanding their social citizenship. The state-sponsored programs also legitimated these workers' input into the policy process, at least at the local, community level that, in turn, enhanced their political citizenship. Many of the women hired by these state-sponsored programs were already working as unpaid caretakers and community leaders within their neighborhoods. They gained increased visibility and legitimacy as well as resources to enhance their community activism and help empower other community members. They also used these positions to contest racist institutional policies and practices. Like the U.S. community workers, the Aboriginal health care workers emphasized that their mission included an engagement with antiracism, both personal and institutional forms, and the promotion of Aboriginal self-determination. Their everyday struggles to enhance the social and political citizenship of their communities and their commitment to participatory democratic practices offer valuable lessons for those of us interested in working towards a multicultural, multiracial feminist-social-democratic praxis.

Conclusion

Feminist state scholars often privilege an individualist construction of citizenship and fail to incorporate the more collectivist vision offered by low-income women of color and indigenous women activists. The

Aboriginal health care workers and the U.S. community workers were drawn to their work as an extension of their commitment to serve their indigenous communities, further social justice, and oppose institutional racism. The community workers of color in the United States and the Australian Aboriginal health care workers explained their commitment as a logical response to inequality, injustice, and a concern for their communities. Many of the community and health care workers also challenged manifestations of inequality and discrimination in the state-funded programs in which they worked. Most Aboriginal health care workers interviewed saw their work in dialogue with the efforts of a broad-based indigenous rights movement.

Recent scholarship contests historical accounts of the civil rights and women's movements that neglect women of color's central role (see, e.g., Robnett 1997). Women's community activism is an essential component of the struggle for social justice. For example, the African American women used their networking skills and central role in their communities to promote and sustain the civil rights movement. Aboriginal women defined the struggle for equitable access to biomedical services and their attempt to provide these services in a culturally sensitive way as linked to the fight for indigenous rights. This commitment to social change was often expressed as a source of empowerment for these women as they struggled within a bureaucracy that supports embedded institutionalized forms of racism, and with the larger social structure of an often hostile, racist society.

While participation in health care and state-sponsored community work became an opportunity for Aboriginal women and U.S. women of color to challenge and transform discriminatory services, their power to achieve more systematic progressive change was limited. Located in community-based programs or in mid-level positions within government bureaucracies, these community and health care workers were rarely able to influence government policy or resource allocation beyond their local community. Consequently, women from low-income African American, Puerto Rican, and Aboriginal communities have less power to achieve the kind of social and political rights they seek than femocrats or others located in strategic decision-making positions within the state. However, despite the contradictions of state employment, community-based service and advocacy provide sites for articulation among civil rights, indigenous rights movement goals, and the state apparatus.

The Aboriginal women interviewed reported little contact with femocrats and complained that their concerns were not reflected in state-sponsored women's programs. According to Eisenstein, femocrats have made a progressive difference in policy design and implementation in Australia (1995). However, in a more recent assessment, Marian Sawer points out that women's ministries "became captured by the bureaucracy over time. [They] became more a public relations exercise than a longitudinal analysis of progress in improving gender equity in design and delivery of mainstream policy and programs" (1999, 93). Collaboration between femocrats and Aboriginal women activists and Abocrats might help to curtail the depoliticization of women's ministries and to diversify women's policy design and delivery.

The African American, Puerto Rican, and Aboriginal women all stressed the value of community-based organizations for providing an institutional base from which indigenous community workers like themselves could develop their skills and create alternative approaches that more directly meet their community's needs. In his analysis of the Civil Rights Movement in the U.S., Aldon Morris (1984) stressed the important role of *local movement centers*. These centers helped promote, sustain, and coordinate civil rights movement activities as well as provide training for indigenous and outside organizers. Local movement centers can function as "visible organizational structures and a site for the development of tactics that can be adopted by other discontented groups" (286). While workers in state-sponsored community-based programs do not have the autonomy enjoyed by activists in the movement centers, the women we interviewed strove to insert movement goals into state policy design and implementation. In this way, the state can be viewed as a resource for movement mobilization through its incorporation of movement participants in community-based and community-controlled programs and organizations.

Many critics argue that the advance of global economic restructuring and a top-down, international, political agenda undermine the effectiveness of local resistance strategies. However, as Vandana Shiva points out, the politics of "localization" provides "the countervailing citizens' agenda for protecting the environment and people's survival and people's livelihood" (1997, 43). It involves "subjecting the logic of globalization to the test of sustainability, democracy and justice" and "reclaiming the state to protect people's interest" (Shiva 1997, 43). In the light of global economic and political restructuring, the feminist praxis we envision also incorporates a transnational perspective, one that acknowledges the many dimensions of power and inequalities of access and resources within and across different nation-states. Many of the lessons we have learned through more nationally defined feminist politics will continue to serve us as we expand the horizons of feminist organizing. These lessons include how to negotiate the dilemmas of organizing across class, race-ethnicity, culture, sexualities, space, and religious and political perspectives; how to sustain feminist activist engagement over time; how to build and mobilize effective coalitions; how to create democratic structures at all levels of organization; and how to negotiate the contradictions of the state and expand the social and political citizenship rights of all women.

Notes

Earlier versions of this article were presented at the conference on Women Transforming the Public, University of California, Santa Barbara, April 23–25, 1999, and the conference on Carework: Research, Theory, and Advocacy, in the session on Conceptualizing Care/Theorizing Care, Howard University, Washington, DC, August 11, 2000.

1. Of all seventeen industries specified in employment statistics, health and community services employ the largest number of Aboriginal women while government administration and defense industries employ the largest number of Aboriginal men. Of all employed Aboriginals, 25 percent of Aboriginal women and 15 percent of Aboriginal men are employed in health and community services. While only 2.2 percent of people employed in health and community services are Aboriginals, indigenous people make up only 1.5 percent of the total population in Australia. Of all indigenous persons employed in health and community services (16, 124), 57 percent, or 9,251 are women; 6,873 are men. As a percentage of the total number of people employed in health and community services, Aboriginal women form 1.3 percent, and Aboriginal men comprise 0.9 percent of this work force (Australian Bureau of Statistics 1998).

2. For example, a National Aboriginal Health Strategy policy recommended the involvement of Aboriginal people in health service provision.

3. All names of the community workers and health care workers in both the United States and Australia are pseudonyms. Quotations in this article without attribution are from this combined field research.

4. Thomas Humphrey Marshall differentiated between civil, political, and social citizenship rights (1964). Civil citizenship included "such basic issues as the freedom of speech, rights to a fair trial and equal access to the legal system" (Turner 1992, 35). Political citizenship is defined as the right to participate in the political process through voting and other political acts such as serving on juries. Social citizenship refers to access to resources like welfare and health care which enable one to sustain a household and "to live the life of a civilized being according to the standards prevailing in the society" (Marshall qtd. in Orloff 1993, 306). For the most part, however, access to social resources presumes some form of political citizenship (see Naples 1998b; Sarvast 1997).

5. Until the latter part of the twentieth century, Australian law denied Aboriginal people "the right to vote, the right to move as one wishes, the right to

marry whom one pleases and the right to drink intoxicating beverages" (Collman 1988, 13).

6. In her study of the Kaytej Aboriginals in Central Australia, Diane Bell points out that their concept of health is "one which entails the maintenance of harmonic relations between people and place" (1993, 146).

7. For example, Puerto Rican community activists discussed participating in the National Conference of Puerto Rican Women, the National Council of Puerto Rican Women, the National Puerto Rican Women's Caucus, and the National Latina Caucus, among other organizations and networks.

8. An emphasis on collective empowerment is also evident in accounts of American Indian women's activism in the United States (see Jaimes 1997).

9. In 1974, the Royal Commission on Australian Government Administration, responding to the recommendations made by the Women's Electoral Lobby, set up a web of women's ministries within the central policy arm of the government. The goal of "women's policy machinery" was to monitor government "policy at the point of initiation" (Sawer 1999, 91; also see Yeatman 1990).

References

Abramovitz, Mimi. 1988. *Regulating the Lives of Women: Social Welfare Policy from Colonial Times to the Present.* Boston: South End Press.

Amott, Teresa L., and Julie A. Matthaei. 1991. *Race, Gender & Work: A Multicultural Economic History of Women in the United States.* Boston: South End Press.

Australian Bureau of Statistics. 1998. "Indigenous Profile, 1996 Census of Population and Housing, Commonwealth of Australia." Canberra, Australia: Australian Bureau of Statistics.

Bell, Diane. 1993. *Daughters of the Dreaming.* Minneapolis: University of Minnesota Press.

Boris, Eileen. 1995. "The Racialized Gendered State: Constructions of Citizenship in the United States." *Social Politics* 2(2):160–80.

Broom, Dorothy. 1991. *Damned If We Do: Contradictions in Women's Health Care.* NWS, Australia: Allen & Unwin.

Burgmann, Meredith. 1984. "Black Sisterhood: The Situation of Urban Aboriginal Women and Their Relationship to the White Women's Movement." In *Australian Studies: Australian Women and the Political System,* ed. Marian Simms, 20–47. Melbourne, Australia: Longman Cheshire.

Clarence, Emma. 1999. "Citizenship and Identity: The Case of Australia." In *Practising Identities: Power and Resistance,* eds. Sasha Roseneil and Julie Seymour, 199–222. New York: St. Martin's Press.

Cohen, Cathy, Kathleen Jones, and Joan Tronto, eds. 1997. *Women Transforming Politics: An Alternative Reader.* New York: New York University Press.

Collman, Jeff. 1988. *Fringe-Dwellers and Welfare: The Aboriginal Response to Bureaucracy.* St. Lucia, Australia: University of Queensland Press.

Cowlishaw, Gillian, and Barry Morris, eds. 1997. *Race Matters: Indigenous Australians and "Our" Society.* Canberra, Australia: Australian National University Press.

Dietz, Mary. 1992. "Context Is All: Feminism and Theories of Citizenship." In *Dimensions of Radical Democracy,* ed. Chantal Mouffe, 63–85. London: Verso.

Dobson, Marnie. 1999. "Living in Two Worlds: Aboriginal Women's Community Work within the Australian Health Care System." Masters Thesis, University of California, Irvine.

Eisenstein, Hester. 1996. *Inside Agitators: Australian Femocrats and the State.* Philadelphia: Temple University Press.

———. 1995. "The Australian Femocratic Experiment: A Feminist Case for Bureaucracy." In *Feminist Organizations,* eds. Myra Marx Ferree and Patricia Yancey Martin, 69–83. Philadelphia: Temple University Press.

Ferree, Myra Marx, and Patricia Yancey Martin, eds. 1995. *Feminist Organizations.* Philadelphia: Temple University Press.

Giddings, Paula. 1984. *When and Where I Enter: The Impact of Black Women on Race and Sex in America.* New York: William Morrow & Co.

Glenn, Evelyn Nakano, Grace Chang, and Linda Rennie Forcey, eds. 1994. *Mothering: Ideology, Experience, and Agency.* New York: Routledge.

Gluck, Sherna Berger, with Maylei Blackwell, Sharon Cotrell, and Karen Harper. 1998. "Whose Feminism, Whose History? Reflections on Excavating the History of (the) U.S. Women's Movement(s)." In *Community-Activism and Feminist Politics Organizing Across Race Class and Gender,* ed. Nancy A. Naples, 31–56. New York: Routledge.

Green, Rayna. 1990. "American Indian Women: Diverse Leadership for Social Change." In *Bridges of Power: Women's Multicultural Alliances,* eds. Lisa Albrecht and Rose M. Brewer, 61–73. Philadelphia: New Society Publishers.

Grewal, Inderpal, and Caren Kaplan, eds. 1994. *Scattered Hegemonies.* Minneapolis: University of Minnesota Press.

Gupta, Akhil, and James Ferguson. 1992. "Beyond 'Culture': Space, Identity, and the Politics of Difference." *Cultural Anthropology* 7(1):6–23.

Hunter, Ernest. 1993. *Aboriginal Health and History: The Australian Women's Movement 1950s–1990s.* NSW, Australia: Allen & Unwin.

Hurtado, Aida. 1999. *The Color of Privilege: Three Blasphemies on Race and Feminism.* Ann Arbor: University of Michigan Press.

Jaimes, Guerrero M. A. 1997. "Exemplars of Indigenism: Native North American Women for De/Colonization and Liberation." In *Women Transforming Politics: An Alternative Reader,* eds. Cathy Cohen, Kathleen Jones, and Joan Tronto, 205–22. New York: New York University Press.

Kunitz, Stephen J., and Maggie Brady. 1995. "Health Care Policy for Aboriginal Australians: The Relevance of the American Indian Experience." *Australian Journal of Public Health* 19(6):549–58.

Marris, Peter, and Martin Rein, eds. 1972. *Dilemmas of Social Reform: Poverty and Community Action in the United States.* London: Routledge and Kegan Paul.

Marshall, Thomas Humphrey. 1964. *Class. Citizenship, and Social Development.* Garden City, NJ: Doubleday.

Morris, Aldon D. 1984. *The Origins of the Civil Rights Movement: Black Communities Organizing for Change.* New York: The Free Press.
Mouffe, Chantal, ed. 1992. *Dimensions of Radical Democracy.* London: Verso.
Naples, Nancy A. 1998a. *Grassroots Warriors: Activist Mothering. Community Work and the War on Poverty.* New York: Routledge.
———. 1998b. "Toward a Multiracial, Feminist Social-Democratic Praxis: Lessons from Grassroots Warriors in the U.S. War on Poverty." *Social Politics* 5(3):286–313.
O'Shane, Pat. 1976. "Is There any Relevance in the Women's Movement for Aboriginal Women?" *Refractory Girl*, 12 September:31–4.
Pearl, Arthur, and Frank Riessman. 1965. *New Careers for the Poor: The Nonprofessional in Human Service.* New York: The Free Press.
Pettman, Jan. 1992. *Living in the Margins: Racism, Sexism and Feminism in Australia.* North Sydney, Australia: Allen & Unwin.
Prindeville, Diane-Michele, and John G. Bretting. 1998. "Indigenous Women Activists and Political Participation: The Case of Environmental Justice." *Women & Politics* 19(1):39–58.
Prokhovnik, Raia. 1998. "Public and Private Citizenship: From Gender Invisibility to Feminist Inclusiveness." *Feminist Review* 60:84–104.
Quadagno, Jill. 1994. *The Color of Welfare: How Racism Undermined the War on Poverty.* New York: Oxford Books.
Rodriquez, Clara E. 1991. *Puerto Ricans: Born in the U.S.A.* Boston: Unwin Hyman.
Robnett, Belinda. 1997. *How Long? How Long?: African-American Women in the Struggle for Civil Rights.* New York: Oxford University Press.
Roseneil, Sasha, and Julie Seymour, eds. *Practising Identities: Power and Resistance.* New York: St. Martin's Press.
Rowley, Charles Dunford. 1970. *The Destruction on Aboriginal Society: Aboriginal Policy and Practice—Volume I.* Canberra, Australia: Australian National University Press.
Saggers, Sherry, and Dennis Gray. 1991. *Aboriginal Health and Society: The Traditional and Contemporary Aboriginal Struggle for Better Health.* Sydney, Australia: Allen & Unwin.
Sandoval, Chela. 1991. "U.S. Third World Feminism: The Theory and Method of Oppositional Consciousness in the Postmodern World." *Genders* 10:1–24.
Sarvasy, Wendy. 1997. "Social Citizenship from a Feminist Perspective." *Hypatia*: Special Issue on Citizenship 12(4):54–73.
Sawer, Marian. 1999. "Women's Ministries: An Australian Perspective." *Feminist Review* 63(Autumn):91–107.
Sawer, Marion. 1990. *Sisters in Suits: Women and Public Policy in Australia.* Sydney, Australia: Allen and Unwin.
Shiva, Vandana. 1997. "Democracy in the Age of Globalization." In *Womens, Empowerment and Political Participation*, ed. Veena Poonacha Mumbai, 34–45. India: Reasearch Centre for Women's Studies, S.N.D.T. Women's University.
Simms, M., ed. 1984. *Australian Studies: Australian Women and the Political System.* Melbourne, Australia: Longman Cheshire.
Smith, Dorothy E. 1987. *The Everyday World as Problematic: A Feminist Sociology.* Toronto, Canada: University of Toronto Press.

Smith, Linda Tuhiwai. 1999. *Decolonizing Methodologies: Research and Indigenous Peoples.* London: Zed Books.

Turner, Bryan. 1992. "Outline of a Theory of Citizenship." In *Dimensions of Radical Democracy,* ed. Chantal Mouffe, 33–62. London: Verso.

Watson, Sophia. 1990. *Playing the State: Australian Feminist Interventions.* London: Verso.

Yeatman, Anna. 1990. *Bureaucrats, Technocrats. Femocrats: Essays on the Contemporary Australian State.* Sydney, Australia: Allen and Unwin.

Zinn, Maxine Baca, and Bonnie Thornton Dill. 1996. "Theorizing Difference from Multiracial Feminism." *Feminist Studies* 22(2):321–31.

CHAPTER ELEVEN

Lesbians in Academia

ESTHER D. ROTHBLUM

> But for job security
> I must pretend to be
> One of the enemy
> —R. Romanovsky and P. Phillips

In the Closet or Out

Being closeted or open about one's sexual orientation is a complex issue and one that may or may not be in one's control. Academic settings differ with regard to their level of heterosexism, and consequently lesbian faculty differ in how open they are about their sexual orientation. On the one hand, female faculty who are not legally married may be suspected of being lesbians even if they are heterosexual. On the other hand, many lesbian faculty who are fairly out still find themselves in situations in which they are presumed to be heterosexual. Some lesbian faculty are hired when heterosexual and come out later.

There are several advantages to being out of the closet. Lesbians who are out as faculty members will not have to pretend to be heterosexual. They can answer openly when asked about their personal lives, including their sexual lives. As professionals, they serve as role models for gay and lesbian as well as heterosexual students and colleagues.

As one graduate student stated,

> I couldn't help thinking about the impact on students of knowing a faculty member is gay or lesbian but also knowing it is not okay to talk about it—that the man/woman is not "out." Raises ambivalent feelings—wanting to respect the personal choice but also feeling very much that it symbolizes a not so positive future for the student. Makes it hard to feel like there's a place for us when we finish graduate school.

Openly lesbian faculty will also find it easier to connect with other lesbians and gay men in the academic community.

There can also be disadvantages to being out, however. Many people have biased attitudes toward or are misinformed about lesbians. As J. B. Rohrbaugh has stated, "It is no longer fashionable to persecute lesbians, at least not in liberal academic communities. Despite this 'instant' cure, however, things have not changed dramatically. Some of our colleagues now profess to 'know a nice lesbian' or, even more likely, 'a nice gay

---

Originally published in the *National Women's Studies Association Journal*, 1995 (7.1).

couple.' This does not prevent them from discriminating against us, however" (115).

In the face of lingering discrimination against lesbians in academia, being closeted is one way to avoid contending directly with heterosexism. Sometimes lesbians are closeted, yet people seem to know about their sexual orientation anyway. For example, I was told of two lesbian faculty members, in separate departments at the same college, who have been lovers for more than twenty years. They live together, come to college social functions together, and collaborate on research and writing. However, they have never come out to anyone on campus. No one had ever heard either of them use the word *lesbian* in conversation. In this example, people knew that the two women were lesbians because of their behavior, even though they did not speak about it.

There are varying degrees of being out. At one extreme, no one knows or even guesses that the faculty member in question is a lesbian. At the other extreme, she is known all over campus and in the community as a lesbian. Most faculty are somewhere in between these extremes. They may be out to just a few friends or relatives but not to anyone on campus. They may be out in the campus lesbian and gay community. They may or may not attend lesbian and gay events.

The facts of one's sexual orientation may or may not correspond to what others perceive. Some lesbians are seen to be straight. One faculty woman in my survey had been married for over twenty years. She was currently divorced from her husband and was living with a woman in a lesbian relationship. She and her lover did not attend campus gay or lesbian events and were out only to a few friends. No one on campus knew she was a lesbian. Sometimes, by contrast, straight women are viewed as being lesbians. A faculty woman at a state university was a nun in a religious order. She decided to inform only the colleagues in her department about her religious affiliation. Several colleagues in other departments assumed that she was a lesbian because she was not in a relationship with a man.

For decades, the lesbian and gay male communities have protected the confidentiality of their members. Coming out to other lesbians and gay men, even if these are other faculty, students, or even complete strangers, has usually not resulted in violation of this confidence. Knowing the risks that disclosure of sexual orientation could mean for people's jobs and lives, lesbians and gay men have kept this information from the heterosexual community. Similarly, many heterosexual women and men are sensitive about keeping their lesbian and gay friends' and colleagues' sexual orientation confidential. Nevertheless, lesbians and gay men in academia have experienced times when heterosexual colleagues have failed to observe the rule of confidentiality. For example, a graduate student stated that, "[when] it became known to a professor of mine that I was a lesbian (not sure exactly how), he let it be known he knew and accepted it, which was nice. However, later that week in a public setting with others around, he specifically asked me what I thought about the gay community in this city compared to another city in which I had lived."

The difficulties related to coming out may be compounded by many factors. Some lesbians may choose to be closeted when newly hired and be more out after some time has gone by or after tenure. Others may become more closeted over time because of changes in their lives, such as the wish to adopt children, a new relationship with a more closeted partner, or reactions to homophobia on campus. Bisexual women[1] may find that they are more accepted than are lesbians and gay men in some situations and less accepted in others. Their level of "acceptability" may also depend on whether they are currently in a relationship with a person of the same or of the opposite gender. Faculty who are hired when heterosexual and who come out later, as well as faculty who are hired when lesbian and who are later in heterosexual relationships, will experience considerable stress with the new role and its concomitant expectations.

Research and Scholarship on Lesbian Issues

Whether to conduct research and scholarship on lesbian issues is the most frequent question asked by lesbian graduate students. There is a common belief that female faculty and graduate students who conduct research on lesbian and gay issues are themselves lesbian. Not all research on lesbian and gay issues is conducted by lesbians and gay men; there are some prominent heterosexual researchers in this field. Nevertheless, people tend to conduct research on topic areas with which they have some personal connection. Thus, this belief has a great deal of truth to it.

The political climate in a research or scholarly institute may or may not be conducive to lesbian and gay research. In very conservative institutions (e.g., religious schools or military academies) women who conduct research on women's issues may be viewed as lesbian, since feminism may be equated with lesbianism. Graduate students (and junior faculty) looking for faculty supervisors may be told not to conduct research on gay or lesbian issues. At other institutions some of the faculty may be supportive of gay and lesbian issues and collaborate on this research. Gay or lesbian graduate students and faculty gravitate to gay-affirmative institutions, so that some universities may become known for having a core of researchers on lesbian and gay issues. For example, the Committee on Lesbian and Gay Concerns of the American Psychological Association (APA) periodically conducts surveys of faculty about research on gay and lesbian issues. The results, which are published by APA, publicize which institutions have gay-affirmative researchers and research supervisors.

Conducting research and scholarship on lesbian issues may present difficulties outside the home institution or department. Journal reviewers and editors may decide that the research is inappropriate for publication, or in many disciplines there may not be journals available that focus on lesbian research and theory. Survey research on lesbians rarely uses a random sample, since so few lesbians are out. Thus, reviewers and tenure committees may criticize such research as biased in its sampling procedure. Lesbian faculty who conduct research in lesbian and gay topic areas may be considered biased, since they are a member of the group they are studying. (This concern is not raised, by contrast, when heterosexual researchers study heterosexual topics such as birth control, abortion, or divorce.)

Closeted graduate students and faculty may fear that doing research on lesbian and gay issues will break their "cover." Graduate students and junior faculty may be concerned that publications and conference presentations on lesbian or gay topics may not be considered serious scholarship or may negatively affect their applications for jobs or their chances for tenure. Senior faculty may have enough publications to their credit to be able to select which ones appear on their vitae, but their reputations as lesbians may precede them nevertheless.

Researchers in the area of lesbian issues have dealt with these concerns in several ways. Some have decided not to conduct research in this area, feeling that they do not want to risk the possible negative effects on their careers. Some scholars conduct research in which lesbian and gay issues are only a small component and are not reflected in their publication titles. Other scholars conduct research and publish on lesbian and gay issues openly. They may be at gay-affirmative institutions or consider this research more important than advancing their careers. Some graduate students and faculty have stated that they list lesbian and gay publications on their vitae because they would not want to be hired by homophobic institutions. Being open about their research is one way to ensure that they are hired by a gay-affirming employer.

These strategies are not unlike those used by researchers on feminist issues a decade ago. At that time many institutions would not hire graduate students and faculty who had conducted research on women's issues. Some faculty chose not to do such research, fearing for their jobs, tenure, or promotion. Others conducted research on women but did not admit this to superiors on their vitae. Still others openly conducted research on women, adding significantly to this body of research. Today many universities encourage research and scholarship on women's issues. In many institutions scholarship on women has become fairly mainstream.

If everyone routinely surveyed lesbians and gay men in their research and analyzed data by sexual orientation, lesbian and gay research would be less stigmatized and would become more commonplace. We would also have a much greater knowledge of issues affecting lesbians and gay men, since this knowledge is currently still very limited. An APA task force completed guidelines for conducting nonheterosexist research (Herek et al. 1991). Faculty at gay-affirmative institutions, those in positions of power and seniority and those who are conducting research even at the risks of their own jobs or tenure, are adding significantly to this body of research. Their efforts will also pave the way for future generations of scholars to conduct lesbian and gay research with greater ease and acceptability.

Teaching and Speaking about Lesbian and Gay Issues

Whether or not lesbians are out in their departments, they may or may not choose to be out in their classes. At large universities, undergraduates may not have close contact with all faculty and will thus be unaware of their professors' sexual orientations. Faculty may choose to be closeted in their classes because they feel that it is not appropriate to discuss their personal life in the classroom. Other faculty come out in their classes because they feel that the nature of the course material (e.g., human sexuality, women in cross-cultural society) is enriched by such disclosure. Still others feel that students need a positive lesbian role model.

Many heterosexual faculty, particularly if they are married, "come out" in their classes. Faculty who wear a wedding ring or who mention their spouse in their lectures are announcing their heterosexuality. In fact, some faculty who caution lesbians not to be "blatant" about their sexual orientation are themselves "blatantly" heterosexual in their own classes.

Faculty who teach women's studies courses are sometimes assumed to be lesbian. For example, one person surveyed related that a student asked his instructor, during a lecture on women's history, whether she was a lesbian. The instructor, a heterosexual woman, responded that his question had nothing to do with the history of women. In another case, a lesbian instructor had never come out to her students. One day, a student in her psychology of women course left a message on her telephone answering machine, accusing her of being a lesbian.

M.A. Barale has described the lesbian instructor as both sexualized and exotic in the eyes of her students. As she states in "The Lesbian Academic" (1988),

> [An instructor's] lesbianism is often perceived as an act of intimate self-disclosure by both lesbian and nonlesbian students. While heterosexual instructors are certainly known as such, although their husbands/lovers and families may be the subject of classroom anecdote, these instructors' sexuality, because it is the norm, tends to fade into the background (185–86).

Lesbian teachers will need to decide on their boundaries of personal self-disclosure in the classroom in case personal questions arise. In contrast, heterosexual faculty are rarely asked, for example, to explain what heterosexual relationships are like.

Lesbian instructors, as well as those who are presumed to be lesbians by their students, may find that they are the subject of curiosity and rumor on campus. Gay and lesbian students will seek them out as role models or come to their offices to discuss personal issues and dilemmas. Some students will feel threatened or alarmed in their presence. A 30-year-old lesbian faculty member was closeted in her classes but came out to gay and lesbian undergraduate students. One day, she was summoned to see the dean of students. The dean had received a call from his former college roommate, now the father of one of the students to whom the faculty member had come out. She was asked to stop "converting" students to become lesbians.

Lesbian faculty, as well as heterosexual faculty who are gay-affirmative, can provide a model for classroom teaching by using gay-affirmative language. Faculty should not indicate by their use of examples that all people are heterosexual. They can use gender-neutral pronouns when referring to lovers or partners (e.g., "the men's partners" rather than "the men's girlfriends" or "the men's wives"). They can avoid humor that assumes heterosexuality. Or they can refer specifically to heterosexuals when the occasion so warrants (e.g., "partners of heterosexual women should use condoms" rather than "women's partners should use condoms").

Whether or not lesbian faculty are out to students, they may be asked by lesbian and gay students to become faculty advisers or sponsors of campus gay organizations. They may be asked by other faculty to give guest lectures on lesbian and gay topics. They may be sought out by graduate students as advisers of theses on lesbian or gay topics. They will need to think about these eventualities and determine what role they want to play in lesbian and gay student-related activities.

One advantage of being a lesbian in most parts of the United States is that the new faculty member will quickly be networked into a supportive lesbian and gay community. In fact, female heterosexual faculty have remarked that they do not have as easy a time becoming acquainted with their peers as do lesbian faculty, who have an immediate connection with other lesbians and gay men on campus. Thus, lesbian instructors may meet faculty from other departments as well as senior professors and administrators, who serve an important mentoring function as academic peers and superiors.

Ironically, some lesbians and gay men may be accused of belonging to a "clique" from which heterosexual faculty are excluded. This illustrates that being lesbian or gay is becoming accepted in some parts of the country, with the result that heterosexuals are beginning to feel left out! Heterosexual graduate and undergraduate students may also feel that lesbian and gay students have something special in common with lesbian and gay faculty, causing them to feel similarly left out. Lesbian faculty may be accused of being anti-men (gay men, by contrast, are rarely accused of being anti-women). Thus, lesbians in academic settings face issues that involve both professional and personal identities. It is important to acknowledge the significant improvements that have occurred on campuses for lesbians while not losing sight of the salience of heterosexism.

Acknowledgment

A version of this chapter was presented at the annual convention of the American Psychological Association (August 1992), and portions of this chapter were excerpted in the newsletter *APA Monitor* (September 1993). The author gratefully acknowledges the comments and feedback of George Albee, Pamela Brand, Phyllis Bronstein, Diane Felicio, Arnold Kahn, Joy Livingston, Beth Mintz, Debra Srebnik, and Jacqueline Weinstock.

Note

1. This article focuses specifically on lesbians; bisexual women may have very different experiences depending on such factors as the degree of acceptance of bisexuality by lesbians or heterosexuals, their marital or relationship status, etc.

References

Barale, M. A. 1988. "The Lesbian Academic: Negotiating New Boundaries." *Women and Therapy* 8(1): 183–194.
Herek, G. M., D. C. Kimmel, H. Amaro, and G. B. Melton. 1991. "Avoiding Heterosexist Bias in Psychological Research." *American Psychologist* 46 (9): 957–963.
Rohrbaugh, J. B. 1989. "Issues Confronting Lesbian Academics." *Career Guide for Women Scholars.* Ed. S. Rose. New York: Springer.
Romanovsky, R., and P. Phillips. 1991. *Be Political, Not Polite.* Recording. Fresh Fruit Records. Santa Fe, NM.

CHAPTER TWELVE

Secretarial Work, Nurturing, and the Ethic of Service

IVY KEN

Women enact many of the nurturing and service activities that sustain nations, organizations, communities, and families. This work, vital as it is, has been routinely ignored, minimized, and even scorned. In the realm of paid work in the United States, occupations that require nurturing tasks, such as social work and teaching, carry a wage penalty, and women disproportionately fill those jobs (England et al. 1994). To a large degree, the aggregate gender makeup of jobs is a result of the myriad of structural forces at work on women's and men's lives, and on the organizations for which they are employed. Yet even within these constraints, it would be very difficult to make someone nurture her coworkers, or to force an employee to have the kind of desire to serve her community that would inspire her to go beyond her assigned work responsibilities. Some women in the labor force make the choice to nurture and serve. In this era of expanded opportunities, why would women participate in such devalued work? If we are to believe geneticists, various religious groups, and the fodder of popular culture, women's propensity to participate in activities of service and assistance is "natural." Women are inherently more responsive and relational, they say (e.g., Mayhall 1998), and may even have a "nurturing gene" (John and Surani 1999).

My study of women who work in secretarial positions adds compelling evidence for the sociological—rather than genetic or natural—character of women's nurturing and service practices. I examine three dimensions of these practices. First, the study confirms that not all women engage in nurturing activities, which, when combined with evidence of men's nurturing and service practices (e.g., Coltrane and Galt 2000), severely undercuts "nature" arguments. Second, I find that the nurturing some secretaries do at work may be a response to the social events of their lives, especially including their parenting experiences. And finally, I reveal that a good portion of what might otherwise be characterized as assisting or nurturing is really what I call an ethic of public service—similar to what our culture tends to admire in doctors, clergy, and some other occupations typically associated with men. By examining the social reasons women engage in nurturing and service activities, and analyzing the race- and class-related opportunity structures under which these activities are enacted, interpreted, and rewarded, I demonstrate that whether or not women have any "natural" or genetic predis-

---

Originally published in the summer 2006 issue of the *NWSA Journal* (18.2).

position to act on their concern for others, those who participate in organizational and community service in their positions as secretaries do so at least in part as a response to the events and constraints they experience in their social lives.

Women, Nurturing, and Public Service in Paid Labor

Nurturing

Caretaking and nurturing are often linked with the responsibilities of motherhood, even in the paid workplace. Scholars have detailed the ways that jobs associated with women incorporate more extensive demands for "emotion work" than jobs affiliated with men (Hochschild 1989; Kilbourne, England, and Beron 1994; England 1992; Steinberg et al. 1986), and found that even women in men-affiliated jobs tend to have disproportionate responsibilities for emotion work (e.g., Benjamin 1997; Clawson 1999). Since motherhood is one of the primary identities that has defined women throughout U.S. history, emotion work has followed women into the paid labor force and, in a "sex-role spillover" (Kelly and Stambaugh 1991), becomes part of their expected workload. Inside paid workplaces this transference is frequently race-specific, as negative motherhood imagery is often associated with women of color and more positive images of motherhood are attached to white women (Collins 1991; Kennelly 1999; Sokoloff 1980).

While scholars have examined the processes through which *employers* conflate women's mothering and paid work roles, they have not fully revealed whether women in the paid labor force engage in a similar association process (Kennelly 1999; Sokoloff 1980). Do women see themselves as mothers in their jobs? Those women who have worked to uncouple the automatic association between "women" and "mothers" may be offended even at the question. Women who have benefited from the individual and collective battles feminists fought to be allowed into the paid work force continue to face the burden of having to demonstrate that they want and deserve to be there. For some women, this has meant downplaying and deprioritizing family responsibilities or forgoing parenthood altogether. These "work-first" postures have made some women critical of feminism for seeming to require them to devalue their families for the supposed glamour of paid careers. Yet other women argue that feminism has provided women with more alternatives. As anyone with a family or a job knows, choices among these alternatives are not simple or easy. The facts remain that most women do not have the option of not working for pay and half (49% in 1994) of pregnancies are unintended (Santelli et al. 2003). In addition, women's opportunities are very clearly patterned by the class and race dynamics that structure all of our life chances. Yet the array of options available to women, however limited, in regard to both paid work and family (and their various combinations) is undeniably wider now than it was 50 years ago. For example, some women forgo having children altogether to concentrate fully on paid work; some forgo paid work to have families; others transition from full-time family responsibilities into full-time paid work, or the reverse; and some somehow manage to nurture both families and careers at the same time.

Women—especially those who cannot opt out of the paid workforce—have yet another option, which has not been given much attention: They can mold their workplace relationships into something akin to families. While scholars have been preoccupied with the conceptual divide between "work and family," some women have quietly ignored that boundary and nestled into a way of life that resists dichotomization. These women treat their colleagues like family and take on mothering tasks that they believe make their work organizations more pleasant. An executive in Arlie Hochschild's study of working parents, for example, strove to achieve a "homey atmosphere" among the people she managed and was well liked at work because of her mother-like qualities (1997, 75). This executive enjoyed her workplace more because of the family-like feeling she was able to create there.

This kind of activity, however well-intentioned, may put women in a particularly precarious position since, within the current economy, the practice of creating "family" at work opens up great opportunities for exploitation. In her classic study, Rosabeth Moss Kanter skillfully elucidated some forms of this phenomenon, in which men in a large corporation were unable to define the secretaries who worked there in ways that did not conjure up motherly and wifely images (1977/1993). Being interpreted in these ways, of course, had very deleterious effects on women's opportunities for advancement within the corporation. Other studies demonstrate similar processes. A recent analysis of workers in a *maquiladora* in Mexico, for example, focused on the "family-like" atmosphere managers and workers established there, and found that the multi-national corporation that owned the plant was able to exploit these workers even more than workers from more rigid, hierarchical plants. Ironically, the workers within the family atmosphere enjoyed their jobs more than other workers, but their personal investment in the company and their desire to prioritize their relationships with each other within the company made them more vulnerable to exploitation and mistreatment (Salzinger 2003). Given the undeniable perils of adopting a mothering persona at work, it is especially interesting to investigate women who voluntarily work to create family-like relationships at their jobs.

It may be the case, however, that some of the women who choose to directly associate, rather than disassociate, motherhood with their paid work are women who have not had children themselves, for reasons of choice or circumstance. Yvonne Vissing studied childless women in a range of jobs, from accounting and advertising to social work and health care (2002). Whether their jobs were specifically constructed around tasks of nurturing or not, many of these women "found a niche in which they could care for their colleagues or clients" (2002, 197). This did not come "naturally" for many of them, especially those who felt unnurtured as children and wanted to learn the skills they were not taught by their parents. Not all women in Vissing's study chose to construct their work lives in a nurturing fashion. Those who did, though, developed powerful rationales for what they came to see as their responsibility to nurture and care. As one woman reasoned, "I thought it was better to go into a career where I could care for hundreds of children instead of just one or two of my own. It seemed my attention would be better spent that way" (2002, 184). A CEO of a multi-million-dollar company explained that she has "tried to make work an extension of home for my employees. I want them to feel supported here and that we can work together like a family. . . . My company is my baby," she said, "and my employees are my family" (2002, 203).

Scholars from a variety of perspectives, including feminism, have attempted to explain nurturing practices like these as manifestations of women's "nature." Essentialists in the radical-cultural feminist vein, for example, argue that women who mothered in early human societies had a deep connection with nature because of their ability to participate in the "natural" processes of birthing and feeding, making mothers indispensable in societies' survival (French 1985). Characteristics like nurturing, these scholars argue, are present-day manifestations of women's "nature" and should be valued as such. Psychoanalytic feminists like Carol Gilligan argue that women and men operate with different moral orientations, with men focused on separation and women focused on connectedness (1982). Women's desire to nurture may be an articulation of what Gilligan would call a mature stage in their moral development in which women are able to take both their own interests (to participate in satisfying work that pays) and the interests of others (who need to be helped) to heart (1982).

Yet Vissing's research reveals two important points. First, not all women engage in nurturing practices. Some do, and other research shows that some men (with and without children) do as well. Second, the desire to nurture can clearly be born out of social experiences. Women in Vissing's study who enjoyed and prioritized tasks of nurturing at work were significantly influenced by their childlessness. Some had wanted children and, in accepting that they would not have any, sought out other ways to mother. Others were not interested in having children of their own but did want the chance to nurture and mother as part of their overall life experiences. And, as noted above, some women in Vissing's study were completely uninterested in participating in nurturing activities at all. Each of these, Vissing found, was at least in part a response to the social events in their lives (2002). When studying nurturing, then, it is as important to understand the social influences that distinguish women from each other as it is to study assumed differences between women and men.

Public Service

We often think of nurturing as an interpersonal activity and use other terms to describe the kind of work that goes into caring for whole communities or populations. Here I focus on activities that I call public service. The wish to be of service to the public is not uncommon for women in the paid work force. Many studies on women in scientific and health-related occupations, for example, "provide supporting evidence that helping others and doing something worthwhile for society serve as powerful motivators to attract women" (Miller et al. 2000, 132). Among students who study science in college, for example, women are more likely than men to be interested in the field because of their desire to help people. Studies like this, however, often focus on women's entry into occupations, like physician, that are primarily filled with men. The studies assume that this ethic of service helps explain why women would take on the challenges involved in entering men-affiliated occupations in which women may face hostility. This kind of trade-off between possible poor treatment and the chance to serve is an example of "compensating differentials" (Filer 1989), or the idea that people give up possible positive aspects associated with work, like high pay or good working conditions, if they value something else even more about that job. Women who value the chance to fulfill their life's mission to serve may, indeed, put themselves in the position of being "tokens" in men-affiliated jobs, which often comes with the possibility of harassing treatment (Kanter 1977/1993).

Men-affiliated occupations are not the only ones to incorporate public service, however. Teaching and social work are women-affiliated occupations with very strong public service components. In their study of teachers, Miech and Elder found that about one-third ranked service first and often solely as their reason for entering the profession, and most at least included service as an important job choice criterion (1996). Yet there is a class barrier to entering this profession since it requires a college degree (which parallels the gender barrier of entering a men-affiliated occupation). The job of secretary is not a prestigious, men-affiliated occupation like politician or physician. It is also not an occupation that requires a college degree in most situations. It does, however, allow many of its occupants the opportunity to engage in public service, even though this aspect of the job is not commonly recognized, appreciated, or compensated.

Scholarship on carework has focused on exactly this kind of occupation—low wage, low prestige, women-affiliated—and argued that such occupations have these characteristics *because* they are filled by women without college educations who value caring, which is otherwise seriously devalued (England 1992; Litt and Zimmerman 2003; Meyer 2000). The market fails to reward the caring women do in their occupations because employers and even clients assume that women perform these activities "out of love" (Folbre 2001), which, employers reason, is difficult and possibly even inappropriate to compensate monetarily (England and Folbre 1999). While the occupation of secretary is sometimes included among occupations that are conceptualized as having a carework component, I argue here that what is often characterized as carework in this job is really public service work, and secretaries are not generally recognized as working in a job with a strong public service component. Further, I argue that women's—specifically secretaries'—public service work, because it is not acknowledged or recognized, fails to command sufficient recompense.

Some types of service in the paid labor force do receive compensation, however meager. Tasks completed in "service sector" jobs, which have come to be a vital foundation for the economy of the United States since the shift in the 1970s from domestic industrialization, are ironically able to be compensated because they have come to be so oppressively routinized (Ritzer 2004). Workers in fast food stores, telephone call centers, and other low-wage service industries are expected to mediate between their organizations and customers through a series of scripts handed down to them from employers. These scripts include more than verbal lines, however: "Employers may try to specify exactly how workers look, exactly what they say, their demeanors, their gestures, their moods, even their thoughts" (Leidner 1993, 8). This can include even the smallest detail, such as folding the top of a customer's bag at McDonald's rather than rolling it up, or saying, "Can I help you?" instead of, "Can I help someone?" However restrictive and authoritarian these details may seem, these are measurable aspects of service workers' occupations and are often written directly into job descriptions. Because of this documentation, workers are evaluated and paid in accordance with their performance on these factors.

Secretaries also have a responsibility to facilitate relationships between organizations and outsiders, yet because they are classified within the "administrative support" sector rather than the service sector, secretarial job descriptions rarely include every dimension of service their positions actually require. This is also true of the public service dimensions required by this occupation. Most public service-related occupations like physician, public administrator, and teacher, are classified by the U.S. Bureau of Labor Statistics as "professional specialties" (1998).

Although secretarial organizations have established dimensions of professionalization, such as the Certified Professional Secretary rating, and have demanded for decades that secretaries be recognized as professionals, the balkanization of secretaries under the support classification obscures the public service work they may do. Without this recognition, secretaries' performance in the public service aspects of their positions generally does not get evaluated or compensated.

In general, the phenomena of women's public service and nurturing activities at work have not been recognized or studied together. Carework literature has spotlighted many gender-segregated occupations, such as nursing and childcare, but women's public service has been recognized primarily in volunteer organizations, community organizing, and social movement activities (e.g., Stall and Stoecker 1998). Studies that do conceptually meld the activities of nurturing with public service reveal practices such as "activist mothering," in which women extend the mothering activities they have honed in their families onto their communities (Naples 1992). Some multiracial/ethnic feminists have found that this practice is particularly common among Black women. Patricia Hill Collins discussed how African American women's notions of community, which developed historically in the United States distinctively from white, mainstream, "public, market-driven, exchange-based community models," are characterized by connectedness and mutual obligation around a sense of extended family (1991, 53). As she explained: "Women's activism within Black families meshed smoothly with activism as community othermothers in the wider Black community as 'family'" (1991, 147). A study of upward mobility by Elizabeth Higginbotham and Lynn Weber also found support for this stronger sense of community ties among Black women, who articulated a hardy sense of obligation to their networks of family and friends more so than white women in the study (1992). These studies provide a basis for understanding how women, not only in their own communities but also in the realm of paid work, may seek out opportunities to engage in public service in concert with carework.

In the context of studies on community organizing, secretarial work may seem like an odd focus for a study of public service. Indeed, before conducting this study even I did not anticipate the commitment many secretaries have to use their occupations to serve their communities. As I concluded each interview with the 49 secretaries in my study, I asked each woman to explain to me in a sentence or two why she is a secretary. This statement made by Elise Cushman, an African American administrative coordinator in her early 40s, is emblematic: "It is a profession in which I am able to be of service to others, which I see as my mission in life—to be able to help others." Secretarial work clearly involves more than the discrete acts of word processing, organizing, and filing for many women. Secretaries' convictions about service incorporate feelings that they are "on this earth for a purpose" (Dominique Daigh, African American secretary in her 30s). That purpose, according to interviewees, is to "do good" in some way, which they have been able to translate into tasks of public service in their occupations. In this article I examine secretaries' ethic of service and their activities of nurturing within a sociological context. One of my primary tasks is to demonstrate the existence of this ethic of service among those in the secretarial profession, and to analyze its form. In doing so, I tease out the ways gender, race, ethnicity, and class give structure to women's opportunities and ambitions to serve.

Data and Methods

The data for this study are 49 intensive interviews with women employed as secretaries in the Atlanta metropolitan area. From May 1997 to October 1998 I conducted open-ended, loosely structured interviews with women working in this gender-segregated occupation, which was 98.5 percent filled with women in 1997 (U.S. Department of Labor 1998).[1] I consciously chose to limit this sample to an occupation that does not necessarily require more education than a high school degree in order to build on previous studies that pay particular attention to the status of workers on the poorly compensated end of formal urban labor markets (Kennelly 1999; Moss and Tilly 1996; Wilson 1987). Only 10 percent of the participants in this study, however, discontinued their education after high school. More than one-quarter of the participants attained college degrees, and many older participants, who may have been the least likely to attend college, participated in an extensive continuing education and testing program that enabled them to be classified as Certified Professional Secretaries. Atlanta was an advantageous setting for the study because of the substantial class and racial variation in its metropolitan labor market. Eighteen of the 49 secretaries in my sample are African American, one is Jamaican American, four are Mexican American, one is Cuban American, and 25 are non-Hispanic white. More than half of participants are in their 30s and 40s, most have children, and just under half are married. About half of the secretaries in the sample earn salaries between $20,000 and 29,999, and very few make more than $40,000. (Please see Appendix A for a full summary of sample characteristics.)

I obtained my purposive sample from a range of businesses primarily by approaching secretaries in their workplaces and asking if they would be willing to be interviewed for my study. A few of the women I interviewed knew other secretaries and directed me to them, but the large majority of participants were original contacts rather than referrals. All participants provided pseudonyms for themselves, which I use in all discussions of these data. I recorded interviews on tape with participants' consent, and transcribed and coded them following the strategies of Glaser and Strauss (1967), Strauss and Corbin (1990), and Rubin and Rubin (1995). I carried out the interconnected processes of gathering, coding, analyzing, writing, and framing data throughout the duration of this project. The questions I asked focused primarily on participants' work histories and orientations toward their jobs. It may be important to note that I did not ask questions about nurturing and public service, specifically. Rather, these themes emerged in the interviews, primarily in response to questions about what the women enjoy (or do not enjoy) about their work as secretaries. In what follows, I detail the conceptual categories of "nurturing" and "the ethic of service" that emerged in my analyses.

Nurturing and the Ethic of Service

Secretaries, as support personnel, are often expected to nurture and help their bosses, coworkers, and clients. Some distance themselves from these expectations, while others cultivate and welcome the opportunity. In this section, I focus on those who enjoy nurturing in order to explore what they hold in common and what motivates them. I then highlight some secretaries' "ethic of service," which is distinctive from nurturing, and describe the structure of constraints within which women are able to provide public service through their secretarial occupation.

Nurturing

Although other studies have documented many administrative professionals' desire to disassociate themselves from stereotypical gender characteristics (e.g., Kennelly 2002), some secretaries in my sample enthusiastically discuss their enjoyment of the voluntary caretaking activities they do at work. These women compose a small proportion of my sample (about 14%), but their views are perhaps even more interesting than other secretaries' because they are somewhat unexpected, given the opportunities for exploitation to which they open themselves with this posture. Consistent with the premise that women bring unique characteristics into the workplace because of their gender, these women say they feel comfortable as nurturers and even seek out work that allows them to engage in mother-like activities. Annette McCoy, for example, a white woman in her early 50s, had a son in the early 1970s. He was sick through most of that decade and died when he was in his late teens. McCoy talks about how, after her son's death, her work as a secretary "filled a spot" for her, enabling her to continue to use her mothering skills at work:

> I really like the work . . . I like, I guess, the nurturing part of me and that's what a secretary does. My boss Nancy, she keeps saying—we are the very same age—she says that I'm from the very, "the old world," as she calls it.
>
> INTERVIEWER: *What does that mean?*
>
> I still feel very nurturing. I still feel like, you know, secretaries would probably be insulted today if they were asked to do, you know—well she doesn't ask me to, you know, go get her coffee or anything like that, but I always make sure that she has certain things on her desk right. And my other boss, I always make sure that he has—I know the way he wants things. And I feel like that I'm just very nurturing and I know how he wants things rather than just saying, you know, "Go do it yourself." And if he asked me to do something, you know, I don't, I don't—he said, "If you're up there, get something for me while you're on your way back." He's very, he's very considerate. But I guess that [is what "old world" means]. And very protective, of being a secretary. I'm very protective. I keep them out of harm's way. And I don't know if the modern secretary, you know, does that because, I don't know. But around here we do. We're kind of very protective and very nurturing of our team and the people that are on our team. Kind of protective of them. And I think that goes along with the job, I mean, that I know anyway. Maybe not in the new world of secretaries or whatever.

Annette McCoy takes comfort in the fact that as a secretary, she can be nurturing to her team members at work and continue her mothering activities, which she did full-time for fourteen years.

Tammy Yearby, a white, 48-year-old woman, talks in a similar way about her 31-year tenure as a secretary. She and her husband of 26 years planned to have children early in their relationship but were unable to do so. In our interview, Tammy Yearby directly relates her childlessness to the great satisfaction she receives from "mothering" the men at work: "I like to take care of people. I think because I don't have children, I like, I can mother my men in the office. You know? Keep everybody on track." Her expression is gendered not only in the fact that Yearby, as a woman, is taking on woman-associated activities of mothering, but also because she specifically names men as the people in her office who need and receive her caretaking.

Still another woman without biological children brings up the prominence of nurturing in her duties as a secretary. Margaret Loomis has been married a number of times and has cared for some of her husbands' children but has not had any children of her own. Divorced now and living alone, this white woman in her late 40s discusses how she appreciates the fact that her work gives her a chance to be a "caregiver":

> I like helping my managers do their job better, and making them look good. It also makes me look good. When I do my work well, then it's a give-and-take thing. And that's what I like doing. What's that? Care . . . that's called a caregiver? [laughs] No. [laughs]

INTERVIEWER: *Ahhh. [laughs] Well . . . ?*

Care . . . is that, is that the right term I want? Yeah. [slight pause] Okay, I'm sorry, what were you gonna ask?

INTERVIEWER: *That's okay. Well, maybe say more about that? Do you, do you see yourself in that role generally?*

To a certain degree, yeah. Even though I don't have [pause] kids, or any [pause], well I have, I had stepsons, from my second marriage. And I have a [pause], well, ex-daughter-in-law now, but [laughs]. She still calls me "Mom." And, I have, [pause] the two daughters that she had with my stepson, and now she's had another daughter by her next husband. But they all call me "Grandma." [laughs] So, you know, that's the family that I have, other than my brother. That family. But, um, to a certain degree, yeah. I like taking care of other people [makes a face with crossed eyes, indicating that she thinks what she just said is dumb, even if it is true].

INTERVIEWER: *Mmhm. Why do you make a face?* [laughter by both] *It's a great thing to do.*

I guess [not said as though she believes it is valuable].

Here, Margaret Loomis seems caught between how she enjoys nurturing and how she thinks she should somehow feel guilty for wanting to nurture, either because nurturing is not a desirable cultural activity generally or because she feels that it is inappropriate for her, specifically, to want to nurture since she has no biological children. Despite this, she indicates that this is one of the most enjoyable parts of her position as a secretary.

The secretaries who say they like this sort of mothering activity comprise a relatively small portion of my sample—seven out of 49. They tend to be among the older women in my sample, and almost all of them are white. One African American woman, Mary Reynolds, who is in her late 60s and has two grown daughters, also speaks of how much she enjoys a secretary's support role since it is so closely akin to caring for and nurturing children. Yet it appears in my sample that African American, Jamaican American, and Mexican American women are less inclined than white women to don the characteristics of motherhood, such as nurturing and caretaking, in their paid work positions.

It is not clear from these data whether Black women and Latinas are reluctant to mother at work because they do not encounter any expectations for taking on these "positive" motherhood roles, or because they reject the association for other reasons. While the overwhelming majority of the secretaries in this sample from all racial, ethnic, age, and class groups enjoy the occupation generally, different orientations to its nurturing aspect specifically, on the basis of race and ethnicity, are not unexpected. I demonstrate elsewhere (see Kennelly 2002) that some young

African American women in the sample work to distance themselves from the associations of an occupation that effectively trapped their foremothers. This may provide some insight into why women of color of all ages may be less enthusiastic about nurturing their employers than this group of white women are. One African American woman in her 40s, Gloria Rains, says that when she goes home from work, she often has to defend her occupation to her children: "My daughters in particular, they always say, 'Oh, I would never be a secretary.'" [Interviewer: *Oh really? Do they say why?*] "Because it's like, you know, you're being a servant to somebody. You're, you know, catering to somebody else." Because secretaries of every race are most likely to work for white men employers, the sort of "servitude" that can be associated with mothering may make women of color in this occupation less likely to voluntarily engage in these activities. The expectation that Black women should "appear warm and nurturing" is what Collins (1991, 71) has called a "controlling image" that has contributed to this group's continued oppression. Their resistance to this form of power should not be surprising. Black women may be more likely than white women, in some contexts, to engage in mother-like activities for their communities (Higginbotham and Weber 1992), but I find little evidence that women of color who work as secretaries wish to put themselves in mothering positions at work. For the women who do voluntarily engage in mothering activities at work, their opportunities (or lack of opportunities) to mother in their families appear to have a great deal to do with how they approach their jobs.

The Ethic of Service

Distinct from nurturing, and also unlike routinized service-sector job tasks, a dimension of their occupation that a good deal (41%) of secretaries in my sample discuss is something I call an "ethic of service." This ethic involves the desire to be of service to people in ways that stem from what some of these women term a "calling" to "do good" with their lives. For example, an African American woman in her early 40s named Elise Cushman says that she is an administrative coordinator because, "It is a profession in which I am able to be of service to others, which I see as my mission in life, is to be able to help others."

Meredith Taggart, a white woman in her 50s, moved, like Elise Cushman, from the private sector into a job with the government and enjoys the opportunities she has there to be of service to others:

> I saw this ad in the paper (my husband had been government, federal government work all his career), and I thought, I really love people. I'm going to have to take a big, big salary decrease, but I did it. I got the job and so I've never

regretted coming here. It's not the high-pace, it's not the dog-eat-dog atmosphere. It's service-oriented, it's people-oriented, and so this is where I fit, better than probably anywhere I've ever been.

For most of the women in my sample who express this ethic of service, their sentiments about public service are tied up with the organizations for which they work. Many of them, like Meredith Taggart and Elise Cushman, work for the government. Some work for nonprofit agencies, some for churches and synagogues, and others work in more corporate settings but are given opportunities to deal with people in ways that meet their desire to serve.

Reagine Draper, for example, a 28-year-old African American woman, has worked for three major organizations throughout the Atlanta metropolitan area that provide social work services to children. She did not intentionally seek out an organization like this in her first job, but every occupational move she has made since gaining exposure to this kind of organization has been based in part on her desire to continue to serve children:

> When I walked in [to interview for this job] I felt a vibe of family, people caring. When I was interviewed, the interview went good and I still wanted to stay in a field where I would be helping children. I worked with [another children-centered organization], so I still wanted to be an active part in helping children or teenagers in our society. So this would kind of [be] the reasons why I got this job. Because they do, this company do work with the [school] system and we have academies in different locations that help kids that are likely to drop out. So I'm still in that social work position where I'm seeing the kids, or try [pause], people are trying to help the kids.

Reagine Draper would liked to have stayed at either of the other organizations where she previously worked, but she reached the top of the administrative ladder at both places and had to look elsewhere for career growth opportunities. She feels that her current organization has many opportunities for promotion to other secretarial positions, although there does not seem to be a ladder between these secretarial positions and other professional jobs in the organization.

Grace Perenich is another interviewee who loves to help children and has even held off on her retirement in part because she cannot bear the idea of not continuing with this kind of public service. She is a white, 68-year-old woman who has worked for a nonprofit social service organization for 26 years. Somewhat like Reagine Draper, she loves what her organization does and she is a vital part of it, although her efforts to take positions in the organization that are recognized and compensated as service-oriented have been thwarted because of her competence as a secretary: "I didn't think I could ever leave the children. I enjoyed the work at the [children's branch] so much. . . . [But] once they find out that you can do it behind the desk, they don't like to lose you and let you leave them." The service-oriented work Perenich does in her position, including working with children and their families, counseling clients, and being a liaison to other organizations, has now simply become part of what is expected of her:

> And we still get telephone calls all the time from people who just want to call in and talk, and I enjoy, you know, talking to them over the phone and trying to get them help or send them to one of the agencies under the [another service organization] umbrella. So we do a lot of networking with that organization. So that's always interesting.
>
> INTERVIEWER: *So they call in and are routed to you to talk with on the phone?*
>
> Yeah. Sometimes you get calls you're not supposed to get but sometimes I think it's an opportunity god gives you that, you know, you can, like, can help that person. But ordinarily, they would only do things that comes to the division and to me. But I've been on so long, somebody might have a person that they think I can talk to and see if I can help in some way. So there are many ways to service if you really look.

Clearly, Grace Perenich does many tasks in her position that are beyond normal secretarial duties but seem normal to her because of the organizational context in which she works. After 26 years and with all these additional duties, Grace makes about $29,000 a year.

Dominique Daigh, an African American woman in her 30s, also incorporates extra service activities into her position as church secretary:

> INTERVIEWER: *So what are your normal hours here in this job?*
>
> Normal? [laughs]
>
> INTERVIEWER: *There is no normal?*
>
> No. There isn't. There isn't. [The bishop] is—he wouldn't like to admit it—he is a taskmaster because he's the type of man that's just a visionary. So you have to catch the vision when he gets it and it may be at six at night. Because he just has a lot of responsibilities, period. Being the chairman of the board of [an organization], over [a] District, which has over 500 churches, which has I don't know how many laypeople. And I end up doing ministering to laypeople. You know, his members of his church. You know, praying. Trying to get them—"Now you call in here complaining about something, is there any really God in what you're talking about? Have you prayed about that first before I even try to get it to the bishop?" Some of that is just stuff folks just need to let go of. "Get over and move on and look to what you need to be looking to." So I do a lot of that and with the ministers, too. Some of them have problems and things. So I do some ministering and counseling. Really it's what I should be in.
>
> INTERVIEWER: *Really? So why aren't you?*

> Well, I kind of do it on a consistent basis anyway just with people I meet and in this job. But I have learned that a lot. And then I did it at my other [secretarial] job because I was in criminal law so I had a lot of prisoners that I talked to on a daily basis. You know, [a famous convicted criminal] came to Christ while he was in jail finally. You know, different things like that. You know, so you get to talk to people.

Dominique Daigh shields her boss from aspects of his job that would consume his time, and she actually takes on part of his job to protect his schedule, as many other secretaries in the sample do. This dimension of the ethic of service appears to be at least somewhat related to secretaries' desire to nurture their bosses, but Daigh takes on a very selective piece of his work, the ministering, because she clearly enjoys the public service aspect of it. Much like Reagine Draper, who has moved from organization to organization in search of opportunities to be of service, Daigh has actively incorporated the aspect of ministering into her positions at different organizations.

Another church secretary, 38-year-old white woman, Lucy Horacek, is not only able to participate in the public service activities she finds so important, but she can also enact some of the nurturing described in the previous section. She says:

> In this job you have to be almost a mothering kind of person, too. A caring person. This isn't the regular secretary/receptionist kind of job because we have to deal with a lot more than just paperwork and scheduling and things like that. We have homeless who come here. We have people who are in need of food and I just have to do that, too, on that end. And I have to occasionally hear someone crying because they're upset about this or that. You know, that kind of thing.
>
> INTERVIEWER: *So does that sort of thing appeal to you or is that a drawback of the job?*
>
> Oh, no, it doesn't bother me one bit because I know if I was in their position, I would want to carry on, too, at the time. I get a phone call and someone's crying, I would want that, too, when they don't know where to turn.

Much like the community "othermothers" in studies of women's activism who use their mothering skills to serve their communities, Horacek directs her nurturing and mothering onto people she encounters through her job.

Other church and synagogue secretaries in my sample also indicate that "prescreening" and counseling people are parts of their jobs, but some of them are much less fond of the task than Lucy Horacek and Dominique Daigh. Marlene Sims, for example, a white church secretary in her early 50s, is annoyed rather than invigorated by this kind of public service:

INTERVIEWER: *Are there any things about your job that you don't care for, that you wish you could change if you could?*

Oh, yeah. I don't think anybody's got a job they don't wish some things were different. I guess part of it is, and I guess it has to do with being in a church, is that organized religion attracts people who are emotionally unstable and people who are emotionally needy. And they can be very draining and hard, sometimes hard to deal with. But, you know, you work in a church, you have to kind of expect that those people will be here. But sometimes it's just . . . it seems a little overwhelming sometimes, that constantly trying to be rational with people who aren't necessarily rational.

Sims's sentiment shows that it is as important to explore why some women do not relish these activities in their positions as secretaries as it is to determine why some women do. Her statement suggests that the difference may be simple and clear-cut: some women may just be uninterested in public service. We see a more complex picture, though, by investigating the lack of public service orientation among a group of secretaries who have concrete plans to leave the occupation. Compared to my whole sample of secretaries, more of the public service-oriented secretaries tend to be white or Mexican American, be in their 30s or 40s, have some college, come from working-class backgrounds, and earn salaries in the $20,000s. Another group of women, most of whom are young, college educated, and African American, is uninterested in staying in an occupation that they feel stifles and confines them. These women work in a range of settings, including religious and nonprofit organizations, which seem to be the most common organizational contexts in which the secretaries in my sample with public service orientations work. They are disgruntled with the occupation in general, and resent some of the public service demands in particular. The fact that they do not welcome opportunities to provide public service in their occupations may seem somewhat inconsistent with Higginbotham and Weber's (1992) study of professional African American women who note their sense of commitment to their communities much more than white professional women.

What is striking about them, though, is that their plans for the future include occupations that are partially based on the ethic of service, including lawyer and biology teacher. It is possible that these women see their opportunities to serve as more valuable when incorporated into professional occupations like lawyer and teacher, but feel underutilized doing secretarial work. Every secretary does not revel in the "opportunity" to go beyond her assigned responsibilities in order to follow an ethic of service. Many do not find out about any public service requirements of their job until after they take the positions, and they do not necessarily receive proportional compensation for them. Unlike a job in the service sector, where norms for "serving" people are spelled out in workers' job descriptions and also compensated, or in a professional specialty occupation, where public service may be an employee's primary responsibility, a job classified as administrative support obscures rather than highlights public service activities. Nonetheless, almost half the secretaries in this sample remark specifically that what they enjoy about their occupation is that it provides them with the chance to serve the public.

Discussion

Adopting a "motherly," nurturing persona at work is a fairly controversial move. Although not many secretaries in this sample enjoy going beyond their formal job descriptions to do the emotion work of nurturing, those who do indicate that they receive a distinctive sense of value from it. Put simply, it makes them feel good. It is striking how prominent the life experience of childlessness is to most of these nurturing women. Many other women in the sample who do not enjoy nurturing are childless; therefore, it is not my contention that women have a "natural" need to nurture, and without kids for which to care they automatically seek to nurture their colleagues. Additionally, some women, like Lucy Horacek above, have children of their own and still enjoy nurturing and mothering at work. Still, what is clear from the ways most of the nurturing women describe their jobs is that enacting motherhood at work is related to the lack of opportunity they have had to nurture within family contexts. Nurturing, for them, is at least in part a response to the social experience of childlessness in their lives.

What makes the practice of nurturing within jobs somewhat controversial is the willingness to engage in it without compensation. If it were built into job descriptions, many women would undoubtedly resist it, but at least they would be rewarded for doing it. The same may be true of the issue of public service. Secretaries in organizational settings from churches to high profile corporations go beyond their required duties to provide extra measures of service to the communities and clients they serve. Many of those I highlight here work for service-oriented organizations, and women in these organizations who take on responsibilities like counseling parishioners, throwing parties for disadvantaged children, and helping educate teenagers in need of social services are certainly not compensated more highly than secretaries in more business-oriented contexts. These tasks do not seem to be part of their reward structures, at least not the way that learning new software or mastering a filing system would be.

Because my data are not longitudinal, I am not able to conclusively determine whether the secretaries I describe here had the desire to engage in public service before they became secretaries or whether it developed over the time they worked in the occupation. From the chronology of their stories, it seems likely that it is a mixture of both. However, if we could project from this evidence that the women in my sample who describe how they build this service ethic into their current occupations are the ones most committed to it, and that they had a sense of this ethic before becoming paid workers, or at least before becoming secretaries, we can imagine that these women may have sought out occupations that would allow them to live in accordance with their belief systems. Secretarial work, at least within certain organizational contexts, allows them to do this. Other gender-segregated occupations, such as teaching, nursing, and social work, would also fit in with this ethic of service, but many of the secretaries in my sample who wanted to be teachers, nurses, or social workers did not attain those occupations largely because they were not able to finish the educations they would have needed to do so.

This indicates that many secretaries are our would-be politicians, think-tank activists, ministers, and secretaries of state—service occupations that require a degree of gender, class, and race privilege to attain, and that come with the prestige that such privilege demands. Few people would immediately imagine that secretaries and politicians have similar jobs, yet these data indicate that some of the rationale behind entering these types of occupations may be the same. Unsurprisingly, the public service occupations with the most prestige are also mostly filled by men.

As in so many other studies that confirm the pattern of devaluation of occupations that are associated with women (Kemp 1994; Reskin and Roos 1988; Roos and Jones 1994), these women's orientation toward the opportunities to be of service in their occupations, and their subsequent placement in secretarial positions, should leave little doubt that the structural factors guiding women's pathways into particular occupations are strong and steady. Class and gender combine here, in ways that are also racialized, to ensure that some women will be more likely to live out their ethic of service in a devalued, gender-segregated occupation than in prestigious occupations that would allow them similar opportunities to serve. Some women did not enter or finish college because they could not afford to; some because their family obligations did not leave them any time; some because they never thought of it in the first place; some because they did not see any need to. The category listed here that is particularly laced with irony, though, is the one that deals with women's family situations. Many women in this sample felt they had to make a choice between college and children, and when they entered the workforce after years of full-time parenting they were able to land jobs as secretaries in which they could serve the public. This contrasts with the situations of women who enjoy the nurturing aspects of the job, since most of these women are childless. While the presence of both sets of women in this occupation may indicate that it is a good landing spot for women with a range of family circumstances, the degree to which secretaries' nurturing and public service activities are devalued more likely signals that women with and without children who wish to pursue these activities should feel prepared to be exploited in this occupation.

Since secretarial work is one of the few paid labor market options available to many women who desire a career of public service, and since so many women do enact their ethic of service in their secretarial jobs, it is important that organizations recognize and compensate the public service work that secretaries do. When we, as a society, attribute valor to individuals who commit their lives to public service occupations, we must not overlook the ethic of service that guides so many secretaries and compels them to contribute to the society's greater good.

Note

1. I completed these interviews as part of a larger project, in which I also interviewed 26 women who work in the gender-integrated occupation of furniture sales (47.0 percent women in 1997 [U.S. Department of Labor 1998]). In this paper, my focus is secretaries.

References

Benjamin, Lois. 1997. *Black Women in the Academy: Promises and Perils.* Gainesville: University Press of Florida.
Clawson, Mary Ann. 1999. "When Women Play the Bass: Instrument Specialization and Gender Interpretation in Alternative Rock Music." *Gender & Society* 13(2): 193–210.
Collins, Patricia Hill. 1991. *Black Feminist Thought: Knowledge, Consciousness, and the Politics of Empowerment.* New York: Routledge.
Coltrane, Scott, and Justin Galt. 2000. "The History of Men's Caring: Evaluating Precedents for Fathers' Family Involvement." In *Care Work: Gender, Labor, and the Welfare State*, ed. Madonna Harrington Meyer, 15–36. New York: Routledge.
England, Paula. 1992. *Comparable Worth: Theories and Evidence.* New York: Aldine de Gruyter.
England, Paula, and Nancy Folbre. 1999. "The Cost of Caring." *Annals of American Academy of Political and Social Science* 561: 39–51.
England, Paula, Melissa S. Herbert, Barbara Stanek Kilbourne, Lori L. Reid, and Lori McCreary Megdal. 1994. "The Gendered Valuation of Occupations and Skills: Earnings in 1980 Census Occupations." *Social Forces* 73(1): 65–99.
Filer, Randall K. 1989. "Occupational Segregation, Compensating Differentials, and Comparable Worth." In *Pay Equity: Empirical Inquiries*, eds. Robert T.

Michael, Heidi I. Hartmann, and Brigid O'Farrell, 153–71. Washington, D.C.: National Academy Press.
Folbre, Nancy. 2001. *The Invisible Heart: Economics and Family Values*. New York: The New Press.
French, Marilyn. 1985. *Beyond Power: On Women, Men, and Morals*. New York: Summit Books.
Gilligan, Carol. 1982. *In a Different Voice: Psychological Theory and Women's Development*. Cambridge: Harvard University Press.
Glaser, Barry G., and Anselm L. Strauss. 1967. *The Discovery of Grounded Theory: Strategies for Qualitative Research*. New York: Aldine de Gruyter.
Higginbotham, Elizabeth, and Lynn Weber. 1992. "Moving Up with Kin and Community: Upward Social Mobility for Black and White Women." *Gender & Society* 6(3): 416–40.
Hochschild, Arlie. 1997. *The Time Bind: When Work Becomes Home and Home Becomes Work*. New York: Metropolitan Books.
Hochschild, Arlie, with Anne Machung. 1989. *The Second Shift: Working Parents and the Revolution at Home*. New York: Viking.
John, Rosalind M., and M. Azim Surani. 1999. "Agouti Germ Line Gets Acquisitive." *Nature Genetics* 23: 254–6.
Kanter, Rosabeth Moss. 1977/1993. *Men and Women of the Corporation*. New York: Basic Books.
Kelly, Rita Mae, and Phoebe Morgan Stambaugh. 1991. "Sex Role Spillover: Personal, Familial, and Organizational Roles." In *The Gendered Economy: Work Careers and Success*, ed. Rita Mae Kelly, 59–76. Newbury Park, CA: Sage.
Kemp, Alice Abel. 1994. *Women's Work: Degraded and Devalued*. Englewood Cliffs, NJ: Prentice Hall.
Kennelly, Ivy. 2002. "'I Would Never Be a Secretary': Reinforcing Gender in Segregated and Integrated Occupations." *Gender & Society* 16(5): 603–24.
———. 1999. "'That Single Mother Element': How White Employers Typify Black Women." *Gender & Society* 13(2): 168–92.
Kilbourne, Barbara, Paula England, and Kurt Beron. 1994. "Effects of Individual and Occupational Characteristics on Earnings: An Intersection of Race and Gender." *Social Forces* 72: 1149–76.
Leidner, Robin. 1993. *Fast Food, Fast Talk: Service Work and the Routinization of Everyday Life*. Berkeley: University of California Press.
Litt, Jacqueline S., and Mary K. Zimmerman. 2003. "Guest Editors' Introduction: Global Perspectives on Gender and Carework: An Introduction." *Gender & Society* 17(2): 156–65.
Mayhall, Carole. 1998. *Come Walk with Me: A Practical Guide to Knowing Christ Intimately and Passing It On*. New York: WaterBrook Press.
Meyer, Madonna Harrington, ed. 2000. *Care Work: Gender, Class, and the Welfare State*. New York: Routledge.
Miech, Richard Allen, and Glen H. Elder, Jr. 1996. "The Service Ethic and Teaching." *Sociology of Education* 69(3): 237–53.
Miller, Patricia H., Sue V. Rosser, Joann P. Benigno, and Mireille L. Zieseniss. 2000. "A Desire to Help Others: Goals of High-Achieving Female Science Undergraduates." *Women's Studies Quarterly* 28(1&2): 128–42.

Moss, Phil, and Chris Tilly. 1996. "'Soft' Skills and Race: An Investigation of Black Men's Employment Problems." *Work and Occupations* 23: 252–76.

Naples, Nancy. 1992. "Activist Mothering: Cross-generational Continuity in the Community Work of Women from Low Income Urban Neighborhoods." *Gender & Society* 6(3): 441–63.

Reskin, Barbara, and Patricia Roos. 1988. *Job Queues, Gender Queues: Explaining Women's Inroads to Male Occupations*. Philadelphia: Temple University Press.

Ritzer, George. 2004. *The McDonaldization of Society*. Thousand Oaks, CA: Pine Forge Press.

Roos, Patricia A., and Katharine Jones. 1994. Shifting Gender Boundaries: Women's Inroads into Academic Sociology." *Work and Occupations* 20: 395–428.

Rubin, Herbert J., and Irene S. Rubin. 1995. *Qualitative Interviewing: The Art of Hearing Data*. Thousand Oaks, CA: Sage.

Salzinger, Leslie. 2003. *Genders in Production: Making Workers in Mexico's Global Factories*. Berkeley: University of California Press.

Santelli, John, Roger Rochat, Kendra Hatfield-Timajchy, Brenda Colley Gilbert, Kathryn Curtis, Rebecca Cabral, Jennifer S. Hirsch, Laura Schieve, and Unintended Pregnancy Working Group. 2003. "The Measurement and Meaning of Unintended Pregnancy." *Perspectives on Sexual and Reproductive Health* 35(2): 94–101.

Sokoloff, Natalie. 1980. *Black Women and White Women in the Professions: Occupational Segregation by Race and Gender, 1960–1980*. New York: Routledge.

Stall, Susan and Randy Stoecker. 1998. "Community Organizing or Organizing Community? Gender and the Crafts of Empowerment." *Gender & Society* 12: 729–56.

Steinberg, Ronnie, Lois Haignere, Carol Possin, Cynthia H. Chertos, and Donald Treiman. 1986. *The New York State Pay Equity Study: A Research Report*. Albany: Center for Women in Government, SUNY.

Strauss, Anselm, and Juliet Corbin. 1990. *Basics of Qualitative Research: Grounded Theory Procedures and Techniques*. Thousand Oaks, CA: Sage.

U.S. Department of Labor, Bureau of Labor Statistics. 1998. *Employment and Earnings*, 29–45, 1. Washington, D.C.: U.S. Government Printing Office.

Vissing, Yvonne. 2002. *Women Without Children: Nurturing Lives*. New Brunswick, NJ: Rutgers University Press.

Wilson, William Julius. 1987. *The Truly Disadvantaged: The Inner City, the Underclass, and Public Policy*. Chicago: University of Chicago Press.

APPENDIX A
Summary of Sample Characteristics

Total		49	100%
Race	African American	18	36.7%
	Jamaican American	1	2.0%
	Cuban American	1	2.0%
	Mexican American	4	8.2%
	White	25	51.0%
Age	20s	9	18.4%
	30s	14	26.5%
	40s	14	26.5%
	50s	8	16.3%
	60s	4	8.2%
Income	$0–19,999	4	8.2%
	$20–23,999	9	18.4%
	$24–27,999	10	20.4%
	$28–29,999	6	12.2%
	$30–33,999	10	20.4%
	$34–37,999	6	12.2%
	$38–39,999	1	2.0%
	$40–44,999	1	2.0%
	$45–49,999	1	2.0%
	$50–54,999	1	2.0%
Education	High School	5	10.2%
	Business School (including Certified Professional Secretary certificate)	9	18.4%
	Some College	12	24.5%
	Associate's Degree	5	10.2%
	College Degree	14	28.6%
	(Don't know)	4	8.2%
Children	0	11	22.5%
	1	5	10.2%
	2	7	14.3%
	3–4	10	20.4%
	Some (did not specify #)	8	16.3%
	(Don't know)	8	16.3%
Married	Yes	24	49.0%
	No (could include divorced)	14	28.6%
	Divorced	7	14.3%
	(Don't know)	4	8.2%

CHAPTER THIRTEEN

Between L=A=N=G=U=A=G=E and Lyric: The Poetry of Pink-Collar Resistance

KAREN KOVACIK

> In the theater of eating out, the waitress plays multiple parts, each reflecting a female role. To fulfill the emotional and fantasy needs of the male customer, she quickly learns the all-too-familiar scripts: scolding wife, doting mother, sexy mistress, or sweet, admiring daughter.
> —Dorothy Sue Cobble (1991)

> Invariably courteous, gentle, cheerful, tactful, sunny, courageous, optimistic, she creates the atmosphere of the office. . . . [The secretary] is merely the channel for the message, and her own personality for the time being is lost in the impersonal act.
> —Sarah Louise Arnold (qtd. in Perkins 1910)

Readers of contemporary American poetry, familiar with the often heated ideological clashes between so-called Language poets,[1] known for their vanguardist linguistic experiments, and more mainstream lyric poets, whose work is typically more representational, might be surprised to find a group of working-class writers who borrow frequently from the aesthetic approaches of both of these divergent camps.[2] The poets who are the subject of this paper—clerical workers Chris Llewellyn, Karen Brodine, and Carol Tarlen, and former waitresses Jan Beatty and Lenore Balliro—make use of such wide-ranging formal strategies to reject what sociologist Arlie Hochschild calls the "emotional labor" of women's work (1983). Along with depressed wages (tips excluded) and relatively low status, performing some caricature of femininity on the job is an enduring characteristic of pink-collar work, as Cobble and Arnold, writing at different historical moments, attest in the epigraphs above. The feminized service occupations of waitressing and clerical work seem to solicit performances of self-denial, which involve nurturing co-workers and customers and suppressing anger. While the development of computer technologies has altered the pace and texture of clerical work—resulting in what Eileen Appelbaum has called "upskilling" and "downwaging"—vestiges of those confining gender scripts remain (1993, 75).[3] The poetry of Llewellyn, Brodine, and others resists such scripts by offering counter-performances, alternative rhetorics, in which secretar-

---

Originally published in the Spring 2001 issue of the *NWSA Journal* (13.1).

ies and waitresses emphatically call attention to their presence as individuals and as members of a collective.

Ironically, that sense of presence is sometimes enacted via the defamiliarizing techniques associated with the Language poets. Brodine and Llewellyn, for example, refer to the materiality of typography; eschew conventional punctuation to highlight syntactic and semantic ambiguities; and include non-standard spellings or deliberate "errors" to denaturalize the linguistic conventions of the commercial sphere. Yet while the Language poets generally employ such techniques to destabilize a sense of human presence, Llewellyn and Brodine use them to assert the clerical worker's subjectivity.

In "In Memoriam: Carolyn Johnson," Chris Llewellyn humanizes a fellow secretary, recently dead, by writing her an elegy in the form of a business letter (1990, 109–10). As an elegy, the poem challenges the notion that secretaries are interchangeable by giving its subject a name and describing some of her personal effects. The form of the professional letter—terse, factual, revealing nothing intimate—is an ironic choice for a poet seeking to mourn and memorialize the dead, as we can see from the first stanza:

> Carolyn Johnson:
> you died two weeks ago.
> I am the secretary
> sent to take your place.
> Your glasses and cupcakes
> are still in your desk
> and I write this
> with your pen.
> I am angry at your life.
> I am angry at your death.
> cause Carol I'm all keyedup
> and I feel it in my bonds
> in my tissues in my
> correctype liquidpaper brain. (109)

The stanza moves from concise, absurdly self-evident statements through un-businesslike avowals of rage to punning expressions of solidarity, and, through them, we see that the speaker is constructing her own persona as much as she is her predecessor's by calling attention to their differences and commonalities. Indeed, Carolyn Johnson has left material traces of her life, a palpable presence. To the new secretary, Carolyn represents the lingo and expertise that clerical workers share, but she is also a specific individual who wore glasses and enjoyed cupcakes. When the speaker says she feels "keyedup" in her "bonds"—a substitute, of course, for bones—she is referring not only to reams of office stationery but also to the sense of being shackled and perhaps to her sense of "bonding" with Carolyn Johnson.

The next stanza opens with more linguistic play and an increasingly irreverent tone:

> Say after breathin whiteout
> mimeofluid typecleaner
> thirty (30) years were you
> hi when you died?
> Glad you were cremated
> not filed ina drawer under
> watermarked engraved letterhead.
> Carolyn Johnson. (109)

The middle-class norms of "professional" etiquette and language—a courteous, but distant tone; the use of standard English; the avoidance of controversial topics—are challenged here and replaced with the wisecracking shop talk of a sisterly comrade. Lynda J. Ames, who studied how secretaries resist bureaucratic standardization in offices, noted that "collegiality" is a favored avenue; rather than succumbing to their bosses' attempts to create a divisive and competitive workplace, secretaries in the offices Ames studied shared limited resources and helped each other on projects assigned to an individual worker (1996, 37–60). In Llewellyn's poem, the chief means of enacting that collegiality is by parodying conventions of business writing, particularly the fetishizing of accuracy. The best way to elegize a fellow secretary, Llewellyn suggests, is to relax the strictures of spelling, grammar, spacing, and punctuation, by which the clerical worker was bound everyday on the job.

The speaker closes with a frenzied litany of regret and rebellion, rich in semantic multiplicity, directed to herself and to all surviving secretaries:

> Reachout fingers on homerows
> deathrows of the world &
> touch home touch my face touch
> Carolyn's ashes somewhere in
> Pennsylvania touch away
> machinated lives mere extensions
> of machines clicking tapping
> thudding tiny nails in coffin lids
> ticking clocks in mausoleumed
> officebuildings and deliver us
> from margins comma cleartabs . . .
> space bar lock shift index return

It is precisely at this moment, when the deathlike quality of the alienating job is enacted in language, that the speaker merges with the secretary to whom the poem is dedicated as she articulates their common fate, their "machinated" lives, to all the secretaries "of the world" (Unite!) with fingers poised on homerows. The abrupt swerve into prayer, "deliver us," precedes a catalogue of keys that, with the exception of the comma, leave no imprint. They represent movement—a life lived but not recorded—blanks that the rhetoric of the poem aims to fill. Llewellyn's elegy gives the lie to the notion that secretaries are interchangeable and also stresses the subversive collegiality among clerical workers. The poem closes with a final pun, a last appeal: "return / return / return Carolyn Johnson."

In a similar effort to emphasize both the clerical worker's individuality and her membership in a collective, Karen Brodine interweaves the jargon of computer typesetting with images from the inner life of a data-entry operator in "Woman Sitting at the Machine Thinking" (1990, 4). As with Llewellyn's mention of Carolyn Johnson's cupcakes and glasses, Brodine includes sensual references to the operator's body in the poem— her rituals of coffee-drinking and lovemaking—as counterpoints to her routinized, mechanized stints at the keyboard, to suggest that the worker is more than a medium for the transmission of text and to assert her sexual agency. Still, that sense of being a mere medium or conduit recurs throughout Brodine's poem because of the inclusion of repetitive typesetting codes and commands:

> Call format o five Reports, Disc 2, quad left
> return. name of town, address zip. quad left
> return. rollalong and there you are
> done with one. start the next
>
> call format o five. my day so silent yet taken up with words
> floating through the currents and cords of my wrists . . .

The staccato commands underscore the monotony of the speaker's work. But Brodine switches to longer sentence rhythms when contrasting the worker's alienated and instrumental performance of her body on the job with her emotional and physical engagement during lovemaking:

> Call file Oceana. name of town, Pacifica. name of street, Arbor.
> thinking about lovemaking last night, how it's another land,
> another set of sounds, the surface of the water, submerged,
> then floating free, the delicate fabric of motion and touch
> knit with listening and humming and soaring
> never a clear separation of power because it is both our power. . . .
> a speaking together from body to mouth to voice. (5)

While Brodine doesn't abandon the typesetting commands, she does introduce a more representationally lyrical language and expansive syntax. The meaningless address blanks in the earlier stanzas have been filled in with words suggesting an absent natural world: "Oceana," "Pacifica," and "Arbor." Images of floating and humming have replaced the clacking of keys and the harsh-sounding commands like "quad left" and "execute." And the idea of the lovers' intimate sharing of a "power" that relies on bodily "speech"—a clear assertion of their agency as well as pleasure—contrasts with the speaker's sense of being silenced by the machine's power. Both the linguistic disjunctions that we typically associate with Language poetry and the more imagistic, voice-based qualities of the lyric serve Brodine here as she depicts the "woman sitting at the machine, thinking."

Later in the poem, Brodine moves from this image of the individual clerical worker escaping her alienating work through erotic reverie to envisioning a socialist-feminist utopia. Because of the materiality of text for these data-entry operators—the sense that language is to them what cloth is to garment workers in a sweatshop—language, in Brodine's poetry, can never be a wholly transparent medium designated for self-expression as it can for some mainstream lyric poets: it is too much the stuff of oppression, too much the instrument of routine. Yet common to the poem's five stanzas, each with a different tone and rhetorical approach, is the idea that the language passing through the bodies of data-entry operators is a potentially revolutionary force. The poem refers to an image from the Mexican muralist, Diego Rivera, of "women, rows of them / similar, yet unique." All individuals, "bodies solid, leaning forward," the female data-entry operators are nonetheless bound by collective interests, and language, despite being the stuff of piecework, may also constitute a common means of resistance: "it flows through our hands and into metal," writes Brodine; "they [the managers] think it doesn't touch us" (17). In "Woman Sitting at the Machine, Thinking," symbolic but meaningful examples of linguistic resistance abound: a typesetter changing "man" to "person," the speaker filing jobs under words like "union," "red," "fury," "strike," and "tiger." These linguistic challenges to the status quo prompt the speaker to question more broadly, "what if you could send anything in and call it out again?" Suddenly, she imagines working-class women in control of the technology that currently controls them. "[W]e could circle our words around the world," she asserts, "like dolphins streaking through water their radar / if the screens were really in the hands of experts: us." With this image of working-class women in charge of producing their own texts rather than reproducing someone else's, the speaker builds to a final crescendo: "think of it—our ideas whipping through the air / everything stored in an eyeflash / our whole history, ready and waiting." Rather than accepting the notion of pink-collar workers as mute conduits, Brodine's poetic sequence emphasizes both their individual intelligence and collective power.

For both Brodine and Llewellyn, poetic resistance involves calling attention to the working conditions of clerical employees—the fetishizing of accuracy, management's expectation that secretaries are interchangeable, the reliance on deskilling (or "upskilling") machines—in a sometimes denaturalizing language that does not, however, deny clerical workers' subjectivity. At this point, I want to emphasize how Llewellyn's and Brodine's approaches differ from those advocated by Language poets Charles Bernstein and Bruce Andrews, two of the main polemicists for vanguardist poetics. Bernstein, in his essay "The Dollar Value of Poetry," envisions a poetry that would not be "in the service of this economic and cultural—social—force called capitalism" (1984). By "avoiding standard patterns of syntax and exposition," such a poetry would have no "exchange value" in the capitalist market and would, thereby, resist commodification (139). Here is an excerpt from Bernstein's own "Sentences My Father Used," a text which presumably would illustrate his claim (1993):

> Casts across otherwise unavailable fields.
> Makes plain. Ruffled. Is trying to
> alleviate his false: invalidate Yet all is
> "to live out," by shut belief, the
> various, simply succeeds which.[4]

In this poem, Bernstein attempts to avoid the commodification he associates with the "most accessible" linguistic codes. Indeed, there is no clear human referent, except perhaps for the father in the title, yet the poem's "sentences," fragmented and oblique, suggest neither the father's reported speech nor provide a psychologically probing portrait. A reader trained to look for the subtle repetitions that help make poems mean might notice sound patterns asserting themselves. The repetition of v in this brief stanza, for example, alerts us to the possibilities of regret, pain, and stunting in such phrases as "unavailable," "alleviate," "invalidate," and " 'to live out.' " But of course the imagery, specificity of voice, and emotional logic of more representational poems are absent here. That "illegibility *within* the legible"—to borrow the phrase of another Language poet, Bruce Andrews—becomes an avenue, Bernstein and Andrews would have us believe, for resisting the dominant culture's intrusive linguistic conventions (1990, 25). While not all Language-affiliated writers strive for such a degree of non-referentiality in their work—indeed Rae Armantrout has suggested that because women "need to describe the conditions of their lives," they are less inclined to make non-representational poems—they all "demand that the reader, deprived of the conventional ordering systems of consistent grammar, syntax, theme, and voice, participate in the construction of the work" (Armantrout 1986, 544; Keller 1993, 561).

For Language poets, then, linguistic resistance tends to occur at the levels of syntax and grammar. Peter Middleton, in a *Social Text* article on the Language poets, raises a potential problem with the "generality" of their approach: "If ideology is equated with naturalistic reference . . . , or with grammar, or with any generally defined structure, then an aesthetic of resistance can only be understood at the same level of generality. The specifics of semanticized social relations cannot be accounted for" (1990, 250). Without content, expression, or communication, one cannot account for, or challenge, as Middleton puts it, particular instances of elitism or social control. Indeed Bruce Boone, in a response to "The Dollar Value of Poetry," asks whether a project like Bernstein's—which holds out the democratic promise of a "participatory writerliness"—may, in the end, prove to be useful to the forces of reaction (1984, 142). Walter Kalaidjian, writing about historical avant-garde movements, shows how easily that co-opting might occur, since "earlier [waves of] dadaist experimentation" were "incorporated by American advertising and other fashionable discourses of the culture industry" (1991, 326–7). Given this precedent, Kalaidjian warns that the "political shock value of . . . linguistic estrangement" should not be overrated (327).

Although I have no evidence that Brodine and Llewellyn have been influenced by the Language poets or even that they have read them, it seems clear from their records of activism that both women would reject a merely formalist approach to critiquing capitalism. Brodine, a socialist and lesbian activist until her death in 1987, fought for better working conditions for data-entry operators, taking part in periodic walkouts and protests at her workplace. Llewellyn, a longtime secretary and the author of an award-winning book of poems about the infamous Triangle fire of 1911, in which 146 garment workers, mostly women, lost their lives, gives public readings of her poems in workplaces to broaden understanding of landmark struggles in labor history.[5] Both would no doubt agree with Cary Nelson's statement that poems offering "images of working-class suffering, discontent, and resistance certainly promote more awareness of the material consequences of class difference. Abstractions about democracy and justice are thereby articulated to specific social and economic disparities" (1989, 167–8).

Indeed, to promote more "awareness of the material consequences of class [and gender] difference," Llewellyn, Brodine, and other poets who have written about pink-collar work—Carol Tarlen, Lenore Balliro, and Jan Beatty, among others—use a broad range of poetic styles, genres, and modes. Some of the poems employ no techniques of linguistic estrangement, favoring instead a more imagistic or lyrical treatment of pink-collar workers' lives and concerns. Carol Tarlen has written a poem contrasting time off (with its relaxed, anarchic rhythms) and time on the job (rigidly controlled). Tarlen, a secretary and AFSCME member in San Francisco, wrote her poem "Today" to celebrate a paid day off after she earned a Master's degree in creative writing while working full time. The poem makes use of sweeping liturgical cadences, with anaphoric repetitions recalling the rhythms of the Old Testament, because, as Tarlen has remarked, "paid days off are rare and miraculous and holy!" (1995, 390):

> Today I slept until the sun eased
> under my eyelashes. The office phone
> rang and rang. No one answered.
> Today I wrote songs for dead poets,
> danced to Schubert's 8th Symphony
> (which he never had time to finish),
> right leg turning andante con moto,
> arms sweeping the ceiling as leaves fell,
> green and golden, autumn in Paris
> I sat in a bistro and sipped absinthe
> while Cesar Vallejo strolled past,
> his dignity betrayed by the hole
> in his pants, and I waved, today
>
> and the dictaphone did not dictate
> and the files remained empty
> and the boss's coffee cup remained empty (330)

Anything can happen on this secretary's day off: the dead walk and the unsung earn overdue applause. Yet in the midst of the festivities, Tarlen acknowledges the limitations of time in her songs for dead poets, in the example of Schubert dying before he could finish his symphony, in the autumn leaves falling, in markers of a moribund modernism (such as absinthe) and in Cesar Vallejo, the great Peruvian poet (d. 1938), who wrote poems of anguish about human suffering and poverty. Implicit in these meditations is the speaker's awareness of her own mortality and of how she surrenders so much of her time to the office. In her absence, an eerie stillness has descended upon the workplace. Setting the voiceless dictaphone and the boss's empty coffee cup to Biblical cadences underscores the mundanity of the speaker's routine while elevating her role, making her appear omnipotent. The boss, by contrast, comes off as a "helpless husband" type.

Later in the poem, Tarlen's speaker indulges in middle-class, individualist pleasures such as reading the *New Yorker* and "nibbling croissants" in bed, but she extends that private fantasy into a collective one, drawing on images of Christ caring for society's outcasts and of a socialist utopia:

> And rain drenched the skins of lepers
> and they were healed.
> Red flags decorated the doorways
> of senior centers, and everyone
> received their social
> security checks on time. (330)

Similarly, she writes that she "praised the sun / in its holiness, / led a revolution, / painted my toenails purple, / and meditated in solitude" on her day off, again inflecting individual indulgences with a collective consciousness. In the end, the leisure time does sound "rare and miraculous and holy," not only because Tarlen has dignified it with rhetorical flourishes, but also because her utopic vision extends to others.

Waitress-poet Lenore Balliro, in "French Restaurant, 1982," depicts the solidarity among restaurant workers both on the job and off by using, to subversive effect, the formal devices of American lyric poetry: concrete language, compelling images, and a strong sense of voice. Balliro juxtaposes scenes from a stuffy restaurant, where waitresses are sexually harassed by customers, with images of a working-class bar, where they relax after work (1995). The disdain that servers often feel for customers is evident in Balliro's terse description of the restaurant's patrons:

> We write down on a pad
> what it is they want,
> but we don't let them see it.
> They think we remember,
> so we let them.
>
> They watch what moves
> under the black swing of skirt,
>
> how the candles underlight
> the faces that lean to clear
> their plates. (32)

Balliro observes the patrons sexualizing the waitresses, romanticizing them as they do their job. But instead of feeling demeaned, the waitresses engage in subtle power plays of their own. This is in keeping with what Greta Foff Paules witnessed in her useful ethnographic study of New Jersey waitresses: "For the most part [the waitress's] resistance is unseen, taking place behind a facade of subservience or behind the lines, out of sight of customers" (1991, 164).

Later, one waitress invites her co-worker to shoot pool,

> far from Beaujolais Nouveau,
> anything from East Side or Ivy League . . .
> to drink shots and beer at Mike's 17 bar, downtown. . . .
>
> The game is good, the sharp clack
> of those balls that we whack
> across Mike's table. (32)

Clearly, the waitresses find relief from the uptown snobs at Mike's unpretentious bar, drinking boilermakers instead of "Beaujolais Nouveau" and indulging in a game of pool, that barroom sport of bravado and innuendo. Balliro concludes her poem with a more explicit image of sexual tension between the women: "We work the same shift. / And when we pass / in the aisles of our stations, / the small hairs on the back of our wrists / stiffen." This delicate frisson, like so much that passes among servers or between waiters and kitchen staff, is invisible to the customers.

Tarlen and Balliro, like Llewellyn and Brodine, would no doubt be in accord with Lynn Keller's assessment of the inadequacy of "the mainstream lyric and Language categories," into which contemporary American poems, like sheep and goats, are typically assigned. Such categories, Keller argues, "are a particularly uneasy fit for feminist poetries. Indeed, although there are numerous feminist practitioners in each mode, some feminists would see the presumption of individualized speaking subjectivity in mainstream lyric and its rejection in Language poetry as inverse reflections of the privilege accorded to (white) male subjectivity" (1999, 312). Surely, there's a class bias built into the mainstream vs. Language binary, as well, which renders invisible poetries that don't fit into either camp.

Consider the following poem by Jan Beatty, who worked her way through the University of Pittsburgh's MFA program as a waitress. Brusque, unlyrical, and packed with commands, Beatty's "A Waitress's Instructions on Tipping or Get the Cash and Don't Waste My Time" challenges popular notions of waitresses as deferential servants who would do anything for a tip:

> 20% minimum as long as the waitress doesn't inflict bodily harm
> If you're two people at a four top, tip extra.
> If you sit a long time, pay rent.
> Double tips for special orders
> Always tip extra when using coupons.
> Better yet, don't use coupons
> Never leave change instead of bills, no pennies.
> Never hide a tip for fun.

Overtip, then tip some more.
Remember, I am somebody's mother or daughter.
No separate piles of change for large parties.
If people in your party don't show up, tip *for* them.
Don't wait around for gratitude.
Take a risk. Don't adjust your tip so your credit card total is even.
Don't ever, ever pull out a tipping guide in public.
If you leave 10% or less, eat at home
If I call a taxi for you, tip me.
If I get cigarettes for you, tip me.
Better yet, do it yourself.
Don't fold a bill and hand it to me like you're a big shot.
Don't say, *There's a big tip in it for you if*
Don't say, *I want to make sure you get this,* like a busboy would steal it.
Don't say, *Here, honey, this is for you—ever.*
If you buy a $50 bottle of wine, pull out a ten.
If I serve you one cocktail, don't hand me 35 cents
If you're just having coffee, leave a five. (1996a, 54)[6]

Not once does the speaker bother to say "please" or "sir" or "ma'am." Here Beatty is "inverting the symbolism of tipping," to borrow a phrase from Paules' ethnography.[7] Instead of deferring to the customers who are paying part of her livelihood, she suggests it is they who are so gauche, so déclassé, that they need to be schooled in the proper etiquette of being restaurant patrons. Refusing the notion of the tip as "a small present of money given to an inferior," as the *Oxford English Dictionary* defines it, she instead regards the gratuity as her earned right. Therefore, she reserves her sternest rebuke for those male customers who make ostentatious displays of their generosity. And because cheap patrons of either gender sometimes forget that she is more than their personal servant, someone with a life outside the restaurant, she reminds them, "I am somebody's mother or daughter."[8] At this moment, we see her manipulating two of the feminine roles mentioned in the Cobble epigraph that began this essay; Beatty invokes them not to "fulfill the emotional and fantasy needs of the male customer" but rather to assert a subjectivity that extends beyond the job. Unapologetically, she employs the jargon of her trade such as "four top" to communicate the waitress's perspective on restaurant work, including the notion that tables and customers are there to be "processed."[9] More than anything, Beatty says that she wished to communicate in the poem what she often felt on the restaurant floor: "I don't care how much money you make; I won't give you your lunch if you don't act right" (1996b).

Not surprisingly, Beatty received mixed responses to "A Waitress's Instructions." After the poem first appeared in the *Pittsburgh Post-Gazette,* waiters and waitresses from restaurants around the city would come up to Beatty in the street, thank her for the poem, and mention they had posted it in their restaurant's bus stand. However, Beatty also received irate letters that charged her poem was aesthetically deficient and complained that she was telling customers how to tip. We might also imagine how Beatty's poem of working-class anger and assertion would be received by critics affiliated with the mainstream lyric or Language camps. Because Beatty's poem eschews the aesthetic favored by what we might call the Helen Vendler school—one featuring imagistic density, a tone of regret or ambivalence, and dense, allusive language that the critic can unpack[10]—it would probably merit a mixed response, similar to that of Vendler herself in a review of Adrienne Rich's socially engaged collection, *An Atlas of a Difficult World* (1991).

In that review, Vendler praises Rich's "deep attachment to the beautiful," but snipes at the poet's "sociological" approach of dividing the world into "victims" and "victimizers"—a "simplification" in Vendler's view. She complains that "we do not, in Rich, see the malathion-sickened migrant worker beating his wife, or the murdered lesbian being indifferent to her sick mother"; too often, she claims, Rich overlooks the "sins" of the oppressed "without extending a similar charity to the oppressors" (50). Although I don't wish to reduce Vendler's complex and at times, anguished remarks on Rich, I see her making a critical move that is common in American letters. A poetry that takes sides, one that dares to abandon ambivalence, gets labeled "simple" by critics who believe that art should transcend the social world. Imagine a reviewer who would applaud the mention of malathion in a poem, who would appreciate a harangue against bad tippers, who would not expect or require that "charity" be extended to oppressors. Such a criticism is nowhere to be found in the mainstream lyric camp.

Nor can one expect to find it in the writings of Language-affiliated critics, such as Jerome McGann or Marjorie Perloff, who favor a poetics of disjunction, ruptured syntax and sense, and often elaborate sound play. Perloff, for example, writes approvingly of a sonically rich though, at times, inscrutable poetic sequence by Language poet Susan Howe about English colonists' early encounters with the Indians of New England (1990). After unpacking a particularly obscure quatrain by Howe ("rest chondriacal lunacy / velc cello viable toil / quench conch uncannunc / drumm amonoosuck ythian"), Perloif poses a series of rhetorical questions about Howe's difficult poem, which she then answers herself:

> Is this then jabberwocky, nonsense verse? If Howe wants to talk about [New England preacher] Hope Atherton's mission to the Indians or apply the "themes" implicit in the tale—Colonial greed, Puritan zeal, the fruits of imperialism, the loneliness of exile, the inability to communicate with the

Other—to the contemporary situation, why doesn't she just get on with it? . . .
It would be easy to counter that the breakdown of articulation, which is the poem's subject, is embodied in the actual breakdown of the language, that the fragmentation of the universe is somehow mirrored in the fragmentary nature of the text. But the fact is that in Howe's work, as in Charles Bernstein's or Lyn Hejinian's [another often-cited Language poet], demilitarization of syntax may well function in precisely the opposite way—namely, as a response to the all-too-ordered, indeed formulaic, syntax that characterizes the typical "workshop" [or what I have been calling "mainstream lyric"] poem. (1990, 304-5)

Like her rival critic Helen Vendler, Perloff privileges poetic form over content. Favoring a "demilitarized" syntax (!) and a radical dismantling of subjectivity, Perloff and other Language-affiliated critics would no doubt find little to admire in a poetic manifesto like "A Waitress's Instructions."[11]

Nomen est omen, as the Germans would say: one's name is one's destiny. Lacking a name, a category, one faces a perilous fate. For pink-collar poets and other writers of the working classes, a weak class consciousness that is peculiarly American jeopardizes the wider reception of their work. David Hogan, in an article on class formation, compares English and American working-class cultures: "American working-class culture is not as cohesive, thickly textured, or self conscious; it is more diffuse, fractured internally, divided along regional, racial and ethnic lines; its repudiation of bourgeois ideology less deep and incisive; its institutional infrastructure—trade unions, political organizations, voluntary associations—less extensive and weaker" (1982, 32). And Janet Zandy, in her introduction to an anthology of working-class women's writings, affirms the difficulty of analyzing such texts or even getting them published both because of the American denial of class and the literary establishment's inadequate terminology: "To dare to write about working-class literature in a culture where the working class is denied a name, never mind a literary category, is to plunge in over one's head. To try to fit this literature into the neat academic categories of genre or period is like squeezing a wilderness into a cultivated park" (1990, 9). Even critics on the left have sometimes perpetuated this problem of invisibility by clinging to limited notions of what constitutes working-class literary production, having derived their categories and definitions from studying the "proletarian" literature of the 1930s whose representative authors were largely white men.[12]

Surely, in a so-called "post-industrial" economy like ours, pink-collar poetry deserves a literary category of its own and a criticism alert to its aims. But what's subversive about these poems by service-sector workers is not that they offer yet more evidence of the inadequacy of existing critical terminology but that they dare to imagine alternative worlds in which secretaries and waitresses, visible and loud, speak out, talk back, assert their individuality, and, at the same time, honor collective commitments. In an era in which the stock market's ups and downs are front-page news and legislative assaults on poor women are commonplace, there is indeed something salutary in these poetic representations of clerical and waitressing work—especially when the poets erupt in anger. Reading pink-collar writers like Llewellyn, Brodine, Beatty, Balliro, and Tarlen, I am reminded of Robert Creeley's famous dictum: "Form *is* content." However, for these poets that dictum would be better reversed, for it is the subject matter of their literary efforts—particularly the urgent need to establish the pink-collar worker's agency—that determines the divergent formal strategies they adopt. And while poetic practice alone cannot further causes of social justice, the "collaborative process of the ethical and the aesthetic," as Regenia Gagnier has suggested, can help to realize "the dream of relations beyond indifference and domination" (1989, 27).

Acknowledgments

I would like to thank Eric Swank, Marilyn Annucci, Jeredith Merrin, Andrea Lunsford, and the anonymous reviewers who offered helpful comments on earlier drafts of this essay.

"Carolyn Johnson" is part of a long sequence titled "Office for the Dead" in Chris Llewellyn's book *Steam Dummy and Fragments from the Fire*, published by Bottom Dog Press, Firelands College, Huron, Ohio, in 1993.

Notes

1. Sometimes, Language is written as I have spelled it in the title of my paper, as in *The L=A=N=G=U=A=G=E Book*, edited by Andrews and Bernstein (1984).

2. This article is part of a larger project studying the poetry of a recent generation of American women from working-class backgrounds. Of the 21 poets in my sample, three are African American, three Chicana, and fifteen Euro-American. Born between 1940 and 1960, all originally came from families supported by blue-collar, pink-collar, or low-level service sector work, and many were the first in their families to attend college. Together, they've held jobs as donut makers, field workers, gas station attendants, waitresses, cooks, typesetters, and secretaries, and each "performs" class in her poetry. Yet, although many of the poets have supported themselves through blue- or pink-collar

work, 18 out of 21 hold advanced degrees and are in some way affiliated with academia.

3. For a thorough historical account of the feminization of clerical work, see Strom (1992).

4. Cited as a representative text in "L=A=N=G=U=A=G=E poetry" (Preminger, Brogan, and Terry 1993, 675). Also anthologized in Messerli (1987).

5. See Llewellyn (1987).

6. An earlier published version of the poem, which appeared in Coles and Oresick (1995), contained the final line, "If you're miserable, there's not enough money in the world," deleted in the *Mad River* version, published by the University of Pittsburgh Press (1996).

7. According to Paules (1991), tips present some benefits, such as enabling servers to maintain autonomy from restaurant management. Because waitresses typically receive such a small percentage of their income from the restaurant, they feel less beholden to follow restaurant rules that will obstruct or reduce their tip income. Still, the tipping system perpetuates the idea of the server as a mental worker, since it is rooted in the practice of employers offering gratuities and gifts to domestic servants. Paules observes that the historical link between private service and restaurant work encourages customers to treat the waitstaff in a patronizing and even degrading manner: "Virtually every rule of etiquette is violated by customers in their interaction with the waitress: the waitress can be interrupted; she can be addressed with the mouth full; she can be ignored and stared at; and she can be subjected to unrestrained anger. Lacking the status of a person she, like the servant, is refused the most basic considerations of polite interaction" (138). Because customers perceive the waitress's status as lower than their own and her financial need as great, they often believe she will be content with even a meager tip (36). Or customers regard the tip as an "evaluative device," which by its size suggests the customer's approval or dismissal of the service (40–41).

   Yet, as they "invert the symbolism of tipping," waitresses have been known to refuse meager tips, one even throwing the spare change she had been left at the backs of exiting customers (37). Rather than feeling inferior at having received a small tip, the waitress locates blame in the customer.

8. Paules reported that waitresses tended to get better tips when their parents eat at the restaurant. One remarked, "I've never been stiffed when my parents have been sitting there.... They [the customers] see that outside of this place I am a person and I have relationships with other people" (133).

9. Waitresses and other restaurant workers use special lingo and abbreviations for convenience and also for maintaining their in-group. An example can be found in Paules' ethnography. One waitress, explaining how she took good care of special customers, frequently transformed nouns into verbs: "I got my

fifth-grade teacher [as a customer] one night . . . I kept her coffeed. I kept her boyfriend coked all night. Sodaed. . . . I kept them filled up" (34).

10. Here I should mention that a number of Beatty's poems in *Mad River* are indeed imagistically and linguistically dense—more typical of the so-called "lyric" camp.

11. See Keller's (1999) article for examples of dismissive criticism by Language-affiliated critics of Alice Fulton's work Fulton's "obvious interest in language as a means of construction rather than of representation" would seemingly make her work more sympathetic to critics of that school.

12. Tim Libretti (1995), whose research synthesizes Marxist, feminist, and "minority" literary theory, offers an example of a white, working-class category that is not transferable, which can be found in Laguna novelist Leslie Marmon Silko's description of the Great Depression in her *Almanac of the Dead*: "[Indians] never even knew a depression was going on, because in those days people had no money in banks to lose. Indians had never held legal title to any Indian land, so there had never been property to mortgage . . . The Laguna people had heard something about the crash, but they remembered the crash as a year of bounty and plenty" (1992). See Libretti (1995).

References

Ames, Lynda J. 1996. "Contrarieties at Work: Women's Resistance to Bureaucracy." *NWSA Journal* 8(2): 37–60.
Andrews, Bruce. 1990. "Poetry as Exploration, Poetry as Praxis." In *The Politics of Poetic Form*, ed. Charles Bernstein, 23–44. New York: Roof.
Andrews, Bruce, and Charles Bernstein, eds. 1984 *The L=A=N=G=U=A=G=E Book*. Carbondale: Southern Illinois University Press.
Appelbaum, Eileen. 1993. "New Technology and Work Organisation" In *Pink-Collar Blues: Work, Gender & Technology*, ed. Belinda Probert and Bruce W. Wilson, 60–84. Melbourne, Australia: University of Melbourne Press.
Armantrout, Rae. 1986. "Why Don't Women Do Language-Oriented Writing?" In *In the American Tree*, ed. Run Silluman, 544–6. Orono, ME: National Poetry Foundation.
Balliro, Lenore. 1995. "French Restaurant, 1982." In *For a Living*, ed. Peter Oresick and Nicholas Coles, 32. Champaign-Urbana: University of Illinois Press.
Beatty, Jan. 1996a. "Awake in a Strange Landscape." In her *Mad River*, 54. Pittsburgh, PA: University of Pittsburgh Press.
———. 1996b. Interview with author, 25 July.
Bernstein, Charles. 1984. "The Dollar Value of Poetry." In *The L=A=N=G=U=A=G=E Book*, ed. Bruce Andrews and Charles Bernstein, 138–9. Carbondale: Southern Illinois University Press.
———. 1987. "Sentences My Father Used." In *"Language" Poetries Anthology*, ed. Douglas Messerli, 147–54. New York: New Directions.

Boone, Bruce. 1984. "Writing, Power, and Activity." In *The L=A=N=G=U=A=G=E Book*, ed. Bruce Andrews and Charles Bernstein, 140–4. Carbondale: Southern Illinois University Press.

Brodine, Karen. 1990. *Woman Sitting at the Machine, Thinking*. Seattle, WA: Red Letter Press.

Cobble, Dorothy Sue. 1991. *Dishing It Out: Waitresses and Their Unions in the Twentieth Century*. Urbana: University of Illinois Press.

Coles, Nicholas, and Peter Oresick, eds. 1995. *For a Living: The Poetry of Work*. Urbana: University of Illinois Press.

Gagnier, Regina. 1989. *Subjectivities: A History of Self-Representation in Britain (1832–1920)*. New York: Oxford University Press.

Hochschild, Arlie. 1983. *The Managed Heart: The Commercialization of Human Feeling*. Berkeley: University of California Press.

Hogan, David. 1982. "Education and Class Formation: The Peculiarities of Americans." In *Cultural and Economic Reproduction in Education*, ed. Michael Apple, 32–78. London: Routledge and Kegan Paul.

Kalaidjian, Walter. 1991. "Transpersonal Poetics: Language Writing and the Historical Avant-Gardes in Postmodern Culture." *American Literary History* 3(2): 319–36.

Keller, Lynn. 1993. "The Twentieth-Century Long Poem." In *The Columbia History of American Poetry*, ed. Jay Panni and Brett C. Millier, 534–63. New York: Columbia University Press.

———. 1999. "The 'Then Some Inbetween': Alice Fulton's Feminist Experimentalism." *American Literature* (June): 311–36.

Libretti, Tim. 1995. "Is There a Working Class in U.S. Literature? Race, Ethnicity, and the Proletarian Literary Tradition." *Radical Teacher* 46: 22–6.

Llewellyn, Chris. 1990. "In Memoriam: Carolyn Johnson." In *Calling Home: Working-Class Women's Writings*, ed. Janet Zandy, 109. New Brunswick, NJ: Rutgers University Press.

———. 1987. *Fragments from the Fire*. New York: Viking/Penguin.

Messerli, Douglas. 1987. *"Language Poetries": An Anthology*. New York: New Directions.

Middleton, Peter. 1990. "Language Poetry and Linguistic Activism." *Social Text* 8(9): 242–53.

Nelson, Cary. 1989. *Repression and Recovery in Modern American Poetry and the Politics of Cultural Memory, 1910–1945*. Madison: University of Wisconsin Press.

Paules, Greta Foff. 1991. *Dishing It Out: Power and Resistance among Waitresses in a New Jersey Restaurant*. Philadelphia: Temple University Press.

Perkins, Agnes F. 1910. *Vocations for the Trained Woman: Opportunities Other Than Teaching*. New York: Longman's.

Perloff, Marjorie. 1990. "'Collision or Collusion with History': Susan Howe's *Articulation of Sound Forms in Time*." In her *Poetic License: Essays on Modernist and Postmodernist Lyric*, 297–310. Evanston, IL: Northwestern University Press.

Preminger, Alex, T.V.F. Brogan, and V.F. Terry, eds. 1993. *The New Princeton Encyclopedia of Poetry and Poetics*. Princeton, NJ: Princeton University Press.

Silko, Lesli Marmon. 1992. *Almanac of the Dead*. New York: Viking Penguin.

Strom, Sharon Hartman. 1992. *Beyond the Typewriter: Gender, Class, and the Origins of Modern American Office Work, 1990–1930.* Urbana: University of Illinois Press.

Tarlen, Carol. 1995. "Today." In *For a Living,* ed. Peter Oresick and Nicholas Coles, 390. Champaign-Urbana: University of Illinois Press.

Vendler, Helen. 1991 "Mapping the Air." *New York Review of Books*, 21 November: 50–6.

Zandy, Janet. 1990. "Introduction." In *Calling Home: Working-Class Women's Writings,* ed. Janet Zandy, 1–13. New Brunswick, NJ: Rutgers University Press.

CHAPTER FOURTEEN

"Growing the Size of the Black Woman": Feminist Activism in Havana Hip Hop

FARI NZINGA

Black Cubans have long been told by Cuban authorities that they do not need places to express the problems of race and class because there are no such problems: they have all been solved by the Revolution. Nevertheless, Black Cubans do face all manners of discrimination in contemporary Cuba. With few formal political outlets open to young Black Cubans (Fernandes 2003), hip hop has emerged on the island as a powerful form of political expression: a kind of "theater of the oppressed" that addresses the racial and economic problems encountered by Black Cubans (Boal 1985). The all-female group Las Krudas stands out as particularly courageous within this hip-hop scene.

In 2003, I spent four months studying at the University of Havana. While in Cuba, my research partner and I recorded interviews with 23 women of African descent. The members of Las Krudas were among this group. I draw upon these interviews to sketch a portrait of a striking phenomenon: the emergence of a strongly oppositional, Black, feminist activist art in Cuba.

I first saw Las Krudas perform at a concert of women rappers; I was struck by their positive message, and they were kind enough to invite me to their home for an interview. We chatted like old friends before we began tape recording the interview. One of the first topics was how they see their intersecting identities. Odaymara, aka Pasa Kruda, tells me:

> I'm Black, I'm a woman and I'm Cuban. ¿*Entiendes*? I'm not *above all* Cuban. I am more than Cuban; I feel as a woman, I feel Black. . . . But there are moments when I don't know *what* it means to be Cuban. Many times in places like schools and things I'm treated like: 'yes, you're Cuban, but you are not representative of Cuba.' ¿*Entiendes*? So then I ask myself, ¿*Soy cubana o no soy cubana*? Am I Cuban or not?

Olivia, aka Pelusa, is a *guantanamera* by birth. She lived in Guantánamo until she was seventeen and then migrated to the capital city. She made her social location clear during the interview: "Principally, I am a woman. I wake up in the morning and I say: 'I am a woman.'" But she also identifies as an artist, an artist with strong ties to the Afro-Cuban

---

Originally published in the Spring 2007 issue of the *NWSA Journal* (19.1), with the author as Ronni Armstead.

community: "I say: 'I have a social responsibility to represent my new ideas and to make my art, on stilts [with her public theater project], in the street, in hip hop, in my poetry, in our painting ... family too. We are family, in our community." For Pelusa, being family, being part of a community, also means being true to her African roots. She proudly insists that Las Krudas seek to incorporate their African roots into their daily lives as well as into their artistic projects, and rap has been a good way to do that: "This hip-hop movement is a really beautiful way to urbanize and modernize and bring up to date the Afro-descended culture that is here," she explained. And she insists on her class location as well.

> More than being Cuban, I am a poor Cuban. *¿Entiendes?* A more humble Cuban. Because they say that in Cuba there are not classes, that everybody is working class. But in Cuba there has been achieved a differentiation, let's say, of certain social scales; there are people [here] who have a car and a house. There are people here who have neither car nor house. *¿Entiendes lo que estoy diciendo?* Do you understand what I'm saying? And I am one of those people who have neither car nor house. Nothing. So I wake up in the morning wondering if at night I'm going to sleep in the same [bed] where I'm living now. So I tell you that [I identify with the] poor, women, artists, Cuban, Black, hip hop.

I also asked the group: *¿Uds son feministas?* Are you feminists? Pelusa spoke up to clarify:

> We think that for us it is absolutely necessary to be feminists. Here, in this context at least. Because to be feminists, for us—is the balance that we need to live in this society *tan machista* that is so sexist. If society were a little- more open and more balanced, maybe we'd be a little more balanced and less extremist; but we are in an extremist society, and we have to balance our lives, and so we are also extremists. We are absolutely feminists ... we know that women in the world need a lot of support today from other women. We give much solidarity so that our self-esteem becomes higher and higher. Because historically, it has been lower every day, I do not know, at least here in Cuba. It is said that, for example, during the revolutionary process, Cuban women have made some social advances and have gone on to, shall we say, to claim their position in society. But we absolutely know that women in Cuba have the double responsibility to work in the street, whatever work she obtains and soon to arrive home and perhaps work even harder in the house. Because here the domestic customs are [such] that the woman is the one who works in house ... the woman is working all the time. All the time.

Las Krudas and Hip Hop

Olivia, Wanda, and Odaymara—the three members of Las Krudas—are *raperas* and community performance artists. Every afternoon they perform in the streets of Habana Vieja (Old Havana) on stilts. They also direct a camp, introducing children to performance and public art. Pelusa underscores the importance to them of participating in a variety of art forms.

> We are actresses in addition to rappers. . . . [We are] in theater, but we have to do our own theater because we don't want to join the [established] Cuban theater. We don't like what [Cuban theater] is doing. We do our own, where the Black woman has the role of protagonist; because the rest of the time in Cuban theater it's not that way. [Black women play] the classic role of slaves, servants, domestics, of long-suffering women, housewives. We have never had the possibility to have plays where the Black woman is protagonist and her life is a victory. *¿Entiendes?* Understand? So then, we, through our theater projects try to grow the size of the Black woman.

Achieving this goal through their hip-hop practice has not been easy. Pelusa illustrates this point.

> Only young men have much time in their lives to dedicate to listening to music, learning to dance, going to parties, or rapping on the corner. . . . Since we were girls we played in the house and when we arrived at adolescence, we had to preoccupy ourselves with learning how to clean the house, how to keep our kitchens correctly, and all that.

She says that she understands that as men were at the forefront of the hip-hop movement they deserve their due, but at the same time she feels excluded from promoting her own art and talents.

> [We recognize] that men have opened paths, that they have been the warriors, the chief warriors of this tribe . . . we [Las Krudas and other female rappers] are a tribe within a tribe, and we are fighting to prove we are just as strong and that we are going to demonstrate that we are capable of continuing the struggle with as much force as they [the male rappers] are.

Hip hop made its way to Cuba in the late 1970s as an extension of the U.S. rap scene via the eastern outskirts of Havana, in Alamar, home to "one of the largest housing projects in the world" whose residents were and continue to be predominantly Black (Olavarria 2002, 1). U.S. rap music was pirated from Miami radio transmissions by innovative young Alamar residents. It gained very wide popularity in Cuba in the early 1990s, just as hip hop in the United States was taking on distinct regional flavors and spilling across national borders.

Lacking technology and recording equipment, Cuban rappers composed their own lyrics to popular American rap tracks taped from the radio. Because of rap music's immense youth appeal, it can be effectively shaped to accommodate most any message. As in the United States, Cuban rap communicates a youthful sense of struggle and rebellion, anger and aggression, aspirations for social mobility and material well-being, and an unswerving identification with the streets. As a musical form it also opens a space for creativity, dialogue, and criticism (George

1998, 155). Also as in U.S. rap, Cuban rappers sample liberally, calling upon a shared musical heritage and collective memory. Afro-Cuban music, including a strong drum beat and traditional rumba sounds, is blended and combined with rap to form something original acknowledging and paying homage to the legacy of Cuba's African musical heritage.

Rap music—in both the United States and Cuban contexts—speaks directly to the social traumas and dislocations suffered by African-descended peoples living in metropolitan centers. Despite the official, government proclamations of fairness, economic opportunity, social mobility, and racial equality, inequity is the rule for most Black Cubans (Rose 1994, 102). For example, many young Black Cubans experience targeted police repression. In establishments catering to foreign capital, Black Cubans in particular are regularly denied access.[1] Like poor Black Americans, Black Cubans are the overwhelming majority of the island's growing underclass as is evidenced by increasing rates of Black unemployment, crime, and incarceration.

During a time of deep uneasiness about Cuba's post-socialist future, many Cubans fear that racial problems may undermine the notion that all is well in Cuba's revolutionary society. Black Cubans active in the hip-hop movement personify the fissure between the real, lived experience of race and the official ideology promoting the notion that racial harmony has been achieved on the island.

Although Las Krudas cannot represent the experiences of all Black women on the island, they occupy a unique position within a growing Black hip-hop intelligentsia. While their activities and lyrics point to specific issues of contemporary concern around the politics of race and gender in Cuba, they differ from U.S. Black women rappers and their Cuban male contemporaries in that they unwaveringly advance a feminist agenda in which they seek to politicize the social and economic reality of being Black and female in Cuba. Las Krudas therefore calls attention to the situation of Black women in a social and political context that denies the existence of racism, sexism, status, and privilege.

Despite Las Krudas' members' increasingly important position as feminists within the Cuba hip-hop culture, they share with U.S. women rappers a frustrating invisibility. In both Cuba and in the United States, women as fans, advocates, and artists in hip hop are virtually ignored in discussions of the phenomenon. Both in the United States and in Cuba, male artists have been touted for the political awareness and resistant nature of their rap lyrics. For example, male rappers in both the United States and Cuba protest and criticize the multiple ways the Black male body and masculinity is policed and surveilled. By contrast, many themes dominant in Black female rappers' lyrics in both the United States and Cuba articulate and/or question hegemonic notions of femininity and Black female sexuality.

Although in their lyrics many Black U.S. women rappers defend women against sexist assumptions and misogynist assertions made by their Black male counterparts, and they attempt to build their female audience's self-esteem and raise consciousness levels in efforts to encourage solidarity among women, most perceive feminism to be a movement specifically related to white women. Consequently, they are ambivalent about taking on a feminist label or stance for fear that assuming a feminist position will be perceived as "anti-Black male" (Rose 1994, 176). In solidarity with Black men, many U.S. Black women rappers refuse to identify or affiliate themselves with a movement that is perceived as speaking largely to heterosexual, white, upper middle-class women's concerns.

Unlike their North American counterparts, Las Krudas readily identify themselves as feminists and refuse to relinquish their strong critiques of the nature and effects of Cuban patriarchy on the lives of marginalized women. Las Krudas' lyrics encourage Black women to reject the racism and sexism of patriarchal notions of femininity, and they seek to raise the self-esteem of their female audiences. Many U.S. Black women rappers do the same. But Las Krudas' open embrace of feminist ideals makes them unique in the world of hip hop. This open embrace of feminism by Las Krudas has caused problems for them within the state-controlled music marketing entity. One example of the racially inflected sexism routinely experienced by the group occurred during the planning of the all-women's concert where I first saw them perform. The hip-hop agency that organized the concert is state-subsidized and run by a white man and a Black woman: together they manage eleven groups. Of these, only one group has a female member, Obsección (a husband and wife duo). The agency did not want to have to pay any of the groups or artists that they did not represent (which, in this case, included all the female *rapera* groups in this all women's concert). In addition, the director of the theater where the concert was taking place pushed for the inclusion of men on the stage even though the concert was intended to feature women artists exclusively. For instance, he tried to force the women rappers to incorporate male dancers and rappers into their acts, something Las Krudas resisted.

Ultimately, Las Krudas prevailed and successfully performed their own original, pro-woman songs, *without* the "enhancement" of male dancers. Odaymara notes that the hip-hop world in Cuba is very sexist: "the rap world is *(¡hmmmmph!) tan fuerte,* so strong. *Muy machista, muy, muy, muy*: Very sexist, very, very, very." Odaymara explained that she was annoyed and angered at the women's concert not only because of the way the organizers treated the women rappers but also because while the men (of the hip-hop world) showed up, their presence was perceived as counterproductive; the men never lent any real support to the women's cause according to Las Krudas. Also, regarding the other female rappers at the concert, Pelusa noted while the women were very good interpreters of text, *los textos* were not written by them but by men. Las Krudas agreed that the feminist movement as well as the hip-hop movement in Cuba has a "long way to go. Long, long, long."

Growing the Size of the Black Woman

Like their male counterparts, in their lyrics, Las Krudas defend the marginalized social location of the rapper and endeavor to dignify the rappers' claim that their music is authentically Cuban (Hernández 2004, 11). However, Las Krudas' artistic content diverges from Cuban male rappers in significant ways. Embedded in Las Krudas' lyrics and philosophy is a feminist stance that refuses to accept the sexist oppression of Black women. Las Krudas have used their music to speak openly about issues of racial and sexual identity that are not often aired publicly.

The first cut on their demo album, *Cubensi Hip Hop*, deals with the *momentos difíciles* (the difficult moments) women must live through. Those moments are eclipsed by a national discourse calling on all Cubans to sacrifice while asking women and African-descended peoples to sacrifice the most for the goals of the Revolution. In the opening song, "*Vamos a Vence*," (We Will Overcome), Pasa Kruda announces the liberatory commitment of Las Krudas.

> *Vivimos momentos difíciles/ pero seguimos pa'lante*
> *Luchando nuestro derecho/ pa'lante me tiendo el pecho*
> *No obstante el camino estrecho/ juntas sabiendo la brecha*
> *Krudas, ¡prender la mecha!*

> We live [through] difficult moments/ but we continue forward
> Struggling [for] our right/ I turn my chest [facing] forward
> No matter how narrow the path/ together, knowing the injustices
> Krudas, light the torch! (Las Krudas 2004)

To Las Krudas, struggle is neither ugly, nor violent, nor done resentfully. The group promotes liberatory struggle "because life is like a flower, small and delicate/ we will take care of it because it's very precious/ we will maintain it because it's beautiful, we will" (*porque la vida es como una florecita, pequeña y delicada/ vamos a cuidarla porque es muy preciada/ vamos a costarla porque es bonita, vamos*) (Las Krudas 2004).

It is because life is so precious and delicate and beautiful that Las Krudas urges their audience to *vencer la dificultad*, "overcome the difficulty." Concluding the song, Las Krudas sing the following.

> *Vamo' a vencer, orgullo arriba, comunidad,*
> *Vamo' a vencer, Afrocubana viva prosperidad,*

> *Vamo' a vencer, Krudas son parte de tu identidad,*
> *Vamo' a vencer, mucha salud y felicidad . . .*
> *Sexo feminino siempre relegado/ pero Las Krudas el molde han quebrado.*
>
> We will overcome, raise your pride, community,
> We will overcome, *Afrocubana* live [your] prosperity,
> We will overcome, *Krudas* are a part of your identity,
> We will overcome, with health and happiness . . .
> Feminine sex, always relegated/ but Las Krudas have broken the mold.
> (Las Krudas 2004)

By struggling to overcome the difficult moments that they face as Black women, and articulating this struggle as *raperas*, Las Krudas are paying homage to those artists who have gone before them, demanding that their presence in the hip-hop world be taken seriously and encouraging their audiences to take heart.

Las Krudas directly address and challenge their listeners. The group's lyrics remind and exhort their listeners to raise up their pride of self, to embrace the "crude" message of resistance, while securing a space for dialogue, empowerment, and self-definition and breaking the silence about the nature and effects of Cuban patriarchy and racism. The use in this song of the phrase "Vamos a Vence" carries a particularly pungent reference to the Cuban Revolution's long-standing slogan, "Venceremos!" (variously translatable as "We shall overcome," "We shall prevail," or "We will win/conquer"), which continues to be used during all official gatherings, by Fidel Castro during speeches and in countless other situations. This sly turn of phrase by Las Krudas transforms the fading battle cry of the revolution's warriors into a feminist exhortation to refuse sexist oppression.

In the second song on the demo album, *Pa'ketenteres* (*So that You Know*), Las Krudas allude to the stereotype of the long-suffering Cuban woman, destabilizing it by giving voice to her (their) experience(s). The chorus of the song points out that women play games with their lives, often for their very survival, as in the case of *jineteras*, female hustlers, and sex workers. Las Krudas sing the following.

> *Pa'ketenteres, asére/ y sepan el juego jugamos las mujeres*
> *Pa'ketentere y no se desespere/ mi krudeza es la que tu mente quiere*
> So that you know, *asére*/ that you might know the games we women play
> So that you know and don't despair/ my crudeness is what your mind wants. (Las Krudas 2004)

While this lyric in particular might suggest that Las Krudas have constructed their audience to be male, the group raps primarily to female audiences, seeking to help women in the audience name their struggles and recognize the way patriarchy shapes "the games they play" and thus their oppression(s).

As *Pa'ketenteres* continues, the lyrics demonstrate that Las Krudas have as their goal nothing less than the liberation of Black Cuban women. They urge their listeners to embrace their independence and recognize the deeper implications of the experiences they share as Black women, exhorting them to struggle alongside Las Krudas as they rap.

> *Más que uds conocemos la discriminación/ somos clase humildes*
> *Somos color/ pero demás somos mujeres/ necesitamos amor*
> *Conocemos el sudor/ disfrutamos nuestro olor*
>
> *Cierra las piernas/ más hijo de la perra/ si protestas eres diabla*
> *Cerebro de mosquito/ secretaria, salario bajito/ condenas altas/ orgullo poquito*
> *Hasta dónde/ contra la pared/ somos personas/ siempre el mismo drama*
> *El macho pa' la calle/ la hembra pa' la cama*
>
> *[. . .] mujer, eres dueña de ti mismo/ de tu destino/ eres tu quien determina*
> *cómo sigue tu camino/ eliges a quien amar/ eliges como pensar*
> *eliges con quien soñar/ la dueña de la tierra y de la mar*
> *mujer poderosa/ mujer hermosa/ mujer diosa/*
> *femenina criatura sagrada, divina/ eres dueña de ti/ de la cabeza.*

More than you, we [women] know discrimination
we are [a] humble class/ we are [of] color
but what's more, we are women/ we need love
we know sweat/ we enjoy our smell

close your legs/ son of a bitch/ if you protest, you're [a] she-devil
brain of a mosquito/ secretary, low salary/ higher [sentences,]
little pride/ where does it lead/ back against the wall/ we are people
always the same drama/ the man for the street/ and the woman for the bed

[. . .] woman, you rule yourself/ your destiny
you are the one who determines/ how to follow your path
choose who to love/ choose how to think/ choose with whom to dream
the ruler of the earth and the sea/ powerful woman
beautiful woman/ goddess woman/ sacred feminine creature, divine
you rule yourself/ of your [own] head. (Las Krudas 2004)

In *Pa'ketenteres*, Las Krudas reach beyond stereotypes of women as long-suffering or hypersexualized. They refer pointedly to the gendered contradictions implicit in Cuban society. They ask, drawing attention to the low wages of female clerical work, "where does this lead?" They respond with: our backs "against the wall." Las Krudas are never resigned to discrimination. They exhort their female audiences to recognize their power to be their own "ruler," to control their own lives. A good example here is the way the group invokes female deities and goddesses in their lyrics. This incorporation of Afro-Cuban cultural and religious references is a distinctive feature of Las Krudas's message of female dignity and self-determination.

Las Krudas's *Eres Bella* (You are Beautiful) is another anthem to the dignity of the Black Cuban woman. Significantly, Las Krudas dedicated this rap to solidarity with an imagined, global community of women.

> *Dedicado a todas las mujeres del mundo*
> *A todas las mujeres que como nosotras están luchando*
> *A todas las guerreras campesinas, urbanas*
> *A todas las hermanas*
> *Especialmente a las más negras*
> *Especialmente a las más pobres*
> *Especialmente a las más gordas . . .*
>
> Dedicated to all the women in the world,
> To all the women who, like us, are struggling,
> To all the rural, urban warriors,
> To all of the sisters,
> Especially the most Black,
> Especially the most poor,
> Especially the most fat,
> I am . . . (Las Krudas 2004)

Dedicated to the most marginalized women of the world, *Eres Bella* strongly rejects the old Cuban adage that Black women are strictly for work, while *mulatas* are for love. Las Krudas rap to their "sisters."

> *Eres bella siendo tú, ébano en flor, negra luz*
> *Eres bella siendo tú, cuerpo no es única virtud*
> *Eres bella siendo tú, ébano en flor, negra luz*
> *Eres bella siendo tú, inteligencia y plenitud.*
>
> You are beautiful being you, ebony in flower, Black light
> You are beautiful being you, [your] body isn't [your] only virtue
> You are beautiful being you, ebony in flower, Black light
> You are beautiful being you, intelligence and fullness. (Las Krudas 2004)

Las Krudas also demonstrate here a deep understanding of the plight of Black women involved in the world of *jineterismo*. Their lyrics make clear that hustling for dollars is, in many instances, an individual strategy for survival as well as a national one. Las Krudas make the point that even if a woman is caught up in hustling as a way to "get by," using whatever means available to her, her humanity, her personhood are nonetheless deserving of respect.

> *Y hoy seguimos, siendo objeto, desvalorizacíon*
> *que nos queda?/ prostitución, seducción?*
> *esto es solo una costumbre hereda'*
> *pa' ayudar a nuestra gente económicamente*
> *en este mundo tan material/ no somos nalgas y pechos solamente*
> *tenemos cerebros/ mujeres siente, siente*

> And today we continue to be objects devalued
> what does that leave us/ prostitution? seduction?
> this is just a custom inherited/ in order to help our people
> in this world [that is] so material/ we are not simply buttocks and breasts
> we have minds/ women feel, feel (Las Krudas 2004)

Las Krudas's rap lyrics reveal a very keen political analysis, one that recognizes that the viability and livelihood of the very state that oppresses Black women is dependent upon their sexual, domestic, and emotional labor. In contemporary Cuba prostitution, the "black" market and growing consumerism are now more than ever revealing the deficiencies that persist despite state-sponsored notions of egalitarian socialism. New awareness of the gap between official proclamations and living reality has led to unofficial radical movements such as Cuban hip hop and the feminist, oppositional lyrics of Las Krudas.

Krudas, Light[ing] the Torch

In this essay, I have described how Black Cuban women like Las Krudas are beginning to lay claim to their own social spaces within hip hop, increasingly a powerful diasporic expressive form. I have argued that Las Krudas have created an activist art that uniquely fuses Black, Cuban, and feminist perspectives; they are in the process of creating a female audience for their unique version of rap and in so doing have encouraged criticism of and dialogue about the reality of life in Cuba among fans and tourists alike. By rapping *to* women, Las Krudas have helped to cultivate a space where women across the spectrum of race and class can express their own realities. I have proposed that Las Krudas are singularly engaged in revolutionary feminist activism through their art by giving voice to the harshness and inequities of Black female experience in Cuban society, a society which has prided itself on its egalitarianism. Las Krudas have stepped up as the vanguard of Black feminism in Cuba. No one else speaks out as they do on the ways in which race, gender, and class inform not only power relations but also socioeconomic status in Cuba.

They multiply their activist effect through their youth theater camps and public performances, succeeding in imposing a unique oppositional identity onto public space that is otherwise difficult to achieve.

What the future may bring Las Krudas is uncertain. Now that the dollar has been rendered illegal in Cuba, it is possible that the government may crack down on *raperos* and *raperas*, even perhaps on the state-supported or so-called "commercial" rap artists. What will happen to Cuban "underground" rap like that of Las Krudas that so far has been tacitly supported by the government despite its rebellious spirit and expression of political awareness that often run counter to official dogmas? Perhaps Cuban rap of various stripes will become the sanctioned music of rebellion on the island? If so, does it follow that Black women will begin to gain access to more "official" channels of power and the political process?

Las Krudas as activists and artists use hip hop as a consciousness-raising forum in which truths are told and justice is sought, "put[ting] the Revolution to the Revolution" (Hernandez 2002). What remains to be seen is whether up and coming female *raperas* will follow Las Krudas' lead in breaking the mold or whether they will conform to the patriarchal, consumption-oriented style that is more typical of mainstream Cuban hip hop.

Note

1. As a visitor to the island, I discovered that the darker one's skin tone, the more likely one is to be deemed "Cuban" and ejected from these establishments. For instance, I was denied entry to the Cuba Libre Hotel on the suspicion that I was a prostitute.

References

Boal, Augusto. 1985. *Theater of the Oppressed*. Charles A. and Maria-Odilia Leal McBride, trans. New York: Theater Communications Group.
Fernandes, Sujatha. 2003. "Fear of a Black Nation: Local Rappers, Transnational Crossings, and State Power in Contemporary Cuba." *Anthropological Quarterly* 76: 575–609.
George, Nelson. 1998. *Hip Hop America*. New York: Viking.
Hernandez, Ariel. 2002. Interview with author, 4 January.
Hernández, Grisel. 2004. "Demo Krudas: Cubensi." *Movimiento: La Revista Cubana de Hip Hop* 2: 11.
Las Krudas. 2004. *Cubensi*. Compact disc. Havana, Cuba.
———. 2003. Tape-recorded interview with author, Havana, Cuba, 15 December.

Olavarria, Margot. 2002. "Rap and Revolution: Hip-Hop comes to Cuba." *NACLA Report on the Americas.* Retrieved 22 September from www.nacla.org/art_display_printable.php?art=2018.

Rose, Tricia. 1994. *Black Noise: Rap Music and Black Culture in Contemporary America.* Middletown, CT: Wesleyan University Press.

Contributors

FAUZIA ERFAN AHMED's research interests in international development studies focus on gender, globalization, Islam, microcredit, and justice. As a scholar practitioner who speaks six languages, she has worked with the United Nations and NGOs in Indonesia, Thailand, Pakistan, India, the United States, and her native Bangladesh. Her writings have appeared in the *National Women's Studies Association Journal*, the *International Journal of Feminist Politics*, the *Encyclopedia for Women in Muslim Cultures*, *Feminist Formations*, *Comparative Studies of South Asia, Africa and the Middle East*, and *The Muslim World*.

YASEMIN BESEN-CASSINO is an associate professor of sociology at Montclair State University. She is the author of *The Jessie Bernard Reader* (with Michael Kimmel) and *Consuming Politics* (with Dan Cassino). Her work focuses on sociology of work, youth, and gender.

MARNIE DOBSON has an appointment as a research associate at the Center for Occupational and Environmental Health at the University of California, Irvine, and is the associate director of the Center for Social Epidemiology in Los Angeles, California. Her transdisciplinary research interests include gender and work, emotional labor, and work organization and psychosocial stressors. She has recently coedited and contributed to the book *Unhealthy Work: Causes, Consequences, Cures* (Baywood Publishing) and has coauthored multiple journal articles in occupational health, sociology, and women's studies journals.

LYNN S. DUGGAN is an associate professor in the Labor Studies Program at Indiana University Bloomington. Her research interests include comparisons of gendered economic systems, European family policy and women's labor force inclusion, pre- and post-unification East and West Germany, working conditions in retail employment, women in building trades, immigration policy, and gender and development in the global South. She has published in *Comparative Economic Studies*, *Feminist Economics*, the *National Women's Studies Association Journal*, and several anthologies and is a coeditor of *The Women, Gender, and Development Reader*.

MOUSHIRA ELGEZIRI has a Ph.D. in Development Studies from the International Institute of Social Studies of Erasmus University, Rotterdam,

Netherlands. She is a consultant to the Higher Education Program at the Ford Foundation Regional Office in Cairo, Egypt.

SONIA R. GARCÍA is a professor in political science at St. Mary's University in San Antonio, Texas. Her research interests include Chicana/Latina politics, civil rights, women and politics, and Texas politics. She has published articles on Latina politics. She is lead author of *Políticas: Latina Public Officials in Texas*, which examines the first Latinas elected to various positions in Texas.

IVY KEN (née Kennelly) is an associate professor of sociology at George Washington University, where she teaches courses on theory; race, class, and gender; and the sociology of food. Her book *Digesting Race, Class, and Gender: Sugar as a Metaphor* was published in 2010 (Palgrave Macmillan).

KAREN KOVACIK is a professor of English at Indiana University–Purdue University Indianapolis, where she directs the creative writing program. Her articles on working-class women poets have appeared in *Women's Studies Quarterly*, the *National Women's Studies Association Journal*, and *Critical Approaches to Working-Class Literature* (Routledge, 2011). She is currently the poet laureate of Indiana.

NIZA LICUANEN-GALELA is a sociology professor at Kent State University Trumbull, where she does much of her work on gender and development, focusing on women in Southeast Asia. She is interested in the effects of globalization on women in developing areas.

MARISELA MÁRQUEZ is the executive director for associated students and a lecturer for the Department of Chicana and Chicano Studies at the University of California, Santa Barbara. Her research interests include Chicana/Latina politics, Chicano and Chicana communities, and higher education. Her recent publication, coauthored with Dr. Sonia García, examines one of the first national Chicana feminist organizations, the Comisión Feminil.

NANCY A. NAPLES holds a joint appointment in sociology and women's studies at the University of Connecticut. Her research on citizenship, social policy, immigration, and community activism has been published in edited books and numerous journals. Her most recent book is *Feminism and Method: Ethnography, Discourse Analysis, and Activist Research*.

FARI NZINGA (née Ronni Armstead) is a Ph.D. candidate in cultural anthropology at Duke University. Nzinga's dissertation project aims to critically deconstruct the "culture of resistance" in post-Katrina New Orleans by examining Black styles of leadership, organizing, and activism within small community-based nonprofits. Nzinga has written a column interpreting her ethnographic "finds" in "the field" for the *Gris Gris Lab Newsletter* and currently works as an independent writing and research consultant.

SUE V. ROSSER has served since 2009 as provost at San Francisco State University, where she is also professor of women's and gender studies and of sociology. Originally trained as a biologist, she has authored approximately 130 journal articles and 13 books on theoretical and applied aspects of women and gender in science, technology, and health.

ESTHER D. ROTHBLUM, PH.D., is professor of women's studies at San Diego State University, after serving twenty-three years as professor of psychology at the University of Vermont. Her research and writing have focused on lesbian relationships and on the stigma of women's weight. She is editor of the *Journal of Lesbian Studies* and has edited more than twenty books, including *Lesbians in Academia: Degrees of Freedom*.

STACI STROBL is an associate professor in the Department of Law, Police Science and Criminal Justice Administration at John Jay College of Criminal Justice and the 2009 winner of the *British Journal of Criminology*'s Radzinowicz Memorial Prize for her work on the criminalization of domestic workers in Bahrain. Her areas of specialization are gender and policing in the Arabian Gulf, multiethnic policing in Eastern Europe, and comic book portrayals of crime in the United States. Earlier in her career, she worked as a U.S. probation officer and a crime journalist. Dr. Strobl completed her doctorate in Criminal Justice at the City University of New York's Graduate Center; she received her M.A. in criminal justice at John Jay University and her B.A. in Near Eastern Studies at Cornell University.

TIM WISE is one of the most prominent antiracist essayists, educators, and activists in the United States. Author of many books, his most recent titles are *Dear White America: Letter to a New Minority*, *Between Barack and a Hard Place: Racism and White Denial in the Age of Obama*, and *Colorblind: The Rise of Post-Racial Politics and the Retreat from Racial Equity*, all published by City Lights Books.

Index

Aboriginal rights movement, 218–21, 227–28, 230
Aboriginal women, 15, 213–16, 218–30; commitment to community of, 15, 223–29; and feminism, 220–23, 228–29
academia: lesbians in, 15–17, 235–41; as sites of patenting, 130–34; working-class writers within, 271, 273, 277–78
activism, 8; among Black feminists in Cuba, 282; effects of government employment on, 226–27, 228–29; grassroots, 8, 11, 15, 202, 206, 207; Latina and Chicana, 15, 202–10; in post-Soviet Russia, 9; by U.S. women of color, 214–18, 220, 222–30, 248
activist mothering, 15, 17, 68, 213–15, 248
advancement opportunities for women, 111–13, 128, 145, 152–53, 191, 244, 254; lack of, 68
affirmative action, 12, 14, 148–70; benefits to white women of, 149–62; failure of gender-based appeals regarding, 158–70; and the problem of "preference" language, 156–57, 160; "racialization" of, 155–57, 158, 160–61; white women's opposition to, 155–62
African American women, 19, 216–18; and commitment to community, 223–29, 248; and resistance to nurturing in the workplace, 252–53, 257–58; and secretarial work, 248, 252–53, 257–58
Afro-Cuban women, 282–92
age, 11, 32, 33, 34
agency, 2, 268; in the home, 78–80; of the individual vs. collective action, 10, 80, 83; in the workplace, 2, 65–66, 68, 73, 77–78
American Indians, 219, 222, 231, 275, 279

Balliro, Lenore, 264, 270, 272–73, 277
Bangladesh, 8, 73–83; garment industry in, 13, 73; rise of the Industrial Class in, 74, 82

Beatty, Jan, 264, 270, 273–77
benefits, workplace, 8, 12, 19, 43–48, 51–54, 78, 110–11, 116; tips on, 273–75, 278
bisexual women, 237, 241
blue-collar jobs, 92, 109–10, 277. *See also* manual labor
Brodine, Karen, 264–65, 267–70, 273, 277

capitalism, 3–6, 54, 140–41; in Bangladesh, 74–76, 82; neoliberal, 3, 7; poetic resistance to, 269–70; radical free market, 7; in Russia, 9; venture, 14, 140–45
caretaking, 139; community, 15, 213, 220; of elderly parents, 5, 143; inventions related to, 133, 135, 143; needs of those responsible for, 54–55; work influenced by, 223–24, 227; in the workplace (*see* nurturing in the workplace)
cheap labor, 50, 81; women as, 8, 12, 61, 69, 77, 93, 138
Chicana women, political involvement of, 202–10
child rearing, 3, 5, 6, 11, 12, 17, 25; devaluing of, 3, 17, 51, 140; jobs worked affected by, 45–46; political involvement affected by, 205, 214–15; women's work affecting, 88, 242, 250
childbearing, 3, 12; inventions related to, 133, 135, 143; state role in, 87
childcare: availability of, 3–4, 5, 17, 51, 81, 87; cost of, 45–46, 51–52
citizenship: consumer citizens vs. producer citizens, 10; practices, 214, 216–22, 227, 230; responsibilities of, 3, 15; rights of, 6, 87, 230, 224; status, 3, 215, 219, 222
Civil Rights Act of 1964, 4, 149
civil rights movement, 216–18, 229; gains of, 149–52; sexism in, 220–21; women of color in, 214–18, 220–21, 228

class, 2, 7–8, 32, 79–80; barriers to solidarity, 76–77; divisions, 8; hijab as symbolic indicator of, 114; impact of, on education and employment in Egypt, 90–92, 95–98, 100–111; inequities, 12; influence of, on women's opportunities, 243–44, 259; oppression, 8; role of, in shaping technology, 140; segregation in Bangladesh factories, 13, 77, 79, 80. *See also* discrimination; division of labor; wage disparities

class bias, 7; in Cuba, 16, 283, 285; in discussions of women and work, 118–19; among literary critics, 273

collective action, 6, 15, 265–69, 277; among indigenous women, 222, 231; maternalist, 9; valuing individual agency over, 6, 10, 77, 80; among women of color, 222

colonialism: effect on Aboriginal communities, 215–16, 218–22, 230–31; effect on Arab and Muslim societies, 178–79, 190; legacy of, 177, 182, 197; and Puerto Rico, 217; sexism and, 219–20, 221–22; and U.S. policy, 10. *See also* colonization; postcolonial cultures

colonization, 7, 18; resistance to, 7, 190; technologies as reflections of, 138. *See also* colonialism; postcolonial cultures

coming out in the workplace, 235–37, 239

community: involvement among women of color, 202–10, 213–18, 220, 222–30, 248, 283–84; lesbian and gay, 235–37, 240; of performance artists in Cuba, 283–84, 292; political involvement influenced by, 202, 207–8, 209–10, 223–24, 229; of support among women, 18, 137–38; women's service to, 15, 195, 207–10, 242, 248; workers in Australia, 15, 213–16, 218–30; workers in the United States, 15, 213–18, 220, 222–30

corporations: dominance over labor unions of, 44–45; practices and policies of, 2, 12, 45–48, 62–68; and relocation to developing countries, 8, 61–69, 92–93; transnational, 61, 64–69, 73; women in, 5, 6, 134–38; women professionals and, 141–42, 143–44, 154

Cuba: hip hop in, 16, 284–87, 292; underclass in, 282, 285

deskilled labor, 8, 40, 46–48, 68, 96, 269
developing countries, 8, 10, 61, 138. *See also* Bangladesh; Philippines
discrimination: against Aboriginal people, 215, 218–21, 230–31; against Black Cubans, 282, 284–85, 289–90; gender, 6, 12, 137–38, 149–50, 151, 152, 159–60, 166–67; against lesbians, 235–36; against low-income women of color, 50, 214–18; prohibitions on, 4, 54–55, 149–51, 159, 189; race, 149, 150, 158, 165–67, 214–18; against women in Japanese-run organizations, 64; women's patenting affected by, 138; workplace, 52–53

disenfranchisement: of grassroots activists in Russia, 9; of women, 8; of women of color, 6

division of labor: gendered, 4, 7, 17, 57, 88, 140, 210, 214; racial, 7. *See also* domestic duties; gender segregation

domestic duties: women's work affected by, 26, 33, 87–90, 91, 102, 110–11; women's work affecting, 6; inventions related to, 133, 143; women's responsibility for, 5, 87, 121–22, 139, 283–84

domestic servants, 6, 78, 216–17, 278, 284; in Bahrain, 194–95; in Egypt, 99–100, 101, 119–20

economic globalization, 12, 61, 69, 73, 75, 81–82, 92–93. *See also* export industrialization

economic theory, 3, 40–42, 47, 53, 82; feminist, 6–7, 8, 10, 42

economics: neoclassical, 40–41; political, 40–42. *See also* capitalism

education, 11; access to, 3–4, 12, 13; differences between men's and women's, 12, 26, 30, 33; Egyptian system of, 90–92, 106; TANF limits on, 51–52; of U.S. workers, 56; of women in Egypt, 13, 85–86, 91–92, 95–96, 102–3, 115–22

Egypt, 13, 85–121

emotion work, 16, 96, 243, 258, 264, 274, 291

empowerment: through access to work, 1, 2–5, 11, 14; community, 215, 222, 226–28, 231; failures of, 1, 5–6, 8–10, 12, 13, 118, 161; of female workers in Bangladesh, 73, 77–81; in GCC countries, 186, 194; through hip hop, 283, 286, 288; language of, 8–10; in women's NGOs, 113–18, 119, 121
engineering. *See* STEM fields
Equal Pay Act of 1963, 4
ethic of service, 253–59
exploitation of labor: in family-like workplaces, 65–67, 76, 244, 259–60; in the global market, 68–69, 77–80, 81–82, 194; in the United States, 41–48, 52–53, 55
export industrialization, 12, 61–62, 66, 68–69, 73, 75, 92–93

family leave policies, 4, 5, 54, 88; women's hiring dampened by, 89
feminisms, 1; Aboriginal women's concerns not addressed by, 220–23, 228–29; access-based, 1–8, 10, 11, 14, 18–19, 138; borders/borderless, 1; comparative, 177; essentialist, 135, 245; existentialist, 135–36; global, 1; international, 1; liberal, 136–39, 190; liberatory, 1, 7; Marxist, 1; multicultural, 1; in Muslim cultures, 189–90; postcolonial, 138; psychoanalytic, 139, 245; social justice, 1; socialist, 1, 139–41; state-sponsored, 9, 87–90, 185–87, 191, 222–23, 228–29, 231; Third World, 1; transformative, 1–3, 6, 10, 11; transnational, 1, 7, 178; U.S., 3, 4, 10–11; white, middle-class, heterosexual women traditionally associated with, 4–7, 14, 286; and women of color, 1, 7
Feminist Formations, 2, 11, 17
feminists: and access, 4; ambivalence to affirmative action among, 157; English, 3; in hip hop community, 283, 285; indigenous, 222; transformative, 8, 11, 18; U.S., 3, 9, 18; in Western societies, 3
feminization: of poverty, 9; of work, 42, 87, 93, 264, 278
food stamps, 12, 49–51. *See also* welfare
free market: economies of, 8; globalization of, 8; in Russia, 9. *See also* economic globalization; export industrialization
freelance employment, 30–34

garment workers, 268; in Bangladesh, 73–82; poetry about, 270
gender discounting, 141, 153
gender hierarchies in the workplace, 4, 8, 78, 119
gender segregation, 4, 12, 27, 47, 248, 249, 259; in Bangladesh garment industry, 13, 76, 78; in Egypt, 94–95; Islam associated with, 177–78; of police in GCC countries, 179–82, 183, 186–88, 190–93, 195–96; in retail sales industry, 47
gender studies. *See* women's studies
gendered expectations of women, 64, 67, 76, 111, 135, 140, 242, 245
girls studies, 11–12
glass ceiling, 7, 152–53
globalization. *See* economic globalization
government: Bangladesh, 74–75; community work sponsored by, 15, 214–16, 217–18, 219, 224; Egyptian women pressured by, 13, 88; as employer in Egypt, 85–89, 92, 98–99; poverty assistance (*see* food stamps; Medicaid; welfare); presence of women in, 5, 15, 202–10, 223, 228, 253–54; racism in, 152, 154, 218–20, 224; sexism in, 18, 87–88, 154; women's rights supported by, 87–90, 149–50, 185–87, 189, 191, 223 (*see also* feminisms: state-sponsored)
Gulf Cooperation Council (GCC) countries, 14, 177–97

health care: in Aboriginal communities, 15, 219–20, 225–26, 230, 231; costs of, 51; need for universal, 12, 54; in poor U.S. communities, 15, 223; workers in, 1, 177–97
health insurance, 46; Egyptians' access to, 86, 89, 101–2, 110; for part-time employees in the United States, 40, 43–45, 46, 49, 51, 52, 53, 55, 57
hegab. *See* hijab
heterosexism and homophobia, 7, 14, 16, 235–41

heterosexual women, privileging of, 4, 7, 238–40, 286
hijab, 90, 99, 103, 114, 184–85, 193
hip hop: in Cuba, 282–87, 292; feminism and, 16, 285–86, 291–92; homophobia in, 16; invisibility of women in, 285; sexism in, 16; in the United States, 287, 292

immigrant women, 6, 194
imperialism, 7, 18; feminist, 15; intellectual, 15; socioeconomic, 7, 9. *See also* colonialism; colonization
India, 17, 82, 97, 137–38, 188
indigenous people: communities of, 214, 218–20; rights of, 214, 219, 221, 227–28, 230–31; women as activists for, 222, 231
informal sector in Egypt, 13, 93–94, 98, 120–21
intellectual property, 132, 141
International Monetary Fund (IMF), 8, 88–89
intersectionality, 7, 18, 34, 215, 219–21, 259, 282–83, 285–92

Japanese-run organizations, 12, 17, 62–69
job security, 8, 12, 13, 43, 49, 81–82, 235

labor force participation rates: in Egypt, 85–86, 93–94, 118; of U.S. teens, 29, 31, 34; of U.S. women, 56, 150–51
labor unions: in Bangladesh, 8, 13, 77–78, 80, 83; difficulty organizing workers on TANF, 52–53; diminishing political power of, 5, 44–46; discrimination against women of color in, 56, 217; International Labor Organization, 81, 98; in Japanese-run organizations, 65–66, 70; strikes in Egypt, 19; women and, 45, 56, 77–78, 270, 271
Las Krudas, 16, 282–92
Latina women, 217–18; political involvement of, 202–10; as activists, 222, 231
lesbians: in academia, 15–16, 17, 235–41; racist attitudes among, 163
liberalism, 3, 6; in Bangladesh, 75; feminists' use of, 3, 10, 136–38, 139, 190. *See also* neoliberalism

Llewellyn, Chris, 264–67, 269–70, 273, 277
loans to women, 81, 151

managers: control over women by, 64, 244; lack of women, 64; women as, 6, 27, 150, 152
manual labor, 13, 40–58, 61–70, 73–83, 96, 119–21; divide between nonmanual labor and, 91, 95–96, 110, 119
mathematics. *See* STEM fields
Medicaid, 12, 49, 51–52
mentoring, 137, 140–41, 142, 143–45; among Latina and Chicana political candidates, 203, 209
microloans, 81
middle class: aspirations to, 80, 85–88, 92, 96, 108–9, 120; in Bangladesh, 76–80; in Egypt, 106–9, 114–15
Middle East, 9, 10, 14–15, 85–122, 177–97
minimum wage: in Bangladesh, 77, 80; in Egypt, 101–2; in the United States, 28, 31, 42, 56
mobility: employment, 12, 67–68, 73, 77, 86, 98, 101, 119–20, 218; social, 12, 76, 85, 95, 120, 248, 284–85
motherhood: decisions regarding, 243–45; nurturing in the workplace linked to, 107, 243, 244, 250–52, 256, 258–60; racialization of, 243, 253; women workers influenced by, 17, 45–46, 50–53, 54; work influenced by, 3, 5, 88
multiculturalism, problems of, 213–16, 218–30
Muslim cultures: anti-Muslim sentiment in the United States, 9; in Egypt, 88, 90, 103, 106–7, 114–15; gender equity in, 188–90; identity in, 106, 114, 178, 184, 187, 188–90; wearing of the hijab in, 90, 99, 103, 106–7, 114–15, 184–85

National Women's Studies Association (NWSA), 11
neoliberalism, 7–8, 15; in Egypt, 93, 98, 121; feminist opposition to, 7–8, 15; poverty solutions of, 9; women imposed upon by, 10; in Russia, 9
nongovernmental organizations (NGOs), 9, 10, 93–94, 113–18; as providers of welfare, 115–16

nonprofit jobs, 113–18, 254–57
nurturing in the workplace, 16, 27, 242–43; appeal for women of, 137; childlessness affecting, 244–45, 251–52, 258; as part of secretarial work, 244, 247–53, 256–60; as public service, 246–49, 254–60; resistance to, 252–53, 256–58; by women of color, 248, 252
NWSA Journal. See *Feminist Formations*

part-time labor, 40, 45–48, 50, 53–55, 56, 57, 93
patents, women's pursuit of, 12, 18, 130–45
patriarchal structure, 7, 11, 14; in Cuba, 283, 286–91; of Japanese organizational culture, 12; resistance to, 193; views of women in, 16, 17; women's participation in, 183, 187–88, 194
patronage in women's access to work, 66–67, 68–69, 76, 99–100
Philippines, 8, 12, 61–69
pink-collar work: in Egypt, 92, 109–18; poetry about, 276–77; in the United States, 16, 242–60, 264–77
policewomen: in Europe, 179, 181–83; in GCC countries, 14–15, 177–81, 183–97; in India, 188; in Israel, 179; in the United States, 150–51, 179, 181–83
politicians: affirmative action opposed by, 165; Latina and Chicana, 5, 202–10
postcolonial cultures, 178–79, 190, 193, 195, 197
poverty: Aboriginal women and, 213–14, 216, 221; and access to education, 12, 51–52, 90–92; assistance by U.S. government for, 40, 48–51; in Cuba, 283–85, 290; in Egypt, 86, 90–92, 97, 100, 114; feminization of, 9; among rural women in Bangladesh, 76, 78; U.S. retail workers and, 40–58; U.S. women of color and, 6, 213–16, 223, 225–26; War on, 213, 218, 226
power: in communities, 11, 68–69, 221; of corporations, 44–45; earning, 30; in the home, 13, 73, 76, 78–80, 140; inequitable distribution of, 3, 7–8, 51, 229, 292; limits on women's, 9, 11, 67–69, 228–29; political, 2–5, 11, 45, 75, 148, 178, 228; in the workplace, 11, 12, 13, 77–78, 82, 103–4, 113–18, 259, 272

private sphere, 3, 17, 213; men's role in household duties in, 5; power in, 4, 11. See also caretaking; child rearing; domestic duties
property ownership, 3, 279
public sector: in Bangladesh, 82; Egyptian employees in, 13, 85, 87–89, 92–100; in the United States, 42 (see also community, workers in the United States)
public sphere, 3, 6, 17; patriarchal organization of, 10; protected spaces for women in, 186, 191; women in, 88, 121, 192, 213
publication, women's rates of, 132
Puerto Rican women: during the 20th century, 217; as activists, 231; commitment to community of, 223–29; and feminism, 220

racism, 7, 16; in Cuba, 285, 287, 290–92; institutionalized, 219, 224–25, 228; movements against, 15; resistance to, 15, 213, 226–28; among white feminists, 163, 221; among white women, 148–49, 162–64. See also discrimination; wage disparities
religion, women's work affected by, 13, 88–90, 103, 178, 184–88, 224
reproduction. See childbearing
research on lesbian issues, 237–39
restaurant workers, 264–65, 272–77, 278–79; in fast food restaurants, 31, 247; poetry about, 264–65, 272–77
retail sales industry in the United States, 12, 31, 40, 46–49, 52, 55–56; changing demographics of, 47
routinization of work, 67–68, 266
rural communities: Aboriginal, 215, 219; women's status in, 61–69, 76, 78, 80
Russia, post-Soviet, 9

science, gendered nature of, 132, 139
sciences. See STEM fields
secretarial work, 244, 246–60, 289–90; by African American women, 248–49, 252–56; in Egypt, 109–10; and ethic of service, 253–58; poetry about, 264–72, 277; as public service, 246–47
sex segregation. See gender segregation

sex work, 78, 288–91
sexism, 7, 14, 16; in Aboriginal culture, 221–22; in Cuba, 283, 287–91; in government policies, 219–20; in hip hop, 286–87; in Japanese-run organizations, 62; resistance to, 213; among women, 14. *See also* discrimination; division of labor; gender segregation; wage disparities
sexual assault. *See* violence against women
sexual harassment in the workplace, 4, 8, 102, 105, 272
sexuality, 2, 17–18; in the classroom, 239–40; of teachers, 239–241
Social Security, 42, 101, 272; Act of 1935, 49–50
solidarity: class barriers to, 76–77; cross-cultural, 1, 18; across divides, 6, 9–10, 14–15, 18, 229, 283, 290; global feminist, 8; transnational, 1, 18; among working-class employees, 265–67, 272
STEM fields, 13–14, 18, 128–45; rates of patenting in, 13, 130–32; women's participation in, 246; women's rate of entrance into, 13, 128, 150
stop-the-clock policies, 4
sweatshops, 8, 13, 41, 77, 80, 83, 268

Tarlen, Carol, 264, 270–73, 277
tax credits to corporations, 40, 49–50, 52–55, 58
teachers: in Egyptian kindergartens, 106–9; as public servants, 246; and sexuality in higher education, 239–41
technology, 264, 267; jobs in (*see* STEM fields); male control over, 141; women's interest in, 135; women's work affected by, 264, 267, 268
teen employment, 12, 25, 28–34
Temporary Assistance to Needy Families (TANF). *See* welfare
Triangle Factory fire, 270
turnover, employee, 57, 103; reasons for low levels of, 67–68

uncompensated work, 3, 5, 17, 51, 67, 120, 140, 227, 247–48, 254–55, 257–58; of slaves in the United States, 19
United Nations, 4, 9

violence against women, 8, 181, 222, 223

wage disparities: age-based, 27, 33, 34; and attitudes toward earnings, 27, 34; by class, 42; between full- and part-time workers, 46; gender-based, 4, 5, 7, 11–12, 25–34, 42, 78, 153–54, 167; by generation, 44, 154; by occupation, 26, 31–34, 242, 259; race-based, 2, 7, 19, 27, 28, 32, 34, 43, 151–52; between skilled and unskilled workers, 48; years of experience affecting, 26; in the youth labor market, 28
wage subsidies, 40, 49–55
wealth gap, 7
welfare (TANF): benefits to employers, 50–55, 58; racial discrimination in, 49–50, 217; reform of, 12, 40, 49–55
women of color: disenfranchisement of, 6; employment as community workers in the United States, 15, 213–18; and feminism, 220–23; history of work in the United States, 19; as political candidates, 205; and secretarial work, 248–52
women-owned businesses, 81, 151, 154, 157–58, 180
women's studies, 10, 11, 239
work conditions, 8, 40, 81, 85; in Egypt, 85, 119, 121; in factories, 62, 67–68, 73, 80–81; safety of, 8, 42, 48, 52, 56, 57; of secretaries, 246, 269, 270
working class: culture in the United States, 276; jobs (*see* manual labor); negative effects on, 1, 8, 141; opportunities for, 150; status in Cuba, 283; women in Egypt, 92, 95–96, 99–100, 102–13; women in the United States, 40–58, 150, 216–17, 220–21, 257, 264–77; writers, 264–79
World Bank, 8, 82, 89, 93
World Trade Organization (WTO), 8–9